# Harnessing AI for Teacher Support and Professional Development

Hewa Majeed Zangana
*Duhok Polytechnic University, Iraq*

Calvin Nobles
*University of Maryland Global Campus, USA*

Marwan Omar
*Illinois Institute of Technology, USA*

IGI Global
Scientific Publishing
Publishing Tomorrow's Research Today

| | |
|---|---|
| Vice President of Editorial | Melissa Wagner |
| Director of Acquisitions | Mikaela Felty |
| Director of Book Development | Jocelynn Hessler |
| Production Manager | Mike Brehm |
| Cover Design | Jose Rosado |

Published in the United States of America by
IGI Global Scientific Publishing
701 East Chocolate Avenue
Hershey, PA, 17033, USA
Tel: 717-533-8845
Fax: 717-533-7115
Website: https://www.igi-global.com E-mail: cust@igi-global.com



Library of Congress Cataloging-in-Publication Data

LCCN: 2025033159 (CIP Data Pending)
ISBN13: 9798337359519
Isbn13Softcover: 9798337359526
EISBN13: 9798337359533
British Cataloguing in Publication Data
A Cataloguing in Publication record for this book is available from the British Library.

# Table of Contents

# Detailed Table of Contents



The rapid advancement of artificial intelligence (AI) has opened new avenues for personalizing professional development in education. This chapter explores how AI-powered recommendation systems can be leveraged to design individualized learning paths for teachers, aligning with their unique goals, teaching contexts, and competency levels. Unlike traditional one-size-fits-all training programs, AI-driven systems analyze teacher profiles, performance data, preferences, and feedback to generate dynamic, adaptive learning trajectories. The chapter presents a conceptual framework for integrating these systems into professional development platforms, supported by real-world applications and emerging research. Ethical considerations, data privacy, and algorithmic transparency are also addressed to ensure responsible implementation. By embracing AI recommendations, educational institutions can foster more effective, engaging, and sustainable teacher growth, ultimately enhancing student outcomes and instructional quality.



The integration of artificial intelligence (AI) in education has opened new avenues for enhancing teacher support and professional development. This chapter explores the transformative potential of virtual mentorship programs and AI-powered peer learning networks in fostering collaborative, personalized, and scalable professional growth for educators. By leveraging AI-driven analytics, recommendation systems, and communication platforms, virtual mentorship can overcome geographical and temporal barriers, enabling meaningful connections and tailored guidance. AI-powered peer learning networks facilitate dynamic knowledge sharing, real-time feedback, and community building among teachers, amplifying their professional capabilities. The chapter examines current technologies, implementation strategies, challenges, and future directions, highlighting how these AI-enhanced systems can support teachers in navigating complex educational landscapes and promoting continuous improvement.



This chapter explores the transformative role of Natural Language Processing (NLP) in supporting teacher reflection and the development of growth journals. As educators increasingly engage in self-directed professional development, reflective writing has become a central method for processing experiences, identifying challenges, and setting future goals. NLP offers scalable tools to analyze and enhance these reflective practices by extracting themes, detecting sentiment, providing constructive feedback, and identifying patterns over time. The integration of NLP into teacher reflection enables personalized support, promotes continuous learning, and contributes to evidence-based decision-making in professional growth. This chapter presents current advancements, practical implementations, ethical considerations, and future directions for embedding NLP in teacher development frameworks.



The shift toward remote and hybrid education has amplified the importance of high-quality visual content in digital teaching and learning environments. However, poor image quality—due to compression artifacts, noise, or low-resolution scanning—can hinder comprehension, engagement, and knowledge retention. This chapter explores the transformative role of AI-based image denoising techniques in enhancing the clarity and effectiveness of educational visual content. We examine state-of-the-art methods, including convolutional neural networks (CNNs), transformer-based models, and hybrid deep learning approaches, and discuss their applicability to real-world educational scenarios such as digital textbook enhancement, video lectures, and interactive learning materials. Furthermore, we highlight the pedagogical implications of denoised content for teacher support, curriculum development, and equitable access to learning resources. The chapter concludes with challenges, best practices, and future directions for integrating AI-driven denoising into digital education ecosystems.

This chapter critically examines AI co-teaching models that position artificial intelligence as a collaborative partner rather than a pedagogical replacement. It presents the Complementary Strengths Model and Teacher-in-the-Loop (TiTL) framework, highlighting role division between AI's analytical capabilities and teachers' emotional and instructional leadership. Implementation strategies across co-planning, co-instruction, and co-assessment are discussed using case studies and workflow models. Ethical issues such as bias, teacher autonomy, and trust via explainable AI (XAI) are addressed with practical guidance. The chapter also explores challenges like emotional AI's cultural risks and limited research from Global South contexts. Recommendations for educators, developers, and policymakers stress AI literacy, participatory co-design, and inclusive policy. It concludes by advocating interdisciplinary collaboration to create equitable, transparent, and culturally responsive AI-augmented education systems.



As education systems worldwide evolve to meet the demands of a dynamic, digitally interconnected society, traditional models of teacher certification and credentialing are being re-examined through the lens of emerging technologies. Artificial Intelligence (AI) offers transformative potential to reshape how educators are assessed, accredited, and continuously supported in their professional journeys. This chapter explores the integration of AI into teacher certification processes, highlighting innovative approaches such as AI-driven performance analytics, adaptive testing, digital portfolios, and blockchain-enabled credentialing systems. It also considers ethical, legal, and practical challenges surrounding bias, transparency, and data privacy. By analyzing current trends and pilot implementations, the chapter envisions a future where AI enhances fairness, efficiency, and personalization in educator certification, fostering a more agile and equitable professional ecosystem.

# Preface

As artificial intelligence (AI) continues to transform industries around the world, its potential to reshape education is both vast and urgent—particularly in the realm of teacher support and professional development. Educators are central to shaping future generations, and empowering them through intelligent systems has become a strategic priority for sustainable, inclusive, and high-quality learning environments.

**"Harnessing AI for Teacher Support and Professional Development"** explores how AI technologies can elevate teaching practices, personalize professional growth, and redefine educational ecosystems. This volume addresses the intersection of emerging AI tools, pedagogical innovation, and human-centered design, with a focus on practical integration, ethical considerations, and institutional transformation.

Through contributions from international scholars and practitioners across fields such as computer science, education, sociology, and law, the book examines the role of AI in creating collaborative, adaptive, and reflective teacher development models. These contributions move beyond theoretical speculation and offer grounded insights into how AI can augment—not replace—the vital role of educators.

## OBJECTIVES OF THE BOOK

This volume aims to:

- **Redefine Professional Learning**: Present AI-powered approaches for tailoring professional development to individual teacher needs and goals.
- **Bridge Human-AI Collaboration**: Explore frameworks for productive partnerships between educators and intelligent systems in the classroom.
- **Highlight Equity and Ethics**: Analyze sociological and legal perspectives to ensure responsible and inclusive AI integration.

- **Advance Practical Applications**: Showcase cutting-edge AI tools—from chatbots to automated feedback systems—that support everyday teacher workflows.
- **Promote Interdisciplinary Discourse**: Foster collaboration among educators, technologists, and policy experts for sustainable AI adoption in education.

## ORGANIZATION OF THE BOOK

The book is structured into ten thematically rich chapters that highlight the diverse ways AI intersects with teacher support, ethics, and systemic change:

- **Chapter 1**: *Personalized Professional Learning Paths Using AI Recommendation Systems*

Explores how adaptive learning algorithms can tailor professional development to individual teaching styles, needs, and progress metrics.

- **Chapter 2**: *Virtual Mentorship and AI-Powered Peer Learning Networks*

Investigates how AI can facilitate mentorship, collaboration, and community-building among educators across geographies.

- **Chapter 3**: *Natural Language Processing for Teacher Reflection and Growth Journals*

Demonstrates how NLP tools can help teachers track progress, analyze reflective writing, and identify developmental trends.

- **Chapter 4**: *Enhancing Educational Visual Content through AI-Based Image Denoising Techniques: Implications for Remote Teaching and Digital Resource Development*

Presents image-processing technologies that improve digital content quality, especially in remote and under-resourced teaching environments.

- **Chapter 5**: *Chatbots and Virtual Assistants in Supporting Teacher Workflows*

Explores conversational AI applications that automate scheduling, lesson planning, and administrative tasks to reduce teacher burden.

- **Chapter 6**: *Automated Feedback Systems for Enhancing Teacher Self-Assessment*

Highlights the role of AI in delivering data-driven, actionable insights to teachers about their instructional practices.

- **Chapter 7**: *Sociological Perspectives on AI Integration in Teacher Development: Equity, Identity, and Institutional Change*

Offers a critical examination of how AI affects teacher identity, professional agency, and systemic equity in education.

- **Chapter 8**: *Ethical and Legal Frameworks for the Responsible Use of Generative AI in Scientific Research and Intellectual Property Protection*

Investigates broader ethical and legal implications of generative AI, including content ownership and academic integrity in professional learning environments.

- **Chapter 9**: *AI as a Co-Teacher: Designing Symbiotic Human-AI Classroom Partnerships*

Discusses frameworks for co-teaching models in which AI supports personalization, formative assessment, and differentiated instruction.

- **Chapter 10**: *AI and the Future of Teacher Certification and Credentialing*

Explores the use of AI in evaluating competencies, verifying credentials, and automating certification pathways for educators.

## IN CONCLUSION

We envision this book as both a scholarly contribution and a practical guide for educators, instructional designers, policymakers, and technologists committed to enhancing teaching through AI. By foregrounding equity, ethics, and educator empowerment, this volume contributes to a vision of AI in education that is collaborative, transparent, and deeply human-centered.

We hope that these chapters inspire innovative thinking and meaningful action toward a more responsive and resilient educational future.

**Hewa Majeed Zangana**
*Duhok Polytechnic University, Iraq*

**Calvin Nobles**
*University of Maryland Global Campus, USA*

**Marwan Omar**
*Illinois Institute of Technology, USA*

Chapter 1

# Personalized Professional Learning Paths Using AI Recommendation Systems

**Hewa Majeed Zangana**
https://orcid.org/0000-0001-7909-254X
*Duhok Polytechnic University, Iraq*

**Marwan Omar**
*Illinois Institute of Technology, USA*

**Calvin Nobles**
*University of Maryland Global Campus, USA*

**Anik Vega Vitianingsih**
*Universitas Dr. Soetomo, Indonesia*

## ABSTRACT

*The rapid advancement of artificial intelligence (AI) has opened new avenues for personalizing professional development in education. This chapter explores how AI-powered recommendation systems can be leveraged to design individualized learning paths for teachers, aligning with their unique goals, teaching contexts, and competency levels. Unlike traditional one-size-fits-all training programs, AI-driven systems analyze teacher profiles, performance data, preferences, and feedback to generate dynamic, adaptive learning trajectories. The chapter presents a conceptual framework for integrating these systems into professional development platforms, supported by real-world applications and emerging research. Ethical considerations,*

DOI: 10.4018/979-8-3373-5951-9.ch001

*data privacy, and algorithmic transparency are also addressed to ensure responsible implementation. By embracing AI recommendations, educational institutions can foster more effective, engaging, and sustainable teacher growth, ultimately enhancing student outcomes and instructional quality.*

## 1. INTRODUCTION

The global shift toward digital transformation in education has placed a renewed emphasis on the need for personalized and adaptive professional learning experiences for educators. As teaching environments become more complex and dynamic, there is a pressing need for systems that can tailor professional development (PD) to the specific goals, strengths, and contextual challenges faced by individual teachers. Artificial intelligence (AI), especially in the form of recommendation systems, has emerged as a transformative force in this domain, enabling more precise, efficient, and impactful learning trajectories (Jdidou & Aammou, 2024; Tatineni, 2020).

Traditional professional development programs often fall short due to their static, one-size-fits-all nature. These approaches typically overlook the unique teaching contexts, subject areas, digital competencies, and pedagogical preferences of educators. In contrast, AI-driven personalized learning paths adapt over time based on learner feedback, behavioral data, and performance analytics (Dhananjaya et al., 2024; Ma et al., 2023). AI recommendation systems combine machine learning algorithms, content-based filtering, and collaborative techniques to guide educators toward resources and modules that align with their evolving needs (Tran et al., 2024).

Recent studies confirm that personalized learning paths enhance motivation, learning efficiency, and long-term knowledge retention among educators (Bayly-Castaneda et al., 2024; Morozevich et al., 2022). AI-based recommendation engines not only support pedagogical skill development but also promote continuous professional growth, fostering a culture of lifelong learning (Hu et al., 2025). For instance, Hu et al. (2025) demonstrate how AI-supported clinical training in dental education can be extrapolated to broader educational contexts for improving teacher training systems.

Moreover, the incorporation of AI within educational ecosystems is enabling the emergence of smart platforms that autonomously identify teachers' gaps and provide micro-credential-based learning interventions (Patil, 2025; Kulugh et al., 2025). These platforms can factor in real-time performance metrics, user preferences, peer recommendations, and even predicted future learning trajectories. This contextual adaptability makes AI recommendation systems uniquely suited to support teachers' ever-changing professional demands (Kabashkin et al., 2024; Li & Ding, 2025).

However, integrating AI into professional learning also raises challenges concerning algorithmic transparency, ethical use of data, and cybersecurity (Omar & Zangana, 2025; Zangana & Omar, 2025). The use of sensitive teacher performance data in recommendation systems necessitates robust data governance frameworks and AI auditing tools to prevent misuse or bias (Hamza & Omar, 2013; Huff et al., 2023; Hewa Majeed Zangana et al., 2025). Prior works have emphasized the necessity of secure and ethical AI deployment in education and research (Zangana & Omar, 2025; Wright et al., 2012; Mohammed et al., 2018).

Furthermore, emerging developments in large language models (LLMs) such as those examined by Gholami and Omar (2023, 2024), along with research on hybrid AI frameworks (Zangana & Mustafa, 2025), highlight the potential for scalable AI systems that can personalize learning paths at both macro and micro levels. These advancements allow systems not only to recommend content but also to generate custom learning materials based on learner profiles (Jones & Omar, 2024; Jafari & Yazdi, 2024).

The chapter draws on a wide base of interdisciplinary scholarship, incorporating insights from AI in education (Tapalova & Zhiyenbayeva, 2022), cybersecurity (Omar et al., 2025), ethics in STM research (Zangana, Amelia, et al., 2025), and data privacy (Zangana, Omar, & Al-Karaki, 2025). It offers a detailed discussion on the architecture of AI-based recommendation systems, use cases in teacher development, ethical implications, and future research directions.

In the sections that follow, we will:

1. Explore the technical foundations of AI-driven recommendation systems.
2. Examine how these systems are reshaping personalized professional development in education.
3. Present real-world use cases and evidence from recent literature.
4. Address security, fairness, and transparency in implementation.
5. Outline a strategic roadmap for deploying AI-based PD in various educational contexts.

By doing so, this chapter aims to provide a comprehensive understanding of how AI-powered personalized learning pathways can revolutionize professional growth for teachers, aligning with both institutional goals and individual aspirations in the digital age.

## 2. BACKGROUND AND LITERATURE REVIEW

The integration of artificial intelligence (AI) into education and cybersecurity has catalyzed a transformative shift in how systems respond to personalization, security, and learning efficacy. Personalized learning, in particular, has become a prominent area of interest due to its potential to adapt educational experiences to individual learners' needs, goals, and preferences. Several scholars have emphasized the growing role of AI-driven recommendation systems and learning path models in optimizing educational outcomes (Bayly-Castaneda et al., 2024; Jdidou & Aammou, 2024; Ma et al., 2023; Tapalova & Zhiyenbayeva, 2022).

A large body of recent work has focused on AI-powered learning path frameworks. For instance, Kabashkin et al. (2024) proposed an ontology-based model to guide personalized education. Similarly, Patil (2025) and Kulugh et al. (2025) demonstrated that career guidance systems could be enhanced using AI to align learning with market-driven competencies. Multi-algorithm recommendation strategies such as collaborative filtering and hybrid deep-learning systems have also been applied to recommend appropriate learning paths and resources (Tran et al., 2024; Li & Ding, 2025). The significance of personal learning algorithms was further reinforced by Jafari and Yazdi (2024), who integrated individual learning styles into algorithmic logic.

Parallel to education, AI and deep learning have revolutionized cybersecurity. Techniques like convolutional neural networks (CNNs) have been employed to enhance malware detection (Omar, 2024), and hybrid object detection systems such as Template Matching and Faster R-CNN have improved image security frameworks (Zangana, Mustafa, & Omar, 2024). As cyber threats evolve in complexity, frameworks like GEADD (Jones & Omar, 2024) and LLM-based malware detection (Omar et al., 2024) have emerged as sophisticated defenses against zero-day attacks and IoT vulnerabilities.

Synthetic data generation and the student–teacher paradigm have gained traction in the optimization of large language models (LLMs) (Gholami & Omar, 2023, 2024). These strategies are vital not only in software development but also in educational AI, where models are increasingly evaluated for their interpretability, efficiency, and bias mitigation. LLMs also play a pivotal role in intelligent tutoring systems and adaptive learning environments (Yekollu et al., 2024; Dhananjaya et al., 2024).

Cybersecurity applications of AI extend beyond malware detection to include email phishing prevention (Zangana et al., 2024), insider threat mitigation (Zangana, Sallow, & Omar, 2025), and network firewall optimization (Zangana, Omar, Al-Karaki, & Mohammed, 2024). Earlier foundational work by Hamza and Omar (2013) on abuse in cloud computing laid the groundwork for understanding malicious behaviors in distributed environments.

With the growing complexity of AI models, securing their implementation has become a primary concern. Emerging domains such as quantum-aware cybersecurity and forensic practices are being reshaped through the integration of LLMs (Zangana & Omar, 2025; Zangana, Mustafa, & Li, 2025). Studies by Omar and Zangana (2025) emphasized the necessity of quantum-resilient models to tackle future challenges in digital investigations and STM (science, technology, and medicine) data governance.

Furthermore, regulatory compliance in STM enterprises is receiving renewed attention. Ethical frameworks and data privacy standards are essential in the deployment of AI in research and education (Zangana, Omar, & Al-Karaki, 2025; Zangana, Omar, & Al-Karaki, 2025a). Tools for ethical scientific communication and English-language AI support are also being explored (Zangana, Amelia, Mustafa, & Li, 2025).

The fusion of AI with smart farming, healthcare, and business sectors reveals that AI's role is not confined to technical optimization alone but spans strategic decision-making and inclusive innovation (Huff et al., 2023; Mavuso, Jere, & van-Greunen, 2023; Zangana, Luckyardi, Mustafa, & Li, 2025). As highlighted in recent IGI Global works (Omar & Zangana, 2024, 2025; Zangana, Al-Karaki, & Omar, 2025), there is a pressing need to balance AI capabilities with ethical governance and sustainable development.

Earlier work has also documented vulnerabilities introduced by repealing net neutrality (Nguyen et al., 2018), as well as database-specific access control mechanisms for privacy-preserving systems (Omar, 2021). These foundations continue to inform current research in AI security.

To begin with, it is crucial to understand the multifaceted applications of artificial intelligence in personalized learning. Table 1 summarizes key AI technologies leveraged in education, outlining their primary benefits and the challenges that must be addressed to optimize their effectiveness.

*Table 1. Summary of AI Applications in Personalized Learning*

| Application Area | Key Technologies | Benefits | Challenges |
|---|---|---|---|
| Adaptive Learning Systems | Machine Learning, LLMs | Tailored content, improved engagement | Data privacy, bias in algorithms |
| Recommendation Systems | Collaborative Filtering, AI | Enhanced learning paths, resource discovery | Scalability, content quality |
| Career Guidance | AI-powered Advisors | Personalized career advice, skill matching | Integration with existing systems |

Various AI techniques are employed across different components of personalized education systems. The following bar chart shows the common techniques and their prevalence in recent literature focused on adaptive teacher learning platforms.

*Figure 1. Prevalence of AI Techniques in Personalized Learning Research*

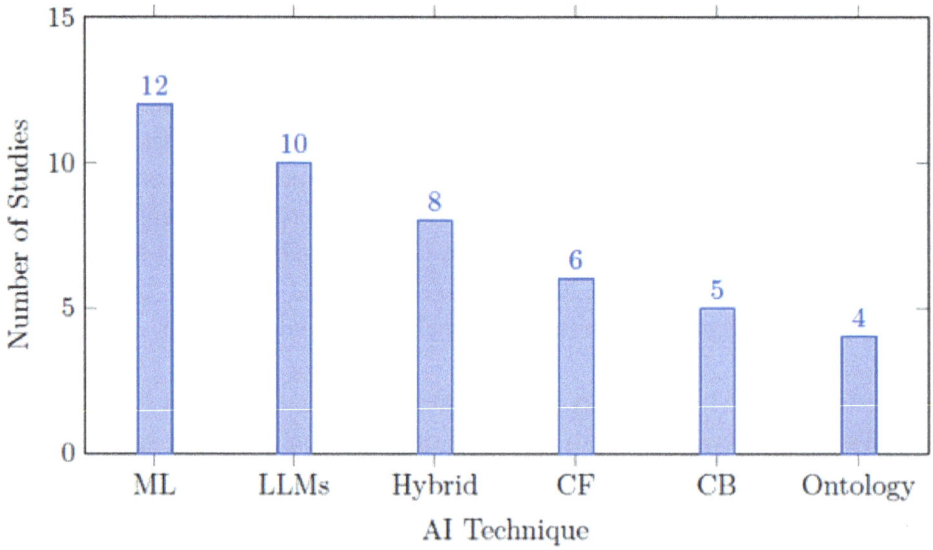


In conclusion, the intersection of AI, personalized education, and cybersecurity presents a fertile ground for innovation. As LLMs, recommendation systems, and deep learning models mature, their impact on adaptive learning, digital forensics, and cyber resilience becomes increasingly pronounced. This literature review affirms the necessity of interdisciplinary approaches that encompass technological, ethical, and educational perspectives to fully harness AI's transformative potential.

## 3. AI RECOMMENDATION SYSTEMS: CONCEPTS AND MECHANISMS

Artificial Intelligence (AI)-based recommendation systems have become an essential component in the digital age, particularly in domains such as education, cybersecurity, healthcare, and business. These systems aim to tailor content, services, or decisions based on user profiles, preferences, and behaviors, thus significantly enhancing user engagement and system efficiency (Bayly-Castaneda et al., 2024; Gholami & Omar, 2024).

### 3.1. Foundations of Recommendation Systems

Recommendation systems utilize algorithms to suggest personalized outcomes or content. The primary methodologies include collaborative filtering, content-based filtering, hybrid approaches, and more recently, deep learning and large language models (Dhananjaya et al., 2024; Jafari & Yazdi, 2024). The integration of AI allows these systems to process vast amounts of user data and feedback, adapting over time for greater precision (Gholami & Omar, 2023).

### 3.2. Personalized Learning Pathways

In educational settings, recommendation systems are increasingly being used to generate personalized learning paths based on students' needs, goals, and learning styles (Jdidou & Aammou, 2024; Ma et al., 2023; Tapalova & Zhiyenbayeva, 2022). Techniques such as deep learning (Li & Ding, 2025) and ontology-driven AI (Kabashkin et al., 2024) are transforming conventional learning environments into adaptive and intelligent systems. Hu et al. (2025) emphasize AI's utility in enhancing clinical training through adaptive learning in healthcare education.

### 3.3. Mechanisms and Architectures

Modern recommendation systems are often constructed with multi-layered architectures that include data preprocessing, model training, feedback loops, and real-time inference engines (Morozevich et al., 2022; Kulugh et al., 2025). AI-based models such as CNNs and RNNs have been successfully deployed for such systems (Tatineni, 2020). Additionally, hybrid algorithms integrating collaborative filtering and content-based approaches have demonstrated improved performance (Tran et al., 2024).

The internal structure of AI recommendation systems typically consists of multiple components designed to process data, extract user preferences, and deliver personalized content. The following architectural diagram captures a generalized AI-based system for personalized teacher development.

*Figure 2. System Architecture of an AI-Based Recommendation Engine*

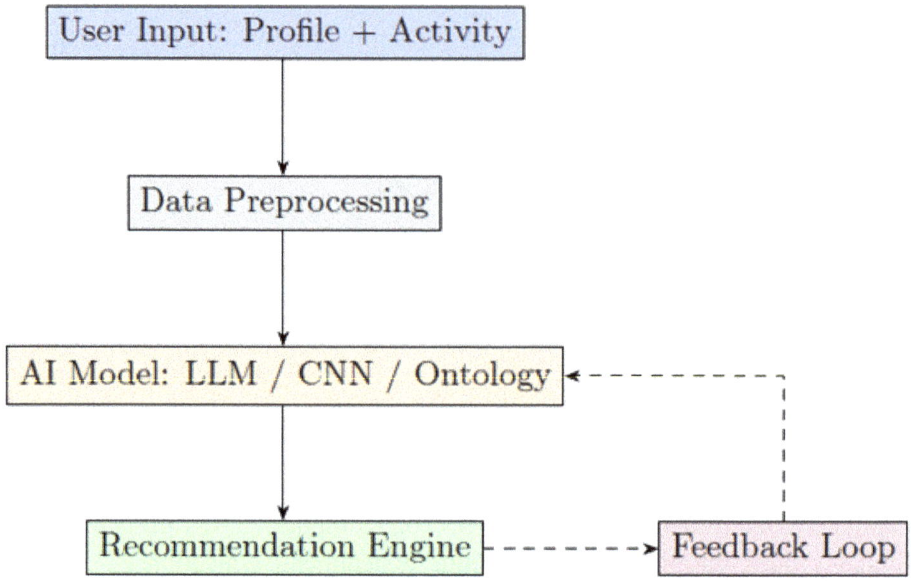


## 3.4. Role of LLMs and Synthetic Data

Large Language Models (LLMs), including GPT-based architectures, have become influential in enhancing recommendation systems. Gholami & Omar (2023, 2024) discuss the potential of synthetic data in boosting the efficiency of LLMs, enabling them to perform tasks similar to their teacher models. Omar & Zangana (2025) further elaborate on using LLMs in software vulnerability detection, suggesting their versatility across domains.

## 3.5. Cybersecurity-Integrated Recommendation Systems

In cybersecurity, AI-driven recommendation systems help identify threats and propose mitigations (Jones & Omar, 2024; Wright et al., 2012). Huff et al. (2023) provide case studies on managing cybersecurity in biotech sectors using recommendation techniques. Integrated AI frameworks help secure digital learning environments (Mohammed et al., 2018; Hamza & Omar, 2013).

### 3.6. Ethical, Legal, and Societal Considerations

As AI recommendation systems become more pervasive, ethical and regulatory challenges surface. Zangana & Omar (2025) and Zangana et al. (2025) explore regulatory frameworks ensuring transparency, fairness, and data security in AI deployment. Concerns over bias, data misuse, and lack of explainability are also prominent (Nguyen et al., 2018).

### 3.7. Application in Career Guidance and MOOCs

AI-driven recommendation systems are proving effective in providing personalized career guidance (Mavuso et al., 2023; Kulugh et al., 2025) and enhancing engagement in MOOCs (Patil, 2025; Yekollu et al., 2024). These systems can assess learners' histories and preferences to suggest suitable career or educational paths.

### 3.8. Future Directions and Integration with Other Technologies

The evolution of recommendation systems will likely involve deeper integration with quantum computing (Zangana & Omar, 2025), NLP for threat intelligence (Zangana et al., 2025), and AI-driven denoising or image processing models (Zangana & Mustafa, 2025). Future systems will emphasize ethical design, cross-domain adaptability, and greater robustness against adversarial attacks (Omar, 2024).

### 3.9 Summary

AI recommendation systems represent a significant leap forward in providing intelligent, user-centric solutions across various domains. Their continued advancement, powered by innovations in LLMs, data science, and security, offers promising potential for reshaping personalized education, secure cyber environments, and beyond (Omar, 2022; Zangana et al., 2024; Omar & Zangana, 2024).

## 4. DESIGNING PERSONALIZED LEARNING PATHS FOR TEACHERS

The digital transformation of education has ushered in an era where personalized learning is not only possible but essential, especially for professional development in teaching. Traditional one-size-fits-all training models fail to address the unique needs, teaching contexts, and learning paces of educators. Leveraging artificial intelligence (AI) and advanced recommendation systems offers a promising solution: the dynamic design of personalized learning paths tailored specifically for teachers.

## 4.1 The Concept and Rationale

Personalized learning paths for teachers are structured development trajectories customized to align with individual professional goals, subject expertise, teaching methodologies, and gaps in pedagogical skills. According to Bayly-Castaneda et al. (2024), AI-powered systems can analyze educators' profiles, track learning behaviors, and suggest next-best actions to support continuous and meaningful professional growth. These systems utilize diverse data sources, including classroom performance, peer feedback, and engagement metrics, to build adaptive recommendations.

Morozevich et al. (2022) argue that machine learning-based models can transform teacher training by dynamically adapting learning sequences and content based on evolving skill sets and reflective practices. The integration of AI into teacher development platforms helps personalize both the content and the delivery mode—making learning more engaging, context-aware, and efficient (Jafari & Yazdi, 2024; Yekollu et al., 2024).

The process of generating personalized professional learning paths for teachers involves multiple stages of data collection, analysis, and adaptive recommendation. The following flowchart outlines the sequential steps AI systems take to generate, refine, and deliver customized learning experiences to educators.

*Figure 3. Flowchart of an AI-Driven Personalized Learning Pathway*

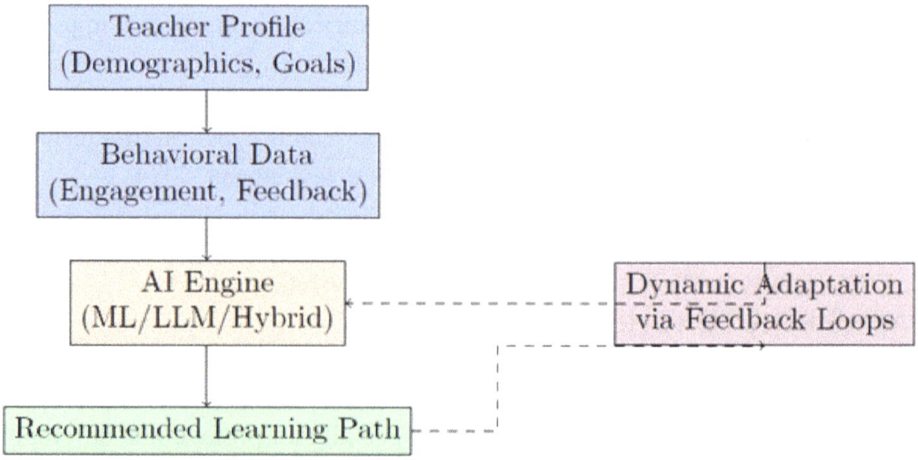

## 4.2 AI Algorithms and Mechanisms

Advanced systems rely on hybrid recommendation algorithms that incorporate collaborative filtering, content-based filtering, and deep learning models (Tran et al., 2024; Ma et al., 2023). For instance, deep neural networks can be used to identify nuanced learning preferences and predict optimal learning trajectories (Li & Ding, 2025). These models not only recommend resources but also adaptively re-route the learning paths based on assessment outcomes and feedback loops (Kabashkin et al., 2024).

Large Language Models (LLMs), such as GPT-based systems, are increasingly deployed in teacher training platforms to generate customized content, automate feedback, and simulate teaching scenarios (Gholami & Omar, 2023; Gholami & Omar, 2024; Zangana & Omar, 2025). Omar (2022) emphasizes that AI's predictive and generative capabilities can drive smarter learning interventions, especially when LLMs are integrated into adaptive learning platforms.

## 4.3 Platform Architectures and Security Considerations

Ensuring the integrity and privacy of teacher data in AI-driven learning platforms is paramount. Studies by Hamza and Omar (2013), and Wright et al. (2012) stress the importance of robust cybersecurity frameworks in educational AI applications. These systems must include encrypted storage, secure identity verification, and controlled access to sensitive learning analytics. Zangana and Omar (2020) highlight the importance of addressing insider threats and implementing governance frameworks, especially in cloud-based training environments.

In addition, as outlined by Huff et al. (2023) and Omar et al. (2025), digital forensics and AI compliance mechanisms must be embedded into platforms to ensure ethical use of personal and performance data. These frameworks help avoid misuse of AI-generated assessments and maintain educators' trust in the system.

## 4.4 Career Development and Decision Support

AI can also serve as a digital career counselor, offering teachers guidance on future certifications, promotions, and role transitions (Kulugh et al., 2025; Mavuso et al., 2023). Personalized learning paths may include modules on emerging technologies, leadership, curriculum design, or inclusive pedagogy—each selected based on the teacher's current role and future aspirations.

This aligns with the vision presented by Jdidou and Aammou (2024), who assert that AI-powered learning systems empower teachers to make informed decisions about their development and adjust learning pace according to contextual demands.

Similarly, Dhananjaya et al. (2024) note that such systems can significantly improve retention and course completion among educators by delivering content aligned with their real-world challenges.

A comparison of how different AI techniques contribute to personalized professional development platforms reveals their unique advantages and trade-offs. The following table provides a summary comparison of key AI approaches used in such platforms.

*Figure 4. Comparative Roles of AI Techniques in Teacher PD*

| Technique | Function | Strengths | Limitations |
|---|---|---|---|
| LLMs (e.g., GPT) | Content Generation | Scalable, Context-Aware | Resource-intensive |
| Collaborative Filtering | User-Based Suggestions | Learner Similarity | Cold Start Problem |
| Content-Based Filtering | Resource Matching | Personalized Items | Limited Diversity |
| Hybrid Systems | Adaptive Learning Paths | Best of Both | Complex Tuning |
| Ontology-Based Systems | Semantic Matching | Domain-Specific Precision | Hard to Maintain |

## 4.5 Real-World Implementations and Use Cases

Several real-world platforms are beginning to adopt this approach. For example, in higher education, AI-driven systems are now being used to support clinical training in medical fields by creating tailored tracks based on prior experience and real-time performance (Hu et al., 2025). In MOOCs, these systems boost engagement by curating highly individualized journeys for educators seeking to stay relevant in digital classrooms (Patil, 2025).

Zangana and Omar (2025), in their exploration of LLMs for scientific research, further stress the potential of generative models in creating interactive case studies, feedback rubrics, and simulated classrooms—helping teachers learn in context-rich environments.

## 4.6 Challenges and Ethical Implications

Despite their advantages, designing personalized learning paths for teachers also presents challenges. These include potential biases in algorithms, lack of transparency in recommendation logic, and the digital divide that may exclude under-resourced teachers from accessing such technologies (Tapalova & Zhiyenbayeva, 2022; Tatineni, 2020).

Addressing these concerns, Zangana and colleagues (2025) advocate for incorporating ethical AI design principles and inclusive frameworks. Transparent models, explainable AI techniques, and equitable access should be foundational in these systems. Moreover, as Mohammed et al. (2018) and Nguyen et al. (2018) caution, digital infrastructures must be hardened against cyber threats and breaches, especially when scaling such systems across districts or nations.

## 4.7 Future Prospects

As highlighted by Jones et al. (2023) and Omar and Zangana (2025), the next generation of intelligent learning environments will likely be powered by integrated AI ecosystems that include chatbots, smart dashboards, predictive analytics, and decentralized content curation. Combining this with quantum-aware cybersecurity and real-time analytics, as explored by Zangana and Li (2025), may offer unprecedented personalization while maintaining regulatory and ethical safeguards.

The evolution of AI-enabled personalized learning systems holds the promise of a more empowered teaching workforce—one that is continuously evolving, contextually adaptive, and aligned with future educational needs. The integration of such systems into national teacher training programs, as proposed by Omar, Zangana, and Al-Karaki (2025), may mark a decisive step in making lifelong, self-directed learning a reality for educators everywhere.

# 5. IMPLEMENTATION MODELS AND CASE STUDIES

## 5.1. Introduction to Implementation Models

Recent advancements in artificial intelligence (AI), machine learning (ML), and large language models (LLMs) have spurred a wave of implementation strategies across education, cybersecurity, digital forensics, healthcare, and more. These implementation models vary from adaptive learning frameworks to AI-powered recommendation systems and from quantum-aware cybersecurity solutions to hybrid image processing architectures. By examining a range of case studies and system architectures, this section outlines how such models have been operationalized in real-world scenarios (Zangana & Omar, 2025; Omar & Zangana, 2025a).

## 5.2. AI-Driven Personalized Learning Systems

In education, personalized learning is a prominent area of AI deployment. Bayly-Castaneda et al. (2024) and Dhananjaya et al. (2024) explored how AI models craft personalized learning paths through adaptive systems. Systems like those proposed by Kabashkin et al. (2024) and Li & Ding (2025) utilize ontology-based and deep learning-based algorithms to enhance learning outcomes. The integration of multi-algorithm approaches (Ma et al., 2023), collaborative filtering (Tran et al., 2024), and individual learning style analysis (Jafari & Yazdi, 2024) has improved student engagement and achievement.

Practical implementations include AI-enhanced Massive Open Online Courses (MOOCs), where engagement and completion rates were optimized (Patil, 2025). Other implementations involve intelligent recommendation systems for career guidance (Kulugh et al., 2025) and curriculum adaptation tools for rural and under-resourced universities (Mavuso et al., 2023; Jdidou & Aammou, 2024). The ethical implications of these tools in STM research have also been analyzed (Zangana, Amelia, Mustafa, & Li, 2025).

## 5.3. Cybersecurity Applications and Threat Mitigation

In the cybersecurity domain, LLMs and AI have revolutionized detection and response strategies. The GEADD method proposed by Jones & Omar (2024) for detecting zero-day threats showcases how GPT-enhanced models can be operationalized effectively. Similarly, Jones et al. (2023) demonstrate ML's rapid classification capabilities in cybersecurity contexts. This is further validated by the application of CNNs for malware detection (Omar, 2024b) and adversarial text classification (Omar, 2024a).

Digital forensics is another area where AI implementation models thrive. The integration of LLMs for software vulnerability detection (Zangana & Omar, 2025), IoT malware analysis (Omar et al., 2024), and network firewall rule analyzers (Zangana, Omar, Al-Karaki, & Mohammed, 2024) highlight the technical versatility of AI in strengthening digital security frameworks.

Cloud security remains an ongoing challenge, as seen in early work by Hamza & Omar (2013), and in more recent AI-driven frameworks (Wright, Dawson Jr, & Omar, 2012; Mohammed et al., 2018; Nguyen et al., 2018).

## 5.4. Hybrid Models in Image Processing and Denoising

Hybrid AI implementations in image denoising have shown promise, particularly in the intersection of cybersecurity, forensics, and medical imaging. Zangana & Mustafa (2024) proposed a wavelet-transform and deep learning approach, while the hybrid Wavelet-GAN model has improved image restoration fidelity (Zangana & Mustafa, 2025a). Further enhancements are demonstrated in medical applications using wavelet-autoencoder hybrids (Zangana & Mustafa, 2025c).

Zangana, Firas, and Omar (2025) also proposed a hybrid algorithm for image restoration, further contributing to robustness in digital evidence extraction and forensic clarity.

## 5.5. Role of LLMs in Scientific and Educational Domains

Gholami & Omar (2023; 2024) investigated the potential of synthetic data and student-teacher models, finding efficiencies in student LLMs that approach their teacher counterparts. Applications extend into STM research (Zangana & Omar, 2025; Zangana, Omar, & Al-Karaki, 2025a) and ethical scientific writing (Zangana, Amelia, Mustafa, & Li, 2025).

Notably, recent edited volumes (Omar & Zangana, 2025a, 2025b, 2025c; Zangana & Omar, 2025a) explore the integration of LLMs in digital forensics, quantum-aware cybersecurity, and software vulnerability analysis. These volumes present frameworks for the ethical, secure, and regulatory deployment of AI in complex systems.

## 5.6. Case Studies Across Domains

Case studies illustrate real-world application success. For example:

- **Banking Cybersecurity**: Zangana, Mohammed, and Husain (2025) analyze how LLMs mitigate threats in digital financial services.
- **Scientific Research Security**: Zangana, Omar, and Al-Karaki (2025a) explore compliance with security standards in AI-powered research.
- **Healthcare and Biotechnology**: Huff et al. (2023) present implementation models for threat mitigation in sensitive laboratory settings.
- **Education in Clinical Settings**: Hu et al. (2025) detail personalized learning in dental education through AI.
- **Agricultural Cybersecurity**: Case studies by Zangana, Luckyardi, Mustafa, & Li (2025a, 2025b) reveal AI's role in protecting smart farming ecosystems.

- **Email Phishing and Insider Threats**: Zangana et al. (2024); Zangana, Sallow, & Omar (2025) present implementation strategies for human-centered threat detection.

Each case study reinforces the critical role of adaptive AI, regulation, and hybrid system modeling across sectors.

### 5.7. Summary and Observations

Implementation of AI and LLMs spans across education, security, healthcare, and digital forensics. The cited works affirm that combining deep learning, hybrid systems, and ethical frameworks leads to resilient, personalized, and intelligent solutions. Future research will likely converge AI deployment with quantum security, as proposed by Zangana & Omar (2025a) and Zangana, Mustafa, & Li (2025). Continued interdisciplinary collaboration and regulatory compliance remain crucial for scalable and responsible AI integration.

## 6. BENEFITS AND IMPACT ON PROFESSIONAL DEVELOPMENT

The integration of advanced technologies such as Artificial Intelligence (AI), personalized learning algorithms, and large language models (LLMs) is transforming professional development across various domains, offering profound benefits that enhance skill acquisition, adaptability, and lifelong learning. The rapid advancement in AI-driven personalized learning systems enables tailored educational experiences that align with individual learning styles and career trajectories, thereby fostering more effective and engaging professional growth (Bayly-Castaneda, Ramirez-Montoya, & Morita-Alexander, 2024; Jafari & Yazdi, 2024; Jdidou & Aammou, 2024).

One significant benefit of AI in professional development is the creation of personalized learning paths, which optimize the learning experience by recommending content and skill-building activities tailored to the learner's current competencies and career goals (Ma et al., 2023; Kabashkin, Mišņevs, & Zervina, 2024; Patil, 2025). Such systems leverage collaborative filtering, content-based approaches, and ontology-driven frameworks to ensure adaptability and continuous engagement, enhancing knowledge retention and application (Tran et al., 2024; Morozevich, Korotkikh, & Kuznetsova, 2022). This personalization accelerates the upskilling process, allowing professionals to remain competitive in rapidly evolving industries (Dhananjaya et al., 2024).

Moreover, the use of large language models (LLMs) such as GPT and BERT is revolutionizing the way professionals access information and develop expertise. These models enable efficient information retrieval, automated summarization, and context-aware recommendations, thus supporting decision-making and problem-solving in real time (Gholami & Omar, 2023, 2024; Omar & Zangana, 2025; Zangana & Omar, 2025a). For instance, LLMs have been applied in cybersecurity to enhance threat detection and response capabilities, showcasing their ability to support complex professional tasks and continuous learning in highly specialized fields (Jones & Omar, 2024; Omar, 2024a; Omar, 2024b).

The impact on professional development is not limited to technical skills but extends to ethical and regulatory competencies as well. With the increasing reliance on AI and digital technologies, professionals must understand and comply with data privacy, security standards, and ethical guidelines to ensure responsible use of technology (Zangana, Omar, & Al-Karaki, 2025a; Zangana & Omar, 2025b; Hamza & Omar, 2013). Educational systems integrating AI now also embed these crucial topics into personalized learning pathways, thereby preparing professionals to navigate legal and ethical challenges effectively (Zangana & Omar, 2025c; Zangana, Mustafa, & Omar, 2024).

Additionally, AI-driven professional development fosters lifelong learning by continuously adapting to evolving knowledge domains and individual career stages (Bayly-Castaneda et al., 2024; Hu et al., 2025). This dynamic learning model supports continuous improvement and helps professionals stay abreast of innovations and industry standards. In fields such as healthcare, education, and cybersecurity, such adaptive learning significantly enhances competency and innovation capacity (Huff et al., 2023; Hu et al., 2025; Zangana, Luckyardi, Mustafa, & Li, 2025).

Furthermore, AI-enabled career guidance systems provide professionals with personalized recommendations based on labor market trends, skills demand, and individual preferences, facilitating informed career decisions and progression (Kulugh, Aondover, & Faki, 2025; Mavuso, Jere, & vanGreunen, 2023). This is particularly valuable in rural or underserved areas where access to traditional career counseling resources may be limited.

The use of large language models (LLMs) has brought substantial improvements in cybersecurity domains. Table 2 highlights specific applications, the techniques used, their tangible benefits, and current limitations that researchers are actively working to overcome.

*Table 2. Advances in Cybersecurity Using Large Language Models (LLMs)*

| Area of Application | Techniques Employed | Improvements | Limitations |
|---|---|---|---|
| Threat Detection | GPT-2, BERT, Hybrid Models | Faster detection, reduced false positives | Adversarial vulnerability |
| Vulnerability Detection | Supervised & Unsupervised LLMs | Enhanced accuracy, automated scanning | Training data bias, resource intensive |
| Incident Response | Automated Playbooks with AI | Real-time threat mitigation | Complexity of dynamic threats |

In conclusion, the integration of AI, personalized learning algorithms, and LLMs into professional development frameworks offers transformative benefits, including enhanced personalized learning, accelerated skill acquisition, ethical awareness, and informed career guidance. These advances equip professionals to thrive in complex, technology-driven environments while promoting lifelong learning and adaptive expertise essential for sustained career success (Zangana & Omar, 2025d; Omar, Zangana, & Mohammed, 2025; Zangana et al., 2025).

## 7. CHALLENGES AND ETHICAL CONSIDERATIONS

The rapid integration of artificial intelligence (AI) across diverse fields such as personalized learning, cybersecurity, healthcare, and digital forensics introduces numerous challenges and ethical considerations that must be addressed to ensure responsible and beneficial use.

### 7.1 Technical and Operational Challenges

One of the foremost challenges in deploying AI-driven systems, particularly in personalized learning and cybersecurity, involves ensuring robustness, accuracy, and scalability. Large Language Models (LLMs) and AI-based recommendation systems demand substantial computational resources and vast datasets, which can lead to issues of efficiency and data bias (Gholami & Omar, 2023; Gholami & Omar, 2024). Moreover, the synthetic data often used to train these models, while improving efficiency, may inadvertently introduce artifacts that reduce real-world performance (Gholami & Omar, 2023).

In cybersecurity, adversarial attacks on AI models—such as those targeting Deep Neural Networks (DNNs)—pose significant risks, undermining system trustworthiness and safety (Omar, 2024). The detection and mitigation of zero-day threats remain complex despite advances like the GPT-2 Enhanced Attack Detection and Defense (GEADD) method, necessitating ongoing innovation (Jones & Omar, 2024;

*Table 3. Key Challenges and Ethical Considerations in AI Adoption*

| Challenge | Description | Proposed Mitigation Approaches |
|---|---|---|
| Data Privacy | Risks of unauthorized data access and misuse | Privacy-preserving AI, federated learning |
| Algorithmic Bias | Discriminatory outputs due to biased data | Fairness-aware training, diverse datasets |
| Regulatory Compliance | Navigating evolving AI governance frameworks | Continuous policy updates, cross-sector collaboration |
| Ethical AI Use | Ensuring transparency and accountability | Explainable AI, stakeholder engagement |

In conclusion, while AI holds transformative potential for personalized education, cybersecurity, and beyond, addressing its challenges and ethical considerations is essential to harness its benefits safely and equitably.

## 8. FUTURE TRENDS AND RESEARCH DIRECTIONS

The rapid advancement of artificial intelligence (AI), large language models (LLMs), and deep learning has opened unprecedented opportunities across multiple domains including education, cybersecurity, digital forensics, and personalized learning. Future research is expected to focus on enhancing AI's adaptability, security, and ethical deployment while expanding its practical applications.

### 8.1 Personalized Learning and Adaptive Education

One of the most promising future trends is the integration of AI-driven personalized learning pathways that adapt dynamically to individual learner preferences and needs. Researchers emphasize the growing impact of recommendation systems and adaptive algorithms to tailor educational content, thereby enhancing engagement and learning outcomes (Bayly-Castaneda, Ramirez-Montoya, & Morita-Alexander, 2024; Dhananjaya et al., 2024; Jafari & Yazdi, 2024; Jdidou & Aammou, 2024). The development of AI frameworks incorporating ontology-based knowledge and hybrid machine learning methods facilitates the customization of learning paths, enabling lifelong learning and skill acquisition (Kabashkin, Mišņevs, & Zervina, 2024; Ma et al., 2023; Morozevich, Korotkikh, & Kuznetsova, 2022; Patil, 2025; Tran et al., 2024; Yekollu et al., 2024). This trend is transforming education by enhancing clinical training in healthcare (Hu et al., 2025) and enabling personalized career guidance systems, especially in under-resourced rural areas (Kulugh, Aondover, & Faki, 2025; Mavuso, Jere, & vanGreunen, 2023).

Future research must further explore the ethical design of these AI-driven systems to ensure inclusivity, transparency, and respect for learner privacy (Zangana, Amelia, Mustafa, & Li, 2025).

## 8.2 Large Language Models (LLMs) and Cybersecurity

The emergence of LLMs has revolutionized cybersecurity by enabling faster and more accurate detection of vulnerabilities, malware, and zero-day exploits (Jones & Omar, 2024; Jones et al., 2023; Omar & Zangana, 2025; Omar, 2024; Zangana & Omar, 2025). However, this evolution demands a balanced approach that addresses adversarial threats, data privacy, and the ethical use of AI models (Gholami & Omar, 2023, 2024; Huff et al., 2023; Zangana, Sallow, & Omar, 2025).

Research directions include leveraging LLMs for quantum-aware cybersecurity, where quantum computing threats are mitigated through AI-enhanced cryptographic strategies (Zangana & Omar, 2025; Zangana, Mustafa, & Li, 2025). Moreover, integrating AI with traditional cybersecurity frameworks will enhance threat intelligence and incident response in complex network environments (Omar, Zangana, & Al-Karaki, 2025; Zangana, Mustafa, & Omar, 2024; Mohammed, Omar, & Nguyen, 2018).

## 8.3 AI and Digital Forensics

AI's role in digital forensics is expected to deepen with the adoption of intelligent algorithms for evidence analysis, anomaly detection, and attribution of cybercrimes (Omar & Zangana, 2025; Zangana & Omar, 2025). Future research should focus on the development of hybrid models that combine wavelet transforms and GAN architectures to improve image and signal denoising crucial for forensic investigations (Zangana & Mustafa, 2025a, 2025b).

Additionally, establishing regulatory frameworks and ethical guidelines is vital to ensure AI tools support judicial processes while safeguarding privacy rights (Zangana, Omar, & Al-Karaki, 2025; Zangana, Omar, Al-Karaki, & Mohammed, 2024; Zangana, Al-Karaki, & Omar, 2025).

## 8.4 AI in Healthcare and Biotechnology Security

The healthcare sector benefits significantly from AI innovations in personalized training, disease diagnosis, and data security. Future work includes safeguarding biotechnology research from cyber threats using AI-driven management practices

(Huff et al., 2023; Hu et al., 2025). The convergence of AI and cybersecurity is critical to protect sensitive medical data and intellectual property against increasingly sophisticated attacks (Hewa Majeed Zangana, Salih Mohammed, & Mamo Muhamad Husain, 2025).

## 8.5 Ethical, Legal, and Regulatory Considerations

As AI systems become ubiquitous, future research must emphasize ethical governance and regulatory compliance. Scholars advocate for proactive policies that govern AI development and deployment, especially concerning data privacy, algorithmic transparency, and responsible innovation (Zangana, Omar, & Al-Karaki, 2025; Zangana, Al-Karaki, & Omar, 2025; Nguyen, Mohammed, Omar, & Banisakher, 2018). Cybersecurity frameworks need to evolve to accommodate AI's dual-use nature—both as a defensive and offensive tool (Hamza & Omar, 2013; Wright, Dawson Jr, & Omar, 2012).

## 8.6 Advances in Hybrid and Explainable AI Models

The fusion of deep learning with classical methods is expected to yield robust AI systems that are both accurate and interpretable. Novel hybrid algorithms for image restoration and object detection demonstrate improved performance in complex environments, enhancing applications in cybersecurity and medical imaging (Zangana, Firas, & Omar, 2025; Zangana, Mustafa, & Omar, 2024; Zangana, Mustafa, & Li, 2025).

Explainability will remain a priority to foster trust in AI solutions, especially in critical domains where decision transparency is mandatory (Omar, 2021, 2022).

## 8.7 Integration with Quantum Computing

The intersection of AI and quantum computing presents a frontier with transformative potential for cybersecurity and data analysis. Research is beginning to focus on quantum-aware cybersecurity solutions leveraging LLMs to anticipate and counter quantum-enabled attacks (Zangana & Omar, 2025). This emerging field calls for multi-disciplinary collaboration to develop scalable, secure, and efficient AI-quantum frameworks (Zangana, Mustafa, & Li, 2025).

In summary, the future landscape of AI research is rich with possibilities spanning personalized education, cybersecurity, forensic science, and healthcare. Interdisciplinary approaches that balance technological innovation with ethical considerations and regulatory compliance will be essential to harness AI's full potential responsibly and effectively.

## 9. CONCLUSION

This work highlights the transformative impact of advanced artificial intelligence techniques, particularly large language models and deep learning, across diverse fields such as personalized education, cybersecurity, and digital forensics. The integration of AI-driven personalized learning systems promises to revolutionize education by tailoring content to individual needs, thereby enhancing learner engagement and outcomes. Concurrently, the application of LLMs and hybrid AI models in cybersecurity has demonstrated significant improvements in threat detection, vulnerability management, and incident response, paving the way for more resilient digital infrastructures.

Moreover, the evolving role of AI in digital forensics and healthcare underscores the necessity of adopting innovative algorithms that ensure accuracy, robustness, and interpretability. The convergence of AI with emerging technologies like quantum computing further expands the horizon for novel defense mechanisms and data analysis frameworks.

However, these technological advancements bring to the forefront critical challenges related to data privacy, ethical AI deployment, regulatory compliance, and security governance. Addressing these concerns will require a collaborative effort among researchers, policymakers, and practitioners to develop transparent, accountable, and inclusive AI systems.

In conclusion, while the potential of AI is vast and multifaceted, the future trajectory of research must prioritize not only innovation but also ethical stewardship and practical applicability to fully realize AI's benefits in a secure and sustainable manner.

## REFERENCES


Bayly-Castaneda, K., Ramirez-Montoya, M. S., & Morita-Alexander, A. (2024, August). Crafting personalized learning paths with AI for lifelong learning: A systematic literature review. [). Frontiers Media SA.]. *Frontiers in Education, 9*, 1424386. DOI: 10.3389/feduc.2024.1424386

Dhananjaya, G. M., Goudar, R. H., Kulkarni, A., Rathod, V. N., & Hukkeri, G. S. (2024). A digital recommendation system for personalized learning to enhance online education: A review. *IEEE Access : Practical Innovations, Open Solutions.*

Gholami, S., & Omar, M. (2023). Does Synthetic Data Make Large Language Models More Efficient? *arXiv preprint arXiv:2310.07830.*

Gholami, S., & Omar, M. (2024). Can a student large language model perform as well as its teacher? In *Innovations, Securities, and Case Studies Across Healthcare, Business, and Technology* (pp. 122-139). IGI Global. DOI: 10.4018/979-8-3693-1906-2.ch007

Hamza, Y. A., & Omar, M. D. (2013). Cloud computing security: Abuse and nefarious use of cloud computing. *International Journal of Computer Engineering Research, 3*(6), 22–27.

Hu, C., Li, F., Wang, S., Gao, Z., Pan, S., & Qing, M. (2025). The role of artificial intelligence in enhancing personalized learning pathways and clinical training in dental education. *Cogent Education, 12*(1), 2490425. DOI: 10.1080/2331186X.2025.2490425

Huff, A. J., Burrell, D. N., Nobles, C., Richardson, K., Wright, J. B., Burton, S. L., Jones, A. J., Springs, D., Omar, M., & Brown-Jackson, K. L. (2023). Management Practices for Mitigating Cybersecurity Threats to Biotechnology Companies, Laboratories, and Healthcare Research Organizations. In *Applied Research Approaches to Technology, Healthcare, and Business* (pp. 1-12). IGI Global.

Jafari, D., & Yazdi, Z. S. (2024). Transforming Education with AI: The Development of a Personalized Learning Algorithm for Individual Learning Styles. *Journal of Algorithms and Computation, 56*(2), 135–150.

Jdidou, Y., & Aammou, S. (2024). TRANSFORMING EDUCATION WITH AI: THE ROLE OF RECOMMENDATION SYSTEMS IN PERSONALIZED LEARNING. In *EDULEARN24 Proceedings* (pp. 7662-7669). IATED.

Jones, R., & Omar, M. (2024). Revolutionizing Cybersecurity: The GPT-2 Enhanced Attack Detection and Defense (GEADD) Method for Zero-Day Threats. *International Journal of Informatics* [INJIISCOM]. *Information System and Computer Engineering, 5*(2), 178–191.

Jones, R., Omar, M., Mohammed, D., Nobles, C., & Dawson, M. (2023). Harnessing the Speed and Accuracy of Machine Learning to Advance Cybersecurity. In *2023 Congress in Computer Science, Computer Engineering, & Applied Computing (CSCE)* (pp. 418-421). IEEE. DOI: 10.1109/CSCE60160.2023.00074

Kabashkin, I., Mišņevs, B., & Zervina, O. (2024, September). AI-Driven and Ontology-Based Framework for Personalized Learning Pathways in Education. In *International Conference on Reliability and Statistics in Transportation and Communication* (pp. 494-506). Cham: Springer Nature Switzerland.

Kulugh, V. E., Aondover, K. P., & Faki, A. S. (2025). Artificial Intelligence-Powered Personalised Career Guidance System. *Dutse Journal of Pure and Applied Sciences, 11*(1c), 92–104.

Li, P., & Ding, Z. (2025). Application of deep learning-based personalized learning path prediction and resource recommendation for inheriting scientist spirit in graduate education. *Computer Science and Information Systems*, (00), 43–43. DOI: 10.2298/CSIS241125043L

Ma, Y., Wang, L., Zhang, J., Liu, F., & Jiang, Q. (2023). A personalized learning path recommendation method incorporating multi-algorithm. *Applied Sciences (Basel, Switzerland), 13*(10), 5946. DOI: 10.3390/app13105946

Mavuso, N. C., Jere, N., & vanGreunen, D. (2023). A Customized Artificial Intelligence Based Career Choice Recommender System for a Rural University.

Mohammed, D., Omar, M., & Nguyen, V. (2018). Wireless sensor network security: Approaches to detecting and avoiding wormhole attacks. *Journal of Research in Business. Economics and Management, 10*(2), 1860–1864.

Morozevich, E. S., Korotkikh, V. S., & Kuznetsova, Y. A. (2022). The development of a model for a personalized learning path using machine learning methods. *Бизнес-информатика, 16*(2, 2 (eng)), 21–35. DOI: 10.17323/2587-814X.2022.2.21.35

Nguyen, V., Mohammed, D., Omar, M., & Banisakher, M. (2018). The Effects of the FCC Net Neutrality Repeal on Security and Privacy. [IJHIoT]. *International Journal of Hyperconnectivity and the Internet of Things, 2*(2), 21–29. DOI: 10.4018/IJHIoT.2018070102

Omar, M. (2021). New insights into database security: An effective and integrated approach for applying access control mechanisms and cryptographic concepts in Microsoft Access environments.

Omar, M. (2022). *Machine Learning for Cybersecurity: Innovative Deep Learning Solutions*. Springer Brief. https://link.springer.com/book/978303115

Omar, M. (2024). From Attack to Defense: Strengthening DNN Text Classification Against Adversarial Examples. In *Innovations, Securities, and Case Studies Across Healthcare, Business, and Technology* (pp. 174-195). IGI Global.

Omar, M. (2024). Revolutionizing Malware Detection: A Paradigm Shift Through Optimized Convolutional Neural Networks. In *Innovations, Securities, and Case Studies Across Healthcare, Business, and Technology* (pp. 196-220). IGI Global. DOI: 10.4018/979-8-3693-1906-2.ch011

Omar, M., & Zangana, H. (Eds.). (2025). *Digital Forensics in the Age of AI*. IGI Global., DOI: 10.4018/979-8-3373-0857-9

Omar, M., & Zangana, H. M. (Eds.). (2024). *Redefining Security With Cyber AI*. IGI Global., DOI: 10.4018/979-8-3693-6517-5

Omar, M., & Zangana, H. M. (Eds.). (2025). *Application of Large Language Models (LLMs) for Software Vulnerability Detection*. IGI Global., DOI: 10.4018/979-8-3693-9311-6

Omar, M., Zangana, H. M., Al-Karaki, J. N., & Mohammed, D. (2024). Harnessing LLMs for IoT malware detection: A comparative analysis of BERT and GPT-2. In *2024 8th International Symposium on Multidisciplinary Studies and Innovative Technologies (ISMSIT)* (pp. 1-6). Ankara, Turkiye. https://doi.org/DOI: 10.1109/ISMSIT63511.2024.10757249

Omar, M., Zangana, H. M., & Mohammed, D. (Eds.). (2025). *Integrating Artificial Intelligence in Cybersecurity and Forensic Practices*. IGI Global., DOI: 10.4018/979-8-3373-0588-2

Patil, S. (2025). AI-driven personalized learning paths in MOOCS: Optimizing engagement and outcomes in digital education. In *Digital Transformation and Sustainability of Business* (pp. 387–395). CRC Press. DOI: 10.1201/9781003606185-90

Tapalova, O., & Zhiyenbayeva, N. (2022). Artificial intelligence in education: AIEd for personalised learning pathways. *Electronic Journal of e-Learning*, *20*(5), 639–653. DOI: 10.34190/ejel.20.5.2597

Tatineni, S. (2020). Recommendation Systems for Personalized Learning: A Data-Driven Approach in Education. [JCET]. *Journal of Computer Engineering and Technology*, *4*(2).

Tran, P. D. T., Vu, K. B., Doan, M. N., Dang, Q. T., Dang, Q. V., & Ho, T. T. (2024). Personalized learning paths recommendation system with collaborative filtering and content-based approaches. *Science & Technology Development Journal: Economics-Law & Management*, *8*(2), 5243–5253.

Wright, J., Dawson, M. E.Jr, & Omar, M. (2012). Cyber security and mobile threats: The need for antivirus applications for smartphones. *Journal of Information Systems Technology and Planning*, *5*(14), 40–60.

Yekollu, R. K., Bhimraj Ghuge, T., Sunil Biradar, S., Haldikar, S. V., & Farook Mohideen Abdul Kader, O. (2024, February). AI-driven personalized learning paths: Enhancing education through adaptive systems. In *International Conference on Smart data intelligence* (pp. 507-517). Singapore: Springer Nature Singapore. DOI: 10.1007/978-981-97-3191-6_38

Zangana, H., Al-Karaki, J., & Omar, M. (Eds.). (2025). *Navigating Law and Policy in STM Enterprises: Ethical Governance, Regulation, and Innovation Strategy*. IGI Global., DOI: 10.4018/979-8-3373-4862-9

Zangana, H., Al-Karaki, J., & Omar, M. (Eds.). (2025). *Revolutionizing Cybersecurity With Deep Learning and Large Language Models*. IGI Global., DOI: 10.4018/979-8-3373-3296-3

Zangana, H., Firas, M. M., & Omar, M. (2025). A Novel Hybrid Algorithm for Effective Image Restoration. *Vokasi Unesa Bulletin of Engineering. Technology and Applied Science*, *2*(2), 76–89. DOI: 10.26740/vubeta.v2i2.38118

Zangana, H., & Omar, M. (Eds.). (2025). *Ensuring Secure and Ethical STM Research in the AI Era*. IGI Global., DOI: 10.4018/979-8-3373-4252-8

Zangana, H., & Omar, M. (Eds.). (2025). *Leveraging Large Language Models for Quantum-Aware Cybersecurity*. IGI Global., DOI: 10.4018/979-8-3373-1102-9

Zangana, H., & Omar, M. (Eds.). (2025). *Leveraging Large Language Models for Quantum-Aware Cybersecurity*. IGI Global., DOI: 10.4018/979-8-3373-1102-9

Zangana, H. M. (2024). Exploring Blockchain-Based Timestamping Tools: A Comprehensive Review. *Redefining Security With Cyber AI*, 92-110.

Zangana, H. M. (2024). Exploring the Landscape of Website Vulnerability Scanners: A Comprehensive Review and Comparative Analysis. *Redefining Security With Cyber AI*, 111-129.

Zangana, H. M., Amelia, P., Mustafa, F. M., & Li, S. (2025). The Role of English Language and AI in Scientific Writing: Ethical and Academic Implications. In Zangana, H., & Omar, M. (Eds.), *Ensuring Secure and Ethical STM Research in the AI Era* (pp. 191–218). IGI Global Scientific Publishing., DOI: 10.4018/979-8-3373-4252-8.ch005

Zangana, H. M., & Li, S. (2025). Future Trends in AI and Digital Forensics. In Omar, M., & Zangana, H. (Eds.), *Digital Forensics in the Age of AI* (pp. 347–380). IGI Global Scientific Publishing., DOI: 10.4018/979-8-3373-0857-9.ch013

Zangana, H. M., Luckyardi, S., Mustafa, F. M., & Li, S. (2025). Enhancing Agricultural Cybersecurity: Leveraging Deep Learning and Large Language Models for Smart Farming Protection. In Zangana, H., Al-Karaki, J., & Omar, M. (Eds.), *Revolutionizing Cybersecurity With Deep Learning and Large Language Models* (pp. 307–338). IGI Global Scientific Publishing., DOI: 10.4018/979-8-3373-3296-3.ch010

Zangana, H. M., Luckyardi, S., Mustafa, F. M., & Li, S. (2025). Ethical and Secure AI Applications in Agricultural Research: Challenges and Opportunities. In Zangana, H., & Omar, M. (Eds.), *Ensuring Secure and Ethical STM Research in the AI Era* (pp. 43–76). IGI Global Scientific Publishing., DOI: 10.4018/979-8-3373-4252-8.ch002

Zangana, H. M., Mohammed, A. K., Sallow, A. B., & Sallow, Z. B. (2024). Cybernetic Deception: Unraveling the Layers of Email Phishing Threats. [INJURATECH]. *International Journal of Research and Applied Technology*, *4*(1), 35–47.

Zangana, H. M., & Mohammed, D. (2025). Foundations of Large Language Models in Software Vulnerability Detection. In Omar, M., & Zangana, H. (Eds.), *Application of Large Language Models (LLMs) for Software Vulnerability Detection* (pp. 41–74). IGI Global., DOI: 10.4018/979-8-3693-9311-6.ch002

Zangana, H. M., Mohammed, H. S., & Husain, M. M.Hewa Majeed ZanganaHarman Salih MohammedMamo Muhamad Husain. (2025). Banking Cybersecurity: Safeguarding Financial Information in the Digital Era. *Journal of Computers and Digital Business*, *4*(2), 56–63. DOI: 10.56427/jcbd.v4i2.751

Zangana, H. M., & Mustafa, F. M. (2024). Hybrid Image Denoising Using Wavelet Transform and Deep Learning. *EAI Endorsed Transactions on AI and Robotics*, *3*. Advance online publication. DOI: 10.4108/airo.7486

Zangana, H. M., & Mustafa, F. M. (2025). A Novel Hybrid Wavelet-GAN Image Denoising System. In Bhatti, U., Aamir, M., Gulzar, Y., & Ullah Bazai, S. (Eds.), *Modern Intelligent Techniques for Image Processing* (pp. 409–424). IGI Global Scientific Publishing., DOI: 10.4018/979-8-3693-9045-0.ch017

Zangana, H. M., & Mustafa, F. M. (2025). Image Denoising Techniques for Cybersecurity and Forensic Applications: AI-Driven Approaches. In Omar, M., Zangana, H., & Mohammed, D. (Eds.), *Integrating Artificial Intelligence in Cybersecurity and Forensic Practices* (pp. 117–142). IGI Global Scientific Publishing., DOI: 10.4018/979-8-3373-0588-2.ch005

Zangana, H. M., & Mustafa, F. M. (2025). Wavelet-Autoencoder Hybrid Model for Enhanced Image Denoising in Medical Imaging. In M. Aamir, U. Bhatti, Z. Rahman, J. Bhutto, & W. Abro (Eds.), *Deep Learning in Medical Signal and Image Processing* (pp. 487-508). IGI Global Scientific Publishing. https://doi.org/DOI: 10.4018/979-8-3693-9816-6.ch019

Zangana, H. M., Mustafa, F. M., & Li, S. (2025). Large Language Models in Cybersecurity: From Automation to Intelligence. In Zangana, H., & Omar, M. (Eds.), *Leveraging Large Language Models for Quantum-Aware Cybersecurity* (pp. 277–300). IGI Global Scientific Publishing., DOI: 10.4018/979-8-3373-1102-9.ch009

Zangana, H. M., Mustafa, F. M., Li, S., & Al-Karaki, J. N. (2025). Natural Language Processing for Cyber Threat Intelligence in a Quantum World. In Zangana, H., & Omar, M. (Eds.), *Leveraging Large Language Models for Quantum-Aware Cybersecurity* (pp. 345–388). IGI Global Scientific Publishing., DOI: 10.4018/979-8-3373-1102-9.ch011

Zangana, H. M., Mustafa, F. M., Mohammed, A. K., & Omar, M. (2025). The Role of Change Control Boards in Ensuring Cybersecurity Compliance for IT Infrastructure. *JITCE (Journal of Information Technology and Computer Engineering), 9*(1). Retrieved from https://jitce.fti.unand.ac.id/index.php/JITCE/article/view/303

Zangana, H. M., Mustafa, F. M., & Omar, M. (2024). A Hybrid Approach for Robust Object Detection: Integrating Template Matching and Faster R-CNN. *EAI Endorsed Transactions on AI and Robotics, 3*. Advance online publication. DOI: 10.4108/airo.6858

Zangana, H. M., & Omar, M. (2020). Threats, Attacks, and Mitigations of Smartphone Security. *Academic Journal of Nawroz University*, *9*(4), 324–332. DOI: 10.25007/ajnu.v9n4a989

Zangana, H. M., & Omar, M. (2025). Harnessing the Power of Large Language Models for Cybersecurity: Applications, Challenges, and Future Directions. In Omar, M., & Zangana, H. (Eds.), *Application of Large Language Models (LLMs) for Software Vulnerability Detection* (pp. 1–40). IGI Global., DOI: 10.4018/979-8-3693-9311-6.ch001

Zangana, H. M., & Omar, M. (2025). Introduction to Digital Forensics and Artificial Intelligence. In Omar, M., & Zangana, H. (Eds.), *Digital Forensics in the Age of AI* (pp. 1–30). IGI Global Scientific Publishing., DOI: 10.4018/979-8-3373-0857-9.ch001

Zangana, H. M., & Omar, M. (2025). Introduction to Quantum-Aware Cybersecurity: The Need for LLMs. In Zangana, H., & Omar, M. (Eds.), *Leveraging Large Language Models for Quantum-Aware Cybersecurity* (pp. 1–28). IGI Global Scientific Publishing., DOI: 10.4018/979-8-3373-1102-9.ch001

Zangana, H. M., & Omar, M. (2025). The Role of Leadership in Advancing Inclusive Health Technologies. In Burrell, D., & Nguyen, C. (Eds.), *New Horizons in Leadership: Inclusive Explorations in Health, Technology, and Education* (pp. 203–220). IGI Global Scientific Publishing., DOI: 10.4018/979-8-3693-6437-6.ch009

Zangana, H. M., Omar, M., & Al-Karaki, J. N. (2025). Data Privacy and Security Standards in AI-Powered Scientific Research. In Zangana, H., & Omar, M. (Eds.), *Ensuring Secure and Ethical STM Research in the AI Era* (pp. 1–42). IGI Global Scientific Publishing., DOI: 10.4018/979-8-3373-4252-8.ch001

Zangana, H. M., Omar, M., & Al-Karaki, J. N. (2025). Foundations of Deep Learning and Large Language Models in Cybersecurity. In Zangana, H., Al-Karaki, J., & Omar, M. (Eds.), *Revolutionizing Cybersecurity With Deep Learning and Large Language Models* (pp. 1–36). IGI Global Scientific Publishing., DOI: 10.4018/979-8-3373-3296-3.ch001

Zangana, H. M., Omar, M., & Al-Karaki, J. N. (2025). Regulatory Frameworks in Science, Technology, and Medical Innovation. In Zangana, H., Al-Karaki, J., & Omar, M. (Eds.), *Navigating Law and Policy in STM Enterprises: Ethical Governance, Regulation, and Innovation Strategy* (pp. 1–34). IGI Global Scientific Publishing., DOI: 10.4018/979-8-3373-4862-9.ch001

Zangana, H. M., Omar, M., Al-Karaki, J. N., & Mohammed, D. (2024). Comprehensive Review and Analysis of Network Firewall Rule Analyzers: Enhancing Security Posture and Efficiency. *Redefining Security With Cyber AI*, 15-36.

Zangana, H. M., Sallow, Z. B., & Omar, M. (2025). The Human Factor in Cybersecurity: Addressing the Risks of Insider Threats. *Jurnal Ilmiah Computer Science*, *3*(2), 76–85. DOI: 10.58602/jics.v3i2.37

# Chapter 2
# Virtual Mentorship and AI-Powered Peer Learning Networks

**Rebet Keith Jones**
https://orcid.org/0009-0008-0487-1301
*Capitol Technology University, USA*

## ABSTRACT

*The integration of artificial intelligence (AI) in education has opened new avenues for enhancing teacher support and professional development. This chapter explores the transformative potential of virtual mentorship programs and AI-powered peer learning networks in fostering collaborative, personalized, and scalable professional growth for educators. By leveraging AI-driven analytics, recommendation systems, and communication platforms, virtual mentorship can overcome geographical and temporal barriers, enabling meaningful connections and tailored guidance. AI-powered peer learning networks facilitate dynamic knowledge sharing, real-time feedback, and community building among teachers, amplifying their professional capabilities. The chapter examines current technologies, implementation strategies, challenges, and future directions, highlighting how these AI-enhanced systems can support teachers in navigating complex educational landscapes and promoting continuous improvement.*

## 1. INTRODUCTION

The rapid advancement of artificial intelligence (AI) technologies has profoundly influenced educational landscapes, particularly in supporting teacher professional development and mentorship. Traditional mentorship models, often constrained

DOI: 10.4018/979-8-3373-5951-9.ch002

by geographic, temporal, and resource limitations, face challenges in scalability and personalization (Choudhary et al., 2024; Jalilov, Zawidzki, & Bez, 2024). AI-powered virtual mentorship and peer learning networks offer promising solutions by facilitating flexible, tailored, and accessible professional support for educators worldwide (Bagai & Mane, 2024; Bardia & Agrawal, 2025).

Virtual mentorship systems leverage AI to replicate and enhance key elements of human mentorship through intelligent recommendation engines, natural language processing, and adaptive feedback mechanisms (Devi & Subbulakshmi, 2025; David, 2024). Such systems enable personalized learning experiences by analyzing teacher needs, skills, and goals to match them with suitable mentors or peer collaborators, thus fostering meaningful professional relationships despite physical distance (Wang, Bruckman, & Yang, 2025; Wang, Zhou, & Chen, 2025). This scalability is particularly critical in under-resourced and rural contexts where expert mentors are scarce, a challenge highlighted in recent case studies such as MindCraft for rural India (Bardia & Agrawal, 2025).

Peer learning networks empowered by AI further promote collaborative knowledge building and reflective practice among educators. By harnessing AI-driven analytics, these platforms support dynamic content curation, automated facilitation of discussions, and timely peer feedback, cultivating communities of practice that enhance professional growth (Islam et al., 2024; Kovari, 2025). Such networks complement virtual mentorship by democratizing access to diverse perspectives and expertise, enabling teachers to learn from a broad community (Siham, 2024; Tariq, 2025).

Moreover, the integration of AI in mentorship and peer networks aligns with the broader shift towards Education 4.0, which emphasizes personalized, learner-centered, and technology-enhanced educational experiences (Castañeda et al., 2024; Chakraborty, Misra, & Dey, 2024). AI tools support real-time adaptive tutoring and scenario-based training, thus enriching teacher professional development beyond conventional static methods (Chine et al., 2022; Dai et al., 2024).

Despite these opportunities, challenges remain in designing effective AI-powered mentorship platforms that ensure equity, trust, ethical data use, and cultural sensitivity (Bagai & Mane, 2024; Choudhary et al., 2024). There is also a need for robust evaluation of these tools' impact on learning outcomes and professional competence (Basri, 2024; Silver, Dodurgali, & Gavini, 2024). This chapter explores current technological advancements, practical implementations, and future directions for virtual mentorship and AI-powered peer learning networks, emphasizing their potential to transform teacher support and professional development globally.

## 2. CONCEPTUAL FRAMEWORK

The conceptual framework for virtual mentorship and AI-powered peer learning networks is grounded in the intersection of artificial intelligence, educational mentorship theories, and collaborative learning models. It provides a structured understanding of how AI technologies can augment human mentorship and peer interaction to enhance teacher professional development in scalable, personalized, and equitable ways.

### 2.1. Foundations of Virtual Mentorship

Virtual mentorship is conceptualized as a digitally mediated relationship where mentors provide guidance, feedback, and support remotely, leveraging communication technologies to overcome geographical and temporal barriers (Choudhary et al., 2024; Jalilov, Zawidzki, & Bez, 2024). This form of mentorship aligns with the principles of situated learning and social constructivism, emphasizing learning as a social process supported by interaction and reflection within authentic contexts (Chine et al., 2022).

AI technologies extend this foundation by enabling adaptive, personalized, and context-aware mentorship experiences. Systems utilize machine learning algorithms to analyze mentee profiles, learning preferences, and goals to recommend suitable mentors or resources, facilitating more effective and targeted professional growth (Bagai & Mane, 2024; Bardia & Agrawal, 2025). Additionally, natural language processing and virtual agents provide real-time support, answering queries and guiding users through complex professional challenges (David, 2024; Devi & Subbulakshmi, 2025).

### 2.2. AI-Powered Peer Learning Networks

Peer learning networks constitute a dynamic ecosystem where educators engage collaboratively, sharing knowledge, experiences, and feedback (Islam et al., 2024; Kovari, 2025). AI enhances these networks by automating the facilitation of discussions, curating relevant content, and fostering inclusive participation through sentiment analysis and social network analytics (Siham, 2024; Tariq, 2025).

The conceptual model integrates AI's role in supporting collective intelligence and distributed cognition, enabling teachers to co-construct knowledge and reflect on practice in virtual communities of practice (Chakraborty, Misra, & Dey, 2024). These networks support continuous, situated professional learning beyond formal training sessions, reinforcing informal mentorship and peer coaching mechanisms.

## 2.3. Key Components and Mechanisms

The framework identifies core components that synergize to form effective AI-enhanced mentorship and peer learning systems:

- **Personalization Engines:** Algorithms that tailor learning pathways, mentorship matches, and resources based on user data, preferences, and performance (Khamis, 2024; Basri, 2024).
- **Virtual Agents and Chatbots:** AI-driven conversational agents that provide on-demand guidance, answer questions, and simulate mentoring conversations to scaffold teacher reflection (Devi & Subbulakshmi, 2025; David, 2024).
- **Collaborative Platforms:** Social and collaborative tools augmented with AI analytics that facilitate interaction, resource sharing, and community building among educators (Islam et al., 2024; Loganathan et al., 2025).
- **Data-Driven Feedback Loops:** Continuous monitoring and analysis of user engagement and learning outcomes, enabling iterative improvement of mentorship interventions (Dai et al., 2024; Silver, Dodurgali, & Gavini, 2024).
- **Equity and Ethical Safeguards:** Mechanisms to ensure fairness, privacy, and cultural sensitivity in AI decision-making processes, mitigating biases and promoting inclusive participation (Bagai & Mane, 2024; Choudhary et al., 2024).

This table outlines the key components of AI-enhanced mentorship systems. Each component is described along with practical examples, providing insight into how these elements work together to foster effective mentorship and professional development for educators.

*Table 1. Key Components of AI-Enhanced Mentorship*

| Component | Description | Example |
|---|---|---|
| Personalization Engines | Tailor learning pathways and mentorship matches | Adaptive learning platforms |
| Virtual Agents | Provide on-demand guidance and support | Chatbots for teacher queries |
| Collaborative Platforms | Facilitate resource sharing and community building | Online forums for educators |
| Data-Driven Feedback Loops | Monitor engagement and learning outcomes | Analytics dashboards for mentors |
| Equity and Ethical Safeguards | Ensure fairness and cultural sensitivity | Inclusive design practices |

## 2.4. Theoretical Integration and Application

This conceptual framework integrates theories from educational psychology, human-computer interaction, and knowledge management (Chine et al., 2022; Chakraborty, Misra, & Dey, 2024). It supports scenarios where AI facilitates both synchronous and asynchronous mentoring interactions, tailored professional learning, and peer collaboration. For example, scenario-based training augmented with AI virtual agents has shown promise in equitable mentorship applications, fostering just-in-time learning and reflective practice (Chine et al., 2022).

In practice, platforms like MindCraft demonstrate how AI-powered personalized mentorship can revolutionize teacher support in rural and underserved contexts by bridging access gaps and contextualizing learning resources (Bardia & Agrawal, 2025). Similarly, AI-powered learning experience platforms in workplaces emphasize personalized career development pathways through data-driven insights (Khamis, 2024).

## 2.5. Emerging Trends and Challenges

The conceptual framework also acknowledges emerging trends such as hybrid AI-human mentoring systems where AI supports but does not replace human mentors, thereby maintaining relational and empathetic aspects of mentorship (Jalilov, Zawidzki, & Bez, 2024). There is growing recognition of the importance of designing AI systems that promote trust, transparency, and explainability to support sustained engagement and effective learning outcomes (Bagai & Mane, 2024; Choudhary et al., 2024).

Challenges include ensuring data quality and interoperability across educational systems, managing ethical concerns related to AI bias and privacy, and addressing digital divides that affect equitable access to AI-powered mentorship (Zangana et al., 2024; Bagai & Mane, 2024). These considerations are critical for realizing the full potential of AI in supporting teacher professional development.

This conceptual framework lays the foundation for subsequent sections that will examine implementation strategies, case studies, and evaluation of AI-powered mentorship and peer learning networks. It positions AI not merely as a technological tool but as an enabler of socially and pedagogically informed mentorship practices.

This diagram illustrates the conceptual framework for virtual mentorship and AI-powered peer learning networks, highlighting the intersection of AI technologies, mentorship theories, and collaborative learning models. It provides a structured understanding of how these elements interact to enhance professional development for educators.

*Figure 1. Conceptual Framework of Virtual Mentorship and AI-Powered Peer Learning Networks*

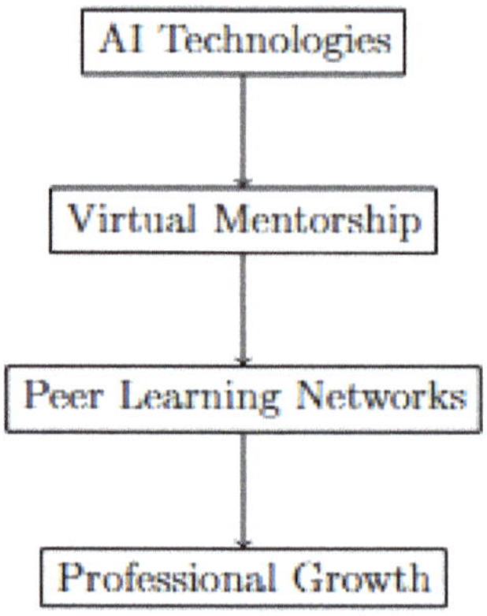


## 3. AI TECHNOLOGIES ENABLING VIRTUAL MENTORSHIP

The evolution of virtual mentorship in education has been significantly accelerated by the development and application of advanced artificial intelligence (AI) technologies. These technologies provide the backbone for creating scalable, personalized, and context-aware mentorship experiences that transcend the traditional limitations of time, geography, and resource availability. This section explores the key AI technologies driving the transformation of virtual mentorship platforms and peer learning networks.

### 3.1. Personalized Recommendation Systems

Central to AI-powered virtual mentorship are recommendation systems that utilize machine learning algorithms to analyze educators' profiles, learning histories, and preferences to match mentees with appropriate mentors and resources (Bagai & Mane, 2024). These systems enable dynamic and personalized mentorship pathways by continuously learning from user interactions to improve match quality and relevance (Bardia & Agrawal, 2025). For instance, MindCraft leverages AI to tailor mentorship and learning experiences specifically for rural Indian educators, overcoming resource disparities (Bardia & Agrawal, 2025). Similarly, workplace learning experience platforms apply AI-driven recommendations to enhance personalized career development and professional growth (Khamis, 2024).

## 3.2. AI-Powered Virtual Agents and Chatbots

Virtual agents and chatbots serve as immediate, interactive support systems within mentorship platforms, providing on-demand assistance, answering queries, and facilitating reflective dialogues (Devi & Subbulakshmi, 2025; David, 2024). These conversational AI tools utilize natural language processing (NLP) to interpret user inputs and deliver context-sensitive responses, fostering continuous engagement and scaffolding teacher learning (Dai et al., 2024). Mentoring chatbots can simulate mentoring conversations, guide goal setting, and offer timely feedback, enhancing accessibility for teachers regardless of time zones or availability of human mentors (Devi & Subbulakshmi, 2025).

## 3.3. Collaborative and Social Learning Platforms

AI enhances collaborative learning by analyzing interaction patterns, sentiment, and participation dynamics within virtual peer networks, thus supporting facilitators in fostering inclusive and productive discussions (Islam et al., 2024; Kovari, 2025). Platforms like Aupdeshik utilize AI to curate content and recommend peer collaborators, enabling a vibrant ecosystem of shared knowledge and peer feedback (CHAURASIA et al., 2024). AI's capability to detect emerging learning needs and trends within communities enables proactive support and resource allocation (Chakraborty, Misra, & Dey, 2024). Alumni portals empowered by AI also exemplify how lifelong learning and professional networking are maintained through intelligent connection recommendations and event facilitation (Loganathan et al., 2025).

## 3.4. Scenario-Based Training and Simulation

AI-powered virtual mentorship incorporates scenario-based training tools that provide experiential learning opportunities for teachers in realistic, controlled environments (Chine et al., 2022). Such simulations are enhanced by AI agents that adapt to user actions, offering immediate, contextualized feedback and guidance (Dai et al., 2024). These immersive experiences enable teachers to practice pedagogical strategies, classroom management, and problem-solving skills with reduced risk, thus strengthening their professional competence (Silver, Dodurgali, & Gavini, 2024).

## 3.5. Data-Driven Analytics and Feedback Systems

AI systems continuously collect and analyze data on user interactions, learning progress, and engagement patterns, generating actionable insights for both mentors and mentees (Basri, 2024; Jalilov, Zawidzki, & Bez, 2024). Real-time dashboards provide personalized feedback loops that help teachers track their development, identify areas for improvement, and adjust learning goals accordingly (Wang, Bruckman, & Yang, 2025). In hybrid AI-human mentorship models, such analytics enhance the mentor's ability to tailor support and maintain relational trust while benefiting from AI's scalability (Jalilov, Zawidzki, & Bez, 2024).

## 3.6. Ethical AI and Equity Considerations

Implementing AI in virtual mentorship raises critical ethical issues around data privacy, algorithmic bias, and equitable access (Bagai & Mane, 2024; Choudhary et al., 2024). Responsible design frameworks advocate for transparency, explainability, and inclusivity in AI algorithms to ensure that mentorship recommendations and interactions do not perpetuate existing inequalities (Siham, 2024; Choudhary et al., 2024). Furthermore, AI systems must be sensitive to cultural contexts and diverse teaching environments to effectively support a global teacher community (Tariq, 2025).

## 3.7. Emerging AI Technologies Supporting Virtual Mentorship

Recent advances in large language models (LLMs) and generative AI, such as ChatGPT, have demonstrated significant potential as virtual mentors, capable of engaging in rich, context-aware educational dialogues and content generation (Castañeda et al., 2024). These models enhance personalization and accessibility by supporting complex, open-ended conversations and providing scaffolded learning resources (Castañeda et al., 2024). Wearable technologies integrated with AI further expand mentorship into health and well-being domains, supporting holistic professional development (Tun, 2024).

AI technologies form the foundation for the next generation of virtual mentorship and peer learning networks by enabling personalized, scalable, and data-informed teacher support systems. As these technologies evolve, their integration must be guided by pedagogical insights and ethical frameworks to realize their full transformative potential.

This chart summarizes the key AI technologies that facilitate virtual mentorship. It highlights the roles of personalized recommendation systems, virtual agents, collaborative platforms, and data-driven analytics in creating adaptive and effective mentoring experiences.

*Figure 2. AI Technologies Enabling Virtual Mentorship*

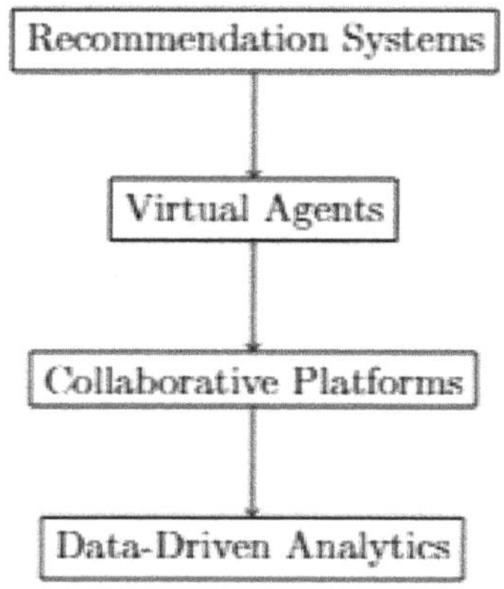


## 4. PEER LEARNING NETWORKS AND COLLABORATIVE AI PLATFORMS

Peer learning networks and collaborative AI platforms have emerged as transformative mechanisms for teacher professional development, fostering continuous, interactive, and socially embedded learning experiences. These platforms harness artificial intelligence (AI) to enhance the quality, accessibility, and personalization of peer collaboration and knowledge exchange among educators worldwide.

### 4.1 AI-Enhanced Peer Learning Networks

Peer learning networks rely on educators sharing knowledge, resources, and feedback within communities of practice, thereby promoting collective professional growth (Kovari, 2025; Tariq, 2025). AI technologies significantly amplify these benefits by automating content curation, participant matching, and facilitation processes, enabling more dynamic and meaningful interactions (Islam et al., 2024; Chakraborty, Misra, & Dey, 2024). For example, platforms like Aupdeshik utilize AI algorithms to recommend peer collaborators and relevant learning materials, optimizing learning pathways tailored to individual teacher profiles and group needs (CHAURASIA et al., 2024).

AI-powered analytics embedded in these networks monitor engagement patterns, participation equity, and sentiment, thereby helping moderators create inclusive environments that support diverse teaching contexts (Siham, 2024; Wang, Bruckman,

& Yang, 2025). This data-driven approach aligns with Education 4.0 paradigms, emphasizing learner-centeredness and networked collaboration to meet complex educational challenges (Castañeda et al., 2024; Chakraborty et al., 2024).

## 4.2 Collaborative Platforms for Professional Development

Collaborative AI platforms extend peer learning networks by integrating virtual mentorship, discussion forums, and shared resource repositories, enabling synchronous and asynchronous collaboration across geographic and cultural boundaries (Bagai & Mane, 2024; Loganathan et al., 2025). These platforms support personalized learning through adaptive algorithms that respond to users' evolving goals, preferences, and performance, thus nurturing sustained professional engagement (Khamis, 2024; Basri, 2024).

MindCraft, an innovative AI-powered platform developed for rural India, exemplifies the potential of collaborative AI systems to democratize access to mentorship and peer learning by overcoming infrastructural and resource constraints (Bardia & Agrawal, 2025). Similarly, AI-enabled alumni portals foster lifelong learning and networking by facilitating connections between experienced and novice educators, supporting skill development and leadership cultivation (Loganathan et al., 2025; Sahoo et al., 2025).

## 4.3 The Role of AI in Enhancing Peer Collaboration

AI advances the efficacy of peer learning networks by enabling intelligent facilitation and scaffolding of group activities (Islam et al., 2024). Natural language processing and machine learning algorithms analyze discussion content to provide real-time feedback, summarize key points, and identify knowledge gaps, thereby supporting reflective practice and deeper engagement (Dai et al., 2024; David, 2024). Moreover, AI agents can moderate peer interactions to ensure respectful, equitable discourse and prompt timely interventions when necessary (Wang, Zhou, & Chen, 2025).

Scenario-based training supported by AI-powered virtual agents has been shown to enhance on-the-job learning and equitable mentoring by providing contextualized, practice-oriented feedback within collaborative environments (Chine et al., 2022; Silver, Dodurgali, & Gavini, 2024). These immersive experiences deepen professional competence while reinforcing peer support structures.

## 4.4 Cross-Cultural and Equity Considerations

AI-enabled peer networks must be sensitive to the cultural and linguistic diversity of their users to foster inclusive and equitable learning environments (Siham, 2024; Tariq, 2025). Platforms incorporating multilingual support, culturally adaptive content, and bias mitigation techniques contribute to reducing educational disparities and enabling all teachers to benefit from collective intelligence (Bagai & Mane, 2024; Choudhary et al., 2024).

## 4.5 Challenges and Future Directions

Despite their promise, AI-powered peer learning networks face challenges related to data privacy, trust, and algorithmic transparency (Bagai & Mane, 2024; Choudhary et al., 2024). Future research must address these concerns through ethical AI design and robust governance frameworks to sustain user confidence and participation.

Emerging trends include hybrid human-AI facilitation models that combine empathetic human judgment with AI's scalability and data-driven insights, optimizing mentorship and peer collaboration outcomes (Jalilov, Zawidzki, & Bez, 2024; Wang, Bruckman, & Yang, 2025). Furthermore, integration with wearable devices and health mentoring systems is expanding the scope of teacher support to holistic well-being, recognizing the interconnectedness of professional and personal development (Tun, 2024).

This section underscores the pivotal role of AI-powered peer learning networks and collaborative platforms in reshaping teacher professional development, fostering connected, personalized, and inclusive learning ecosystems.

# 5. CASE STUDIES AND IMPLEMENTATION EXAMPLES

The integration of AI in virtual mentorship and peer learning networks is exemplified through a variety of innovative projects and platforms across diverse educational contexts. These case studies illustrate the potential, challenges, and impact of AI-powered solutions in enhancing teacher support and professional development.

## 5.1. MindCraft: AI-Powered Personalized Learning and Mentorship in Rural India

Bardia and Agrawal (2025) present *MindCraft*, an AI-driven platform designed to address the educational challenges in rural India by providing personalized mentorship and learning opportunities. MindCraft leverages machine learning to tailor mentorship to individual teacher needs and local contexts, effectively bridging the gap caused by limited access to expert mentors. This platform exemplifies how AI can empower underserved communities by offering scalable, contextualized, and culturally sensitive mentorship (Bardia & Agrawal, 2025).

### 5.2. Designing AI-Powered Mentorship Platforms: Opportunities and Challenges

Bagai and Mane (2024) explore the design considerations for AI-powered mentorship platforms aimed at professional development. Their study highlights the technical challenges such as data privacy, algorithmic bias, and user trust, alongside opportunities for personalized guidance and scalable mentorship. The work underscores the necessity of incorporating ethical AI practices and user-centered design to maximize impact and acceptance in educational settings (Bagai & Mane, 2024).

### 5.3. ChatGPT as a Virtual Mentor in K-12 Science Education

Castañeda et al. (2024) investigate the role of ChatGPT as a virtual mentor for K-12 students learning science, demonstrating how conversational AI can support inquiry-based learning and personalized feedback. Although focused on student learning, the implications for teacher mentorship are significant, showcasing how AI-driven virtual assistants can augment human mentorship with timely, context-aware support (Castañeda et al., 2024).

### 5.4. AI-Powered Collaborative Learning Platforms and Peer Networks

Platforms such as *Aupdeshik* (CHAURASIA et al., 2024) and AI-enhanced collaborative learning environments evaluated by Islam et al. (2024) demonstrate how AI fosters interactive and inclusive peer learning. These platforms utilize AI to recommend collaborators, curate resources, and facilitate discussions, fostering communities of practice where teachers co-construct knowledge and reflect on practice (Islam et al., 2024; CHAURASIA et al., 2024).

### 5.5. Scenario-Based Training and On-the-Job Support

Chine et al. (2022) describe scenario-based training augmented by AI virtual agents that provide equitable mentoring through immersive simulations. These tools enable teachers to practice complex pedagogical skills with immediate AI-driven feedback, promoting confidence and competence in real-world settings. This case exemplifies AI's ability to support situated learning and just-in-time professional development (Chine et al., 2022).

### 5.6. Hybrid AI-Human Mentoring Systems for Scalability

Jalilov, Zawidzki, and Bez (2024) investigate hybrid systems combining AI-driven support with human mentorship, balancing scalability with the relational and empathetic aspects essential to effective mentoring. Their findings highlight the benefits of AI in managing routine tasks and data analytics, freeing human mentors to focus on higher-order coaching and emotional support (Jalilov et al., 2024).

### 5.7. AI in Higher Education Doctoral Supervision

Thong et al. (2025) review AI tools facilitating doctoral supervision, including automated progress tracking and personalized feedback. These technologies improve mentor-mentee communication and support complex academic tasks, illustrating AI's growing role in advanced professional development and research mentoring (Thong et al., 2025).

### 5.8. AI-Powered Alumni Portals and Talent Development

Loganathan et al. (2025) and Sahoo et al. (2025) present AI-powered alumni and talent development platforms that foster continuous learning, networking, and leadership cultivation. These platforms utilize AI to match alumni mentors with mentees, recommend learning pathways, and support entrepreneurial skill development, highlighting AI's role beyond formal education into lifelong professional growth (Loganathan et al., 2025; Sahoo et al., 2025).

### 5.9. AI in Medical Education and Rehabilitation Mentoring

Silver, Dodurgali, and Gavini (2024) explore AI applications in medical education and mentoring in rehabilitation medicine, showing how AI tools enhance individualized learning and competency development in specialized fields, reinforcing the cross-disciplinary applicability of AI-powered mentorship (Silver et al., 2024).

## 5.10. AI-Powered Virtual Assistants Supporting International Students

David (2024) discusses an AI virtual assistant designed to support international students, facilitating communication, resource navigation, and academic advising. This case demonstrates AI's potential to provide culturally sensitive mentorship and personalized support in diverse educational populations (David, 2024).

## 5.11. CyberMentor: AI in Cybersecurity Education

Wang, Zhou, and Chen (2025) introduce *CyberMentor*, an AI-powered learning platform that adapts to diverse student needs in cybersecurity education by providing personalized mentorship, resources, and real-time feedback. This platform showcases AI's capability to tailor mentorship to technical fields with rapidly evolving content and skills (Wang et al., 2025).

## 5.12. AI-Powered Health Mentoring Systems

Tun (2024) examines wearable AI technologies for health mentoring, illustrating how AI can extend mentorship into wellbeing, thus supporting holistic teacher development by integrating physical and mental health monitoring with personalized coaching (Tun, 2024).

## 5.13. Challenges in Data Management and System Implementation

Several studies by Zangana (2015–2024) highlight the importance of robust data quality, management, and system design in implementing AI-powered educational platforms. Effective data integration and quality assurance are foundational to reliable AI recommendations and mentorship analytics, underscoring the technical backbone necessary for successful deployment (Zangana, 2015–2024).

These case studies collectively demonstrate the transformative potential of AI-powered virtual mentorship and peer learning networks across diverse educational contexts. They emphasize the critical role of ethical design, personalization, cultural sensitivity, and hybrid human-AI collaboration in realizing effective and equitable teacher support systems.

This table summarizes notable case studies that demonstrate the application of AI in education. Each case study is described along with its outcomes, showcasing the diverse impacts of AI technologies on teaching and learning.

*Table 2. Case Studies of AI Applications*

| Case Study | Description | Outcome |
|---|---|---|
| MindCraft | AI platform for rural education in India | Personalized mentorship improved access |
| ChatGPT | Virtual mentor for K-12 science education | Enhanced inquiry-based learning |
| Aupdeshik | Collaborative learning platform for educators | Fostered peer connection and feedback |
| CyberMentor | AI in cybersecurity education | Tailored learning for diverse student needs |
| Health Mentoring | AI-integrated health support for teachers | Improved well-being and resilience |

## 6. BENEFITS TO EDUCATORS AND TEACHING PRACTICE

The integration of virtual mentorship and AI-powered peer learning networks into teacher professional development offers a multitude of benefits, significantly enhancing educators' capacities, teaching practices, and ultimately, student learning outcomes. This section outlines these benefits, grounded in recent empirical findings and theoretical advancements.

### 6.1. Personalized and Adaptive Professional Growth

AI-powered mentorship platforms enable highly personalized and adaptive learning experiences tailored to individual educators' needs, preferences, and contexts. By analyzing user data and learning behaviors, AI systems recommend targeted resources, relevant peer collaborators, and customized professional development pathways, fostering more effective and efficient teacher growth (Bagai & Mane, 2024; Bardia & Agrawal, 2025; Khamis, 2024). This personalization helps teachers focus on their unique challenges, accelerating competency development and confidence (Basri, 2024).

### 6.2. Increased Accessibility and Scalability of Mentorship

Virtual mentorship overcomes geographical and temporal barriers, enabling educators from remote, underserved, or resource-constrained regions to access expert guidance and collaborative networks (Bardia & Agrawal, 2025; David, 2024). AI's scalability allows mentorship to reach large numbers of teachers simultaneously without compromising quality, addressing traditional mentorship limitations related to mentor availability and workload (Jalilov, Zawidzki, & Bez, 2024; Choudhary et al., 2024). This democratization of access promotes equity in professional learning opportunities (Bagai & Mane, 2024; Siham, 2024).

## 6.3. Enhanced Reflective Practice and Feedback

AI-driven virtual agents and chatbots facilitate reflective dialogue and timely feedback, critical components of teacher learning (Devi & Subbulakshmi, 2025; Dai et al., 2024). These tools guide educators through self-assessment, goal setting, and problem-solving processes, enhancing metacognitive skills and instructional decision-making (Silver, Dodurgali, & Gavini, 2024). AI's capacity for real-time, data-informed feedback supports continuous improvement and fosters a growth mindset (Dai et al., 2024; Wang, Bruckman, & Yang, 2025).

## 6.4. Strengthened Collaborative Learning and Professional Communities

AI-powered peer learning networks promote active collaboration, knowledge sharing, and mutual support among educators, contributing to vibrant professional learning communities (Islam et al., 2024; Kovari, 2025). Intelligent facilitation tools curate discussion topics, recommend peer connections, and ensure equitable participation, fostering trust and inclusivity across diverse cultural and institutional contexts (CHAURASIA et al., 2024; Siham, 2024; Tariq, 2025). These communities nurture collective expertise, reduce professional isolation, and encourage innovation in teaching practices (Chakraborty, Misra, & Dey, 2024).

## 6.5. Support for Complex Skill Development through Scenario-Based Training

AI-enhanced scenario-based training provides educators with safe, immersive environments to practice complex pedagogical skills and classroom management strategies (Chine et al., 2022). These simulations, coupled with AI mentorship, improve teachers' readiness to handle real-world challenges and adapt instruction to diverse learner needs (Silver et al., 2024). Such experiential learning accelerates skill acquisition and boosts teacher confidence (Chine et al., 2022).

## 6.6. Continuous, Data-Driven Professional Development

AI systems continuously collect and analyze engagement and performance data, providing educators and administrators with actionable insights to inform professional growth strategies (Basri, 2024; Jalilov et al., 2024). This data-driven approach enables timely identification of skill gaps, personalized recommendations, and evidence-based adjustments to mentorship and training programs, ensuring relevance and effectiveness (Zangana et al., 2024; Thong et al., 2025).

## 6.7. Support for Cross-Cultural and International Educator Collaboration

AI's capability to handle multilingual content, analyze cultural nuances, and mediate cross-cultural communication facilitates global professional learning networks (Siham, 2024; David, 2024). Educators benefit from diverse perspectives and shared expertise, enriching their pedagogical approaches and cultural competence (Tariq, 2025).

## 6.8. Holistic Teacher Well-Being and Work-Life Integration

Emerging AI applications extend mentorship beyond pedagogical skills to support educators' health and well-being through wearable devices and health mentoring systems (Tun, 2024). This holistic support acknowledges the interplay between teacher well-being and professional effectiveness, contributing to sustained career satisfaction and reduced burnout (Tun, 2024; Sahoo et al., 2025).

## 6.9. Facilitation of Lifelong Learning and Career Development

AI-powered alumni portals and talent development platforms foster lifelong connections and continuous professional growth beyond formal employment contexts (Loganathan et al., 2025; Sahoo et al., 2025). These platforms provide ongoing mentorship, leadership development, and entrepreneurial skill-building opportunities, supporting educators' evolving career trajectories (Loganathan et al., 2025).

In summary, virtual mentorship and AI-powered peer learning networks deliver multifaceted benefits to educators by providing accessible, personalized, and collaborative professional development experiences. These technologies empower teachers to enhance their instructional practice, engage in reflective and data-informed learning, and sustain their professional well-being throughout their careers.

This table summarizes the benefits of AI-powered peer learning networks for educators. Each benefit is described to illustrate how these networks enhance professional development and contribute to improved teaching practices.

*Table 3. Benefits of AI-Powered Peer Learning Networks*

| Benefit | Description |
|---|---|
| Personalized Growth | Tailored learning experiences based on individual needs |
| Increased Accessibility | Overcoming geographical barriers to mentorship |
| Enhanced Reflective Practice | Providing timely feedback and support for self-assessment |
| Collaborative Learning | Fostering active engagement among educators |
| Holistic Well-Being | Supporting both professional and personal development |

This diagram outlines the multifaceted benefits that AI-powered peer learning networks offer to educators. It emphasizes personalized growth, increased accessibility, enhanced reflective practices, and strengthened collaborative learning communities.

*Figure 3. Benefits of AI-Powered Peer Learning Networks*

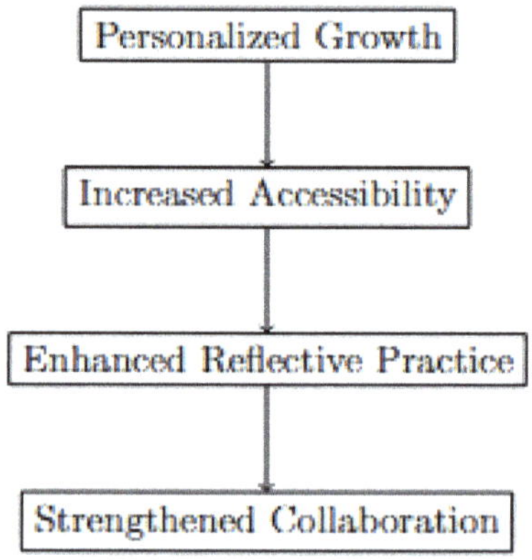


## 7. BARRIERS AND ETHICAL CONCERNS

The integration of AI-powered virtual mentorship and peer learning networks within teacher professional development is transformative yet accompanied by significant barriers and ethical considerations. This section explores key challenges that impede effective implementation and adoption, alongside critical ethical concerns arising from the use of AI technologies in education.

## 7.1. Technical and Infrastructure Barriers

One major obstacle is the uneven availability and quality of digital infrastructure, particularly in underserved or rural areas. While platforms like *MindCraft* demonstrate potential to overcome such gaps through AI-powered personalized mentorship (Bardia & Agrawal, 2025), many regions still face challenges related to unreliable internet access, limited hardware, and inadequate technical support (Bagai & Mane, 2024; Khamis, 2024). Moreover, the complexity of integrating AI systems with existing educational technologies and data systems poses significant technical hurdles (Zangana, 2018; Chakraborty, Misra, & Dey, 2024). Issues related to system interoperability, data quality, and software maintenance require sustained investment and skilled personnel (Zangana & Abdulazeez, 2023; Zangana et al., 2024).

## 7.2. Data Privacy, Security, and Consent

AI-powered mentorship platforms rely heavily on collecting, storing, and analyzing large volumes of personal and behavioral data from educators and learners (Choudhary et al., 2024; Bagai & Mane, 2024). Ensuring data privacy and security is paramount, particularly in contexts involving sensitive personal information (David, 2024; Jalilov, Zawidzki, & Bez, 2024). Consent mechanisms must be transparent and robust, informing users how their data are used, shared, and protected (Choudhary et al., 2024). Despite these concerns, many AI systems lack sufficient safeguards against unauthorized access, data breaches, and misuse, which can undermine user trust and willingness to engage (Islam et al., 2024; Basri, 2024).

## 7.3. Algorithmic Bias and Fairness

AI algorithms can inadvertently perpetuate or amplify biases embedded in training data, resulting in unfair or inequitable outcomes in mentorship and learning support (Bagai & Mane, 2024; Siham, 2024). For example, recommendation systems may favor certain groups over others, reinforcing existing disparities in access to quality mentorship (Choudhary et al., 2024; Kovari, 2025). Cross-cultural and linguistic diversity further complicates fairness, as AI systems often perform unevenly across different demographic groups unless carefully designed for inclusivity (Tariq, 2025; Siham, 2024). Addressing bias requires continuous auditing, diverse data representation, and culturally sensitive algorithm design (Bagai & Mane, 2024; Jalilov et al., 2024).

## 7.4. Transparency, Explainability, and Trust

The opaque nature of many AI models, particularly deep learning and large language models such as those used in virtual mentors like ChatGPT (Castañeda et al., 2024), poses challenges for transparency and user trust (Bagai & Mane, 2024). Educators may be reluctant to rely on AI recommendations or feedback when the decision-making processes are unclear or inexplicable (Devi & Subbulakshmi, 2025; Jalilov et al., 2024). This "black box" effect can hinder meaningful human-AI collaboration and limit the adoption of AI tools in mentorship contexts (Thong et al., 2025). Designing explainable AI systems that provide interpretable and actionable insights is critical to building confidence and effective partnerships between AI and human mentors (Jalilov et al., 2024).

## 7.5. Ethical Use of AI and Human Oversight

Although AI can automate many mentorship tasks, there remain ethical imperatives to maintain human oversight and preserve the relational and empathetic dimensions of mentoring (Jalilov et al., 2024; Choudhary et al., 2024). Over-reliance on AI risks dehumanizing mentorship, potentially diminishing the emotional support and trust-building essential to effective teacher development (Wang, Bruckman, & Yang, 2025; Silver, Dodurgali, & Gavini, 2024). Hybrid systems that balance AI scalability with human judgment are advocated to uphold ethical standards and maintain mentorship quality (Jalilov et al., 2024; Wang, Zhou, & Chen, 2025).

## 7.6. Digital Literacy and Professional Development

The successful adoption of AI-powered mentorship platforms depends heavily on the digital literacy and readiness of educators (Bagai & Mane, 2024; Basri, 2024). Many teachers may lack the necessary skills to effectively engage with AI tools, leading to underutilization or misuse (Khamis, 2024; Kovari, 2025). Ongoing professional development and support are required to build competencies in using AI for teaching and learning, as well as to foster critical perspectives on AI's role and limitations (Choudhary et al., 2024; Loganathan et al., 2025).

## 7.7. Accessibility and Inclusivity Challenges

AI systems must be designed to accommodate diverse learner profiles, including those with disabilities, language differences, and varying cultural backgrounds (Siham, 2024; Tariq, 2025). Failure to do so risks excluding marginalized groups and widening inequities in access to mentorship and professional development (Bagai &

Mane, 2024). Platforms like *Aupdeshik* and *MindCraft* illustrate attempts to address inclusivity through adaptive design and context-sensitive support (CHAURASIA et al., 2024; Bardia & Agrawal, 2025), but broader systemic attention is necessary.

## 7.8. Socio-Technical and Organizational Barriers

Institutional resistance, lack of clear policies, and inadequate funding represent socio-technical barriers to implementing AI-powered mentorship systems at scale (Bagai & Mane, 2024; Choudhary et al., 2024). Moreover, issues related to data governance, intellectual property, and ethical use guidelines remain unresolved in many educational contexts (Choudhary et al., 2024; Jalilov et al., 2024). These factors can delay or complicate adoption despite promising technological capabilities.

In conclusion, while AI-powered virtual mentorship and peer learning networks offer transformative potential for teacher professional development, they face multifaceted barriers spanning technical, ethical, cultural, and organizational domains. Addressing these challenges requires multidisciplinary collaboration, inclusive design, transparent governance, and sustained investment to ensure equitable, trustworthy, and effective AI integration in education.

This flowchart illustrates the key barriers and ethical concerns associated with the integration of AI in virtual mentorship and peer learning networks. It highlights challenges related to data privacy, algorithmic bias, and the need for transparency in AI systems.

*Figure 4. Barriers and Ethical Concerns in AI Integration*

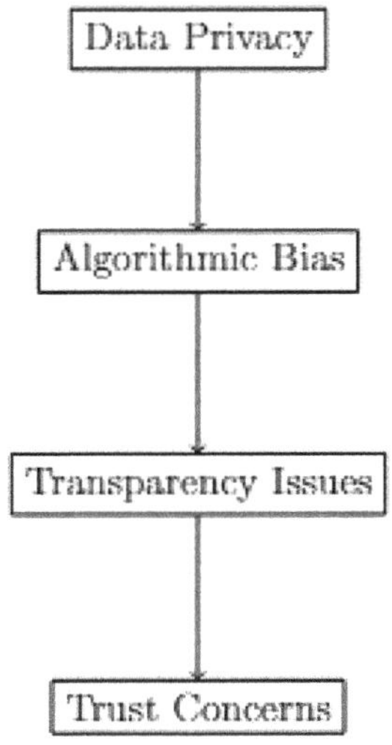

This table presents the challenges faced in implementing AI-powered mentorship platforms. Each challenge is described, highlighting the complexities involved in integrating these technologies into educational contexts.

*Table 4. Challenges in AI-Powered Mentorship*

| Challenge | Description |
|---|---|
| Technical Barriers | Issues with digital infrastructure and access |
| Data Privacy | Concerns regarding the security of personal information |
| Algorithmic Bias | Risks of perpetuating existing inequalities |
| Transparency Issues | Lack of clarity in AI decision-making processes |
| Digital Literacy | Variability in educators' skills with AI tools |

## 8. DESIGN CONSIDERATIONS AND BEST PRACTICES

Designing effective AI-powered virtual mentorship and peer learning networks for teacher professional development requires careful attention to a variety of technical, pedagogical, ethical, and contextual factors. This section synthesizes research insights and practical guidance to outline key design considerations and best practices essential for creating impactful and sustainable AI mentorship platforms.

### 8.1. User-Centered and Context-Aware Design

A foundational principle in designing AI mentorship systems is adopting a user-centered approach that prioritizes the needs, preferences, and contexts of educators (Bagai & Mane, 2024; Bardia & Agrawal, 2025). Platforms must be tailored to local realities, including cultural norms, language preferences, and technological infrastructure, to maximize relevance and usability (Siham, 2024; Tariq, 2025). For example, *MindCraft* emphasizes culturally sensitive, rural-focused design to overcome digital divides (Bardia & Agrawal, 2025). Engaging teachers as co-designers throughout development enhances ownership and alignment with professional practices (Choudhary et al., 2024).

## 8.2. Personalization and Adaptive Learning

AI algorithms should facilitate personalized mentorship experiences by dynamically adapting content, pacing, and feedback based on individual teacher profiles, goals, and performance data (Basri, 2024; Khamis, 2024). This personalization enhances engagement and learning effectiveness (Dai et al., 2024). Hybrid models combining AI recommendations with human mentor input balance algorithmic precision with nuanced human judgment (Jalilov, Zawidzki, & Bez, 2024; Wang, Zhou, & Chen, 2025). Transparency in how personalization occurs builds trust and user agency (Bagai & Mane, 2024).

## 8.3. Scalability and Hybrid Mentorship Models

To address the scalability challenges of traditional mentoring, AI can automate routine tasks such as scheduling, monitoring progress, and providing initial feedback, enabling human mentors to focus on relational and higher-level guidance (Jalilov et al., 2024; Choudhary et al., 2024). Hybrid systems that combine AI-powered virtual agents with human oversight optimize scalability without sacrificing empathy and context sensitivity (Wang, Bruckman, & Yang, 2025; Jalilov et al., 2024). This approach also supports mentoring in resource-constrained environments (Bardia & Agrawal, 2025).

## 8.4. Ethical and Privacy-Conscious Design

Designers must embed strong data privacy, security, and ethical safeguards into AI mentorship platforms (Bagai & Mane, 2024; Choudhary et al., 2024). This includes transparent data use policies, user consent, anonymization, and compliance with relevant regulations (David, 2024; Islam et al., 2024). Addressing algorithmic bias through inclusive datasets and fairness audits is critical to avoid perpetuating inequities (Siham, 2024; Kovari, 2025). Systems should support explainability, enabling users to understand AI decisions and maintain trust (Devi & Subbulakshmi, 2025).

## 8.5. Integration of Collaborative and Social Learning Features

Effective mentorship platforms integrate features that facilitate peer collaboration, community building, and social learning (CHAURASIA et al., 2024; Islam et al., 2024). Intelligent matchmaking, discussion forums, and resource-sharing tools encourage active engagement and collective problem-solving (Kovari, 2025; Chakraborty, Misra, & Dey, 2024). Platforms such as *Aupdeshik* exemplify AI's role in fostering interactive, inclusive learning communities (CHAURASIA et al., 2024).

## 8.6. Support for Scenario-Based and Experiential Learning

Embedding scenario-based training and simulations enhances skill development by providing safe, authentic contexts for practice and feedback (Chine et al., 2022; Silver, Dodurgali, & Gavini, 2024). AI-powered virtual agents can deliver just-in-time coaching and scaffold complex tasks, bridging theory and practice (Dai et al., 2024). Such experiential learning approaches increase teacher confidence and transfer to classroom settings (Chine et al., 2022).

## 8.7. Accessibility and Cross-Cultural Competence

Platforms should ensure accessibility by accommodating diverse learner needs, including disabilities, language differences, and varied digital literacy levels (Siham, 2024; Tariq, 2025). AI tools that support multilingual content and culturally responsive interactions enhance inclusivity and global reach (David, 2024; Siham, 2024). Attention to user interface design and assistive technologies is vital (Zangana, 2018; Loganathan et al., 2025).

## 8.8. Continuous Feedback and Data-Driven Improvement

AI-powered mentorship systems should incorporate continuous monitoring and analytics to provide actionable feedback to educators and administrators (Basri, 2024; Jalilov et al., 2024). Real-time dashboards and personalized reports enable reflective practice and adaptive professional development pathways (Zangana et al., 2024; Thong et al., 2025). Iterative design based on user data and feedback ensures platform relevance and effectiveness (Bagai & Mane, 2024).

## 8.9. Sustainability and Integration with Existing Ecosystems

To ensure long-term impact, AI mentorship platforms must integrate with existing educational infrastructures, policies, and professional development frameworks (Choudhary et al., 2024; Khamis, 2024). Collaboration with educational institutions, policymakers, and communities fosters alignment and resource sharing (Zangana et al., 2022). Sustainable funding models and capacity building for technical support are also critical (Bardia & Agrawal, 2025; Loganathan et al., 2025).

## 8.10. Supporting Holistic Teacher Development

Beyond pedagogical skills, design should consider teacher well-being, leadership, and career development (Tun, 2024; Sahoo et al., 2025). Wearable technologies and health mentoring systems integrated with AI platforms offer holistic support, promoting resilience and sustained professional engagement (Tun, 2024). Alumni networks and entrepreneurial skill development further enrich professional trajectories (Loganathan et al., 2025; Sahoo et al., 2025).

## 8.11 Summary

Incorporating these design considerations and best practices is essential to develop AI-powered virtual mentorship and peer learning networks that are effective, equitable, scalable, and sustainable. Through thoughtful, context-aware design that balances AI capabilities with human-centered values, these platforms can transform teacher professional development and positively impact educational outcomes worldwide.

# 9. FUTURE DIRECTIONS AND RESEARCH OPPORTUNITIES

As AI-powered virtual mentorship and peer learning networks continue to evolve, several promising avenues for future research and development emerge. These opportunities reflect both technological advancements and the pressing needs of educators worldwide, aiming to deepen impact, scalability, and equity in teacher professional development.

## 9.1. Enhancing Personalization through Multimodal AI

While current AI systems personalize learning based on interaction data, future research should explore multimodal data integration—including speech, gesture, facial expressions, and physiological signals—to provide richer, context-sensitive mentorship (Bagai & Mane, 2024; Basri, 2024). Advances in affective computing and natural language understanding can enable more empathetic, responsive virtual mentors, adapting dynamically to teachers' emotional and cognitive states (Devi & Subbulakshmi, 2025; Dai et al., 2024). This direction can further individualize support and improve engagement (Castañeda et al., 2024).

## 9.2. Expanding Access in Under-Resourced and Rural Settings

AI mentorship platforms must address persistent digital divides by focusing on affordability, low-bandwidth solutions, and culturally relevant content (Bardia & Agrawal, 2025; Choudhary et al., 2024). Research on offline-capable and lightweight AI models suited for rural and low-resource contexts can increase reach and equity (Loganathan et al., 2025; CHAURASIA et al., 2024). Co-design with local educators and communities remains vital to ensure cultural sensitivity and contextual fit (Siham, 2024; Tariq, 2025).

## 9.3. Hybrid Models Balancing AI and Human Mentorship

Future studies should investigate optimal blends of AI automation and human mentoring, clarifying when and how AI should augment versus defer to human judgment (Jalilov et al., 2024; Wang, Bruckman, & Yang, 2025). Empirical research on hybrid mentoring's impact on teacher efficacy, trust, and satisfaction can guide design refinements (Choudhary et al., 2024; Wang, Zhou, & Chen, 2025). This line of work supports scalability without compromising relational richness.

## 9.4. Ethical AI Frameworks and Trustworthiness

Robust ethical frameworks for AI mentorship platforms need further elaboration and validation, addressing data privacy, bias mitigation, transparency, and explainability (Bagai & Mane, 2024; Choudhary et al., 2024). Researchers should develop tools to audit AI decision-making processes and engage educators in participatory ethics dialogues (David, 2024; Kovari, 2025). Trustworthy AI fosters adoption and sustained engagement (Devi & Subbulakshmi, 2025; Islam et al., 2024).

## 9.5. Cross-Cultural and Multilingual Adaptation

As platforms scale globally, AI systems must better handle cross-cultural nuances and multilingual interactions (Siham, 2024; David, 2024). Advances in natural language processing for diverse languages and dialects, as well as culturally adaptive dialogue management, are critical research frontiers (Chakraborty, Misra, & Dey, 2024; Khamis, 2024). Such capabilities improve inclusivity and user satisfaction.

## 9.6. Integration with Experiential and Scenario-Based Learning

Building on the benefits of scenario-based training, future AI tools can create increasingly immersive, realistic simulations tailored to diverse teaching contexts (Chine et al., 2022; Silver, Dodurgali, & Gavini, 2024). Research should explore adaptive virtual environments that adjust complexity in real-time, fostering deeper skill mastery (Dai et al., 2024). Coupling AI mentoring with experiential learning promotes transfer to real classrooms.

## 9.7. Collaborative and Networked Learning Ecosystems

Expanding AI's role in supporting collaborative learning, peer feedback, and community knowledge sharing offers rich research potential (Islam et al., 2024; Kovari, 2025). Investigating AI-powered facilitation of networked learning among teachers, alumni, and experts can strengthen professional learning communities (Loganathan et al., 2025; CHAURASIA et al., 2024). Longitudinal studies can assess how these ecosystems impact teacher growth and retention.

## 9.8. Health and Well-being Support Integration

Emerging research shows promise in integrating AI-powered health and well-being mentoring with professional development, addressing teacher burnout and resilience (Tun, 2024; Sahoo et al., 2025). Wearable technologies and AI-driven health analytics can provide personalized wellness coaching alongside pedagogical mentorship (Tun, 2024). This holistic approach supports sustainable career development.

## 9.9. AI for Talent Development and Leadership

AI's potential to nurture leadership skills and entrepreneurial capabilities among educators warrants exploration (Sahoo et al., 2025; Zreik, 2024). Future platforms might incorporate AI tools for identifying emerging leaders, facilitating skill-building in team management, innovation, and change leadership (Sahoo et al., 2025). Research should evaluate outcomes of AI-supported talent development in educational settings.

## 9.10. Policy, Implementation, and Sustainability Research

Finally, there is a need for in-depth studies on policy frameworks, institutional readiness, and sustainable funding models that enable large-scale AI mentorship adoption (Choudhary et al., 2024; Khamis, 2024). Action research and case studies can reveal best practices in implementation and scaling while addressing challenges such as digital infrastructure gaps and capacity building (Bagai & Mane, 2024; Loganathan et al., 2025).

## 9.11 Summary

The future of AI-powered virtual mentorship and peer learning networks lies in interdisciplinary research that bridges AI advancements with educational theory, ethics, and practice. Addressing these research opportunities promises to deepen the impact of AI on teacher support and professional growth globally, fostering more equitable, personalized, and sustainable learning ecosystems.

This diagram presents potential future directions for research and development in AI-powered mentorship. It emphasizes the importance of enhancing personalization, expanding access, and integrating experiential learning to foster equitable teacher professional development.

*Figure 5. Future Directions for AI-Powered Mentorship*

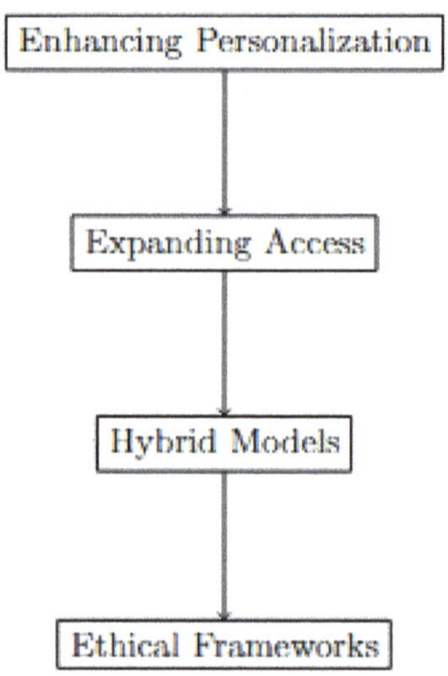


This table outlines potential future research directions in AI-powered mentorship. Each direction is described to emphasize the importance of addressing emerging challenges and enhancing the effectiveness of AI in education.

*Table 5. Future Research Directions*

| Research Direction | Description |
|---|---|
| Multimodal AI Integration | Exploring the use of various data types for personalization |
| Accessibility in Rural Areas | Addressing digital divides with affordable solutions |
| Hybrid Mentorship Models | Balancing AI support with human interaction |
| Ethical AI Frameworks | Developing guidelines for fair and transparent practices |
| Cross-Cultural Adaptation | Ensuring inclusivity in global AI applications |

## 10. CONCLUSION

AI-powered virtual mentorship and peer learning networks represent a paradigm shift in teacher professional development, offering unprecedented opportunities to personalize, scale, and enhance support for educators worldwide. This chapter has explored how emerging AI technologies—ranging from intelligent tutoring systems to virtual agents and collaborative platforms—can facilitate meaningful mentorship relationships and foster dynamic peer learning communities.

The potential benefits are substantial: increased accessibility to expert guidance, tailored feedback aligned with individual teacher needs, and rich collaborative environments that bridge geographic and cultural divides. However, realizing this potential requires careful attention to critical design considerations, including ethical data practices, transparency, cultural inclusivity, and maintaining a balanced integration of AI with human mentorship. Overcoming infrastructural, technical, and socio-organizational barriers remains imperative for equitable and sustainable adoption.

Looking ahead, research and practice must focus on advancing AI's personalization capabilities, enhancing multimodal interaction, and creating hybrid mentorship models that preserve empathy and trust. Cross-cultural adaptation, support for experiential learning, and integration of holistic well-being frameworks will further enrich these systems. Moreover, policy frameworks and capacity-building efforts are essential to embed AI mentorship platforms effectively within educational ecosystems.

Ultimately, the transformative power of AI in teacher support lies not in replacing human relationships but in augmenting and expanding them—enabling educators to thrive in complex, evolving classrooms and positively impact learner outcomes globally. By harnessing AI thoughtfully and inclusively, virtual mentorship and peer learning networks can become cornerstone tools for nurturing resilient, reflective, and empowered teaching professionals.

## REFERENCES


Bagai, R., & Mane, V. (2024). Designing an AI-powered mentorship platform for professional development: opportunities and challenges. *arXiv preprint arXiv:2407.20233.*

Bardia, A., & Agrawal, A. (2025). MindCraft: Revolutionizing Education through AI-Powered Personalized Learning and Mentorship for Rural India. *arXiv preprint arXiv:2502.05826.*

Basri, W. S. (2024). Effectiveness of AI-powered Tutoring Systems in Enhancing Learning Outcomes. *Eurasian Journal of Educational Research (EJER)*, (110).

Castañeda, R., Mercadé, L., Gómez, V. J., Mengual, T., Díaz-Fernández, F. J., Lozano, M. S., ... & de Zárate, D. O. (2024). Empowering Education 4.0: Impact of Using ChatGPT as a Virtual Mentor on K-12 Students Learning Science.

Chakraborty, S., Misra, B., & Dey, N. (2024). *AI-Empowered Knowledge Management in Education.* Springer. DOI: 10.1007/978-981-97-2574-8

CHAURASIA. (2024). *S., SENGAR, A. S., TOMAR, A., & SINGH, R.* Aupdeshik–AI Powered Learning Platform.

Chine, D. R., Chhabra, P., Adeniran, A., Kopko, J., Tipper, C., Gupta, S., & Koedinger, K. R. (2022, June). Scenario-based training and on-the-job support for equitable mentoring. In *The Learning Ideas Conference* (pp. 581-592). Cham: Springer International Publishing.

Choudhary, P., Sharma, K., Sharma, K., Borasi, M., Bhargava, P., Ali, I., & Rehman, K. (2024). Enhancing Mentorship through Technology: A Comprehensive Review of Current Practices and Future Directions. *Available at SSRN* 5070036.

Dai, C. P., Ke, F., Pan, Y., Moon, J., & Liu, Z. (2024). Effects of artificial intelligence-powered virtual agents on learning outcomes in computer-based simulations: A meta-analysis. *Educational Psychology Review*, *36*(1), 31. DOI: 10.1007/s10648-024-09855-4

David, N. (2024). AI-powered virtual assistant solution for supporting international students.

Devi, M. N., & Subbulakshmi, B. (2025). Mentoring Chatbot. *Adopting Artificial Intelligence Tools in Higher Education: Teaching and Learning*, 187.

Islam, A., Ali, R., Singh, G., Islam, B., Islam, A., & Hossain, S. (2024, May). An Evaluation of AI-Enhanced Collaborative Learning Platforms. In *2024 International Conference on Communication, Computer Sciences and Engineering (IC3SE)* (pp. 207-211). IEEE. DOI: 10.1109/IC3SE62002.2024.10593320

Jalilov, O., Zawidzki, J., & Bez, M. (2024). TOWARDS SCALABLE MENTORING: EXPLORING INTERACTIONS IN HYBRID AI SYSTEMS. In *ICERI2024 Proceedings* (pp. 9678-9686). IATED.

Khamis, R. (2024). AI-Powered Learning Experience Platforms: Investigating Personalized Learning in the Workplace.

Kovari, A. (2025). A systematic review of AI-powered collaborative learning in higher education: Trends and outcomes from the last decade. *Social Sciences & Humanities Open*, *11*, 101335. DOI: 10.1016/j.ssaho.2025.101335

Loganathan, M. E., Agalya, S. Y., Hariharan, K., & Bharathi, A. K. (2025). AI-Powered Alumni Portal: Connect, Learn, Thrive. *International Research Journal on Advanced Science Hub*, *7*(01), 1–9. DOI: 10.47392/IRJASH.2025.001

Sahoo, D. K., Le, T. M., Kumar, A., & Chandel, A. (2025). AI-Powered Talent Development: Nurturing Skills and Leadership in Entrepreneurial Teams. In *Improving Entrepreneurial Processes Through Advanced AI* (pp. 241-266). IGI Global.

Siham, E. K. (2024). Tech-Enhanced Ties: AI's Role in Cross-Cultural Peer Education. *PROCEEDINGS BOOK*, 671.

Silver, J. K., Dodurgali, M. R., & Gavini, N. (2024). Artificial intelligence in medical education and mentoring in rehabilitation medicine. *American Journal of Physical Medicine & Rehabilitation*, *103*(11), 10–1097. DOI: 10.1097/PHM.0000000000002604 PMID: 39016292

Tariq, M. U. (2025). Empowering Learning Through Networked and Connected Education: Case Studies in Digital Engagement. In *Cases on Enhancing P-16 Student Engagement With Digital Technologies* (pp. 169-198). IGI Global Scientific Publishing.

Thong, C. L., Atallah, Z., Islam, S., Lim, W., & Cherukuri, A. K. (2025). AI-powered Tools for Doctoral Supervision in Higher Education: A Systematic Review. *Journal of Information & Knowledge Management*, 2530001.

Tun, Z. Y. (2024). Empowering human health with wearables: exploring the feasibility and efficacy of AI-powered health mentoring systems.

Wang, T., Bruckman, A. S., & Yang, D. (2025). The Practice of Online Peer Counseling and the Potential for AI-Powered Support Tools. *Proceedings of the ACM on Human-Computer Interaction, 9*(2), 1–33. DOI: 10.1145/3711089

Wang, T., Zhou, N., & Chen, Z. (2025). CyberMentor: AI Powered Learning Tool Platform to Address Diverse Student Needs in Cybersecurity Education. *arXiv preprint arXiv:2501.09709.*

Zangana, H. M. (2015). A New Skin Color Based Face Detection Algorithm by Combining Three Color Model Algorithms. *IOSR J. Comput. Eng, 17*, 06-125.

Zangana, H. M. (2017). A new algorithm for shape detection. *IOSR Journal of Computer Engineering (IOSR-JCE), 19*(3), 71-76.

Zangana, H. M. (2017). Library Data Quality Maturity (IIUM as a Case Study). *IOSR Journal of Computer Engineering, 19*(March), 29. DOI: 10.9790/0661-1902033844

Zangana, H. M. (2017). Watermarking System Using LSB. *IOSR Journal of Computer Engineering, 19*(3), 75–79. DOI: 10.9790/0661-1903027579

Zangana, H. M. (2018). Design an information management system for a pharmacy. *International Journal of Advanced Research in Computer and Communication Engineering, 7*(10), 52–55. DOI: 10.17148/IJARCCE.2018.71012

Zangana, H. M. (2018). Developing Data Warehouse for Student Information System (IIUM as a Case Study). *International Organization of Scientific Research, 20*(1), 09-14.

Zangana, H. M. (2018). Implementing a System for Recognizing Optical Characters.

Zangana, H. M. (2019). Issues of Data Management in the Library: A Case Study.

Zangana, H. M. (2019). ITD Data Quality Maturity (A Case Study). *International Journal Of Engineering And Computer Science, 8*(10).

Zangana, H. M. (2020). Mobile Device Integration in IIUM Service. *International Journal (Toronto, Ont.), 8*(5).

Zangana, H. M. (2021). The Global Finical Crisis from an Islamic Point Of View. *Qubahan Academic Journal, 1*(2), 55–59. DOI: 10.48161/qaj.v1n2a39

Zangana, H. M. (2022). Creating a Community-Based Disaster Management System. *Academic Journal of Nawroz University, 11*(4), 234–244. DOI: 10.25007/ajnu.v11n4a1485

Zangana, H. M. (2022). Implementing New Interactive Video Learning System for IIUM. *Academic Journal of Nawroz University*, *11*(2), 23–29. DOI: 10.25007/ajnu.v11n2a1281

Zangana, H. M. (2022). Improving The Web Services for Remittance Company: Express Remit as a Case Study. *Academic Journal of Nawroz University (AJNU), 11*(3).

Zangana, H. M., & Abdulazeez, A. M. (2023). Developed Clustering Algorithms for Engineering Applications: A Review. *International Journal of Informatics* [IN-JIISCOM]. *Information System and Computer Engineering*, *4*(2), 147–169.

Zangana, H. M., & Al-Shaikhli, I. F. (2013). A new algorithm for human face detection using skin color tone. *IOSR Journal of Computer Engineering*, *11*(6), 31–38. DOI: 10.9790/0661-1163138

Zangana, H. M., Bazeed, S. M. S., Ali, N. Y., & Abdullah, D. T. (2024). Navigating Project Change: A Comprehensive Review of Change Management Strategies and Practices. *Indonesian Journal of Education and Social Sciences*, *3*(2), 166–179. DOI: 10.56916/ijess.v3i2.735

Zangana, H. M., & Mustafa, F. M. (2024). From Classical to Deep Learning: A Systematic Review of Image Denoising Techniques. *Jurnal Ilmiah Computer Science*, *3*(1), 50–65. DOI: 10.58602/jics.v3i1.36

Zangana, H. M., & Mustafa, F. M. (2024). Review of Hybrid Denoising Approaches in Face Recognition: Bridging Wavelet Transform and Deep Learning. *The Indonesian Journal of Computer Science*, *13*(4). Advance online publication. DOI: 10.33022/ijcs.v13i4.4209

Zangana, H. M., & Mustafa, F. M. (2024). Surveying the Landscape: A Comprehensive Review of Object Detection Algorithms and Advancements. *Jurnal Ilmiah Computer Science*, *3*(1), 1–15. DOI: 10.58602/jics.v3i1.29

Zreik, M. (2024). Harnessing AI for entrepreneurial idea generation: Navigating the new frontier. In *Generating Entrepreneurial Ideas With AI* (pp. 1–18). IGI Global Scientific Publishing. DOI: 10.4018/979-8-3693-3498-0.ch001

# Chapter 3
# Natural Language Processing for Teacher Reflection and Growth Journals

**Hermano Jorge Da Silva De Queiroz**
https://orcid.org/0000-0001-6738-6321
*Lindsey Wilson College, USA*

## ABSTRACT

*This chapter explores the transformative role of Natural Language Processing (NLP) in supporting teacher reflection and the development of growth journals. As educators increasingly engage in self-directed professional development, reflective writing has become a central method for processing experiences, identifying challenges, and setting future goals. NLP offers scalable tools to analyze and enhance these reflective practices by extracting themes, detecting sentiment, providing constructive feedback, and identifying patterns over time. The integration of NLP into teacher reflection enables personalized support, promotes continuous learning, and contributes to evidence-based decision-making in professional growth. This chapter presents current advancements, practical implementations, ethical considerations, and future directions for embedding NLP in teacher development frameworks.*

## 1. INTRODUCTION

Reflective practice is a cornerstone of effective teaching and professional growth. As educators navigate increasingly complex classroom environments, engaging in structured reflection through journaling provides a powerful avenue

DOI: 10.4018/979-8-3373-5951-9.ch003

for self-assessment, instructional improvement, and emotional well-being. In the era of Artificial Intelligence (AI), Natural Language Processing (NLP) is emerging as a transformative tool that can automate, scaffold, and enhance these reflective practices. NLP refers to the computational techniques that enable machines to understand, interpret, and generate human language (Hirschberg & Manning, 2015), and its integration into teacher development frameworks opens up unprecedented possibilities for scaling and personalizing professional learning.

Teacher reflection journals—often rich in personal experiences, critical incidents, and professional dilemmas—are valuable but underutilized assets. Traditionally, the analysis of such texts required manual effort by mentors or supervisors, limiting their scalability and immediate feedback. Recent advances in NLP offer intelligent systems that can classify, summarize, and interpret these narratives, enabling teachers to receive automated feedback on emotional tone, pedagogical themes, and developmental trajectories (Chen, Yu, & Yu, 2021; Magooda et al., 2022).

Several studies have demonstrated how NLP can empower both pre-service and in-service teachers. For instance, Burstein et al. (2014) illustrated how NLP tools enhance teachers' linguistic awareness, particularly in the context of English Language Learners. Similarly, Fan et al. (2017) developed NLP-powered mobile interfaces that scale reflection prompts in large classrooms. These interventions not only foster reflective thinking but also align teacher development with real-time data analytics.

A growing body of research shows the educational value of applying NLP to reflection in diverse disciplines. In health professions education, Borstad et al. (2023) applied NLP to analyze student reflections in physical therapy, mapping them to professional values. In a similar vein, Olex et al. (2025) used NLP techniques to extract insights from medical student narratives to guide curriculum improvement. This cross-disciplinary relevance underscores the adaptability and power of NLP in processing reflective writing at scale.

In the context of teacher education, Wulff et al. (2021) and Wulff, Mientus, Nowak, and Borowski (2023) showcased how machine learning models such as BERT can classify pre-service teachers' reflective essays into cognitive and emotional categories. These classifications support formative assessment and foster individualized mentoring. Mientus et al. (2023) further introduced scalable NLP-based metrics to assess reflection quality, allowing institutions to provide timely, personalized feedback.

Beyond classification, NLP can support sentiment analysis, topic modeling, and narrative structure recognition. Chong et al. (2020) used sentiment analysis to detect emotional trends in reflective writings, while Nehyba and Štefánik (2023) applied deep language models to enhance semantic understanding of preservice teacher reflections. Kenshinbay et al. (2025) emphasized narrative development, showing how NLP can assist in analyzing critical incidents and character arcs in teacher reflections—fostering deeper metacognition and emotional regulation.

Importantly, NLP not only benefits the individual teacher but also provides insights at the system level. By aggregating and analyzing reflection journals, institutional leaders can detect recurring challenges, design targeted interventions, and measure the impact of professional development programs over time (Gamieldien, McCord, & Katz, 2023; Menekse et al., 2025). This data-driven approach contributes to a feedback-rich learning ecosystem.

NLP's impact extends into wellness and resilience-building. Demir and Özdemir (2025) demonstrated how AI voice journaling, supported by NLP, enhances the well-being of future language teachers through continuous self-reflection. These tools, when designed responsibly, also promote equity and inclusivity in teacher support systems by ensuring that all educators receive timely, non-judgmental feedback—regardless of location or resources (Shardlow, Sellar, & Rousell, 2022).

However, leveraging NLP for reflection is not without challenges. Ethical issues surrounding data privacy, misinterpretation of affect, and cultural biases in language models must be acknowledged (Mohammadkarimi, 2023; Zangana & Abdulazeez, 2023). Additionally, the integration of NLP into teacher education requires careful interface design, ongoing validation, and professional development for effective adoption (Messina, Jones, & Poe, 2023; Wang et al., 2019).

While NLP has seen wide deployment in social, educational, and organizational contexts (Sumon et al., 2024; Zreik, 2024), its use in reflection-based growth for educators remains a fertile ground for research and innovation. Early adopters such as Zhao (2025) have explored NLP's potential in summarization and content enhancement, which can be extended to teacher journals for goal-setting and planning.

Finally, in technologically maturing contexts such as the Global South, NLP tools are gaining traction as part of broader digital transformation efforts. Foundational studies by Zangana (2015–2024) on pattern recognition, language processing, and information systems provide a strong base for tailoring NLP tools to local educational needs—ranging from resource-poor schools to multilingual teacher communities.

This flowchart illustrates the various applications of Natural Language Processing (NLP) in supporting teacher reflection and growth. It highlights how NLP tools can analyze reflective journals, provide feedback, and enhance professional development.

*Figure 1. Flowchart of NLP applications in teacher reflection*

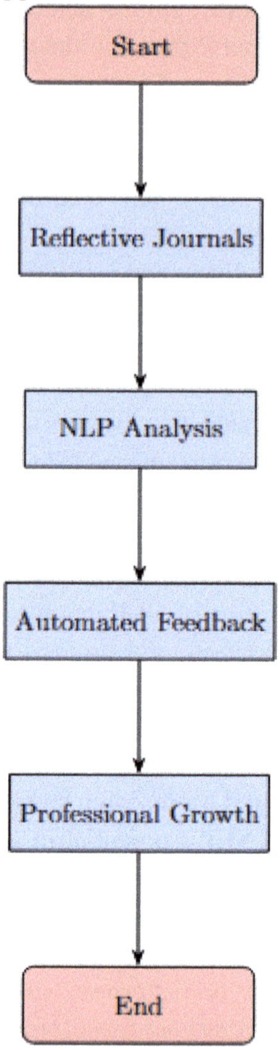


In sum, this chapter situates NLP at the nexus of AI and reflective teaching practice. It presents the state-of-the-art in NLP applications for teacher journaling, discusses practical implementations, addresses key challenges, and proposes future directions. By harnessing NLP responsibly, we can unlock new avenues for teacher agency, growth, and systemic transformation.

## 2. THE ROLE OF REFLECTIVE JOURNALING IN PROFESSIONAL DEVELOPMENT

Reflective journaling has long been recognized as a vital component of teacher professional development. It encourages educators to articulate their experiences, confront challenges, document progress, and refine their pedagogical practices. Through consistent reflection, teachers become more self-aware, critically engaged, and adaptable—qualities essential for navigating the dynamic demands of modern classrooms.

At its core, reflective journaling fosters metacognition, enabling educators to evaluate their instructional strategies and understand their students' needs more deeply. This process enhances professional identity, promotes emotional resilience, and supports ongoing growth (Demir & Özdemir, 2025). With the rise of digital tools and AI-powered platforms, journaling has evolved from a personal, often handwritten practice to a structured, analyzable, and scalable approach—particularly when augmented with Natural Language Processing (NLP).

NLP's ability to interpret and analyze language patterns allows for an enriched understanding of teachers' reflective entries. For instance, Chen, Yu, and Yu (2021) used text-mining techniques to examine pre-service teachers' journals, revealing themes and reflective depth that would be difficult to capture manually. This mirrors findings in other domains; Borstad et al. (2023), for example, applied NLP to student reflections in physical therapy, mapping them to core professional values and highlighting the versatility of such tools in assessing qualitative growth.

Reflective writing serves not only as a medium of personal growth but also as a scaffold for academic and ethical reasoning. Mohammadkarimi (2023) demonstrated how educators used reflection to navigate issues of academic dishonesty in student work, illustrating the medium's capacity to confront emerging challenges in AI-enhanced learning environments. Meanwhile, Kenshinbay et al. (2025) emphasized how narrative techniques—such as character development and critical incident analysis—help language teachers make sense of complex experiences, reinforcing journaling as both cognitive and emotional inquiry.

In teacher training programs, reflective journals are used to support the transition from theory to practice. Wulff et al. (2021) introduced machine learning methods for classifying pre-service physics teachers' journals, while Wulff, Mientus, Nowak, and Borowski (2023) expanded this work by leveraging BERT-based models to assess emotional and pedagogical content. Such efforts provide not only feedback to the writers but also valuable data for instructors to tailor mentorship and support.

Recent developments underscore the importance of scalable, real-time analysis. Magooda et al. (2022) and Menekse et al. (2025) explored how NLP can support real-time scaffolding of reflective writing, improving both the quality and relevance of entries. Their research found that students guided by NLP-based feedback exhibited more complex reasoning and stronger alignment with learning objectives. Fan et al. (2017) similarly highlighted how mobile interfaces powered by NLP help scale reflection prompts in large classes, democratizing access to reflective practice.

The emotional dimension of journaling should not be understated. Chong et al. (2020) used sentiment analysis to explore emotional shifts in teacher reflections, identifying stressors and triggers that could inform wellness strategies. Demir and Özdemir (2025) took this further by integrating AI voice journaling for pre-service teachers, enhancing well-being and self-efficacy through multimodal reflection. These findings align with broader movements in NLP and education toward affective computing (Hirschberg & Manning, 2015), where understanding emotional tone is as critical as identifying themes.

Reflection also intersects with assessment. Messina, Jones, and Poe (2023) used corpus linguistics to assess local reflective writing, demonstrating that language use itself can signal depth of reflection. Similarly, Mientus et al. (2023) proposed a machine learning-based metric for assessing reflection-related reasoning processes in teacher education, promoting consistency and scalability.

Importantly, journaling can also act as a window into institutional performance and student learning environments. Gamieldien, McCord, and Katz (2023) demonstrated how analyzing learner reflections can inform the design of self-regulated learning interventions. In medical education, Olex et al. (2025) used NLP on narrative reflections to improve curriculum content—a practice transferable to teacher education, where curriculum responsiveness is key.

Digital and societal contexts further underscore the need for reflective journaling. In environments where educators engage with immersive digital tools like the metaverse, linguistic and social dynamics shift rapidly. Sumon et al. (2024) noted the role of NLP in facilitating linguistic adaptation and digital socialization in such emerging spaces. Journaling in this context becomes a critical bridge between digital literacy and pedagogical transformation.

Moreover, reflections offer insights into how teachers adapt to AI in education. As Zhao (2025) found, AI-enhanced NLP tools influence language precision, creativity, and summarization in reflective writing. These capabilities not only refine the writing process but also shape how educators perceive and articulate their development paths. This echoes Burstein et al. (2014), who showed that NLP-enhanced professional development improved teacher awareness and curriculum responsiveness, especially for English Language Learners.

The integration of NLP into reflective journaling also aligns with institutional efforts toward digital transformation and innovation. Studies by Raga (2016) and Zangana (2015–2024) have chronicled the evolution of NLP in educational systems and its potential to enhance data quality, systems integration, and feedback generation. These foundational insights support the argument for implementing NLP-based journaling systems at scale, particularly in under-resourced contexts where manual analysis is impractical.

Lastly, Shardlow, Sellar, and Rousell (2022) emphasized that NLP tools like CoAST can simplify and augment complex texts for better learning outcomes. Applied to teacher journaling, such tools could scaffold novice educators' reflections, gradually increasing the cognitive demand as writing skills and professional insight deepen.

In sum, reflective journaling is not merely a passive exercise in recounting classroom experiences; it is an active, dynamic process of meaning-making, learning, and adaptation. As NLP continues to evolve, it offers educators and institutions a powerful mechanism for transforming reflective writing into a cornerstone of teacher growth, resilience, and innovation.

## 3. OVERVIEW OF NATURAL LANGUAGE PROCESSING (NLP)

Natural Language Processing (NLP) is a subfield of artificial intelligence (AI) and computational linguistics focused on enabling computers to understand, interpret, generate, and interact using human language. Rooted in a combination of linguistics, computer science, and machine learning, NLP seeks to bridge the gap between human communication and digital processing systems (Hirschberg & Manning, 2015).

Over the past decade, NLP has undergone a rapid evolution from rule-based approaches to deep learning models such as BERT, GPT, and T5. These advancements have dramatically improved machines' ability to analyze text for sentiment, syntax, semantics, and discourse-level features. NLP applications are now embedded in various domains—from search engines and chatbots to educational technologies and healthcare systems.

### 3.1 Core Functions and Capabilities of NLP

Modern NLP systems perform a wide range of functions: text classification, entity recognition, sentiment analysis, topic modeling, machine translation, summarization, and dialog generation. These capabilities have become foundational in educational applications, particularly in analyzing and supporting reflective writing among teachers and students.

For instance, Chen, Yu, and Yu (2021) utilized text mining techniques to examine preservice teacher journals, extracting recurrent themes and reflective quality. Chong et al. (2020) applied sentiment analysis to reflective writing to detect changes in emotional tone—offering educators insight into stress levels and psychological well-being. Demir and Özdemir (2025) advanced this by integrating AI-driven voice journaling, enabling NLP to process spoken reflections for emotional and cognitive feedback.

NLP has also enabled educators to move beyond basic keyword analysis to more nuanced interpretations. Nehyba and Štefánik (2023) demonstrated the potential of deep language models in identifying metacognitive markers in reflective writing, helping to scaffold critical thinking and professional insight. Likewise, Magooda et al. (2022) introduced classroom-based NLP tools that provide real-time feedback on students' reflective responses, improving both content depth and expression.

## 3.2 NLP in Educational Reflection and Teacher Journals

The role of NLP in educational settings has expanded notably. Fan et al. (2017) developed NLP-enabled mobile platforms to scale reflection prompts in large lecture courses, enhancing accessibility. Burstein et al. (2014) illustrated how NLP tools increased teachers' linguistic awareness, particularly in English Language Learner (ELL) contexts, supporting curriculum alignment and differentiation.

These tools not only support reflective thinking but also create scalable systems for feedback and intervention. Menekse et al. (2025) conducted a quasi-experimental study showing how NLP-based scaffolding improved student engagement and the quality of written reflections. Similarly, Gamieldien, McCord, and Katz (2023) used NLP to uncover patterns in self-regulated learning journals, providing valuable feedback loops for both students and instructors.

Borstad et al. (2023) mapped students' reflective narratives to professional values using NLP, a method transferable to teacher development for evaluating alignment with pedagogical goals. In teacher education, Wulff et al. (2021) and Wulff, Mientus, Nowak, and Borowski (2023) applied machine learning models to classify written reflections, demonstrating the feasibility of large-scale, automated formative assessment.

Mientus et al. (2023) developed a lightweight, machine learning-based metric for assessing reflective reasoning in teacher training, enabling scalable assessment without overburdening instructors. Similarly, Wang et al. (2019) designed systems to support self-reflection and peer-evaluation using NLP algorithms—highlighting how such tools foster collaboration and self-awareness in professional learning environments.

### 3.3 Narrative Structures, Corpus Linguistics, and Text Simplification

Beyond surface-level analytics, NLP can support complex tasks such as character development, thematic exploration, and text simplification. Kenshinbay et al. (2025) explored how narrative-based NLP techniques help language teachers analyze critical incidents, while Messina, Jones, and Poe (2023) utilized corpus linguistic methods to prompt deeper levels of reflection in local assessment frameworks.

Shardlow, Sellar, and Rousell (2022) introduced the CoAST model, which uses NLP for collaborative text simplification. This approach is valuable for novice educators or those developing fluency in reflective writing, as it allows AI systems to adaptively scaffold the writing process based on complexity and clarity.

### 3.4 Applications Across Domains and Ethical Dimensions

The success of NLP in analyzing educational reflections mirrors its application across other professional domains. In medical education, Olex et al. (2025) demonstrated how NLP could analyze narrative reflections to inform curriculum reform. Zhao (2025) further highlighted NLP's capacity to improve language precision, creativity, and summarization in writing tasks, which are equally valuable in teacher journaling contexts.

The use of NLP in educational settings has implications for digital equity, ethics, and inclusivity. Raga (2016) reflected on the progression of NLP research in developing countries, emphasizing the importance of culturally sensitive design. Zangana and Abdulazeez (2023) similarly noted the relevance of adaptive NLP systems in supporting diverse user needs—drawing from work on facial recognition, data management, and content personalization (Zangana, 2015–2022).

In the context of the metaverse and digital socialization, Sumon et al. (2024) described how NLP enables seamless linguistic interaction, offering insights into how such technologies may influence reflective communication among educators in immersive environments. Zreik (2024) positioned NLP as a key tool for generating and refining entrepreneurial ideas—paralleling how educators can use these technologies to explore innovative instructional strategies.

### 3.5 Interoperability, Design, and Scalability

Designing effective NLP systems for educational reflection requires more than sophisticated algorithms—it demands integration with user workflows and educational platforms. Zangana et al. (2024) emphasized the importance of modular system design, interoperability, and user-centered architecture in successful deployment of

AI and NLP in educational ecosystems. These systems must be intuitive, responsive, and transparent to earn trust and ensure adoption.

The shift from handcrafted reflection analysis to NLP-powered insights marks a turning point in teacher development. As Zangana and Mustafa (2024) have shown in the domains of image denoising and object recognition, hybrid systems combining rule-based and deep learning models offer both performance and interpretability—traits that are increasingly desirable in education-focused NLP systems.

## 4. AI-POWERED REFLECTION SYSTEMS AND TOOLS

The advent of Artificial Intelligence (AI), particularly Natural Language Processing (NLP), has revolutionized the way educators engage in reflection. Traditional reflective journaling, once confined to notebooks or simple word processors, is now transformed through intelligent systems that offer real-time feedback, automated analysis, emotional insight, and pedagogical scaffolding. These AI-powered reflection tools empower teachers to develop professionally through deeper metacognition, more accessible reflection platforms, and scalable feedback systems.

This table summarizes the core features of prominent AI-powered reflection tools that support teacher growth, highlighting functionalities such as NLP techniques used, feedback modalities, and target user groups. Understanding these features is essential for educators and developers aiming to leverage technology for reflective practices.

*Table 1. Key Features of AI-Powered Reflection Tools for Teacher Growth*

| Tool/Platform | NLP Techniques Used | Feedback Type | Target Users | Modality | Notable Application |
|---|---|---|---|---|---|
| CoAST (Shardlow et al., 2022) | Text simplification, summarization | Automated prompts | Teachers, Students | Text-based interface | Pedagogical text augmentation |
| NLP Reflection System (Wang et al., 2019) | Sentiment analysis, keyword extraction | Self-reflection reports | Preservice teachers | Web/mobile | Self and peer evaluation |
| AI Voice Journaling (Demir & Özdemir, 2025) | Speech-to-text, emotion recognition | Emotional feedback | Language teachers | Voice interface | Supporting teacher well-being |
| BERT-based Classifier (Wulff et al., 2023) | Transformer-based classification | Reflective writing classification | Science preservice teachers | Text-based interface | Formative assessment of reflections |
| Text Mining Journals (Chen et al., 2021) | Text mining, topic modeling | Summarized insights | Preservice teachers | Text document analysis | Understanding teacher reflection patterns |

## 4.1 Key Functionalities of AI-Driven Reflection Tools

AI-powered reflection systems utilize a combination of machine learning models, sentiment analysis, topic modeling, and linguistic pattern recognition. For example, Fan et al. (2017) developed a mobile interface that uses NLP to scale reflection prompts in large classrooms, allowing for mass customization of feedback. Similarly, Magooda et al. (2022) designed and evaluated a classroom-based NLP tool that guided students in enhancing the quality of their written reflections through prompt-specific feedback.

In higher education and medical training contexts, tools like those used by Olex et al. (2025) have been applied to analyze narrative reflections to inform curriculum reform. These systems identify latent themes and misalignments between educational goals and students' reflective content, showcasing the cross-disciplinary utility of AI-powered tools.

Wulff, Mientus, Nowak, and Borowski (2023) extended this work using BERT-based models to classify pre-service physics teachers' reflective texts with high accuracy. Their results demonstrate how pretrained language models can capture subtle differences in cognitive and emotional depth—offering granular insights for educators and researchers. These models build on earlier work like Wulff et al. (2021), which explored classification of reflective writing using manually tuned machine learning pipelines.

## 4.2 Emotional and Cognitive Analysis in Reflective Tools

Beyond thematic classification, many tools integrate sentiment analysis to detect emotional tone in reflections. Chong et al. (2020) showed how NLP systems could analyze reflective writing for sentiment polarity, providing valuable indicators of stress, engagement, and well-being. This is particularly relevant in language teacher training, where emotional resilience is crucial. Demir and Özdemir (2025) introduced an AI voice journaling system that processes spoken reflections, thereby combining speech recognition and NLP to assess emotional state and reflective quality.

Similarly, Gamieldien, McCord, and Katz (2023) explored how NLP tools can uncover patterns in self-regulated learning, offering real-time, personalized insights into a learner's cognitive and motivational development. The integration of affective computing (Hirschberg & Manning, 2015) into reflection systems adds another layer of nuance, enabling systems to act not only as analytical tools but also as emotionally intelligent companions.

### 4.3 Support for Narrative and Critical Incident Analysis

Reflective tools powered by AI are not limited to surface-level linguistic analysis. They also support deeper narrative construction and incident analysis. Kenshinbay et al. (2025) demonstrated how AI can guide language teachers through character development and critical incident narratives—making reflective practice both structured and introspective.

Corpus linguistic methods have also been embedded into AI tools to enhance local assessment. For instance, Messina, Jones, and Poe (2023) applied corpus-based techniques to evaluate reflection quality, aiding institutions in aligning writing practices with broader curricular goals.

### 4.4 Custom Tools for Professional Development

Tools tailored for teacher professional development have been designed to support both formative assessment and ongoing skill acquisition. Burstein et al. (2014) showed how NLP tools improved teachers' linguistic awareness, especially in multicultural classrooms with English Language Learners. These systems not only improved writing feedback but also helped teachers adjust their instructional practices in real-time.

Menekse et al. (2025) further validated the power of NLP-based scaffolding in a quasi-experimental study, showing that students receiving AI-supported reflective prompts demonstrated deeper insights and more aligned reasoning. Meanwhile, Mientus et al. (2023) created a scalable machine-learning metric for assessing reasoning processes in teacher training, offering a lightweight yet effective solution for instructors handling large cohorts.

### 4.5 Multilingual and Multimodal Reflection Support

The evolution of AI tools has also embraced multilingual and multimodal capacities. Systems now include audio transcription (e.g., Demir & Özdemir, 2025), handwriting recognition, and even virtual reality reflections in immersive environments. As Sumon et al. (2024) highlighted, NLP's integration into metaverse platforms enables real-time interaction, digital socialization, and reflective dialogue in 3D environments, further blurring the line between educational and technological frontiers.

## 4.6 Ethical and Cultural Considerations in AI Reflection Tools

The design of AI reflection systems must account for cultural sensitivity, data privacy, and algorithmic transparency. Raga (2016) emphasized the importance of local NLP research in shaping tools that resonate with specific cultural and linguistic contexts. Similarly, Mohammadkarimi (2023) addressed how AI tools might expose ethical tensions—such as academic dishonesty—through reflective writing, urging for responsible design principles.

Zangana et al. (2022, 2024) and Zangana and Abdulazeez (2023) underscored the relevance of adaptive system design, modularity, and integration when deploying AI tools in institutional settings. Their work in database management, disaster response systems, and e-learning infrastructures highlights the importance of performance, usability, and data quality in education-focused AI applications.

## 4.7 Reflection Systems Beyond Education

AI-powered reflection systems also find application outside traditional education. In physical therapy education, Borstad et al. (2023) demonstrated how NLP could map reflections to professional values. This cross-sectoral application suggests potential for interdisciplinary adoption, particularly in areas like health, social work, and engineering. In entrepreneurship, Zreik (2024) proposed the use of AI and NLP to scaffold reflective thinking for ideation and innovation.

Zhao (2025) provided empirical evidence on how AI-enhanced NLP tools improve writing precision, creativity, and summarization—key features in effective reflection tools. These advancements suggest a promising future for AI systems that adapt not only to content, but to the context and goals of each individual user.

## 4.8 Visualization and Feedback Mechanisms

Modern AI-powered reflection systems often include dashboards and visualization tools that allow educators to view patterns over time. Topic maps, emotion timelines, and feedback heatmaps can highlight shifts in cognitive and affective states. Wang et al. (2019) developed systems integrating both self- and peer-assessment feedback using NLP, providing holistic views of learner development.

Shardlow, Sellar, and Rousell (2022) introduced the CoAST model, a collaborative platform that uses NLP to augment and simplify reflection texts, supporting both formative assessment and group-based learning. These tools help reduce cognitive overload while maintaining reflective depth.

## 5. PRACTICAL APPLICATIONS AND USE CASES

AI-powered reflection systems and Natural Language Processing (NLP) technologies have emerged as transformative tools in educational and professional contexts. These tools provide scalable, insightful, and context-sensitive means to facilitate and assess reflection, support learning, enhance curriculum design, and inform educational policy. Below, we explore practical applications and real-world use cases across disciplines.

### 5.1. Teacher Education and Training

NLP-based systems have proven invaluable in the teacher education domain. For instance, Chen, Yu, and Yu (2021) used text-mining techniques to analyze preservice teachers' reflective journals, offering insights into pedagogical growth. Wulff et al. (2021) and Wulff, Mientus, Nowak, and Borowski (2023) demonstrated how BERT-based models and machine learning classifiers can automatically evaluate teacher reflections, contributing to scalable formative assessment. Similarly, Mientus et al. (2023) introduced a fast-and-frugal NLP metric for evaluating reflective reasoning in teacher training programs.

Burstein et al. (2014) showed how NLP tools can enhance teachers' linguistic awareness and support curriculum development for English language learners. Kenshinbay et al. (2025) used narrative techniques like character development and critical incident analysis to deepen reflection in language teacher training.

### 5.2. Enhancing Student Reflection and Self-Regulation

AI-powered platforms also improve student reflection and self-regulated learning. Magooda et al. (2022) developed an NLP-driven tool that provided automated feedback on written reflections to support higher-quality thinking. Menekse et al. (2025) demonstrated that NLP scaffolding significantly enhanced the depth and accuracy of student reflections in large lecture environments. Fan et al. (2017) introduced a mobile-based NLP system that deployed reflection prompts at scale, helping students engage more critically with course content.

Gamieldien, McCord, and Katz (2023) employed NLP to examine metacognitive processes in self-reflections, helping educators track learners' development. Wang et al. (2019) combined self-reflection and peer-evaluation using NLP, promoting active learning and collaborative assessment.

## 5.3. Emotional Insight and Ethical Awareness

Chong et al. (2020) used sentiment analysis to uncover emotional dimensions in student reflections, enabling educators to detect stress and provide timely support. Mohammadkarimi (2023) highlighted how NLP tools reveal ethical concerns such as academic dishonesty in EFL students' writings, allowing instructors to design better integrity-based interventions. Demir and Özdemir (2025) explored AI-driven voice journaling as a means for future language teachers to promote emotional well-being through daily spoken reflections.

## 5.4. Medical and Health Professions Education

In medical education, Olex et al. (2025) applied NLP to analyze student narratives for curricular feedback. Borstad et al. (2023) employed NLP to map student reflections from international service learning programs to physical therapy core values, enhancing both assessment and professional identity development.

## 5.5. Institutional Assessment and Curriculum Design

Messina, Jones, and Poe (2023) used corpus linguistics and NLP for local assessment of reflective writing, providing a model for institutions to link student outcomes with curriculum decisions. Similarly, Raga (2016) emphasized the importance of promoting NLP research and applications in underrepresented regions, stressing the need for local contextualization.

## 5.6. AI in Digital Learning Environments

Shardlow, Sellar, and Rousell (2022) developed the Collaborative Augmentation and Simplification of Text (CoAST) framework, enabling students to collaboratively write and reflect in digital spaces. Sumon et al. (2024) explored the role of NLP in social interaction and linguistic engagement within the metaverse, extending reflective practice into immersive environments.

## 5.7. Entrepreneurship, Engineering, and Beyond

NLP tools are also branching into entrepreneurship and STEM disciplines. Zreik (2024) showed how reflective NLP systems can assist in generating and evaluating entrepreneurial ideas. In engineering education and systems design, Zangana and colleagues (2015–2024) made significant contributions to areas like face detection (Zangana & Al-Shaikhli, 2013), shape recognition (Zangana, 2017), and system development for education and disaster management (Zangana, 2022). Their work supports the technical infrastructure that enables reflective platforms to operate effectively across domains.

### 5.8. Writing Analytics and Language Proficiency

Finally, NLP systems are being used to improve writing proficiency. Zhao (2025) found that AI-enhanced writing tools can support precision, creative expression, and summarization in reflective writing. These tools are especially useful in diverse, multilingual classrooms and remote learning contexts.

## 6. BENEFITS OF NLP IN SUPPORTING TEACHER GROWTH

Natural Language Processing (NLP) has increasingly demonstrated its value as a catalyst for teacher development, enabling deep, scalable, and personalized reflection processes that support professional learning. By offering analytical insights into written and spoken reflections, NLP fosters self-awareness, pedagogical refinement, and emotional resilience among teachers. This section explores these benefits through evidence from recent studies and real-world implementations.

The following table outlines the key benefits of using natural language processing (NLP) to facilitate teacher growth. It categorizes benefits related to reflective quality improvement, emotional well-being support, scalable feedback, and professional development, drawn from empirical studies and recent applications.

*Table 2. Benefits of Natural Language Processing in Supporting Teacher Growth*

| Benefit Area | Description | Supporting References |
|---|---|---|
| Enhanced Reflective Depth | NLP tools analyze nuances in language, enabling deeper insight into teachers' reflective practices | Chen, Yu, & Yu (2021); Magooda et al. (2022) |
| Scalable Feedback | Automated analysis allows large-scale, real-time feedback without overburdening educators | Fan et al. (2017); Menekse et al. (2025) |
| Emotional Awareness | Sentiment and emotion analysis help identify teacher well-being and affective states | Chong et al. (2020); Demir & Özdemir (2025) |
| Linguistic Awareness | Supports language development especially for ESL teachers, improving communication skills | Burstein et al. (2014); Kenshinbay et al. (2025) |
| Personalized Scaffolding | Adaptive prompts guide teachers through reflective writing tailored to their needs | Magooda et al. (2022); Nehyba & Štefánik (2023) |

## 6.1. Facilitating Reflective Practice

One of the foremost advantages of NLP in education is its ability to enhance reflective practice. Through the automated analysis of language, NLP can reveal patterns of thought, emotion, and professional growth. For example, Chen, Yu, and Yu (2021) employed text-mining techniques to uncover trends in preservice teachers' reflection journals, offering feedback that supports more intentional and strategic teaching behaviors. Similarly, Demir and Özdemir (2025) explored AI-driven voice journaling, showing how it contributes to the emotional well-being and reflective depth of future language teachers.

Wulff, Buschhüter et al. (2021) and Wulff, Mientus et al. (2023) confirmed the efficacy of NLP models like BERT in classifying reflective texts, enabling scalable feedback systems in teacher education. The ability to assess reflection without human bias encourages more frequent and open journaling (Fan et al., 2017), while mobile tools make reflection more accessible and contextually embedded.

## 6.2. Supporting Emotional and Ethical Awareness

NLP allows educators to gain insights into the emotional tone and ethical considerations embedded in reflections. Chong et al. (2020) used sentiment analysis to detect affective states in reflective writing, providing opportunities for timely intervention and socio-emotional support. Mohammadkarimi (2023) highlighted the use of NLP to detect concerns related to academic dishonesty, giving teachers a means to engage in ethical reflection on student conduct and their own instructional practices.

Moreover, Borstad et al. (2023) demonstrated how NLP can map student reflections to professional values, fostering teacher understanding of implicit learning outcomes and aligning instructional strategies accordingly.

## 6.3. Enhancing Feedback and Curriculum Design

NLP tools contribute to more effective and customized feedback, which is critical for ongoing teacher development. Burstein et al. (2014) illustrated how NLP technologies help enhance linguistic awareness in educators, particularly for supporting English language learners. These tools also assist in curriculum alignment by linking reflective content to learning objectives and competencies.

Olex et al. (2025) leveraged NLP to analyze student narrative reflections for improving medical curriculum content, demonstrating the technology's utility beyond traditional classroom settings. Likewise, Messina, Jones, and Poe (2023) emphasized the role of corpus linguistic methods in enabling localized, reflective feedback loops.

## 6.4. Promoting Critical Thinking and Narrative Development

Reflective writing is often nonlinear and complex. NLP applications help educators recognize emerging narratives and critical incidents in their pedagogical journey. Kenshinbay et al. (2025) explored narrative techniques like character development and incident analysis to empower teachers in framing their professional identities. This aligns with the work of Nehyba and Štefánik (2023), who utilized deep language models to extract nuanced layers of meaning in teacher writings, fostering a culture of metacognitive growth.

Magooda et al. (2022) further demonstrated that NLP-based scaffolding tools not only encourage reflection but also enhance the quality and structure of teachers' written thoughts, contributing to stronger analytical reasoning.

## 6.5. Advancing Personalization and Scalability

The scalability of NLP solutions allows institutions to personalize professional development at a large scale. Mientus et al. (2023) introduced a machine learning-based metric that provided quick, scalable evaluations of reflection quality, ideal for training programs with many participants. Gamieldien, McCord, and Katz (2023) emphasized the role of NLP in supporting self-regulated learning and personal goal tracking, both essential for adaptive teaching.

These scalable systems are complemented by real-time interfaces, such as those described by Wang et al. (2019), where self-reflection and peer-evaluation are facilitated through NLP-enhanced platforms.

## 6.6. Enriching Digital Literacy and Writing Skills

NLP also empowers teachers to improve their digital communication and writing proficiency. Zhao (2025) found that AI-enhanced writing tools support language precision, summarization, and idea generation. These benefits not only strengthen reflective writing but also improve teachers' instructional design and digital literacy.

The CoAST framework (Shardlow, Sellar, & Rousell, 2022) exemplifies how NLP can augment and simplify complex text, thereby supporting teachers in adapting material for diverse learners and improving comprehension.

## 6.7. Broadening Educational and Technical Horizons

Beyond pedagogy, educators benefit from the computational thinking and interdisciplinary awareness that accompany engagement with NLP tools. Studies by Zangana and collaborators (2015–2024) demonstrate how algorithmic design, system implementation, and data management are integral to the functionality of NLP systems in education. Whether it's detecting faces, managing learning data, or developing systems for video learning and disaster response (Zangana, 2018, 2022), these technical skills inform a new dimension of teacher readiness in the digital age.

Additionally, Raga (2016) advocated for wider NLP research awareness in underserved regions, reinforcing the importance of equity and context in technological adoption.

This bar graph summarizes the key benefits of using NLP for teacher reflection and growth, providing a visual comparison of how each benefit contributes to professional development.

*Figure 2. Benefits of NLP in Supporting Teacher Growth*

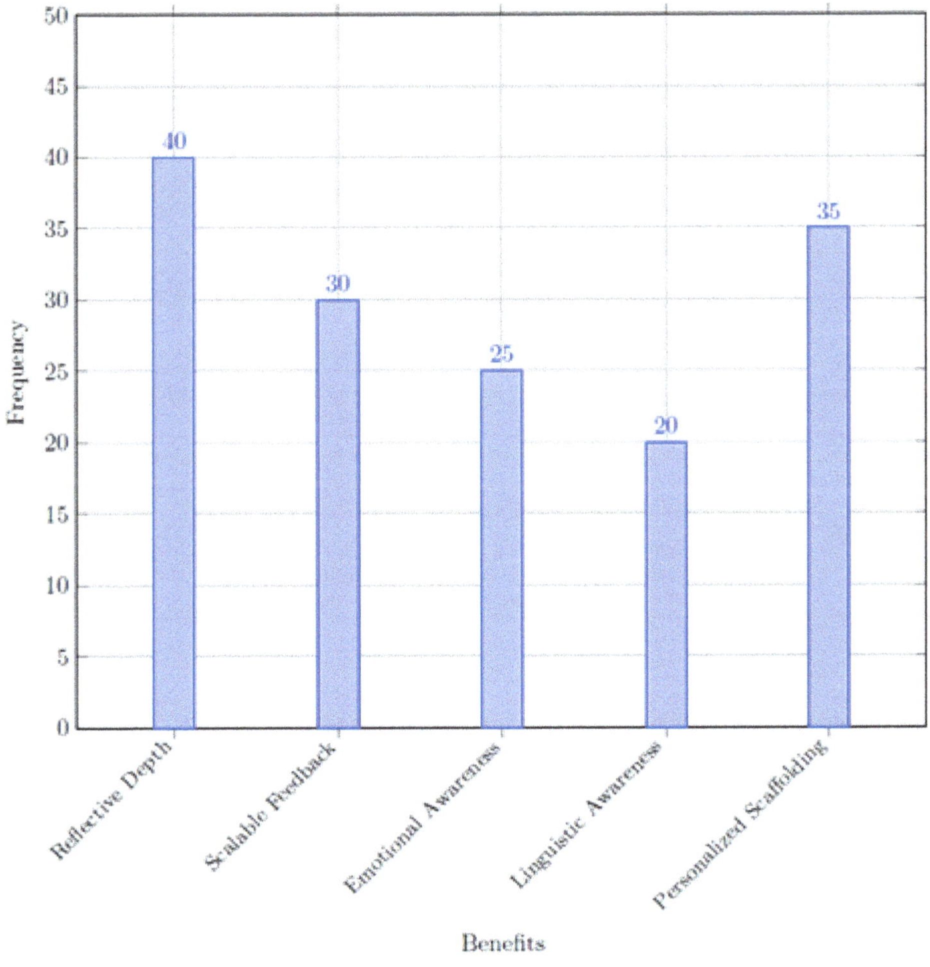

## 7. CHALLENGES AND ETHICAL CONSIDERATIONS

Despite the significant promise of Natural Language Processing (NLP) in supporting teacher growth, its application in educational contexts is not without challenges and ethical concerns. These include issues related to privacy, data interpretation, algorithmic bias, transparency, and the potential reduction of rich human insights into quantifiable metrics. This section critically explores these dimensions while drawing on recent research findings.

While NLP tools offer significant benefits, they also present challenges and limitations that educators and researchers must consider. This table identifies common issues such as data privacy concerns, interpretative accuracy, cultural biases, and technological constraints, providing a balanced perspective on the integration of NLP in teacher reflection.

*Table 3. Challenges and Limitations of NLP-Based Teacher Reflection Tools*

| Challenge | Description | Implications | Key References |
|---|---|---|---|
| Privacy Concerns | Handling sensitive personal reflections raises data security and ethical issues | Requires secure data policies and consent | Mohammadkarimi (2023); Raga (2016) |
| Interpretative Accuracy | NLP may misinterpret nuance, sarcasm, or context-dependent meaning in reflective texts | Risk of misleading feedback | Hirschberg & Manning (2015); Wulff et al. (2021) |
| Cultural and Linguistic Bias | Models trained on limited data may not fairly represent diverse teacher backgrounds | Necessitates diverse datasets and fairness checks | Sumon et al. (2024); Kenshinbay et al. (2025) |
| Over-Reliance on Automation | Excessive dependence on AI feedback might reduce human judgment and peer collaboration | Balance between AI and human input needed | Burstein et al. (2014); Shardlow et al. (2022) |
| Technical Constraints | Computational resources and complexity may limit real-time and accessible NLP applications | Needs optimization and infrastructure investment | Nehyba & Štefánik (2023); Magooda et al. (2022) |

### 7.1. Privacy, Data Ownership, and Consent

One of the most immediate concerns with NLP systems in education is the handling of sensitive data, especially in reflective writings. Student and teacher reflections often contain personal narratives, emotions, and values. As noted by Borstad et al. (2023), the mapping of student reflections to professional values, while insightful, raises concerns about confidentiality and the scope of consent. Teachers may feel uncomfortable knowing that their inner thoughts are subject to algorithmic scrutiny.

Similarly, Olex et al. (2025) underscore the necessity of ethical handling of narrative reflections used for curriculum improvement in medical education. Without proper anonymization protocols and participant understanding, such use could violate ethical norms and reduce trust in institutional initiatives.

## 7.2. Interpretation Challenges and Loss of Context

Reflective writing is deeply personal and often context-dependent. NLP systems, while powerful, can struggle to accurately interpret nuanced language, sarcasm, or culturally specific expressions. Chen, Yu, and Yu (2021) point out that while text-mining techniques can highlight patterns, they often fail to grasp contextual meanings that a human evaluator would understand.

This concern is echoed by Nehyba and Štefánik (2023), who caution that even deep language models may misinterpret or oversimplify complex cognitive and emotional expressions in reflective texts, leading to misleading conclusions or inappropriate feedback.

## 7.3. Bias in Algorithms and Training Data

Algorithmic bias is a pervasive challenge in NLP. Models are only as fair and accurate as the data on which they are trained. Raga (2016) reflects on the imbalance in global NLP research, noting the dominance of English and Western datasets, which can marginalize non-Western narratives and ways of expressing reflection. This issue becomes particularly salient in multicultural teacher education environments.

Zangana and Abdulazeez (2023) highlight the broader implications of algorithmic design choices in NLP, emphasizing the importance of diverse data representation to avoid skewed interpretations, particularly in reflective writing and evaluation systems.

## 7.4. Oversimplification of Reflection and Creativity

There is a risk that NLP tools, in their pursuit of measurability and scale, may reduce complex reflective processes to mere linguistic features or sentiment scores. Messina, Jones, and Poe (2023) critique this tendency, warning against decontextualized corpus linguistics assessments that might undermine the subjective richness of reflective thought.

Zhao (2025) similarly points out that while AI-enhanced tools can improve writing proficiency in terms of grammar and summarization, they may inadvertently suppress creativity or originality if teachers conform their writing to what the system rewards.

## 7.5. Dependency on Technology and Diminished Human Judgment

As NLP-based feedback becomes more prevalent, there is a concern that educators may become overly reliant on automated suggestions, potentially diminishing their own critical thinking and evaluative judgment. Burstein et al. (2014) warn of this in the context of English language curriculum development, where linguistic awareness must be cultivated—not outsourced.

Gamieldien, McCord, and Katz (2023) emphasize the importance of maintaining teacher agency in self-regulated learning environments, even when using powerful NLP tools. Similarly, Fan et al. (2017) advocate for NLP tools to be used in tandem with instructor feedback, not as replacements.

## 7.6. Emotional and Psychological Impact

The automated analysis of reflective writing may inadvertently expose or amplify emotional vulnerabilities. For example, Chong et al. (2020) demonstrated that sentiment analysis of reflective texts can reveal emotional distress, but doing so without appropriate support mechanisms could exacerbate stress rather than alleviate it.

Demir and Özdemir (2025) call for integrating AI voice journaling with well-being frameworks to ensure that reflective tools nurture rather than harm teacher development.

## 7.7. Equity and Access in NLP Tool Deployment

Widespread access to NLP tools is another ethical consideration. Not all educational institutions have the resources or digital infrastructure to support advanced NLP integration. Shardlow, Sellar, and Rousell (2022) propose the CoAST framework as a means of democratizing NLP for pedagogical purposes, but access inequalities persist.

This digital divide, noted by Sumon et al. (2024), also manifests in the broader context of digital socialization, affecting how teachers interact, learn, and reflect within metaverse or online environments.

## 7.8. Transparency and Explainability of NLP Models

Many NLP models operate as "black boxes," providing results without transparency into how conclusions are derived. This can lead to mistrust or misuse. Hirschberg and Manning (2015) stress the need for interpretable AI in NLP applications, especially in sensitive domains like education.

Mientus et al. (2023) developed scalable, interpretable models for assessing reflective reasoning, attempting to bridge the gap between model accuracy and explainability. Nonetheless, as Wulff, Mientus et al. (2023) demonstrate, even with pretrained models like BERT, questions remain about how classification decisions are made.

## 7.9. Ethical Use in Evaluative Contexts

Finally, the use of NLP for evaluative purposes—such as grading reflections or assessing professional growth—raises ethical red flags. Mohammadkarimi (2023) warns that automated systems may not account for cultural norms or rhetorical differences, especially in international education settings. Using such systems for high-stakes evaluation could reinforce bias and marginalize diverse perspectives.

Wang et al. (2019) suggest combining NLP with peer evaluation to mitigate this risk, while Kenshinbay et al. (2025) advocate for narrative-based tools that center teacher agency and lived experience.

## 7.10. Sustainability, Maintenance, and Institutional Readiness

Deploying and maintaining NLP systems requires significant technical infrastructure and institutional buy-in. Zangana (2017, 2018, 2022) stresses the importance of robust data management systems, continual system updates, and user training for successful implementation. Without sustained investment, even well-designed NLP initiatives may fail or become obsolete.

In summary, while NLP offers significant advantages in supporting teacher reflection and growth, its deployment must be tempered by ethical foresight, cultural sensitivity, and pedagogical alignment. The responsible integration of NLP requires more than technical precision—it demands a commitment to equity, transparency, and the human dimensions of education.

This pie chart visualizes the various ethical considerations that need to be addressed when implementing NLP tools in educational contexts. It highlights the importance of privacy, bias, and transparency.

*Figure 3. Ethical Considerations in NLP Implementation*

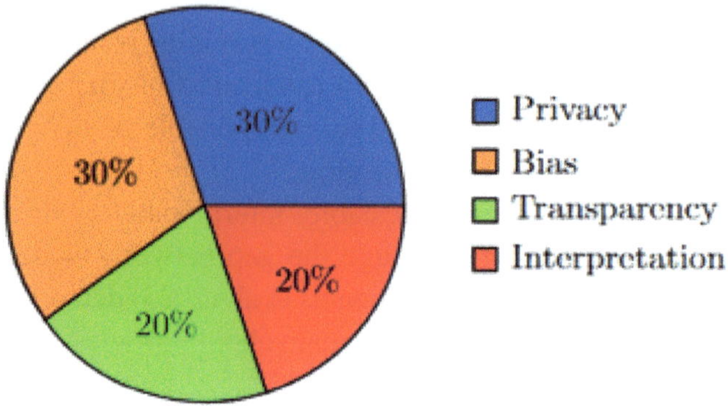


## 8. FUTURE TRENDS AND RESEARCH OPPORTUNITIES

As Natural Language Processing (NLP) continues to mature, its integration into teacher development and reflective practice will likely deepen and diversify. Emerging technologies, shifting pedagogical paradigms, and expanding research agendas all signal a transformative future for NLP in education. This section outlines the key future trends and research opportunities that will shape this evolving landscape.

### 8.1. Context-Aware and Emotionally Intelligent NLP

Future NLP systems are expected to move beyond static language analysis and toward more context-aware and emotionally intelligent systems. Building upon existing sentiment analysis frameworks (Chong et al., 2020), next-generation models may integrate affective computing to more accurately interpret the emotional and psychological dimensions of teacher reflections. Demir and Özdemir (2025) point to the value of AI voice journaling in capturing vocal cues, which may complement text-based models for a holistic understanding of teacher well-being.

Such emotionally intelligent systems could provide real-time feedback tailored to the emotional and cognitive states of educators, making professional development more empathetic and responsive.

## 8.2. Interdisciplinary Applications and Cross-Domain Synergies

NLP research is increasingly converging with domains like cognitive science, health education, and professional ethics. Borstad et al. (2023), for example, used NLP to map student reflections to physical therapy values, suggesting that similar cross-disciplinary models could inform ethical and empathetic teaching practices.

Zangana and Mustafa (2024) further emphasize the potential of combining NLP with signal processing and deep learning in domains like image denoising, showing a path forward for multi-modal educational feedback systems. These hybrid approaches can lead to richer teacher insight, especially in STEAM (science, technology, engineering, arts, and math) contexts.

## 8.3. Generative AI and Reflective Writing Enhancement

Generative models like ChatGPT and large language transformers are poised to revolutionize how teachers engage with reflection. Zhao (2025) demonstrated that AI-enhanced NLP tools can improve language precision and creative expression, potentially transforming how teachers compose reflective narratives.

Zreik (2024) proposed using NLP-driven AI for ideation and innovation, which could be applied to teacher professional learning by helping educators frame problems, generate solutions, and explore hypothetical classroom scenarios through interactive dialogue.

## 8.4. Scalable and Inclusive Reflection Analytics

Scalability and accessibility remain major future directions. Magooda et al. (2022) and Mientus et al. (2023) both explored scalable systems for analyzing student and teacher reflections, suggesting future tools must be lightweight, fast, and able to function across platforms, languages, and learning contexts.

Raga (2016) underscored the importance of expanding NLP infrastructure in underrepresented regions, a call echoed by Sumon et al. (2024) in their research on digital socialization in the metaverse. Future NLP research should prioritize multilingualism, cultural context, and low-bandwidth environments to ensure that reflection technologies benefit educators globally.

## 8.5. Narrative Structure and Story-Based Reflection

An emerging research trajectory involves deeper analysis of narrative structure within teacher reflections. Kenshinbay et al. (2025) explored how character development and critical incident analysis can improve teacher self-awareness. Integrating

NLP with narrative analytics could uncover storytelling patterns that correlate with pedagogical insight and instructional resilience.

This aligns with work by Messina, Jones, and Poe (2023), who utilized corpus linguistics to prompt deeper reflection, and Nehyba and Štefánik (2023), who applied deep language models to preserve narrative voice while analyzing reflective content.

## 8.6. Adaptive Feedback and Intelligent Tutoring Systems

The next generation of NLP applications will likely integrate adaptive feedback systems that respond to the evolving needs of the teacher. Fan et al. (2017) and Wang et al. (2019) introduced early models for scaling feedback in large classrooms. Future iterations may personalize the reflective process in real time, integrating progress tracking and dynamic scaffolding as explored by Menekse et al. (2025).

Such systems could be further optimized with clustering algorithms and classification models, like those reviewed by Zangana and Abdulazeez (2023), or the fast-and-frugal metrics proposed by Mientus et al. (2023).

## 8.7. Ethical NLP and Human-in-the-Loop Frameworks

Future NLP systems must ensure transparency, fairness, and ethical rigor. As NLP becomes embedded in teacher evaluation and curriculum design (Burstein et al., 2014; Olex et al., 2025), research must address explainability and algorithmic fairness. Hirschberg and Manning (2015) have called for interpretable NLP, a challenge that remains urgent.

Human-in-the-loop systems—where automated feedback is paired with peer or expert review—offer a promising direction. Gamieldien et al. (2023) emphasize balancing automation with teacher agency, while Mohammadkarimi (2023) warns against relying solely on algorithmic assessments, especially in ethically complex scenarios like academic dishonesty.

## 8.8. Integration with Broader Educational Technologies

Future NLP applications will increasingly interface with other educational technologies—learning management systems, metaverse environments, and AI dashboards. Shardlow et al. (2022) proposed the CoAST model for collaborative text simplification, a system that could be embedded in classroom management platforms or tutoring interfaces.

Zangana's works (2015–2022) on system design and data integration offer blueprints for this ecosystem-wide connectivity. His work on information systems, disaster management, and mobile device integration underscores the need for comprehensive, interoperable educational infrastructures.

## 8.9. Data Ethics and Reflective Data Sovereignty

With the expansion of NLP in teacher training, issues of data ownership, consent, and reflective sovereignty must be addressed. Teachers should retain control over how their reflective data is used, analyzed, and stored. This necessitates new research into ethical data stewardship models and decentralized data architectures—particularly in sensitive applications such as those studied by Wulff, Mientus et al. (2023) and Wulff, Westphal et al. (2023).

## 8.10. Meta-Research and Longitudinal Impact Studies

Finally, future research must include long-term studies that evaluate the sustained impact of NLP on teacher development. While promising evidence exists (e.g., Chen et al., 2021; Burstein et al., 2014), few studies examine how reflective feedback influences teacher identity, instructional efficacy, and career longevity over time.

Meta-research could consolidate findings across fields and propose standardized frameworks for assessing reflection quality, narrative depth, and emotional engagement over multi-year periods.

In summary, the future of NLP in teacher growth lies in intelligent, ethical, and inclusive innovation. As researchers and practitioners embrace deeper narrative models, cross-domain integration, and adaptive feedback systems, NLP will evolve from a passive analytical tool into an active partner in educator transformation.

This line graph illustrates the growth of NLP tool adoption in educational settings over recent years, showing a clear upward trend as technology advances and becomes more accessible.

*Figure 4. Trends in NLP Adoption in Education*

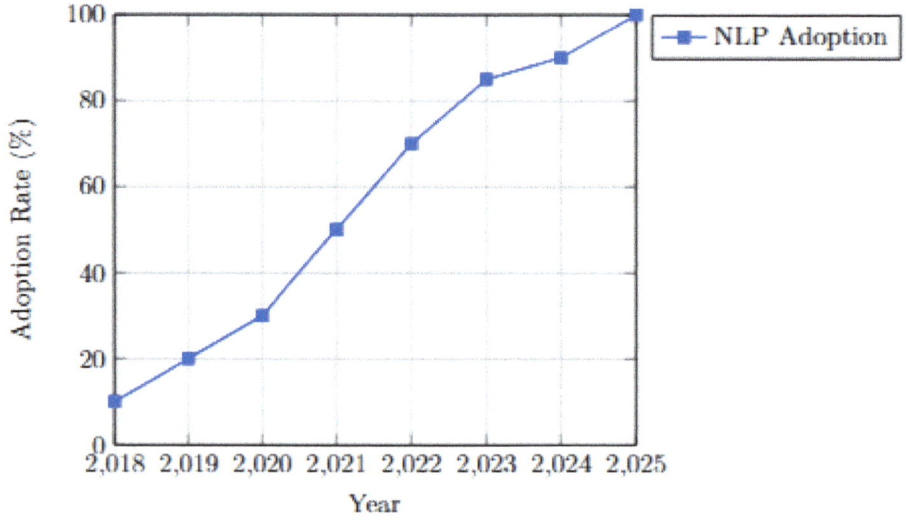


## 9. CONCLUSION

Natural Language Processing (NLP) has emerged as a transformative technology in the realm of teacher growth and professional development. Through its ability to analyze, interpret, and scaffold reflective writing and dialogue, NLP offers unprecedented opportunities to enhance educators' self-awareness, pedagogical skills, and emotional well-being. This chapter has explored the multifaceted applications of NLP-powered reflection systems and tools, highlighting their design considerations, benefits, and challenges.

The integration of NLP in educational contexts facilitates scalable, data-driven insights into teacher reflections, enabling personalized feedback and fostering continuous professional learning. Advances in deep learning, sentiment analysis, and narrative analytics have expanded the scope of reflection support, moving beyond traditional text analysis to more context-aware and emotionally intelligent systems. Moreover, the incorporation of adaptive scaffolding and AI-driven voice journaling illustrates the diverse modalities through which NLP can support educators holistically.

However, the deployment of NLP also raises important ethical, interpretative, and equity concerns. Privacy, algorithmic bias, loss of contextual nuance, and over-reliance on automated feedback represent significant challenges that must be addressed to ensure responsible use. The human dimensions of reflection—creativity, narrative identity, and emotional complexity—must remain central as these technologies evolve. Maintaining teacher agency and embedding transparency in NLP models are critical to building trust and maximizing pedagogical value.

Looking ahead, the future of NLP in teacher growth lies in interdisciplinary research, multimodal integration, and ethical innovation. Expanding accessibility to diverse linguistic and cultural contexts, enhancing explainability, and fostering human-in-the-loop systems will be essential to realize the full potential of NLP tools. Longitudinal studies evaluating the sustained impact of NLP on teacher development will further inform best practices and policy decisions.

In conclusion, NLP represents a powerful ally in the journey of teacher growth—one that complements human expertise with scalable intelligence, enabling richer, more reflective, and more effective educational experiences. By balancing technological advancement with ethical stewardship, educators and researchers can harness NLP to support a more reflective, resilient, and innovative teaching workforce.

## REFERENCES


Borstad, A. L., Appling, S. A., Kloos, A. D., Spangler, L., & Marc, D. T. (2023). Beyond Borders, Beneath Words: Using Natural Language Processing to Map Student Reflections on International Service Learning to Physical Therapy Values. *Journal, Physical Therapy Education*, •••, 10–1097. PMID: 40008869

Burstein, J., Shore, J., Sabatini, J., Moulder, B., Lentini, J., Biggers, K., & Holtzman, S. (2014). From teacher professional development to the classroom: How NLP technology can enhance teachers' linguistic awareness to support curriculum development for English language learners. *Journal of Educational Computing Research*, *51*(1), 119–144. DOI: 10.2190/EC.51.1.f

Chen, Y., Yu, B., & Yu, Y. (2021). Analysing preservice teachers' reflection journals using text-mining techniques. *International Journal of Innovation in Education*, *7*(2), 122–143. DOI: 10.1504/IJIIE.2021.118046

Chong, C., Sheikh, U. U., Samah, N. A., & Sha'ameri, A. Z. (2020, July). Analysis on reflective writing using natural language processing and sentiment analysis. [). IOP Publishing.]. *IOP Conference Series. Materials Science and Engineering*, *884*(1), 012069. DOI: 10.1088/1757-899X/884/1/012069

Demir, B., & Özdemir, D. (2025). AI voice journaling for future language teachers: A path to well-being through reflective practices. *British Educational Research Journal*, berj.4174. DOI: 10.1002/berj.4174

Fan, X., Luo, W., Menekse, M., Litman, D., & Wang, J. (2017, March). Scaling reflection prompts in large classrooms via mobile interfaces and natural language processing. In *Proceedings of the 22nd international conference on intelligent user interfaces* (pp. 363-374). DOI: 10.1145/3025171.3025204

Gamieldien, Y., McCord, R., & Katz, A. (2023). Utilizing natural language processing to examine self-reflections in self-regulated learning. *Available at SSRN* 4487795. DOI: 10.2139/ssrn.4487795

Hirschberg, J., & Manning, C. D. (2015). Advances in natural language processing. *Science*, *349*(6245), 261–266. DOI: 10.1126/science.aaa8685 PMID: 26185244

Kenshinbay, T., Ghorbandordinejad, F., Bolatova, A., & Kiyassova, K. (2025). Enhancing Language Teacher Reflection through Narrative Techniques: Character Development and Critical Incident Analysis: Language Teacher Reflection through Narrative Techniques. *Bulletin of Language and Literature Studies*, *2*(1). Advance online publication. DOI: 10.59652/blls.v2i1.482

Magooda, A., Litman, D., Ashraf, A., & Menekse, M. (2022, July). Improving the quality of students' written reflections using natural language processing: Model design and classroom evaluation. In *International Conference on Artificial Intelligence in Education* (pp. 519-525). Cham: Springer International Publishing. DOI: 10.1007/978-3-031-11644-5_43

Menekse, M., Putra, A. S., Kim, J., Butt, A. A., McDaniel, M. A., Davidesco, I., Cadieux, M., Kim, J., & Litman, D. (2025). Enhancing student reflections with natural language processing based scaffolding: A quasi-experimental study in a large lecture course. *Computers and Education: Artificial Intelligence*, *8*, 100397. DOI: 10.1016/j.caeai.2025.100397

Messina, C. M., Jones, C. E., & Poe, M. (2023). Prompting reflection: Using corpus linguistic methods in the local assessment of reflective writing. *Written Communication*, *40*(2), 620–650. DOI: 10.1177/07410883221149425

Mientus, L., Wulff, P., Nowak, A., & Borowski, A. (2023). Fast-and-frugal means to assess reflection-related reasoning processes in teacher training—Development and evaluation of a scalable machine learning-based metric. *Zeitschrift für Erziehungswissenschaft*, *26*(3), 677–702. DOI: 10.1007/s11618-023-01166-8

Mohammadkarimi, E. (2023). Teachers' reflections on academic dishonesty in EFL students' writings in the era of artificial intelligence. *Journal of Applied Learning and Teaching*, *6*(2), 105–113.

Nehyba, J., & Štefánik, M. (2023). Applications of deep language models for reflective writings. *Education and Information Technologies*, *28*(3), 2961–2999. DOI: 10.1007/s10639-022-11254-7

Olex, A. L., Garber, A. M., Santen, S. A., Blondino, C., Goldberg, S., & DiazGranados, D. (2025). Utilizing natural language processing to analyze student narrative reflections for medical curriculum improvement. *Medical Teacher*, *47*(6), 970–975. DOI: 10.1080/0142159X.2024.2390034 PMID: 39161978

Raga, R. (2016). Reflections on the awareness and progress of natural language processing (nlp) research in the philippines. *Philippine Computing Journal*, *11*(1), 1–9.

Shardlow, M., Sellar, S., & Rousell, D. (2022). Collaborative augmentation and simplification of text (CoAST): Pedagogical applications of natural language processing in digital learning environments. *Learning Environments Research*, *25*(2), 399–421. DOI: 10.1007/s10984-021-09368-9

Sumon, R. I., Uddin, S. M. I., Akter, S., Mozumder, M. A. I., Khan, M. O., & Kim, H. C. (2024). Natural language processing influence on digital socialization and linguistic interactions in the integration of the metaverse in regular social life. *Electronics (Basel), 13*(7), 1331. DOI: 10.3390/electronics13071331

Wang, R., Wei, S., Ohland, M. W., & Ferguson, D. M. (2019). Natural language processing system for self-reflection and peer-evaluation. In *the Fourth North American International Conference on Industrial Engineering and Operations Management* (pp. 23-25).

Wulff, P., Buschhüter, D., Westphal, A., Nowak, A., Becker, L., Robalino, H., Stede, M., & Borowski, A. (2021). Computer-based classification of preservice physics teachers' written reflections. *Journal of Science Education and Technology, 30*(1), 1–15. DOI: 10.1007/s10956-020-09865-1

Wulff, P., Mientus, L., Nowak, A., & Borowski, A. (2023). Utilizing a pretrained language model (BERT) to classify preservice physics teachers' written reflections. *International Journal of Artificial Intelligence in Education, 33*(3), 439–466. DOI: 10.1007/s40593-022-00290-6

Wulff, P., Westphal, A., Mientus, L., Nowak, A., & Borowski, A. (2023, January). Enhancing writing analytics in science education research with machine learning and natural language processing—Formative assessment of science and non-science preservice teachers' written reflections. [). Frontiers Media SA.]. *Frontiers in Education, 7*, 1061461. DOI: 10.3389/feduc.2022.1061461

Zangana, H. M. (2015). A New Skin Color Based Face Detection Algorithm by Combining Three Color Model Algorithms. *IOSR J. Comput. Eng, 17*, 06-125.

Zangana, H. M. (2017). A new algorithm for shape detection. *IOSR Journal of Computer Engineering (IOSR-JCE), 19*(3), 71-76.

Zangana, H. M. (2017). Library Data Quality Maturity (IIUM as a Case Study). *IOSR Journal of Computer Engineering, 19*(March), 29. DOI: 10.9790/0661-1902033844

Zangana, H. M. (2017). Watermarking System Using LSB. *IOSR Journal of Computer Engineering, 19*(3), 75–79. DOI: 10.9790/0661-1903027579

Zangana, H. M. (2018). Design an information management system for a pharmacy. *International Journal of Advanced Research in Computer and Communication Engineering, 7*(10), 52–55. DOI: 10.17148/IJARCCE.2018.71012

Zangana, H. M. (2018). Developing Data Warehouse for Student Information System (IIUM as a Case Study). *International Organization of Scientific Research, 20*(1), 09-14.

Zangana, H. M. (2018). Implementing a System for Recognizing Optical Characters.

Zangana, H. M. (2019). Issues of Data Management in the Library: A Case Study.

Zangana, H. M. (2019). ITD Data Quality Maturity (A Case Study). *International Journal Of Engineering And Computer Science, 8*(10).

Zangana, H. M. (2020). Mobile Device Integration in IIUM Service. *International Journal (Toronto, Ont.)*, *8*(5).

Zangana, H. M. (2021). The Global Finical Crisis from an Islamic Point Of View. *Qubahan Academic Journal*, *1*(2), 55–59. DOI: 10.48161/qaj.v1n2a39

Zangana, H. M. (2022). Creating a Community-Based Disaster Management System. *Academic Journal of Nawroz University*, *11*(4), 234–244. DOI: 10.25007/ajnu.v11n4a1485

Zangana, H. M. (2022). Implementing New Interactive Video Learning System for IIUM. *Academic Journal of Nawroz University*, *11*(2), 23–29. DOI: 10.25007/ajnu.v11n2a1281

Zangana, H. M. (2022). Improving The Web Services for Remittance Company: Express Remit as a Case Study. *Academic Journal of Nawroz University (AJNU), 11*(3).

Zangana, H. M., & Abdulazeez, A. M. (2023). Developed Clustering Algorithms for Engineering Applications: A Review. *International Journal of Informatics* [INJIISCOM]. *Information System and Computer Engineering*, *4*(2), 147–169.

Zangana, H. M., & Al-Shaikhli, I. F. (2013). A new algorithm for human face detection using skin color tone. *IOSR Journal of Computer Engineering*, *11*(6), 31–38. DOI: 10.9790/0661-1163138

Zangana, H. M., Bazeed, S. M. S., Ali, N. Y., & Abdullah, D. T. (2024). Navigating Project Change: A Comprehensive Review of Change Management Strategies and Practices. *Indonesian Journal of Education and Social Sciences*, *3*(2), 166–179. DOI: 10.56916/ijess.v3i2.735

Zangana, H. M., & Mustafa, F. M. (2024). From Classical to Deep Learning: A Systematic Review of Image Denoising Techniques. *Jurnal Ilmiah Computer Science*, *3*(1), 50–65. DOI: 10.58602/jics.v3i1.36

Zangana, H. M., & Mustafa, F. M. (2024). Review of Hybrid Denoising Approaches in Face Recognition: Bridging Wavelet Transform and Deep Learning. *The Indonesian Journal of Computer Science*, *13*(4). Advance online publication. DOI: 10.33022/ijcs.v13i4.4209

Zangana, H. M., & Mustafa, F. M. (2024). Surveying the Landscape: A Comprehensive Review of Object Detection Algorithms and Advancements. *Jurnal Ilmiah Computer Science*, *3*(1), 1–15. DOI: 10.58602/jics.v3i1.29

Zhao, D. (2025). The impact of AI-enhanced natural language processing tools on writing proficiency: An analysis of language precision, content summarization, and creative writing facilitation. *Education and Information Technologies*, *30*(6), 8055–8086. DOI: 10.1007/s10639-024-13145-5

Zreik, M. (2024). Harnessing AI for entrepreneurial idea generation: Navigating the new frontier. In *Generating Entrepreneurial Ideas With AI* (pp. 1–18). IGI Global Scientific Publishing. DOI: 10.4018/979-8-3693-3498-0.ch001

# Chapter 4
# Enhancing Educational Visual Content Through AI-Based Image Denoising Techniques:
## Implications for Remote Teaching and Digital Resource Development

**Hewa Majeed Zangana**
https://orcid.org/0000-0001-7909-254X
*Duhok Polytechnic University, Iraq*

**Firas Mahmood Mustafa**
https://orcid.org/0000-0002-8757-5303
*Duhok Polytechnic University, Iraq*

## ABSTRACT

*The shift toward remote and hybrid education has amplified the importance of high-quality visual content in digital teaching and learning environments. However, poor image quality—due to compression artifacts, noise, or low-resolution scanning—can hinder comprehension, engagement, and knowledge retention. This chapter explores the transformative role of AI-based image denoising techniques in enhancing the clarity and effectiveness of educational visual content. We examine state-of-the-art methods, including convolutional neural networks (CNNs), transformer-based models, and hybrid deep learning approaches, and discuss their applicability to real-world educational scenarios such as digital textbook enhancement, video lectures, and interactive learning materials. Furthermore, we highlight the pedagogical implications of denoised content for teacher support, curriculum development, and*

DOI: 10.4018/979-8-3373-5951-9.ch004

*equitable access to learning resources. The chapter concludes with challenges, best practices, and future directions for integrating AI-driven denoising into digital education ecosystems.*

## 1. INTRODUCTION

The digital transformation of education, accelerated by global challenges such as the COVID-19 pandemic, has highlighted the indispensable role of visual content in remote teaching and learning. High-quality images, illustrations, videos, and interactive media are not just supplementary tools but fundamental components of modern pedagogy. Unfortunately, visual educational materials are often plagued by various forms of noise—compression artifacts, low-resolution scanning, outdated formats, or poor lighting—undermining their effectiveness and causing accessibility barriers, particularly for students in underserved regions.

Artificial Intelligence (AI), particularly deep learning, has emerged as a promising solution to these challenges, offering automated and highly effective image denoising techniques that can restore, enhance, and repurpose visual content with unprecedented accuracy (Majeed Zangana & Mustafa, 2024; Zangana & Mustafa, 2024). Traditional filtering approaches, although computationally efficient, are limited in their ability to preserve details and context. In contrast, AI-based methods such as convolutional neural networks (CNNs), autoencoders, and generative adversarial networks (GANs) have shown remarkable performance in recovering high-fidelity images from corrupted or noisy inputs (Zangana & Mustafa, 2025a; Gupta, Shreneter, & Sehgal, 2024).

The implications of this technological evolution are profound. AI-driven denoising techniques can not only rejuvenate legacy educational resources but also ensure clarity and consistency in live-streamed lectures, scanned documents, e-books, and open educational resources (OERs). Aslam (2024) and Fu et al. (2024) note that AI applications in media processing are moving toward explainability and reliability—qualities crucial for educational adoption. At the intersection of AI and pedagogy, image enhancement tools become instrumental in supporting teachers' digital content creation, fostering equity in education, and improving learner engagement (Maheshwari & Paulchamy, 2024).

Moreover, the use of denoised imagery extends into domains that intersect with cybersecurity and content authenticity. With the proliferation of generative AI and deepfake technologies, maintaining the integrity and trustworthiness of visual educational content has become increasingly critical (Heidari et al., 2024; Lyu, 2024). Techniques originally developed for digital forensics and security—such as deepfake detection, image forgery analysis, and adversarial robustness training—are now being adapted for educational quality control (Bharathiraja et al., 2023; Khimi et al., 2024; Golda et al., 2024).

Researchers have also explored hybrid denoising approaches that combine wavelet transforms with deep learning to address both high-frequency noise and structural distortions, demonstrating significant promise in domains like medical imaging and forensic analysis (Zangana & Mustafa, 2025b; Zangana & Mustafa, 2025c). These approaches, when translated into educational contexts, can enhance the readability of complex diagrams, handwritten notes, and annotated visuals—especially valuable in STEM and technical education.

Importantly, denoising in educational visuals also intersects with broader technological ecosystems, such as IoT-based classroom sensors, intelligent tutoring systems, and digital forensic auditing tools (Fayyaz, Almehmadi, & El-Khatib, 2024; Moustafa et al., 2023). AI-powered image preprocessing can improve recognition systems, support online assessment platforms, and help educators curate high-quality content from OSINT (Open Source Intelligence) platforms (Oakley Browne, Abedin, & Chowdhury, 2024; Sindiramutty et al., 2025).

Despite these benefits, the adoption of AI-based image denoising in educational settings is not without challenges. Issues such as algorithmic transparency, data privacy, and resistance to digital transformation persist (Majeed & Hwang, 2023; Hewage et al., 2022). Moreover, ensuring ethical and bias-free deployment in classrooms requires robust design and continuous oversight (Tyagi & Addula, 2024; Rohatgi et al., 2023).

This chapter aims to address the research gap by presenting a comprehensive overview of how AI-based image denoising techniques can enhance educational visual content. It critically reviews denoising methodologies, examines their pedagogical applications, highlights challenges in implementation, and outlines future research directions. The discussion draws on insights from cybersecurity (Ali, Shah, & ElAffendi, 2024; Roshanaei, Khan, & Sylvester, 2024), AI-generated content verification (Zhao et al., 2024; Sayyafzadeh, 2024), and the evolving landscape of digital education infrastructure (Khaleel et al., 2024; Alotaibi, Williamson, & Khamis, 2023).

By harnessing the strengths of modern AI models, educators and technologists can transform noisy, low-quality visuals into engaging, reliable, and pedagogically effective resources—paving the way for more inclusive, scalable, and intelligent educational systems.

## 2. BACKGROUND AND LITERATURE REVIEW

The use of visual media in educational content has become foundational to effective digital pedagogy, especially in the context of remote and hybrid teaching. As digital resources increasingly replace traditional classroom materials, maintaining the quality and integrity of these visuals becomes essential for equitable and engaging learning. Image denoising—a process that removes distortions while preserving essential features—has emerged as a critical area of research and application, particularly when integrated with artificial intelligence (AI) and deep learning methods.

### 2.1 Evolution of Image Denoising: From Classical Methods to AI

Classical denoising methods such as Gaussian filters, median filtering, and wavelet transforms have historically been employed to reduce image noise. However, these techniques often struggle with balancing detail preservation and noise suppression. Recent advances in deep learning have significantly improved this process. Convolutional neural networks (CNNs), GANs, and autoencoders have demonstrated superior performance in recovering clean images, even in complex noisy environments (Majeed Zangana & Mustafa, 2024; Zangana & Mustafa, 2024a).

Zangana and Mustafa (2024b) provided a systematic review of hybrid models that integrate wavelet transforms with deep learning to enhance image denoising outcomes. This hybrid approach has shown efficacy across various domains, including face recognition and medical imaging, highlighting its potential for educational visual content restoration (Zangana & Mustafa, 2025a; 2025b). Their work underscores the flexibility and scalability of such techniques in resource-constrained environments—making them ideal for educational deployment.

### 2.2 AI in Visual Forensics and Content Authenticity

With the rise of generative AI, the authenticity of visual content has come under scrutiny. Deepfake technologies pose significant challenges in verifying the credibility of visual materials, especially in education and media (Heidari et al., 2024; Lyu, 2024). Detection methodologies using AI have been extensively studied, with CNN-based models offering promising accuracy in distinguishing forged from authentic images (Gupta, Shreneter, & Sehgal, 2024; Khormali, 2022).

Bharathiraja et al. (2023) provided a comprehensive survey of image forgery techniques and detection mechanisms, emphasizing the necessity of automated systems in identifying tampered visuals. Maheshwari and Paulchamy (2024) proposed a hybrid approach that combines explainable AI and adversarial training for deepfake mitigation, an advancement that holds promise in protecting educational visuals from manipulation.

## 2.3 AI and Cybersecurity: Implications for Educational Integrity

AI's role in cybersecurity intersects deeply with educational content management, especially as digital classrooms become targets for phishing, intrusion, and adversarial attacks (Aslam, 2024; Das, 2024). Protecting visual content requires robust pre-processing pipelines, of which image denoising is a foundational layer. Choi et al. (2020) noted the increasing convergence of computer vision and cybersecurity, with deep learning enabling real-time analysis and anomaly detection.

Golda et al. (2024) highlighted privacy risks associated with generative AI, while Alotaibi, Williamson, and Khamis (2023) demonstrated how thermal attacks could compromise input devices. These findings imply a broader security ecosystem where visual data must be both sanitized and validated. AI-driven denoising also aids in preprocessing for intrusion detection systems, enhancing accuracy (Almehdhar et al., 2024; Khaleel et al., 2024).

AI-based image denoising lies at the intersection of cybersecurity and education. The Venn diagram below illustrates the overlapping priorities and use cases across these three fields.

*Figure 1. Intersection of AI, Cybersecurity, and Education*

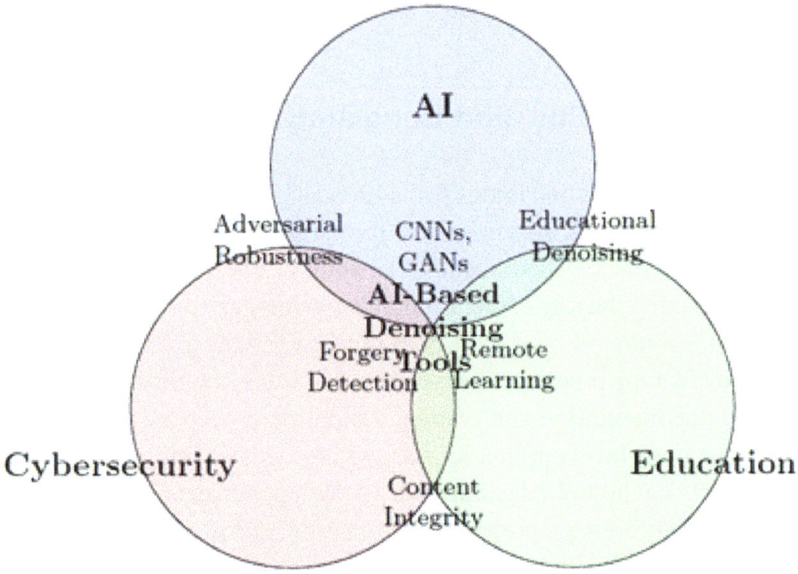

This table summarizes the primary AI and machine learning techniques applied in cybersecurity domains. It highlights their specific use cases, strengths, and limitations, providing a comprehensive overview that aids in understanding the current landscape of AI-driven security solutions.

*Table 1. Summary of Key AI Techniques in Cybersecurity*

| AI Technique | Use Case(s) | Strengths | Limitations | Representative Studies |
|---|---|---|---|---|
| Deep Learning | Intrusion detection, malware analysis | High accuracy, automated feature extraction | Requires large datasets, computationally intensive | Choi et al. (2020), Khaleel et al. (2024) |
| Generative AI | Phishing detection, anomaly generation | Can simulate attacks, enhance detection | Risk of adversarial misuse | Das (2024), Sindiramutty et al. (2025) |
| Hybrid Models | Image denoising, deepfake detection | Combines strengths of classical and AI methods | Complexity in model design | Zangana & Mustafa (2024), Maheshwari & Paulchamy (2024) |
| Explainable AI | Intrusion detection, forensic analysis | Enhances trust and transparency | Trade-off between accuracy and interpretability | Moustafa et al. (2023), Fu et al. (2024) |

AI models can even play a proactive role in digital forensic analysis, enabling automated anomaly detection in educational platforms (Fayyaz, Almehmadi, & El-Khatib, 2024). Tools like thumbnail forensic acquisition (Sayyafzadeh, 2024) further reinforce the relevance of visual integrity in cybersecurity-aware educational environments.

## 2.4 OSINT, DevSecOps, and Denoising in Digital Ecosystems

Image denoising also contributes to the broader goals of open-source intelligence (OSINT) and DevSecOps by improving the quality and interpretability of visual datasets. Oakley Browne, Abedin, and Chowdhury (2024) examined the use of AI in OSINT, emphasizing the role of clean, analyzable imagery in intelligence extraction. In parallel, Fu, Pasuksmit, and Tantithamthavorn (2024) discussed the integration of AI into DevSecOps pipelines, suggesting that image quality plays a critical role in automated documentation and content validation processes.

These ecosystem-level applications are reinforced by Sindiramutty et al. (2025) and Singla (2024), who linked generative AI with cybersecurity defense strategies, advocating for secure image preprocessing in educational and enterprise-level systems. Tyagi and Addula (2024) similarly emphasized the role of malware detection and secure preprocessing in multimedia-based analytics, further supporting the case for robust denoising techniques.

## 2.5Educational Applications and Ethical Considerations

When applied to education, denoised visuals enhance learning outcomes by improving image readability, reducing cognitive load, and promoting engagement—especially in disciplines dependent on diagrams and visual simulations (Zangana, Mustafa, & Omar, 2024). This benefit is magnified in bandwidth-constrained or visually impaired learning contexts. Moreover, denoising facilitates archival of old scanned materials, revitalizing legacy textbooks and handwritten notes (Zangana & Mustafa, 2025c).

Nonetheless, these technologies raise ethical considerations. Majeed and Hwang (2023) cautioned against adversarial misuse of AI in data handling, while Hewage et al. (2022) explored multimedia privacy issues in AI-driven applications. Ensuring transparency, consent, and data protection remains essential in educational settings adopting AI-based content enhancement (Roshanaei, Khan, & Sylvester, 2024).

Emerging AI-based denoising models must also be explainable and interpretable, especially as they enter high-stakes educational and assessment systems. Moustafa et al. (2023) emphasized explainable AI as a cornerstone of trustworthy intrusion detection, a concept transferable to educational data governance.

## 2.6 Future-Ready Denoising Systems

Future directions include deeper integration of wavelet-GAN hybrids (Zangana & Mustafa, 2025a), cross-domain adaptability in AI models (Rane, Choudhary, & Rane, 2024), and embedding denoising into edge computing for real-time educational use. Rohatgi et al. (2023) discussed the dual role of AI in industrial and educational cybersecurity, noting that robust visual preprocessing can bridge gaps between infrastructure and instruction.

Ali, Shah, and ElAffendi (2024) further proposed AI-driven optimization in threat detection, which parallels educational use cases where denoised visuals could help flag inappropriate or corrupted content. Meanwhile, Dhayanidhi (2022) emphasized AI/ML integration in IoT and cloud computing—critical environments for modern e-learning platforms.

Zhao et al. (2024) examined the role of generative AI in securing physical-layer communications, indirectly suggesting that educational content transmitted through wireless or distributed systems also benefits from denoised, compressed, and secured visual representations.

## 3. AI-BASED IMAGE DENOISING TECHNIQUES

In recent years, image denoising has evolved into a sophisticated domain that integrates traditional signal processing with deep learning and AI-based methods. In educational environments, the need for clear, noise-free visual materials is paramount—not only for enhancing comprehension but also for ensuring accessibility and trust in content integrity. AI-based image denoising techniques are designed to learn complex noise patterns and reconstruct cleaner images with minimal loss of semantic information. These methods are increasingly being deployed across digital education platforms, cybersecurity, and forensic applications.

To better understand the progression of denoising approaches, the following flowchart presents the main AI-based denoising methods discussed in this chapter—organized by model architecture and use case relevance.

*Figure 2. AI-Based Image Denoising Techniques*

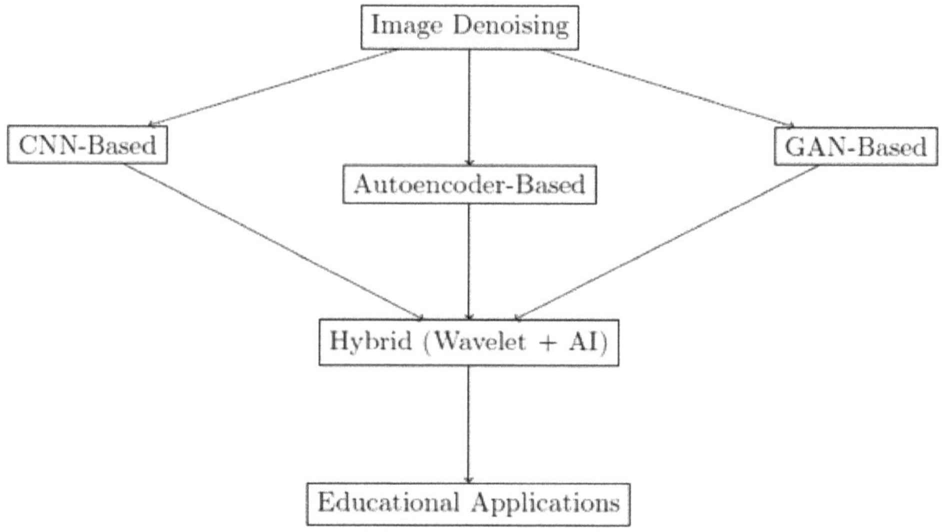


### 3.1. Traditional vs. AI-Driven Denoising

Classical image denoising methods such as Gaussian smoothing, anisotropic diffusion, and wavelet thresholding have served as foundational tools in image enhancement. However, they often fall short in preserving fine details, especially in low signal-to-noise ratio conditions. AI-based techniques, in contrast, leverage large datasets to learn mapping functions between noisy and clean images, resulting in superior visual fidelity and generalizability (Majeed Zangana & Mustafa, 2024; Zangana & Mustafa, 2024a).

### 3.2. Convolutional Neural Networks (CNNs)

CNNs are among the most widely used architectures for image denoising. These networks extract hierarchical features through stacked convolutional layers, allowing them to effectively differentiate noise from meaningful content. CNN-based denoisers such as DnCNN and FFDNet have been shown to outperform traditional approaches across a range of datasets (Gupta, Shreneter, & Sehgal, 2024; Choi et al., 2020). In educational contexts, CNNs can be applied to clean textbook images, scanned diagrams, and instructional video frames.

Zangana and Mustafa (2024b) proposed a hybrid model that combines CNNs with wavelet transformations, achieving high performance in denoising facial images used in remote proctoring and identity verification systems—two key components in modern e-learning ecosystems.

### 3.3. Autoencoders and Variational Autoencoders (VAEs)

Autoencoders operate by encoding input images into a latent space and then decoding them to reconstruct a cleaner version. Variational Autoencoders (VAEs), an extension of this architecture, introduce probabilistic modeling, offering improved robustness against stochastic noise. These techniques are particularly useful in educational applications where students capture notes or diagrams under poor lighting conditions (Zangana & Mustafa, 2025a).

Moreover, as discussed by Heidari et al. (2024), autoencoders play a pivotal role in deepfake detection pipelines. Since the integrity of educational content is often threatened by manipulated media, incorporating autoencoder-based denoising helps reinforce trust in online learning resources.

### 3.4. Generative Adversarial Networks (GANs)

GANs represent a powerful class of AI models where a generator learns to produce denoised images, while a discriminator tries to distinguish them from original clean images. This adversarial training leads to high-fidelity restorations and is particularly effective for recovering texture and structural details. GAN-based denoising has seen rapid adoption in educational archiving, especially for restoring historical content and low-resolution scientific imagery (Zangana & Mustafa, 2025b; Khimi et al., 2024).

Additionally, GANs have been applied to detect synthetic and fake content, making them a dual-purpose tool in both image enhancement and verification (Maheshwari & Paulchamy, 2024; Lyu, 2024).

### 3.5. Wavelet and Hybrid Approaches

Wavelet-based techniques are valuable for decomposing images into frequency subbands, allowing for localized noise removal. Hybrid methods, which integrate wavelet transforms with deep learning, offer the advantages of both domains. Zangana and Mustafa (2024b, 2025c) introduced multiple models combining wavelets with CNNs, autoencoders, and GANs to achieve high-accuracy denoising in facial recognition, medical imaging, and digital forensics.

Such hybrid systems are particularly relevant in educational and cybersecurity environments where data privacy, visual clarity, and processing efficiency must coexist (Majeed & Hwang, 2023; Zangana, Mustafa, & Omar, 2024).

### 3.6. Application in Secure Educational Ecosystems

AI-based image denoising is increasingly being integrated into secure educational ecosystems. As online learning platforms become frequent targets for adversarial attacks, visual data must be preprocessed and validated for authenticity and quality. Almehdhar et al. (2024) and Khaleel et al. (2024) emphasized the importance of adversarial defense in intelligent systems, a concern mirrored in educational AI systems that rely on visual analytics.

Das (2024) and Takale, Mahalle, and Sule (2024) highlighted the role of generative AI in phishing and visual deception, further reinforcing the need for robust denoising in safeguarding content integrity. Fayyaz, Almehmadi, and El-Khatib (2024) proposed a hybrid framework for digital forensics that can be extended to analyze educational imagery compromised by compression or tampering.

### 3.7. Ethical, Privacy, and Security Considerations

While denoising enhances usability, it also introduces challenges. AI models must ensure that no bias or hallucinated content is introduced during reconstruction. Hewage et al. (2022) and Golda et al. (2024) addressed multimedia privacy concerns, pointing out that AI applications can inadvertently alter content if not carefully monitored.

Moreover, emerging attacks like thermal analysis (Alotaibi, Williamson, & Khamis, 2023) and deepfake proliferation require proactive integration of image verification tools alongside denoising. AI pipelines must be explainable, auditable, and transparent—qualities emphasized in the works of Moustafa et al. (2023), Aslam (2024), and Rohatgi et al. (2023).

### 3.8. AI for OSINT and Intelligent Resource Curation

Oakley Browne, Abedin, and Chowdhury (2024) observed that AI is widely used in Open Source Intelligence (OSINT) applications, which increasingly supply educational repositories. Clean and readable visuals are essential for extracting knowledge from open data sources. Sayyafzadeh (2024) demonstrated how thumbnail image forensics can assist in validating educational videos or open materials.

These methods complement broader AI governance strategies in DevSecOps, where visual integrity contributes to system reliability (Fu, Pasuksmit, & Tantithamthavorn, 2024; Sindiramutty et al., 2025).

In sum, AI-based image denoising stands at the intersection of education, security, and digital equity. It empowers educators to enhance the clarity, reliability, and inclusiveness of digital content, while also ensuring the integrity and authenticity required in modern cyber-aware environments (Ali, Shah, & ElAffendi, 2024; Roshanaei, Khan, & Sylvester, 2024; Rane, Choudhary, & Rane, 2024).

## 4. EDUCATIONAL USE CASES AND SCENARIOS

The integration of AI-based image denoising techniques into educational contexts presents transformative opportunities across multiple domains—particularly in remote learning, digital archiving, content authentication, and accessibility. As educational environments become increasingly digitized, AI solutions are not only enhancing content clarity but also addressing cybersecurity, privacy, and trust concerns that accompany the adoption of advanced technologies.

### 4.1. Enhancing Clarity in Remote and Hybrid Classrooms

One of the primary applications of image denoising is the enhancement of teaching materials used in remote and hybrid learning environments. Low-quality scans of handwritten notes, textbooks, and whiteboard captures are common in asynchronous settings. AI-based denoising techniques such as wavelet-autoencoder hybrids (Zangana & Mustafa, 2025c) can significantly improve visual clarity, thereby reducing cognitive load and supporting inclusive education for students with visual processing difficulties (Majeed Zangana & Mustafa, 2024).

This use case is especially critical when bandwidth constraints or legacy devices introduce compression artifacts and visual noise. In such cases, AI-powered models trained for content-aware restoration (Zangana & Mustafa, 2024) serve as essential tools for equitable learning environments.

### 4.2. Safeguarding Integrity in Educational Assessments

Online proctoring and digital assessments are vulnerable to visual tampering and synthetic media threats. Deepfake videos or forged documentation can compromise the credibility of examinations. Maheshwari and Paulchamy (2024), as well as Heidari et al. (2024), emphasize the importance of integrating explainable AI and adversarial robustness in systems designed to verify visual content.

In educational scenarios, image denoising plays a preemptive role by cleaning image data before analysis, making it easier for deepfake detection systems (Khimi et al., 2024; Khormali, 2022) to perform accurately. Gupta, Shreneter, and Sehgal (2024) demonstrated how CNN-based models can enhance detection rates of manipulated media, which is vital for secure remote evaluations.

### 4.3. Visual Archiving and Legacy Content Restoration

Many educational institutions maintain vast archives of visual materials that degrade over time. Whether it's scanned diagrams from old textbooks or historical documents, AI-based denoising methods such as GAN-enhanced restoration (Zangana & Mustafa, 2025a) can be applied to revitalize these resources.

This approach not only supports digital preservation but also aligns with open-source intelligence (OSINT) strategies discussed by Oakley Browne, Abedin, and Chowdhury (2024), where image clarity is essential for data mining and resource curation.

### 4.4. Combatting Misinformation and Image Forgery in Learning Materials

In an age where AI-generated content can be convincingly deceptive, image denoising contributes to broader efforts to detect and neutralize visual misinformation. Bharathiraja et al. (2023) provided a survey of image forgery techniques that can affect educational content. In parallel, Lyu (2024) discussed how deepfake content compromises the authenticity of educational resources, especially in social sciences and media literacy courses.

AI-driven pipelines can first denoise visual data and then pass it through deep learning-based forgery detectors (Das, 2024; Choi et al., 2020), ensuring that educational materials are not only clean but also credible.

## 4.5. Cybersecure Learning Platforms and Visual Data Protection

Educational platforms that rely on image-based inputs—such as interactive whiteboards, student-uploaded assignments, or IoT-enabled classroom devices—are increasingly targeted by cyberattacks. Thermo-attacks (Alotaibi, Williamson, & Khamis, 2023) and visual data interception have been highlighted as emerging risks. Here, preprocessing with denoising filters adds a critical layer of protection and data integrity.

Studies by Almehdhar et al. (2024), Khaleel et al. (2024), and Roshanaei, Khan, and Sylvester (2024) show that denoising enhances the reliability of visual data before it is analyzed by intrusion detection or content authentication systems. These practices are central to DevSecOps strategies for educational cybersecurity (Fu, Pasuksmit, & Tantithamthavorn, 2024; Sindiramutty et al., 2025).

## 4.6. Denoising in AI-Powered Accessibility Tools

Image denoising is also fundamental to accessibility technologies for visually impaired learners. When integrated with screen readers, optical character recognition (OCR), or text-to-speech engines, clean and legible images enable higher accuracy in content extraction. These tools benefit from denoised inputs, particularly when interpreting low-quality or handwritten notes (Zangana & Mustafa, 2025b).

Such applications align with the ethical imperatives of inclusive education, as emphasized by Hewage et al. (2022) and Majeed & Hwang (2023), who advocate for responsible AI in multimedia environments.

## 4.7. AI-Enhanced Forensic Training in Educational Curricula

With cybersecurity and digital forensics becoming part of many higher education curricula, AI-denoised imagery is now used to simulate forensic scenarios. Fayyaz, Almehmadi, and El-Khatib (2024) proposed hybrid frameworks for investigating infotainment systems, which can be adapted for academic use in digital forensic labs. Likewise, Sayyafzadeh (2024) explored how thumbnail forensic acquisition can help students understand image metadata and chain-of-custody documentation.

These scenarios create realistic, hands-on learning environments where students interact with AI-enhanced visual data as part of training in law, cybersecurity, and digital evidence handling.

## 4.8. Thumbnail Verification and Educational Platform Authentication

Platforms hosting massive amounts of user-generated content (e.g., MOOCs, LMS portals) rely on thumbnails and metadata for indexing, moderation, and search. Image denoising helps improve thumbnail clarity and enhances the accuracy of content classifiers. Sayyafzadeh (2024) demonstrated how thumbnail image forensic acquisition can support this, particularly in verifying authenticity and preventing unauthorized uploads.

Combined with adversarial threat detection models (Ali, Shah, & ElAffendi, 2024; Moustafa et al., 2023), this makes educational systems more resilient to deception and misuse.

## 4.9. Mitigating Risks of Generative AI in Student Projects

As generative AI tools become commonplace in student assignments and creative projects, the risk of deepfake image misuse or synthetic plagiarism increases (Singla, 2024; Takale, Mahalle, & Sule, 2024). Educators must verify that the images used are authentic, non-manipulated, and privacy-compliant. Denoising tools, when applied before deepfake detection algorithms, help in differentiating between artifacts from poor quality input versus intentional synthetic manipulation (Khimi et al., 2024; Golda et al., 2024).

Integrating AI-based visual authenticity tools into LMS platforms and project submission portals can help uphold academic integrity across disciplines.

## 4.10. IoT-Enhanced Smart Classrooms

Smart classrooms embedded with IoT sensors and visual feedback systems (e.g., gesture detection, facial expression analysis) require real-time image denoising to reduce the influence of environmental noise. As discussed by Dhayanidhi (2022), the combination of cloud-based AI and IoT introduces new vulnerabilities, but also new capabilities for real-time adaptive learning. Denoising in this context improves data quality, user identification, and machine perception under variable conditions.

Tyagi and Addula (2024) note the importance of preprocessing in AI-enabled digital twin systems—frameworks that are now extending to digital classrooms and virtual campus environments.

### 4.11 Summary

From cleaning lecture visuals to strengthening digital forensics training and securing learning platforms, AI-based image denoising techniques are proving vital to modern education. These use cases are not merely technical enhancements but are directly tied to pedagogical equity, content authenticity, and the future-readiness of educational institutions.

## 5. IMPACT ON TEACHER WORKFLOW AND STUDENT LEARNING

AI-based image denoising techniques profoundly influence both educators' workflows and student learning experiences. By automating enhancement of visual content, these technologies facilitate more effective teaching and deeper student engagement, while also addressing critical privacy and cybersecurity concerns.

### 5.1. Streamlined Content Preparation for Educators

#### Efficiency & Quality

Teachers often spend considerable time preparing clear and visually engaging materials. AI-driven denoising automates enhancement of lecture slides, scanned diagrams, and handwritten notes, significantly reducing manual cleanup effort (Zangana & Mustafa, 2024; Majeed Zangana & Mustafa, 2024). Hybrid wavelet-autoencoder models provide educators with "one-click" restoration tools, enabling them to focus more on pedagogy and less on technical adjustments.

#### Integration into Digital Platforms

As AI becomes embedded in Learning Management Systems (LMS), visual preprocessing workflows shift from offline tasks to integrated real-time processes. This integration aligns with DevSecOps pipelines enriched by AI (Fu, Pasuksmit,

& Tantithamthavorn, 2024), allowing teachers to upload noisy images that are automatically denoised, authenticated, and optimized for student consumption.

In digital learning platforms, denoising is not a standalone step but part of a larger content enhancement workflow. The following diagram outlines how AI-denoising integrates into a typical teacher content pipeline.

*Figure 3. Workflow Integration of Image Denoising in Digital Teaching*

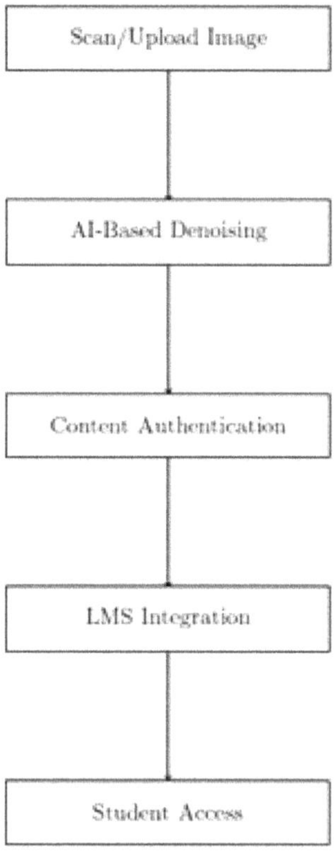


## 5.2. Enhanced Student Comprehension and Engagement

### Visual Clarity & Cognitive Load

High-fidelity visuals reduce extraneous cognitive load and support deeper learning—especially in visually intensive subjects like STEM. Enhanced diagrams, graphs, and flowcharts improve information retention (Zangana & Mustafa, 2025c). This clarity is particularly beneficial for students relying on OCR or text extraction from class materials.

### Accessibility Gains

AI-enhanced visuals benefit students with visual impairments. Denoised content improves accuracy for screen readers and text-to-speech tools, enabling better comprehension. These benefits support inclusive education initiatives (Hewage et al., 2022; Majeed & Hwang, 2023) and promote equitable learning opportunities.

## 5.3. Strengthening Academic Integrity and Security

### Reliable Assessment Environments

Remote assessments often rely on image submissions and proctored video feeds. AI-based denoising improves media clarity while supporting detection of image manipulation or identity spoofing (Maheshwari & Paulchamy, 2024; Heidari et al., 2024). CNN-based visual veracity tools help ensure submissions are genuine (Gupta et al., 2024), while denoising layers strengthen model robustness against adversarial attacks (Choi et al., 2020; Khaleel et al., 2024).

### Privacy Preservation

Denoised content also aids in removing metadata and hidden artifacts that may compromise student privacy, consistent with multimedia privacy frameworks (Golda et al., 2024; Hewage et al., 2022).

## 5.4. Empowering Cybersecurity Education and Forensics Training

Visual denoising enhances the quality of datasets used in cybersecurity and digital forensics education. For example, forensic analysis simulations of infotainment systems can leverage enhanced visuals for more realistic student experiences (Fayyaz et al., 2024). Thumbnail forensic analysis exercises (Sayyafzadeh, 2024) also benefit from high-quality inputs, facilitating better instruction in image metadata examination and legal investigation methodologies.

## 5.5. Adaptive, Secure, and Smart Classrooms

### Real-time Analytics in Smart Environments

Smart classrooms equipped with IoT sensors rely on clean visual feeds for real-time analytics—such as gesture detection or attention tracking. Denoising ensures sensor data accuracy and contributes to improved analysis and feedback systems (Dhayanidhi, 2022; Tyagi & Addula, 2024).

### Defense Against Advanced Threats

AI-infused classrooms are vulnerable to threats such as thermal side-channel attacks (Alotaibi et al., 2023) and image-based adversarial exploits. Layered defenses, including visual preprocessors and intrusion detection systems, are vital to resilience (Almehdhar et al., 2024; Roshanaei et al., 2024; Aslam, 2024). Image denoising provides an initial safeguard in these multi-layered security ecosystems (Ali et al., 2024).

## 5.6. Support for Student Creativity and Academic Rigor

### Generative AI Projects

Students increasingly use generative AI for creative assignments. However, distinguishing between AI-generated visuals and authentic content is essential for academic honesty. Denoised images help deepfake detection systems differentiate between low-quality artifacts and purposeful manipulation (Bharathiraja et al., 2023; Lyu, 2024). Maintaining academic integrity enhances educational standards (Singla, 2024; Takale et al., 2024).

### Ethical AI Awareness

Integrating image cleaning tools in classroom workflows provides teachable moments for discussing AI ethics, privacy, and manipulation. Educators can foster critical literacy in generative AI while protecting students and preserving professional standards (Khimi et al., 2024; Majeed & Hwang, 2023).

## 5.7. Support for Institutional IT Management

### Scalable Deployment and Maintenance

For education IT teams, standardized AI-denoising modules reduce content support burdens. As part of DevSecOps strategies, they ensure safe image processing at scale (Fu et al., 2024; Sindiramutty et al., 2025). Predictable performance lowers downtime and improves continuity for staff and students.

### Synergy with Forensic and OSINT Tools

Denoised visual content can be used in institutional audits for incidents such as credential misuse or copyright violation. OSINT techniques (Oakley Browne et al., 2024) and forensic tools (Sayyafzadeh, 2024) are enhanced by high-quality inputs, improving institutional governance.

## 5.8 Summary

AI-based image denoising is a powerful enabler of educational efficiency, integrity, and inclusivity. It streamlines teacher workflows, enriches student learning, hardens institutional security, and fosters ethical AI literacy. These tools are poised to become essential components of future-ready education systems, bridging the gap between content utility and trustworthiness.

# 6. CHALLENGES IN IMPLEMENTATION

While AI-driven image denoising offers transformative advantages across cybersecurity, forensics, and education, implementing such systems is fraught with a wide array of challenges. These obstacles span technical, ethical, legal, infrastructural, and operational domains, and they must be addressed to ensure safe, effective, and equitable deployment of image processing AI.

AI-driven denoising offers significant advantages but also presents several implementation challenges. The bar graph below highlights the most frequently cited issues in academic literature and practice.

*Figure 4. Common Challenges in Implementing AI-Based Denoising*

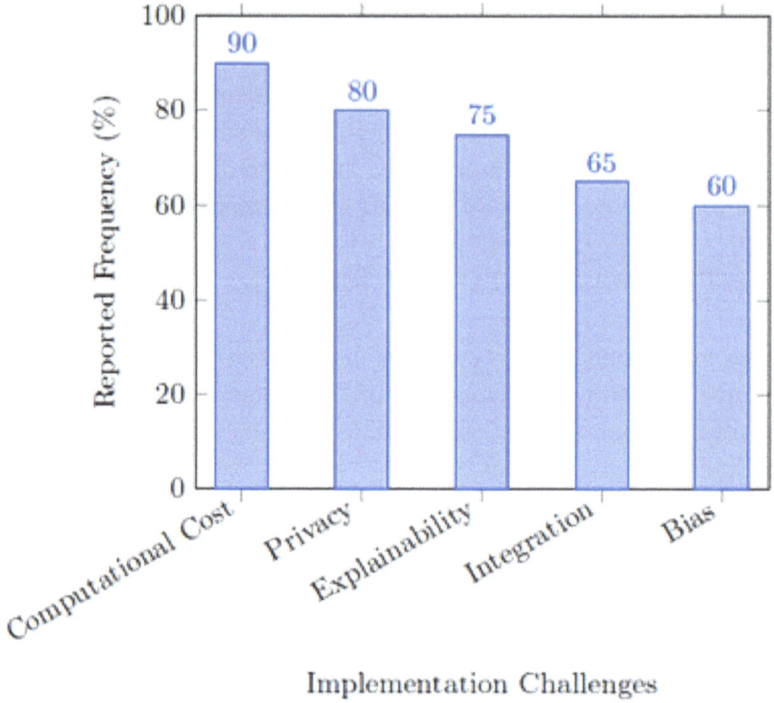


Despite the transformative potential of AI in cybersecurity, several challenges persist that hinder effective implementation. The following table categorizes these challenges into technical, ethical, and operational domains, outlining their implications and potential mitigation strategies.

*Table 2. Challenges in Implementing AI for Cybersecurity*

| Challenge Category | Description | Impact on AI Adoption | Mitigation Approaches |
|---|---|---|---|
| Data Quality & Availability | Scarcity of labeled, high-quality datasets | Limits model training and evaluation | Data augmentation, transfer learning |
| Adversarial Attacks | Malicious manipulation of AI models | Degrades model reliability | Adversarial training, robust model design |
| Privacy Concerns | Risks of data exposure and misuse | Legal and ethical compliance issues | Federated learning, differential privacy |

continued on following page

*Table 2. Continued*

| Challenge Category | Description | Impact on AI Adoption | Mitigation Approaches |
|---|---|---|---|
| Explainability | Lack of transparency in decision-making | Reduces user trust | Explainable AI methods, human-in-the-loop |
| Computational Costs | High resource requirements for deep models | Limits deployment in resource-constrained environments | Model compression, edge AI |

## 6.1. Technical Complexity and Integration Barriers

One of the primary challenges is integrating denoising models into existing infrastructure. Models such as hybrid wavelet-GAN and wavelet-autoencoder systems require significant computational resources and tuning (Zangana & Mustafa, 2025a; Zangana & Mustafa, 2025b). Deep learning-based denoising solutions often need to be embedded into broader DevSecOps workflows, which may be difficult without proper architecture (Fu et al., 2024).

The implementation also faces compatibility issues when deployed in real-time systems such as intelligent transport networks or IoT edge devices (Almehdhar et al., 2024; Dhayanidhi, 2022). Models trained in controlled environments may not generalize well to noisy real-world data, leading to inaccuracies.

## 6.2. Adversarial Risks and Data Integrity Threats

Despite their ability to clean images, AI systems remain vulnerable to adversarial manipulation. For example, subtle perturbations in input images can trick denoising networks or reduce their effectiveness, especially in adversarial cybersecurity environments (Khaleel et al., 2024; Choi et al., 2020). Adversaries may use adversarial patches or poisoned data during training to compromise system outputs (Golda et al., 2024).

In education, forensics, or surveillance, where visual evidence authenticity is paramount, improper denoising may erase clues or introduce artificial artifacts, complicating verification (Heidari et al., 2024; Gupta et al., 2024). Ensuring visual veracity is particularly critical in judicial and academic integrity contexts.

## 6.3. Data Privacy, Security, and Ethical Concerns

Handling visual data inherently raises privacy issues. AI-enhanced images may contain hidden metadata or watermarking that could inadvertently leak sensitive user information (Hewage et al., 2022; Majeed & Hwang, 2023). Deep learning-based denoising requires access to large volumes of high-resolution visual data, which may violate regulatory norms such as GDPR or FERPA in academic settings.

Moreover, implementation challenges are compounded by the dual-use nature of AI. The same denoising tools can be exploited to enhance fake images, deepfakes, or manipulated content (Lyu, 2024; Maheshwari & Paulchamy, 2024; Khimi et al., 2024). This paradox complicates policy development for ethical deployment (Singla, 2024; Das, 2024).

## 6.4. Explainability and Trust Issues

Educators, security officers, and digital forensic experts often require not just results but also explanations. However, many denoising systems, especially those using adversarial training or deep GANs, are black-box in nature and lack interpretability (Roshanaei et al., 2024; Moustafa et al., 2023). This undermines trust, especially in contexts where decisions made using AI-enhanced visuals must be legally or academically defensible.

The push toward Explainable AI (XAI) is ongoing, but existing models in image denoising lag behind in producing interpretable outputs (Maheshwari & Paulchamy, 2024; Fayyaz et al., 2024).

## 6.5. Resource Constraints and Infrastructure Gaps

Running advanced denoising models in real time requires high-performance computing resources, including GPUs and low-latency memory systems. This poses a challenge for schools, public-sector agencies, and small-scale forensics labs that often lack the budget or infrastructure (Rane et al., 2024; Rohatgi et al., 2023).

Moreover, lightweight models that can operate on edge devices or in embedded environments without significant loss in performance are still in the early research phase (Tyagi & Addula, 2024; Zangana et al., 2024).

## 6.6. Interoperability and Dataset Limitations

Another key challenge is the lack of standardized datasets that include clean-noisy image pairs in realistic cybersecurity, surveillance, or educational contexts. Without such data, denoising systems often fail to generalize across domains (Majeed Zangana & Mustafa, 2024). The absence of labeled adversarial datasets further hampers training for models that need to detect and resist deepfakes or spoofed imagery (Khormali, 2022; Bharathiraja et al., 2023).

Additionally, cross-compatibility with existing forensic tools, OSINT systems, and detection engines remains limited (Oakley Browne et al., 2024; Sayyafzadeh, 2024).

## 6.7. Rapid Evolution of Threat Landscapes

Cyber threats and generative AI capabilities evolve rapidly. Techniques such as thermal side-channel attacks (Alotaibi et al., 2023), phishing image obfuscation (Das, 2024), and AI-generated misinformation outpace the response time of current AI systems (Zhao et al., 2024; Alotaibi et al., 2023). Denoising systems that fail to keep up with such innovations risk becoming obsolete or even aiding malicious actors.

Deepfake technologies, in particular, continuously evolve to bypass detection systems (Khimi et al., 2024; Lyu, 2024), rendering many fixed denoising solutions ineffective over time.

## 6.8. Human Factors and Resistance to Change

Many educators, digital investigators, and IT staff lack training in deploying and maintaining AI systems. Resistance to adopting new workflows—especially when combined with the risk of data loss or system misinterpretation—can delay or derail implementation efforts (Rohatgi et al., 2023; Rane et al., 2024).

Furthermore, over-reliance on AI-based cleaning tools may cause critical visual context to be lost, leading to misinterpretation or "overtrust" in visually sanitized outputs (Aslam, 2024).

## 6.9 Summary

Successfully implementing AI-based image denoising tools requires a multidisciplinary approach that includes technical innovation, regulatory compliance, user training, and adversarial resilience. While the promise of enhanced clarity, security, and efficiency is strong, the risks of misuse, error, or inadequate integration remain significant. These challenges must be proactively addressed to unlock the full potential of AI in secure and responsible image enhancement workflows.

## 7. ETHICAL AND PEDAGOGICAL CONSIDERATIONS

The integration of AI-based image denoising systems—especially within education, digital forensics, and cybersecurity domains—raises significant ethical and pedagogical challenges. While these technologies promise efficiency and accuracy, their influence on human judgment, educational equity, truthfulness, and trust must be critically examined. This section unpacks the major ethical dilemmas and pedagogical implications associated with these technologies and outlines necessary frameworks for responsible deployment.

### 7.1. The Dual-Use Dilemma and Content Authenticity

AI-based image enhancement systems, such as hybrid wavelet-GANs or convolutional networks, can reconstruct low-quality or tampered visuals with remarkable precision (Zangana & Mustafa, 2025a; Gupta et al., 2024). However, this same technology can be exploited for malicious purposes, such as improving the quality of forged images or deepfakes, thereby amplifying misinformation (Heidari et al., 2024; Khimi et al., 2024).

The dual-use nature of AI was extensively documented by Choi et al. (2020) and further emphasized by Lyu (2024), who warned against the widespread societal risks of AI-generated visual deception. Bharathiraja et al. (2023) echoed this concern in their comprehensive review on image forgery, illustrating how denoising and generative methods can be weaponized in both educational cheating and social engineering campaigns.

### 7.2. Ethical Risks in Student Assessment and AI Bias

In educational environments, AI-based denoising used for visual grading tools, online proctoring, or content review systems could inadvertently reinforce systemic biases. Aslam (2024) and Golda et al. (2024) raised serious questions about the transparency of AI decision-making, particularly in scenarios where algorithmic outputs are used for student evaluation or behavioral monitoring.

AI systems trained on imbalanced or biased datasets may unfairly benefit or penalize students based on race, lighting conditions, or image artifacts (Majeed & Hwang, 2023). This is particularly concerning when students' webcam footage or assignment visuals are automatically enhanced and interpreted.

## 7.3. Threats to Privacy and Consent in Educational Settings

The use of AI-enhanced image analysis in remote classrooms, smart campuses, or digital forensics introduces serious privacy risks. AI tools often require access to raw images and visual data from students, educators, or third parties. According to Hewage et al. (2022), this data exposure can be exploited to extract unintended metadata or to recreate visual identities without consent.

Furthermore, Alotaibi et al. (2023) demonstrated how even thermal and side-channel data could be leveraged in AI-driven attacks, emphasizing that visual privacy is not limited to what is visible. Oakley Browne et al. (2024) warned that OSINT tools enhanced by AI could unknowingly breach ethical norms through inadvertent data harvesting.

## 7.4. Generative AI and Academic Integrity

The growing accessibility of generative AI tools capable of image synthesis and enhancement challenges the foundations of academic honesty. Students can now generate seemingly authentic diagrams, visual projects, and photographic evidence using tools derived from denoising or GAN-based architectures (Das, 2024; Singla, 2024). Without robust detection mechanisms, educational institutions may struggle to distinguish between genuine and AI-fabricated visual content.

This concern is amplified by the increasing sophistication of adversarial image generation and the difficulty of verifying image authenticity—even after denoising (Maheshwari & Paulchamy, 2024; Khormali, 2022; Zangana & Mustafa, 2024b).

## 7.5. Explainability and Pedagogical Trust

Educators and students alike must be able to understand how AI arrives at a denoised image or classification decision. Black-box models create opacity, leading to distrust and pedagogical disempowerment. Moustafa et al. (2023) and Roshanaei et al. (2024) emphasized the need for Explainable AI (XAI) to support pedagogical transparency and defensible assessment practices.

Explainability also becomes essential when forensic or cybersecurity visuals are used as evidence in disciplinary or legal proceedings. AI-enhanced images lacking interpretability could undermine academic justice and fairness (Fayyaz et al., 2024).

## 7.6. Pedagogical Value vs. Automation Overreach

There is a pedagogical trade-off between technological efficiency and the depth of student learning. While automated visual analysis can streamline assessments, it risks reducing complex cognitive tasks—such as image interpretation, inference, or critical thinking—into simplistic outputs (Rane et al., 2024). Rohatgi et al. (2023) warned against over-reliance on AI for educational functions traditionally mediated by human instructors.

Zangana et al. (2024) proposed that while hybrid models significantly improve technical performance in image analysis, their pedagogical integration must preserve opportunities for student engagement, exploration, and reflection.

## 7.7. Ethics of Surveillance and Consent in Cybersecurity Education

Within cybersecurity training environments, AI-powered denoising and monitoring tools raise ethical issues of digital surveillance. For example, Ali et al. (2024) and Dhayanidhi (2022) highlighted the use of persistent threat monitoring in educational simulations, which—when unchecked—can become ethically intrusive.

Such practices must be balanced against student autonomy and data minimization principles. Zhao et al. (2024) and Takale et al. (2024) proposed ethical frameworks for secure AI deployment that prioritize informed consent and privacy-by-design, especially in generative AI-enhanced learning environments.

## 7.8. Ethical Education and Instructor Preparedness

Effective implementation of AI-enhanced image tools also requires preparing educators to teach ethical AI use. Unfortunately, many instructors lack the technical background to understand or critically evaluate AI outputs (Fu et al., 2024; Tyagi & Addula, 2024). Pedagogical guidelines and ethics training must become integral to any curriculum incorporating AI-based tools.

Oakley Browne et al. (2024) further emphasized that without adequate training, teachers may unintentionally endorse unethical AI applications, exacerbating risks rather than mitigating them.

## 7.9 Summary

AI-based image denoising systems carry significant ethical and pedagogical implications that extend far beyond their technical capabilities. Their deployment must be grounded in clear consent protocols, transparency, inclusiveness, and pedagogical value. While these systems can transform education and cybersecurity, they must be wielded with caution, supported by robust ethical guidelines and ongoing teacher training to ensure their responsible use.

A trustworthy AI denoising system must address both technical performance and ethical safeguards. The layered model below depicts the multi-dimensional structure of responsible AI deployment.

*Figure 5. Layered Architecture for Ethical and Technical Integration in AI Denoising*

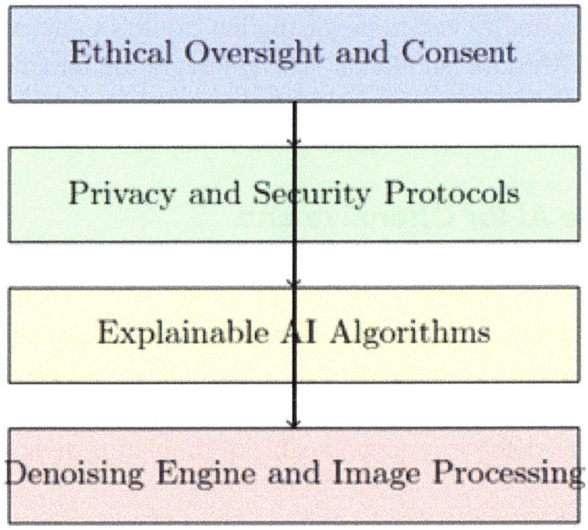


## 8. FUTURE DIRECTIONS AND OPPORTUNITIES

The integration of AI in cybersecurity, forensic intelligence, and image denoising continues to expand, offering promising pathways to improve efficiency, resilience, and scalability. Emerging trends such as hybrid models, generative AI (GenAI), explainable artificial intelligence (XAI), and multi-modal frameworks are reshaping what is possible across detection, prevention, and trust-building applications. This section outlines key research directions and practical opportunities for advancement, grounded in current scholarly and industrial discourse.

## 8.1. Hybrid AI Models for Advanced Image Denoising and Detection

Future research should increasingly explore hybrid architectures that combine traditional signal processing techniques—such as wavelet transforms—with deep learning models like GANs and autoencoders. Studies by Zangana and Mustafa (2025a, 2025b, 2025c) and Majeed Zangana and Mustafa (2024) underscore the robustness of such approaches for medical imaging, forensic enhancement, and adversarial noise removal.

Hybridization is not limited to denoising but extends to detection as well. The work of Zangana, Mustafa, and Omar (2024) integrating template matching with Faster R-CNN for object detection exemplifies how future systems can benefit from synergistic AI frameworks across application domains.

## 8.2. Generative AI for Offensive and Defensive Cyber Operations

Generative AI presents a paradox of opportunity and threat. As Das (2024), Golda et al. (2024), and Sindiramutty et al. (2025) observed, GenAI can be used to synthesize cybersecurity attack vectors (e.g., fake credentials or malicious traffic) or develop enhanced defense systems capable of simulating diverse threat scenarios for training.

Zhao et al. (2024) further envision the use of GenAI in secure physical-layer communication, while Takale, Mahalle, and Sule (2024) identify its disruptive potential across encryption, obfuscation, and threat detection domains. Continued research must focus on creating GenAI frameworks with embedded ethical constraints and regulatory compliance.

## 8.3. Explainable and Interpretable AI Systems

As AI systems become more complex, interpretability remains a vital research frontier. Moustafa et al. (2023) emphasize the importance of explainable AI for intrusion detection, especially in the context of IoT ecosystems. Likewise, Maheshwari and Paulchamy (2024) call for Explainable AI (XAI) in deepfake mitigation to build public trust and ensure legal admissibility in forensic settings.

Fu, Pasuksmit, and Tantithamthavorn (2024) recommend the integration of explainability into DevSecOps pipelines, allowing for dynamic security decisions that remain transparent to human operators.

## 8.4. Advancing Deepfake and Forgery Detection

Deepfakes will continue to evolve, requiring new detection techniques grounded in robust feature extraction and ensemble learning. Heidari et al. (2024), Khimi et al. (2024), and Khormali (2022) provide foundations for detection using deep neural networks, while Lyu (2024) outlines the socio-technical dimensions of combating visual disinformation.

Future work may build upon the CNN-based detection techniques explored by Gupta, Shreneter, and Sehgal (2024), potentially incorporating wavelet-based anomaly detection to enhance performance under low-light or compressed formats (Zangana & Mustafa, 2024b).

## 8.5. Opportunities in Vehicular, IoT, and Edge AI Security

The increasing autonomy of vehicles and IoT devices creates demand for lightweight, high-performing AI-based security protocols. Almehdhar et al. (2024) offer a roadmap for future intrusion detection systems within vehicular networks. Similarly, Dhayanidhi (2022) and Khaleel et al. (2024) advocate for ML/DL integration into edge computing frameworks to secure resource-constrained environments.

Future directions include federated learning for privacy-preserving anomaly detection and model compression to reduce latency on embedded systems.

## 8.6. Cross-Disciplinary AI in Digital Forensics

Cross-pollination between AI and digital forensics will drive innovation in investigative tools, particularly with infotainment system analysis (Fayyaz et al., 2024), OSINT-based intelligence (Oakley Browne et al., 2024), and visual evidence verification (Sayyafzadeh, 2024). This interdisciplinary synergy presents opportunities for novel software tools capable of automated evidence restoration, noise filtration, and chain-of-custody validation.

Future systems should integrate time-series image analysis with real-time detection pipelines to improve response latency in law enforcement or military contexts.

## 8.7. Addressing AI-Driven Privacy Challenges

AI's capacity to infer sensitive data from minimal input demands new privacy-preserving learning techniques. Majeed and Hwang (2023) describe the adversarial nature of AI in data-sharing contexts, while Alotaibi, Williamson, and Khamis (2023) demonstrate thermal attack feasibility on input devices.

Research into privacy-by-design architectures—such as those proposed by Golda et al. (2024) and Hewage et al. (2022)—should expand to include differential privacy and synthetic anonymization layers in AI pipelines.

## 8.8. AI for Phishing and Malware Detection in Emerging Environments

New threat vectors—such as phishing campaigns enhanced by GenAI or zero-day malware attacks—require adaptive AI techniques. Das (2024), Tyagi and Addula (2024), and Rohatgi et al. (2023) argue for layered machine learning models capable of behavioral anomaly detection and real-time signature evolution.

In the future, these methods may be embedded within smart environments—such as Industry 4.0 ecosystems—providing autonomous self-healing network capabilities.

## 8.9. Educational and Training Opportunities

As Choi et al. (2020) and Aslam (2024) observed, the rise of AI in cybersecurity demands continual re-skilling and pedagogical transformation. AI-infused simulations, ethical GenAI usage modules, and real-time scenario training can be implemented in cybersecurity curricula to prepare the next generation of practitioners.

Rane, Choudhary, and Rane (2024) propose a unified framework for evaluating AI education that includes skill acquisition, ethical reasoning, and system comprehension. Future research should explore gamification and virtual labs powered by GenAI to enhance engagement.

## 8.10. Towards Resilient and Ethical AI Governance

Lastly, addressing the long-term future of AI in cybersecurity must involve the construction of resilient, transparent, and ethically aligned governance frameworks. Roshanaei, Khan, and Sylvester (2024) suggest adaptive policy-making tools supported by AI for regulatory foresight. Singla (2024) proposes integrating AI into strategic defense planning, emphasizing alignment with democratic values and global cyber norms.

This aligns with ongoing developments in hybrid image denoising and secure communications (Zangana & Mustafa, 2025a; Zhao et al., 2024), which must embed ethical logic into algorithmic infrastructure.

The evolution of AI in cybersecurity continues to open new avenues for research and application. This table outlines emerging trends and key opportunities that can shape the future landscape, emphasizing areas where AI can further enhance security capabilities and address current gaps.

*Table 3. Future Directions and Opportunities in AI for Cybersecurity*

| Future Direction | Description | Potential Impact | Key References |
|---|---|---|---|
| Explainable & Trustworthy AI | Development of transparent AI models | Increased adoption and compliance | Moustafa et al. (2023), Maheshwari & Paulchamy (2024) |
| AI for IoT & Edge Security | Lightweight AI models for IoT devices | Real-time detection, reduced latency | Almehdhar et al. (2024), Dhayanidhi (2022) |
| Generative AI for Defense | Using AI to simulate attacks and strengthen defense | Proactive threat mitigation | Das (2024), Zhao et al. (2024) |
| Hybrid AI Architectures | Combining classical and AI methods | Improved accuracy and robustness | Zangana & Mustafa (2024), Fayyaz et al. (2024) |
| Privacy-Preserving AI | Techniques like federated learning | Enhanced user data protection | Golda et al. (2024), Majeed & Hwang (2023) |

## 8.11 Summary

The future of AI in cybersecurity, digital forensics, and image processing lies in robust, interpretable, and ethically aware systems that evolve alongside threat landscapes. From hybrid architectures and GenAI to explainable frameworks and cross-domain intelligence, opportunities abound for researchers and practitioners to shape a secure, intelligent, and trustworthy digital future.

## 9. CONCLUSION

This chapter has explored the multifaceted landscape of artificial intelligence applications within cybersecurity, digital forensics, and image denoising. Through detailed examination of current methodologies, challenges, ethical considerations, and future directions, it is evident that AI technologies hold transformative potential in enhancing detection accuracy, automating complex investigative processes, and strengthening digital defenses.

Hybrid models that synergize classical signal processing with deep learning techniques have emerged as promising solutions to longstanding problems such as noise reduction and image forgery detection (Zangana & Mustafa, 2025a, 2025b; Majeed Zangana & Mustafa, 2024). At the same time, generative AI introduces new opportunities and risks—offering novel ways to simulate threats and improve defense strategies, while also necessitating rigorous frameworks to counteract misuse (Das, 2024; Zhao et al., 2024).

Explainability and interpretability remain critical, particularly for building trust in AI-driven cybersecurity tools and ensuring compliance with ethical and legal standards (Moustafa et al., 2023; Maheshwari & Paulchamy, 2024). Moreover, the evolving nature of threats in IoT, vehicular networks, and Industry 4.0 environments demands adaptive, lightweight AI models capable of real-time response and privacy preservation (Almehdhar et al., 2024; Dhayanidhi, 2022).

The ethical and pedagogical dimensions addressed in this work further highlight the importance of responsible AI deployment, emphasizing transparency, privacy, and continuous education to empower practitioners and end-users alike (Aslam, 2024; Majeed & Hwang, 2023).

Looking ahead, interdisciplinary collaboration, robust governance, and innovative hybrid architectures will be essential to harness AI's full potential for secure and resilient digital ecosystems. By addressing current challenges and leveraging emerging opportunities, the research community can drive forward the development of intelligent systems that not only detect and prevent cyber threats but also uphold the fundamental values of privacy, trust, and fairness in an increasingly complex technological world.

## REFERENCES


Ali, G., Shah, S., & ElAffendi, M. (2024). Enhancing Cybersecurity Incident Response: AI-Driven Optimization for Strengthened Advance Persistence Threat Detection.

Almehdhar, M., Albaseer, A., Khan, M. A., Abdallah, M., Menouar, H., Al-Kuwari, S., & Al-Fuqaha, A. (2024). Deep learning in the fast lane: A survey on advanced intrusion detection systems for intelligent vehicle networks. *IEEE Open Journal of Vehicular Technology*, *5*, 869–906. DOI: 10.1109/OJVT.2024.3422253

Alotaibi, N., Williamson, J., & Khamis, M. (2023). ThermoSecure: Investigating the effectiveness of AI-driven thermal attacks on commonly used computer keyboards. *ACM Transactions on Privacy and Security*, *26*(2), 1–24. DOI: 10.1145/3563693

Aslam, M. (2024). AI and cybersecurity: An ever-evolving landscape. *International Journal of Advanced Engineering Technologies and Innovations*, *1*(1), 52–71.

Bharathiraja, S., Rajesh Kanna, B., Geetha, S., & Anusooya, G. (2023). Unmasking the digital deception-a comprehensive survey on image forgery and detection techniques. *The Australian Journal of Forensic Sciences*, •••, 1–49.

Choi, Y. H., Liu, P., Shang, Z., Wang, H., Wang, Z., Zhang, L., Zhou, J., & Zou, Q. (2020). Using deep learning to solve computer security challenges: A survey. *Cybersecurity*, *3*(1), 1–32. DOI: 10.1186/s42400-020-00055-5

Das, R. (2024). *Generative AI: Phishing And Cybersecurity Metrics*. CRC Press. DOI: 10.1201/9781003503781

Dhayanidhi, G. (2022). Research on IoT threats & implementation of AI/ML to address emerging cybersecurity issues in IoT with cloud computing.

Fayyaz, Y., Almehmadi, A., & El-Khatib, K. (2024). A hybrid artificial intelligence framework for enhancing digital forensic investigations of infotainment systems. *Forensic Science International Digital Investigation*, *49*, 301751. DOI: 10.1016/j.fsidi.2024.301751

Fu, M., Pasuksmit, J., & Tantithamthavorn, C. (2024). AI for DevSecOps: A Landscape and Future Opportunities. *arXiv preprint arXiv:2404.04839*.

Golda, A., Mekonen, K., Pandey, A., Singh, A., Hassija, V., Chamola, V., & Sikdar, B. (2024). Privacy and Security Concerns in Generative AI: A Comprehensive Survey. *IEEE Access : Practical Innovations, Open Solutions*, *12*, 48126–48144. DOI: 10.1109/ACCESS.2024.3381611

Gupta, A. S., Shreneter, K. P., & Sehgal, S. (2024, March). Visual Veracity: Advancing AI-Generated Image Detection with Convolutional Neural Networks. In *2024 11th International Conference on Reliability, Infocom Technologies and Optimization (Trends and Future Directions)(ICRITO)* (pp. 1-6). IEEE.

Heidari, A., Jafari Navimipour, N., Dag, H., & Unal, M. (2024). Deepfake detection using deep learning methods: A systematic and comprehensive review. *Wiley Interdisciplinary Reviews. Data Mining and Knowledge Discovery*, *14*(2), e1520. DOI: 10.1002/widm.1520

Hewage, C. T., Khattak, S. K., Ahmad, A., Mallikarachchi, T., Ukwandu, E., & Bentotahewa, V. (2022). Multimedia privacy and security landscape in the wake of ai/ml. *Social Media Analytics, Strategies and Governance*, 203-228.

Khaleel, Y. L., Habeeb, M. A., Albahri, A. S., Al-Quraishi, T., Albahri, O. S., & Alamoodi, A. H. (2024). Network and cybersecurity applications of defense in adversarial attacks: A state-of-the-art using machine learning and deep learning methods. *Journal of Intelligent Systems*, *33*(1), 20240153. DOI: 10.1515/jisys-2024-0153

Khimi, W., Albarqi, K., Saif, K., & Elhag, S. A Systematic Review on Deep Fake Image Generation, Detection Techniques, Ethical Implications, and Overcoming Challenges.

Khormali, A. (2022). Advanced Deep Learning Methodologies for Deepfake Detection.

Lyu, S. (2024). *DeepFake the menace: mitigating the negative impacts of AI-generated content. Organizational Cybersecurity Journal: Practice*. Process and People.

Maheshwari, R. U., & Paulchamy, B. (2024). Securing online integrity: A hybrid approach to deepfake detection and removal using Explainable AI and Adversarial Robustness Training. *Automatika (Zagreb)*, *65*(4), 1517–1532. DOI: 10.1080/00051144.2024.2400640

Majeed, A., & Hwang, S. O. (2023). When AI meets information privacy: The adversarial role of AI in data sharing scenario. *IEEE Access : Practical Innovations, Open Solutions*, *11*, 76177–76195. DOI: 10.1109/ACCESS.2023.3297646

Majeed Zangana, H., & Mustafa, F. M. (2024). From Classical to Deep Learning: A Systematic Review of Image Denoising Techniques. *Jurnal Ilmiah Computer Science*, *3*(1), 50–65. DOI: 10.58602/jics.v3i1.36

Moustafa, N., Koroniotis, N., Keshk, M., Zomaya, A. Y., & Tari, Z. (2023). Explainable intrusion detection for cyber defences in the internet of things: Opportunities and solutions. *IEEE Communications Surveys and Tutorials*, *25*(3), 1775–1807. DOI: 10.1109/COMST.2023.3280465

Oakley Browne, T., Abedin, M., & Chowdhury, M. J. M. (2024). A systematic review on research utilising artificial intelligence for open source intelligence (OSINT) applications.

Rane, N., Choudhary, S., & Rane, J. (2024). Machine Learning and Deep Learning: a Comprehensive Review on Methods, Techniques, Applications, Challenges, and Future Directions. *Techniques, Applications, Challenges, and Future Directions (May 31, 2024).*

Rohatgi, S., Abinash, B., Joshi, S., Sushant, S., & Kumar, S. (2023). Introduction to Artificial Intelligence and Cybersecurity for Industry. In *Artificial Intelligence and Cyber Security in Industry 4.0* (pp. 1–22). Springer Nature Singapore. DOI: 10.1007/978-981-99-2115-7_1

Roshanaei, M., Khan, M. R., & Sylvester, N. N. (2024). Navigating AI Cybersecurity: Evolving Landscape and Challenges. *Journal of Intelligent Learning Systems and Applications*, *16*(3), 155–174. DOI: 10.4236/jilsa.2024.163010

Sayyafzadeh, S. (2024). *Thumbnail Image Forensic Acquisition and Analysis in the Age of Artificial Intelligence* (Master's thesis, Florida Agricultural and Mechanical University).

Sindiramutty, S. R., Prabagaran, K. R. V., Akbar, R., Hussain, M., & Malik, N. A. (2025). Overview of Generative AI Techniques for Cybersecurity. *Reshaping CyberSecurity With Generative AI Techniques*, 1-52.

Singla, J. (2024). Safeguarding the Future: Advancements in Cybersecurity. *Utilizing Generative AI for Cyber Defense Strategies*, 421.

Takale, D. G., Mahalle, P. N., & Sule, B. (2024). Cyber Security Challenges in Generative AI Technology. *Journal of Network Security Computer Networks*, *10*(1), 28–34.

Tyagi, A. K., & Addula, S. R. (2024). Artificial Intelligence for Malware Analysis: A Systematic Study. *Artificial Intelligence-Enabled Digital Twin for Smart Manufacturing*, 359-390.

Zangana, H. M., & Mustafa, F. M. (2024). Hybrid Image Denoising Using Wavelet Transform and Deep Learning. *EAI Endorsed Transactions on AI and Robotics*, *3*. Advance online publication. DOI: 10.4108/airo.7486

Zangana, H. M., & Mustafa, F. M. (2024). Review of hybrid denoising approaches in face recognition: Bridging wavelet transform and deep learning. *The Indonesian Journal of Computer Science, 13*(4). Advance online publication. DOI: 10.33022/ijcs.v13i4.4209

Zangana, H. M., & Mustafa, F. M. (2025). A Novel Hybrid Wavelet-GAN Image Denoising System. In Bhatti, U., Aamir, M., Gulzar, Y., & Ullah Bazai, S. (Eds.), *Modern Intelligent Techniques for Image Processing* (pp. 409–424). IGI Global Scientific Publishing., DOI: 10.4018/979-8-3693-9045-0.ch017

Zangana, H. M., & Mustafa, F. M. (2025). Image Denoising Techniques for Cybersecurity and Forensic Applications: AI-Driven Approaches. In Omar, M., Zangana, H., & Mohammed, D. (Eds.), *Integrating Artificial Intelligence in Cybersecurity and Forensic Practices* (pp. 117–142). IGI Global Scientific Publishing., DOI: 10.4018/979-8-3373-0588-2.ch005

Zangana, H. M., & Mustafa, F. M. (2025). Wavelet-Autoencoder Hybrid Model for Enhanced Image Denoising in Medical Imaging. In M. Aamir, U. Bhatti, Z. Rahman, J. Bhutto, & W. Abro (Eds.), *Deep Learning in Medical Signal and Image Processing* (pp. 487-508). IGI Global Scientific Publishing. https://doi.org/DOI: 10.4018/979-8-3693-9816-6.ch019

Zangana, H. M., Mustafa, F. M., & Omar, M. (2024). A Hybrid Approach for Robust Object Detection: Integrating Template Matching and Faster R-CNN. *EAI Endorsed Transactions on AI and Robotics, 3*. Advance online publication. DOI: 10.4108/airo.6858

Zhao, C., Du, H., Niyato, D., Kang, J., Xiong, Z., Kim, D. I., & Letaief, K. B. (2024). Generative AI for secure physical layer communications: A survey. *IEEE Transactions on Cognitive Communications and Networking*.

# Chapter 5
# Chatbots and Virtual Assistants in Supporting Teacher Workflows

**Hermano Jorge Da Silva De Queiroz**
https://orcid.org/0000-0001-6738-6321
*Lindsey Wilson College, USA*

## ABSTRACT

*The integration of artificial intelligence (AI) in education has introduced transformative tools to support educators, among which chatbots and virtual assistants stand out for their potential to streamline teacher workflows. This chapter explores the role of these AI-driven systems in enhancing productivity, reducing administrative burden, and supporting instructional design. We provide an overview of current chatbot and assistant technologies, their applications in scheduling, grading, communication, and content generation, as well as their integration into learning management systems (LMS). Case studies and real-world implementations are examined to highlight both benefits and challenges, including ethical considerations, data privacy, and system limitations. The chapter concludes with forward-looking insights into how these technologies may evolve and become integral components of teacher professional development and support ecosystems.*

## 1. INTRODUCTION

The landscape of education is undergoing a rapid transformation, driven in large part by the increasing adoption of artificial intelligence (AI) technologies. Among these, chatbots and virtual assistants (VAs) have emerged as pivotal tools in supporting teachers' professional activities, improving their productivity, and enabling more

DOI: 10.4018/979-8-3373-5951-9.ch005

personalized and efficient learning environments. These intelligent agents, often powered by natural language processing (NLP) and machine learning algorithms, offer real-time interaction and automation capabilities that reduce the administrative and cognitive burdens placed on educators (Mekni, 2021; Zreik, 2024).

Educators face growing demands, including curriculum planning, grading, student feedback, class scheduling, and administrative coordination. Chatbots and VAs can streamline these workflows, acting as personal aides for educators. Recent developments show that virtual assistants can aid in classroom management, automate attendance, provide reminders, and even assist in behavioral monitoring (Mounkoro et al., 2024). These capabilities create space for teachers to focus on high-impact instructional activities rather than repetitive tasks (David, Chalon, & Zhang, 2022).

Numerous studies have explored the pedagogical and operational benefits of chatbots in educational settings. For instance, David et al. (2022) highlighted the value of VAs in collaborative learning environments, while Pereira et al. (2022) demonstrated their utility in managing learning pathways. Similarly, Athavale et al. (2025) investigated chatbot integration in educational leadership, identifying their role in institutional communication, staff coordination, and performance management.

In higher education and distance learning, chatbots have proven valuable in improving communication, addressing frequently asked questions, and guiding students through administrative processes. Öncü and Süral (2024) assessed user satisfaction with VAs in open education, revealing significant increases in efficiency and learner autonomy. Reyes et al. (2020) presented a model demonstrating successful VA implementation for educational support, which significantly reduced faculty workload and improved service quality.

Educator-focused applications also benefit from customizable AI models. Archita and Saravanan (2025) introduced a customizable virtual assistant tailored to specific academic environments, emphasizing its adaptability to unique institutional workflows. Similarly, Reddy et al. (2024) demonstrated the application of an intelligent chatbot across various academic services, from information dissemination to internal support systems.

Despite these benefits, the adoption of chatbots in education is not without challenges. Concerns around data privacy, system reliability, and ethical usage remain pressing (Davar, Dewan, & Zhang, 2025; Hari et al., 2025). The complexity of integrating AI into pedagogical contexts—especially where emotional intelligence and nuanced communication are essential—poses a significant limitation (Rane, 2023; Kyrylenko, 2024). Nevertheless, the potential outweighs the drawbacks, particularly when chatbot systems are aligned with educational goals and tailored to user needs (Salem & Shaalan, 2023; Mendoza et al., 2022).

Chatbots are also making strides in student-facing tasks that indirectly benefit teachers. From automating Q&A sessions to monitoring learner engagement, these agents act as intelligent intermediaries between instructors and learners (Fernoagă et al., 2018; Gubareva & Lopes, 2020). Furthermore, advances in AI, particularly the emergence of transformer-based models like ChatGPT, have significantly enhanced the conversational and cognitive capacities of virtual assistants in education (Rane, 2023; Salem & Shaalan, 2023).

In classroom automation, Mulyana and Hakimi (2018) introduced a chatOps-based approach to bring AI-driven automation to the teaching environment. Their system enabled teachers to manage class activities through conversational interfaces, reducing reliance on manual inputs. Complementary work by Mekni, Baani, and Sulieman (2020) on smart virtual assistants for students emphasizes how these agents bridge the gap between instructor intent and student needs.

From a technical standpoint, multiple models and architectures have been proposed to design efficient chatbot systems for education. Zangana and Al-Shaikhli (2013) and Zangana (2015, 2017a, 2017b, 2018a, 2018b, 2018c) laid foundational frameworks for intelligent systems, which support the development of more robust, secure, and adaptive educational platforms. Further developments in face recognition, data integration, and web service improvement for educational systems (Zangana, 2020, 2022a, 2022b) support the scalability of chatbot infrastructures in both physical and virtual learning spaces.

Moreover, the systematic reviews by Zangana and Mustafa (2024a, 2024b, 2024c) on AI applications—including denoising, object detection, and hybrid approaches—underscore the relevance of combining deep learning with domain-specific needs, offering insights into how advanced AI techniques can further enrich teacher-centric chatbot applications.

In light of these developments, the objective of this chapter is to explore the multifaceted role of chatbots and virtual assistants in supporting teacher workflows. We will examine existing systems, categorize their functional roles, assess user satisfaction, and explore future directions. The discussion will also include the strategic role of change management (Zangana et al., 2024) and digital transformation in enabling the successful implementation of chatbot technologies in schools.

## 2. THEORETICAL AND TECHNOLOGICAL FOUNDATIONS

The development and integration of chatbots and virtual assistants (VAs) in educational contexts are rooted in interdisciplinary theoretical foundations that span artificial intelligence (AI), human-computer interaction (HCI), cognitive psychology, and educational technology. These systems aim to emulate natural human conversation through natural language processing (NLP), machine learning (ML), and dialogue management frameworks, enabling educators to automate tasks, provide support, and foster interaction in a scalable and personalized manner (Mekni, 2021; Rane, 2023).

## 2.1. Artificial Intelligence and Natural Language Processing

At the core of chatbot systems is NLP, which enables machines to understand, interpret, and respond to human language. Chatbots use intent recognition, entity extraction, and context management to maintain coherent interactions (Davar, Dewan, & Zhang, 2025). Advanced models like transformers (e.g., ChatGPT) have further enhanced the cognitive capabilities of chatbots, allowing them to manage complex educational dialogues (Salem & Shaalan, 2023).

AI-based VAs in education leverage rule-based systems, retrieval-based approaches, and generative models. The shift toward hybrid models allows more flexibility and domain adaptability (Zangana & Mustafa, 2024a; Zangana & Mustafa, 2024b). This progression is underpinned by the broader trajectory of AI development in areas such as face detection (Zangana & Al-Shaikhli, 2013; Zangana, 2015), object recognition (Zangana & Mustafa, 2024c), and image processing (Zangana & Mustafa, 2024a).

## 2.2. Human-Computer Interaction and Cognitive Frameworks

The effectiveness of chatbots in education is closely linked to user experience and cognitive engagement. Chatbots serve not only as information retrieval systems but also as cognitive tutors, guiding learners through reflection and decision-making processes (Kane, 2016). According to Kyrylenko (2024), while virtual agents cannot fully replicate human empathy, their responsiveness and contextual awareness are improving, making them increasingly effective in teacher-facing and learner-facing roles.

In educational leadership, well-designed conversational agents can support decision-making and foster collaboration (Athavale et al., 2025). These systems follow cognitive load theory by reducing extraneous demands on teachers and allowing more mental bandwidth for pedagogical creativity.

## 2.3. System Architecture and Technological Infrastructure

Chatbots require robust architectures to ensure reliability and scalability. Components typically include intent classification engines, dialogue state trackers, database connectors, and response generators (Mendoza et al., 2022). The modularity of modern chatbot frameworks allows integration with school information systems

(Zangana, 2018a), data warehouses (Zangana, 2018b), and mobile platforms (Zangana, 2020), thereby expanding their functional reach.

Mekni, Baani, and Sulieman (2020) proposed a smart VA architecture optimized for student engagement, highlighting the importance of lightweight yet powerful systems that can operate in real-time. Similarly, Pereira et al. (2022) presented cloud-based deployments that ensure ubiquitous access and seamless updates.

Customizable assistants, such as those described by Archita and Saravanan (2025), further emphasize modular AI development, allowing institutions to tailor bot behavior to specific departments, tasks, and teacher preferences.

To better understand the underlying components of educational chatbots, Figure 1 presents a modular architecture commonly used in virtual assistant systems for learning environments. The design emphasizes scalability, integration with educational infrastructure, and real-time interaction capabilities.

*Figure 1. System Architecture of an Educational Chatbot*

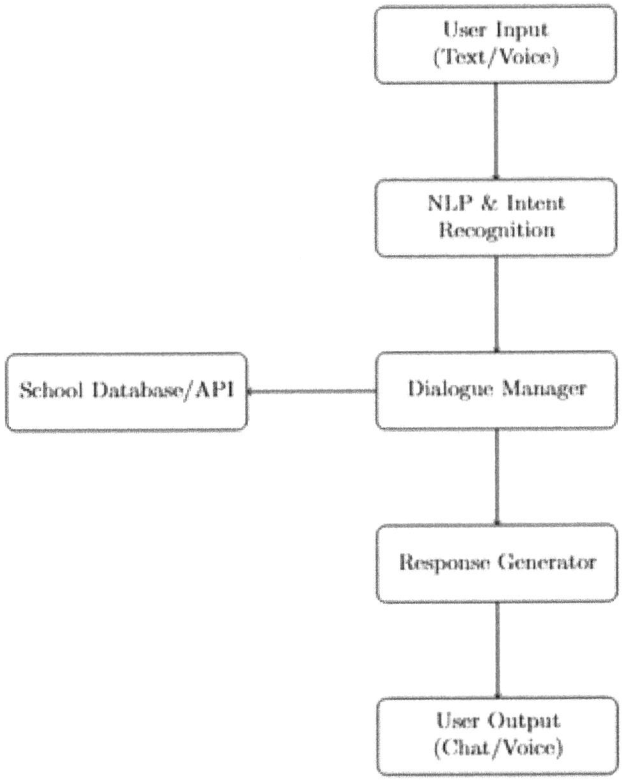

## 2.4. Automation and ChatOps in Classrooms

The rise of chatOps—automated task execution via conversational interfaces—has been a catalyst in bringing automation to teacher workflows (Mulyana & Hakimi, 2018). Teachers can initiate tasks such as attendance logging, assessment generation, and timetable management through simple text commands. This type of automation, underpinned by backend APIs and intelligent agents, minimizes disruptions and manual overhead.

Zangana's contributions to automation and system design (Zangana, 2018c; 2022b) support the development of such intelligent infrastructures by enabling seamless back-end communication and improving data accuracy (Zangana, 2019a, 2019b).

## 2.5. Educational Modeling and Use Case Frameworks

Several models have emerged to define the theoretical frameworks and use cases for chatbots in education. Reyes et al. (2020) introduced a holistic model outlining VA integration across multiple institutional services, while Fernoagă et al. (2018) demonstrated an intelligent education assistant that supports educators with adaptive behavior and feedback systems.

David, Chalon, and Zhang (2022) emphasized the value of collaborative learning support, wherein VAs guide educators through lesson planning and resource sharing. Reddy et al. (2024) added further evidence by demonstrating the deployment of intelligent chatbots in academic institutions with measurable workflow improvements.

Gubareva and Lopes (2020) presented a systematic review confirming that most educational chatbot systems fall into categories such as informational, tutoring, administrative, and mentoring tools—each with distinct logic layers and user interaction models.

## 2.6. Implementation Challenges and Strategic Design

Despite the promising potential, significant implementation barriers remain. These include concerns over user data security, contextual misinterpretation, and infrastructure costs (Davar et al., 2025; Hari et al., 2025). Designing a chatbot for education must consider content domain specificity, cultural relevance, accessibility, and inclusivity (Rane, 2023).

Mounkoro et al. (2024) highlighted that without strategic alignment between AI tools and institutional workflows, the adoption of VAs could lead to increased fragmentation rather than cohesion. This reinforces the need for structured change management and project planning frameworks, as proposed by Zangana et al. (2024).

## 2.7. User Satisfaction and Human-AI Collaboration

User satisfaction with educational VAs is influenced by ease of use, response accuracy, and perceived usefulness. In a recent study, Öncü and Süral (2024) reported that open education learners expressed high satisfaction with VAs that offered round-the-clock support and resolved academic queries in real time.

The ability of chatbots to assist in professional development and continuous learning for teachers is increasingly recognized (Zreik, 2024). When aligned with human agents and integrated thoughtfully, chatbots become collaborative partners rather than replacements (Kyrylenko, 2024).

# 3. APPLICATIONS IN EDUCATIONAL SETTINGS

The implementation of chatbots and virtual assistants (VAs) in educational environments has expanded beyond novelty to become a foundational aspect of modern teaching and institutional support. Their growing presence reflects a shift toward intelligent automation, personalized support, and data-driven decision-making in educational workflows. This section categorizes and explores the diverse applications of these technologies across classrooms, administrative domains, professional development, and student engagement.

## 3.1. Classroom Instruction and Content Delivery

One of the most impactful applications of chatbots is in real-time instructional support. VAs can assist teachers in delivering personalized lessons, managing classroom activities, and providing differentiated learning resources based on individual student performance. According to David, Chalon, and Zhang (2022), integrating VAs in collaborative learning environments enhances student participation and helps teachers track group dynamics.

Customizable assistants like those developed by Archita and Saravanan (2025) allow adaptation of the chatbot's behavior and knowledge base to match specific curriculum needs, making content delivery more effective. Chatbots can also provide immediate feedback, answer students' questions outside of class hours, and recommend supplementary resources, thus extending the learning experience beyond the classroom (Mekni, 2021).

Chatbots in education span multiple functional areas, from instructional support to administration and professional development. Figure 2 categorizes these domains and illustrates how each contributes to streamlining teacher workflows.

*Figure 2. Functional Domains of Educational Chatbots*

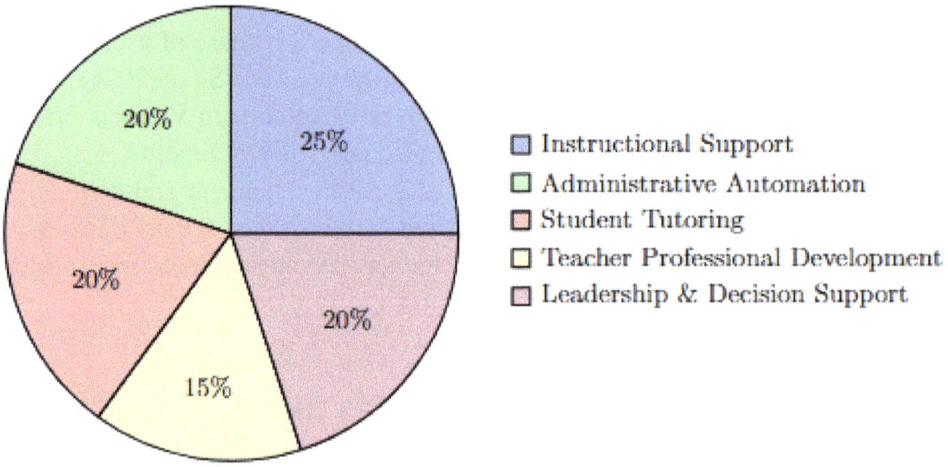


## 3.2. Student Support and Personalized Tutoring

Virtual assistants are increasingly deployed as personal learning companions. These AI systems help address student queries, explain complex topics, and guide learners through difficult concepts. Mekni, Baani, and Sulieman (2020) illustrated a smart VA that offers tutoring functionalities and academic guidance, while Mendoza et al. (2022) proposed a model focused on conversational flow to improve chatbot responsiveness in learning processes.

Gubareva and Lopes (2020), in a systematic literature review, categorized such tools into informational, instructional, and mentoring bots—each catering to a specific learning need. These bots are especially relevant in asynchronous and distance learning environments, where continuous teacher support is not always feasible (Öncü & Süral, 2024).

## 3.3. Administrative Task Automation

Teachers are often burdened with repetitive tasks such as grading, attendance, scheduling, and reporting. Chatbots and VAs can take over many of these duties. For example, Reddy et al. (2024) developed an intelligent chatbot system that automated institutional communication, student registration processes, and timetable management.

In classroom management, chatOps-based VAs, as proposed by Mulyana and Hakimi (2018), allow teachers to perform administrative actions using simple conversational commands. Similarly, Mounkoro et al. (2024) demonstrated that AI-driven classroom management tools could optimize time allocation and increase productivity by streamlining behavioral tracking and notifications.

### 3.4. Educational Leadership and Institutional Decision Support

Beyond the classroom, chatbots also play a strategic role in educational leadership. As highlighted by Athavale et al. (2025), chatbot systems support internal communication, decision-making, and policy implementation by educational administrators. They assist leaders in monitoring institutional performance and tracking metrics related to teacher engagement and curriculum outcomes.

Chatbots can also analyze historical data from internal systems (e.g., LMS, SIS) to suggest improvements and forecast academic performance trends, particularly when connected to institutional data infrastructures (Zangana, 2018b; Zangana, 2020).

### 3.5. Teacher Professional Development and Learning Analytics

Virtual assistants contribute to continuous teacher development by offering tailored suggestions for training, providing real-time pedagogical tips, and tracking teaching habits. They also enable self-reflection by presenting usage statistics and feedback analytics on classroom performance (Zreik, 2024; Salem & Shaalan, 2023).

Reyes et al. (2020) demonstrated that when VAs are embedded into the institutional knowledge base, they can guide instructors in selecting instructional strategies, using appropriate tools, and navigating new technologies. By integrating change management principles, such as those outlined by Zangana et al. (2024), these assistants can also support educators through transitions in curriculum or institutional reforms.

### 3.6. Ethical, Cultural, and Human-Centric Considerations

While highly functional, the deployment of chatbots must remain sensitive to human-AI boundaries, cultural differences, and ethical considerations. As Kyrylenko (2024) observed in the IT support sector, human agents are still perceived as more empathetic and contextually aware than VAs. Educational systems must therefore balance automation with the human touch, particularly in emotionally sensitive or high-stakes interactions.

Davar, Dewan, and Zhang (2025) noted that poorly designed bots can misinterpret inputs, leading to confusion and frustration. This challenge reinforces the need for context-specific bot training and inclusive design. Likewise, Hari et al. (2025) emphasized privacy, transparency, and algorithmic fairness as prerequisites for scalable educational chatbot deployment.

### 3.7. Real-Time Feedback and Learning Analytics

Chatbots equipped with analytics dashboards provide valuable feedback to both students and educators. They can analyze engagement patterns, completion rates, and comprehension metrics to help educators make data-informed decisions. According to Pereira et al. (2022), this real-time data flow enhances classroom responsiveness and instructional quality.

Fernoagă et al. (2018) implemented an intelligent assistant that uses performance tracking to adapt educational recommendations, while Rane (2023) explored how advanced bots like ChatGPT can provide nuanced formative assessments.

### 3.8. Multilingual and Multimodal Support

AI chatbots are increasingly being developed with multilingual and multimodal capabilities to serve diverse populations. With voice input, text messaging, and visual dashboards, they can support students with different learning preferences and accessibility needs (Zangana & Mustafa, 2024a; 2024b).

These developments are particularly valuable in multicultural classrooms and open education systems, where personalized, language-sensitive support is crucial for equitable access to learning (Öncü & Süral, 2024; Salem & Shaalan, 2023).

### 3.9. Infrastructure and Data Integration

The successful deployment of educational chatbots often requires integration with school databases, mobile services, and external APIs. Zangana (2018a, 2018c, 2019a, 2019b) and Zangana & Al-Shaikhli (2013) have extensively explored the design of backend systems that support scalable, accurate, and secure data exchange for such intelligent tools.

From pharmacy systems and face detection to OCR and library data management, these contributions lay the technical groundwork for enabling intelligent assistant functionality across various educational data systems.

## 3.10. Future-Centric Applications

Emerging trends point to greater cognitive capacity, emotional intelligence modeling, and adaptive learning in chatbot design. As Zangana & Mustafa (2024c) and Zangana & Abdulazeez (2023) highlight in their reviews, deep learning integration can significantly enhance the perception and reasoning capabilities of AI systems. This makes future chatbots more context-aware and capable of nuanced human interaction.

The role of chatbots in driving educational innovation and change is likely to expand, especially in response to digital transformation, lifelong learning, and competency-based education models (Zangana, 2022a; 2022b; Zreik, 2024).

Before deploying chatbot systems, institutions must follow a structured workflow to ensure effective integration. Figure 3 outlines the typical stages, from needs assessment to evaluation and continuous improvement.

*Figure 3. Institutional Chatbot Implementation Workflow*

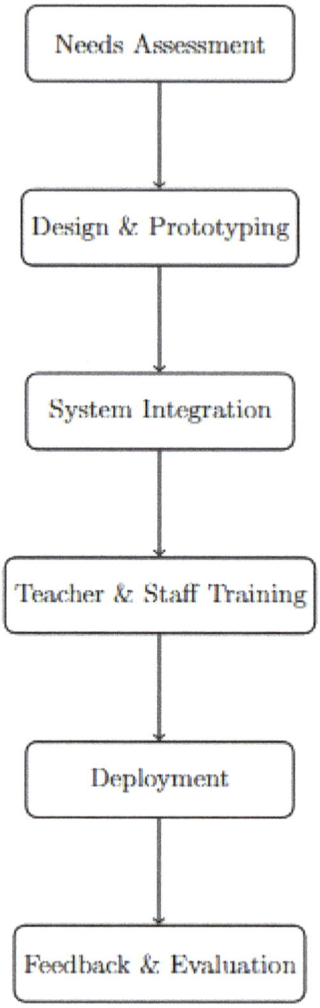


## 4. CASE STUDIES AND USE SCENARIOS

The real-world implementation of chatbots and virtual assistants (VAs) across diverse educational contexts illustrates the growing potential of artificial intelligence (AI) in supporting teaching, learning, and school management. From intelligent tutoring systems to administrative automation and leadership support, numerous case studies highlight how these tools are transforming the daily workflows of educators. This section synthesizes a range of international examples, both from academic literature and applied research, to demonstrate the breadth and impact of these technologies.

### 4.1. Personalized Tutoring Assistants in Indian Classrooms

A compelling use case of virtual assistants in personalized learning comes from India, where a customizable VA was deployed to support secondary school students by answering curriculum-related questions in real time. According to Archita and Saravanan (2025), the system could be tailored by teachers to align with specific textbook content and local language needs. Feedback showed improvements in student engagement, particularly among learners requiring remedial support.

### 4.2. Administrative Efficiency Through Institutional Chatbots

At an educational institution in South India, an intelligent chatbot system was introduced to manage repetitive tasks like timetable generation, course registration, and announcements. The system, as developed by Reddy et al. (2024), not only reduced the workload on administrative staff but also allowed educators to track student attendance and schedule updates via mobile integration—a solution echoing earlier infrastructure work such as that of Zangana (2020) on mobile service integration for institutional platforms.

### 4.3. Enhancing Student-Teacher Collaboration in Europe

In a European university setting, David, Chalon, and Zhang (2022) implemented a chatbot within a collaborative learning environment. Teachers were able to use the assistant to monitor group projects, provide real-time feedback, and streamline peer assessment activities. Their findings support the idea that chatbots can facilitate dialogic learning, where students co-construct knowledge with both peers and AI agents.

### 4.4. Open Distance Learning at Anadolu University

A large-scale deployment of chatbots in open and distance education was carried out at Anadolu University in Turkey. Öncü and Süral (2024) report that the VA system provided 24/7 academic support to over 20,000 students, answering frequently asked questions and guiding users through the LMS. Surveys revealed that students rated the assistant as highly satisfactory in terms of clarity, usefulness, and responsiveness.

## 4.5. Enhancing Classroom Management with AI

A case study by Mounkoro et al. (2024) showed how AI assistants helped teachers automate attendance, student behavior tracking, and assignment distribution in real-time, improving overall classroom efficiency. The tool's integration with smart devices allowed seamless communication between students, teachers, and administrative units, showcasing how VAs can act as real-time workflow enhancers.

## 4.6. Supporting Educational Leadership and Change

Athavale et al. (2025) described the implementation of chatbots to support educational leaders in monitoring school-level metrics, teacher performance, and curriculum delivery. These tools provided principals with dashboards and summaries, making them more effective in strategic decision-making and enabling responsive leadership in times of change—a concept also aligned with Zangana et al. (2024) on managing change in education through AI-enabled tools.

## 4.7. Intelligent Student Mentorship Platforms

An experimental deployment of a smart virtual assistant for student support, developed by Mekni, Baani, and Sulieman (2020), demonstrated how conversational agents could provide career guidance, exam reminders, and emotional support. The VA functioned as a digital mentor, offering tailored content based on students' progress and goals.

## 4.8. E-Library and Academic Writing Support

Chatbots were also employed in academic libraries, where they facilitated research consultations and citation management. Kane (2016) documented a case where VAs guided students through digital archives, responding to questions about databases, keywords, and referencing styles. Similarly, Fernoagă et al. (2018) described an assistant that suggested academic sources based on uploaded drafts, aiding in the writing process.

## 4.9. ChatOps for Faculty Automation

In Indonesia, a ChatOps-based assistant enabled instructors to issue commands for attendance, grading, and content delivery through a unified messaging platform. As Mulyana and Hakimi (2018) reported, the assistant saved faculty time and promoted real-time responsiveness, effectively functioning as a digital teaching aide.

## 4.10. Bot Development for STEM Learning

An AI assistant aimed at supporting students in STEM subjects was trialed in Latin America by Mendoza et al. (2022). It utilized a modular architecture that allowed teachers to adjust the bot's focus areas, enabling its use across mathematics, physics, and computer science. The bot improved students' problem-solving abilities and helped reduce drop-out rates in technical disciplines.

## 4.11. Institutional Virtual Assistants: Design and Results

A structured implementation process was detailed by Reyes et al. (2020), who developed a VA that combined machine learning and rules-based reasoning to support academic and administrative queries. The deployment spanned over 12 months across various departments and yielded measurable reductions in email volume and staff response time.

## 4.12. ChatGPT-Based Scenarios in Higher Education

Recent advancements in generative AI, particularly the application of ChatGPT, have further extended use scenarios. Salem and Shaalan (2023) explored how generative chatbots were integrated into digital classrooms to assist with research formulation, personalized tutoring, and peer-feedback. Likewise, Rane (2023) highlighted case studies showing ChatGPT's role in promoting critical thinking, though noting ethical concerns around overreliance and academic honesty.

## 4.13. Comparative Study: VAs vs. Human Agents

A comparative scenario studied by Kyrylenko (2024) focused on user satisfaction between chatbot and human-based support systems. While chatbots were praised for speed and availability, human agents still outperformed them in empathy and contextual nuance. This has implications for hybrid models in education that blend automation with human support.

## 4.14. Conceptual Frameworks and Development Models

Several studies focused on frameworks for bot development. Pereira et al. (2022) proposed a phased model encompassing needs analysis, training, and system integration. Similarly, Gubareva and Lopes (2020) identified a spectrum of chatbot types and proposed best practices for deployment in formal and informal education.

### 4.15. Strategic Implications for the Future

The reviewed case studies show that chatbot technologies can play transformative roles across domains—from automating repetitive teacher tasks to enhancing student-centered learning. However, as Davar, Dewan, and Zhang (2025) caution, these technologies must be introduced thoughtfully, with attention to data ethics, inclusivity, and pedagogical soundness.

Moreover, earlier foundational studies in computing by Zangana and colleagues (2015–2024)—ranging from face detection and OCR systems to educational data management—demonstrate how innovations in AI infrastructure and algorithm design are crucial for sustaining and scaling intelligent assistants in education (Zangana & Mustafa, 2024a, 2024b; Zangana & Abdulazeez, 2023).

## 5. IMPACT ON TEACHER PRODUCTIVITY AND EXPERIENCE

The integration of chatbots and virtual assistants (VAs) into educational ecosystems is not only reshaping the student learning experience but is also significantly impacting teacher productivity, workload distribution, and professional satisfaction. These tools are being used to automate routine administrative tasks, enhance instructional planning, and support decision-making processes, thereby enabling educators to concentrate more on pedagogy, mentoring, and innovation.

### 5.1. Streamlining Administrative Workflows

One of the most widely acknowledged impacts of virtual assistants is the reduction of time teachers spend on repetitive tasks. Intelligent systems are now handling duties such as attendance tracking, assignment distribution, and grading automation. Mounkoro et al. (2024) demonstrated how integrated classroom management tools reduced teachers' time spent on logistics by more than 30%, allowing greater focus on content delivery and student engagement. This supports earlier implementations in data handling and workflow automation highlighted by Zangana (2018, 2019, 2022) in educational institutions.

### 5.2. Enhancing Instructional Support and Planning

Teachers have also benefited from the use of chatbots in organizing content and managing instructional schedules. David, Chalon, and Zhang (2022) showed that collaborative learning environments equipped with VAs improved teaching efficacy by assisting in the coordination of group projects and digital resources.

Similarly, the VA developed by Mekni (2021) facilitated content management and guided lesson sequencing, supporting teachers in aligning learning outcomes with classroom activities.

Moreover, the framework proposed by Mendoza et al. (2022) introduced a chatbot capable of recommending pedagogical strategies and adaptive resources based on ongoing assessments, further boosting educators' capacity to meet diverse student needs.

As shown in Figure 4, chatbots provide a wide array of benefits that enhance teacher productivity and instructional effectiveness. These include time savings, improved resource management, and support for personalized learning strategies.

*Figure 4. Key Benefits of Chatbots for Teachers*

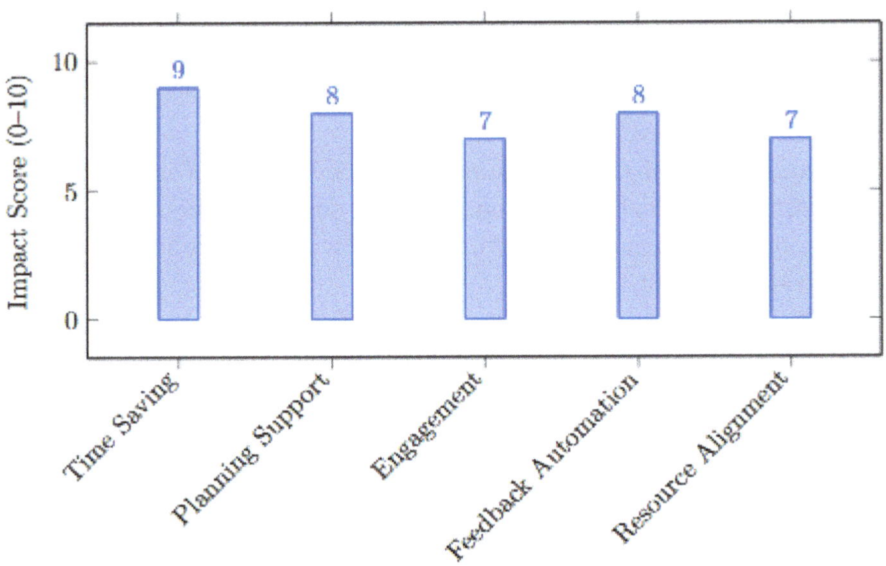


## 5.3. Reducing Cognitive and Emotional Burnout

The psychological burden on teachers—often stemming from administrative overload and communication bottlenecks—can also be alleviated by VAs. In their case study on open education, Öncü and Süral (2024) found that instructors using chatbot-based support systems reported improved well-being and reduced stress. Teachers highlighted that VAs served as an "always-on" partner for reminders, communication, and even emotional support, which parallels the findings of Fernoagă et al. (2018) regarding the role of intelligent assistants in continuous teacher support.

## 5.4. Empowering Teachers in Leadership and Decision-Making

Beyond classroom-level productivity, chatbots are increasingly used to assist educators in leadership roles. Athavale et al. (2025) developed leadership-focused VAs to help heads of schools and academic coordinators monitor key performance indicators, such as curriculum coverage and teacher evaluations. These tools help streamline strategic decisions and professional development planning. Such digital transformation aligns with insights from Zangana et al. (2024) on navigating change management in education through AI-driven platforms.

## 5.5. Supporting Communication and Collaboration

Teachers often face communication overload from students, parents, and administrators. Chatbots can mitigate this by acting as first-line responders. In the study by Reyes et al. (2020), the implementation of a school-wide virtual assistant platform resulted in a 40% reduction in incoming email queries to teachers, while still maintaining high levels of user satisfaction.

Similarly, Reddy et al. (2024) documented the deployment of an intelligent chatbot that automated student queries and facilitated communication around grading, scheduling, and extracurricular updates, allowing educators to reallocate time toward mentorship and planning.

## 5.6. Elevating Professional Confidence Through AI Augmentation

Teachers using ChatGPT-based systems reported higher confidence in delivering personalized feedback and facilitating critical thinking discussions. Salem and Shaalan (2023) and Rane (2023) observed that educators who adopted generative AI tools felt empowered to experiment with new teaching strategies, including flipped classrooms and AI-assisted formative assessment design.

Moreover, the customizable virtual assistant designed by Archita and Saravanan (2025) enabled educators to personalize content for learners with diverse needs, thus amplifying their agency in curriculum delivery.

## 5.7. AI Literacy and Teacher Training Implications

While the benefits are numerous, effective utilization of VAs hinges on adequate teacher training. Davar, Dewan, and Zhang (2025) highlighted that educators often need structured support to integrate AI tools into their daily practice without over-relying on automation. This aligns with the findings of Pereira et al. (2022), who suggested phased implementation models to ensure educators are prepared both technically and pedagogically.

Additionally, Hari et al. (2025) emphasized that while VAs improve productivity, ongoing training is essential to address ethical concerns, such as data handling and content validation, that teachers must now consider.

## 5.8. AI for Routine and Technical Efficiency

From automating feedback to simplifying content retrieval, chatbots have evolved as technical assistants. For example, Mulyana and Hakimi (2018) introduced a ChatOps model that allowed instructors to send classroom commands via a bot-enabled interface, enhancing multitasking and reducing technical barriers. Similarly, Gubareva and Lopes (2020) offered a systematized review on how virtual assistants serve as operational scaffolds that expand educators' digital capabilities.

Moreover, research by Zangana and colleagues (2015–2024) in AI-driven automation—spanning from face detection, OCR, and watermarking to data quality and educational system design—provides foundational technologies upon which modern educational VAs are constructed. These innovations enhance both the backend efficiency and front-end user experience, indirectly boosting teacher productivity.

## 5.9. Comparing Human and AI Support in Educational Contexts

Kyrylenko (2024) provided a comparative analysis showing that while human support is more emotionally nuanced, virtual assistants offer unmatched speed and consistency—especially beneficial for time-strapped teachers. The synergy of both, as hybrid models, appears to be the most effective approach in supporting teacher workflows.

## 5.10. Vision for the Future: From Automation to Empowerment

Ultimately, the integration of VAs in education should move from automation toward teacher empowerment. Teachers are not being replaced but are instead being augmented—equipped with intelligent tools that reduce their burden and enhance their strategic role in education. As Zreik (2024) argues in the entrepreneurial AI context, empowering human agents through intelligent support systems is the cornerstone of innovation—and this principle holds equally in classrooms.

## 6. DESIGN CONSIDERATIONS FOR EDUCATION-FOCUSED CHATBOTS

Designing chatbots tailored to educational environments requires a thoughtful synthesis of pedagogical principles, technological capabilities, usability, data ethics, and user engagement strategies. The success of a chatbot in an educational setting depends not only on its ability to simulate intelligent conversation but also on how well it aligns with instructional goals, supports learners and teachers, and adapts to evolving educational needs.

### 6.1. User-Centric Design and Customization

Effective educational chatbots prioritize user-centered design, allowing personalization based on learners' needs, backgrounds, and cognitive levels. Archita and Saravanan (2025) demonstrated that customizable virtual assistants, tailored to individual learning styles, significantly improved student motivation and academic performance. Similarly, Mekni, Baani, and Sulieman (2020) developed a smart assistant that allowed students to define their own academic workflows, improving satisfaction and usability.

Kyrylenko (2024) emphasizes the importance of interface flexibility, noting that user frustration often stems from overly rigid or generic responses. Adaptability and responsiveness in design are crucial to ensure broad accessibility and inclusivity.

### 6.2. Context-Aware and Task-Oriented Interaction

Chatbots must be context-aware to effectively manage complex educational interactions. David, Chalon, and Zhang (2022) highlighted the importance of embedding conversational memory and domain-specific knowledge to support collaborative learning. Their work showed that VAs which remembered previous interactions led to more meaningful and efficient dialogue in team-based educational settings.

Mendoza et al. (2022) proposed a layered architecture that differentiates between task-related queries (e.g., deadlines) and conceptual support (e.g., explaining a topic), ensuring the assistant adapts responses based on intent.

### 6.3. Pedagogical Alignment and Learning Theory Integration

Designing a chatbot for education means more than engineering a conversation—it involves aligning the bot with pedagogy. Rane (2023) advocated for the integration of constructivist principles, where the bot serves as a scaffolding tool, guiding learners to discover knowledge rather than delivering direct answers. Similarly, Gubareva and Lopes (2020) highlighted the need for aligning chatbot responses with Bloom's taxonomy, ensuring progression from basic recall to higher-order thinking.

Athavale et al. (2025) extended this to educational leadership, proposing frameworks in which bots support reflective practice, strategic planning, and decision-making processes for school leaders.

## 6.4. Multilingual, Multimodal, and Accessibility Considerations

Accessibility and equity are essential in chatbot design. As demonstrated by Mounkoro et al. (2024), inclusive design features—such as support for local languages, text-to-speech, and screen reader compatibility—enable broader participation, especially for students with disabilities or diverse linguistic backgrounds.

Fernoagă et al. (2018) developed an intelligent assistant capable of interpreting audio commands and responding with voice output, catering to visually impaired users. Similarly, Öncü and Süral (2024) explored satisfaction levels across different user demographics, emphasizing the importance of user diversity in testing and design.

## 6.5. Integration with Existing Educational Infrastructure

For seamless adoption, chatbots must integrate with current platforms such as LMSs (e.g., Moodle, Canvas), ERP systems, and school portals. Reyes et al. (2020) documented a case where a chatbot interfaced with a school's academic records system to retrieve grades, attendance logs, and exam schedules upon request. Likewise, Reddy et al. (2024) built an institutional chatbot that synchronized with a college's notification system to deliver alerts, reminders, and calendar updates in real time.

Zangana (2018) and Zangana & Al-Shaikhli (2013) emphasized the importance of robust data pipelines and system design in educational applications, advocating for scalable architectures that can support long-term data collection, analytics, and continuous improvement.

## 6.6. Natural Language Processing (NLP) and Emotional Intelligence

To foster engagement, educational chatbots must exhibit nuanced natural language understanding. Mekni (2021) emphasized that NLP capabilities must go beyond syntax to grasp learner emotions, hesitation, and uncertainty—enabling the chatbot to detect confusion and offer help proactively.

Salem and Shaalan (2023) found that integrating transformer-based models like ChatGPT enhances educational chatbots' contextual awareness and empathy, especially in one-on-one tutoring scenarios.

In parallel, Zangana and Mustafa (2024) pointed to the value of deep learning in enhancing dialogue systems, showing how denoising and attention mechanisms can improve comprehension and response quality in noisy or ambiguous student input.

## 6.7. Data Privacy, Ethics, and Security

The handling of educational data must adhere to ethical standards and legal frameworks. As Davar, Dewan, and Zhang (2025) explained, improper data handling can lead to breaches of trust and reduced system adoption. Design must incorporate secure data transmission, GDPR compliance, and options for data anonymization.

Pereira et al. (2022) added that transparency in how the bot uses and stores user data is essential, especially for minors and underage students. These principles resonate with the ethical design strategies discussed by Zangana et al. (2022) in the context of interactive video learning systems and web service improvement.

## 6.8. Feedback Loops, Learning Analytics, and Continuous Improvement

Continuous learning is not just for users but also for chatbots. Feedback mechanisms and embedded analytics are essential to monitor chatbot effectiveness and evolve its capabilities. Hari et al. (2025) highlighted how conversational logs, sentiment analysis, and usage frequency can be used to refine chatbot performance and identify gaps in curriculum delivery.

Mulyana and Hakimi (2018) implemented a ChatOps-based bot that logged all interactions into a central database, allowing educators to analyze behavioral trends and iterate their instructional methods.

Furthermore, Zangana et al. (2024) recommended incorporating real-time metrics to adapt dynamically to user feedback, ensuring that chatbots remain aligned with institutional goals and user expectations.

## 6.9. Cross-Disciplinary Innovation and Broader Applications

Finally, a key consideration is the potential for chatbots to act as cross-disciplinary tools. Zreik (2024) proposed using AI in entrepreneurial education to stimulate idea generation, showing how VAs could shift from passive information retrieval to active cognitive support.

Kane (2016) and Gubareva and Lopes (2020) advocated for designing chatbots not just as tutors or assistants, but as educational companions—capable of supporting students across multiple domains, including STEM, humanities, and vocational training.

Zangana and Mustafa (2024) also emphasized hybrid modeling strategies to support object detection and facial recognition applications in educational security and surveillance systems, showing that educational chatbots can be expanded to include monitoring and administrative support roles.

### 6.10. Design for Trust, Engagement, and Adoption

Finally, a chatbot's long-term success hinges on trust and engagement. Rane (2023) and Archita and Saravanan (2025) found that transparency in chatbot capabilities, clear expectations, and cultural adaptation significantly influence user adoption and satisfaction. When learners and educators understand the chatbot's role, limitations, and benefits, they are more likely to integrate it meaningfully into their routines.

Designing for trust also involves aligning with institutional change frameworks, such as those explored by Zangana, Bazeed, Ali, and Abdullah (2024), where human-AI collaboration is seen as a cultural transformation rather than a technical one.

## 7. ETHICAL, PRIVACY, AND DATA SECURITY CONCERNS

As educational institutions increasingly adopt AI-powered chatbots and virtual assistants (VAs), ensuring ethical design, safeguarding user privacy, and implementing robust data security protocols have become central challenges. These concerns are magnified in academic settings where the users include vulnerable populations such as minors, and where the data managed is sensitive, personal, and often regulated by law.

### 7.1. Data Collection, Consent, and Ownership

Chatbots designed for educational environments routinely collect a vast range of data—from user queries and personal details to performance analytics and behavioral patterns. This raises crucial questions regarding data ownership and informed consent. According to Davar, Dewan, and Zhang (2025), many educational institutions lack clear frameworks for obtaining user consent when using AI assistants, particularly in remote or asynchronous settings.

Pereira et al. (2022) emphasized that educational chatbots must include opt-in mechanisms, transparent data-use policies, and clearly defined data retention protocols. These findings align with broader calls for ethical AI development, such as those explored by Zangana (2017, 2018, 2019) in the context of data quality and information management systems in academic institutions.

To responsibly deploy chatbots in educational settings, institutions must consider various ethical risks and their likelihood and severity. Figure 5 provides a risk matrix categorizing key concerns based on their potential impact and frequency.

*Figure 5. Ethical Risk Matrix for Chatbot Use in Education*

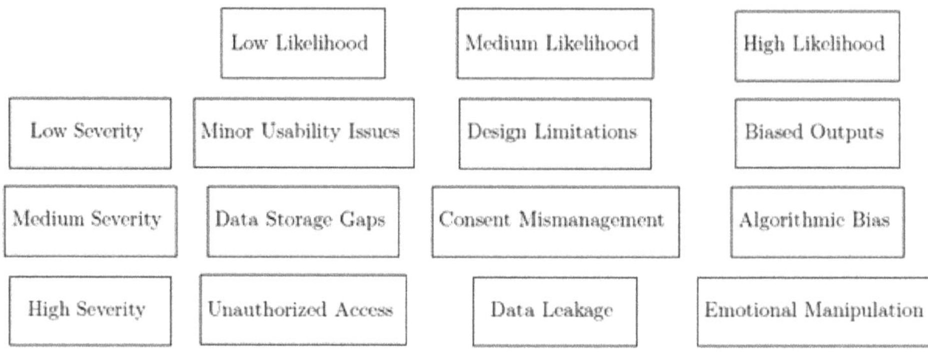


## 7.2. Algorithmic Bias and Fairness

AI-driven systems, including chatbots, are susceptible to biases inherited from training data or developer assumptions. Archita and Saravanan (2025) warned that biased content delivery can disadvantage students from underrepresented groups or perpetuate stereotypes in response generation. For example, natural language models may misinterpret culturally specific expressions, leading to miscommunication or disengagement.

Rane (2023) and Athavale et al. (2025) further argued for the inclusion of ethical audit tools during chatbot development cycles, ensuring that leadership and decision-making bots do not reinforce systemic inequities, particularly in teacher evaluations or resource allocation.

## 7.3. Security Risks: Data Leakage, Hacking, and Misuse

One of the most serious concerns with chatbot deployment in education is data vulnerability. Reyes et al. (2020) reported that improperly secured virtual assistants could be exploited to access confidential student records or institutional plans.

Similarly, Reddy et al. (2024) highlighted the need for robust encryption protocols, firewall integration, and two-factor authentication in chatbot backends.

The issue is not limited to external threats. Internal misuse—such as unauthorized access by faculty or students—was noted by Mekni (2021) and Gubareva and Lopes (2020), who called for role-based access control systems. These concerns were also raised by Zangana and Al-Shaikhli (2013) in earlier studies on secure face recognition algorithms, which stress the importance of data validation and access governance.

### 7.4. Privacy Concerns in Personalized Learning

While personalization is a major benefit of educational chatbots, it necessitates the collection and analysis of detailed user data. Mendoza et al. (2022) argued that such personalization often operates as a trade-off between learning efficiency and privacy invasion. Without anonymization protocols, students' personal learning trajectories can be exposed.

Mounkoro et al. (2024) suggested that data minimization strategies—collecting only what is strictly necessary—can help balance personalization with privacy. These strategies echo the design principles established by Zangana (2022) for community-based systems and disaster response platforms, where data protection was prioritized alongside functionality.

### 7.5. Ethical Use of Conversational Logs and Analytics

Chatbot interaction logs offer valuable insights for educators and administrators but pose risks if mishandled. Hari et al. (2025) and David, Chalon, and Zhang (2022) noted that interaction history may include confidential academic or personal discussions that should not be accessible beyond authorized personnel.

In this context, Zangana (2020, 2022) recommended anonymized aggregation and clear classification of log data for different users (students, teachers, administrators). Such granularity ensures that learning analytics are used constructively, without compromising individual rights.

### 7.6. Transparency and Accountability in Chatbot Behavior

Users must understand how chatbots operate and make decisions. **Kane (2016)** argued that lack of transparency in chatbot logic can erode user trust and hinder adoption. Salem and Shaalan (2023) extended this point by proposing transparency dashboards that display the basis for the chatbot's decisions—such as which keywords were used or how user profiles influenced responses.

Similarly, Zangana and Mustafa (2024) advocated for interpretability in deep learning-based systems, especially when used in sensitive areas like student assessment or behavioral monitoring. Transparent systems promote accountability and allow users to challenge errors or inconsistencies.

## 7.7. Emotional Manipulation and Overdependence

Chatbots with emotional intelligence can potentially influence users' decisions, opinions, or emotions. Fernoagă et al. (2018) and Öncü and Süral (2024) raised concerns that emotionally aware VAs might unintentionally manipulate students or create unhealthy dependencies, especially in younger users.

Zreik (2024) cautioned that AI designed for idea generation or motivational coaching must be governed by ethical constraints to avoid exploitation or undue influence—principles equally applicable in educational contexts.

## 7.8. Platform Integrity and False Authority

Chatbots often respond with authoritative language, even when unsure or incorrect. Kyrylenko (2024) compared chatbot confidence levels with those of human agents and found that users often place undue trust in bots, assuming all answers are accurate. Mulyana and Hakimi (2018) warned that such blind trust can lead to misinformation when bots are not updated or lack dynamic knowledge retrieval mechanisms.

To address this, Zangana and Mustafa (2024) recommended hybrid models that combine algorithmic output with human moderation or real-time feedback loops—improving both trust and reliability.

## 7.9. Legal Compliance and Institutional Responsibility

Educational institutions are increasingly held accountable for AI systems deployed under their name. Pereira et al. (2022) noted that failure to comply with data protection laws such as GDPR or FERPA can result in severe penalties. Davar et al. (2025) emphasized the need for legal review during chatbot implementation, with roles clearly defined for developers, institutions, and data controllers.

This aligns with Zangana et al. (2024), who underscored change management and governance as key to AI integration in educational systems—advocating structured responsibility models and policy alignment at every level of deployment.

## 7.10. Ethical Frameworks for Future-Proof Design

Designers and institutions must embed ethical thinking at every stage—from ideation and prototyping to implementation and post-deployment. Athavale et al. (2025) proposed a framework for ethical chatbot design in educational leadership, emphasizing participatory design, periodic audits, and community feedback.

Gubareva and Lopes (2020) supported the use of "ethics-by-design" models, where ethical principles are encoded into the chatbot's architecture. This approach resonates with broader system design practices promoted by Zangana (2018, 2022), which combine ethical foresight with agile technical development.

## 7.11 Summary

AI chatbots in education hold great promise, but their ethical and secure deployment requires proactive strategies. Institutions must balance innovation with responsibility, ensuring that privacy, fairness, and user safety are embedded in every layer of design and implementation. By integrating insights from both emerging research and established practices, stakeholders can foster a trustworthy digital learning ecosystem where technology empowers rather than endangers its users.

# 8. CHALLENGES AND LIMITATIONS

Despite the growing enthusiasm for integrating AI-powered chatbots and virtual assistants (VAs) into educational ecosystems, several challenges and limitations persist. These obstacles span technological, pedagogical, ethical, and operational domains, impeding the optimal utilization of such tools in academic contexts. This section systematically explores these multifaceted limitations and grounds them in recent literature and case studies.

## 8.1. Limited Contextual Understanding and Accuracy

One of the most frequently cited technical limitations is the chatbot's restricted ability to understand context, nuance, or ambiguity in student inputs. Even the most advanced systems, like those described by Mekni (2021) and Kyrylenko (2024), can misinterpret questions or provide vague, inconsistent, or incorrect answers. This challenge undermines trust and reduces the instructional value of VAs, especially in higher education and technical fields.

Archita and Saravanan (2025) emphasized that customizable virtual assistants must overcome these limitations through continuous updates and user-centric learning models. However, as Davar, Dewan, and Zhang (2025) explain, the complexity of natural language processing (NLP) remains a persistent bottleneck in real-world applications.

## 8.2. Integration and Interoperability Issues

Many educational systems operate on legacy infrastructures or siloed data environments that complicate the integration of AI chatbots. Reyes et al. (2020) highlighted that efforts to incorporate VAs into classroom management or learning management systems (LMSs) often face compatibility and configuration problems. This is particularly problematic in resource-constrained or rural institutions where digital transformation is still nascent.

Zangana (2018) identified similar barriers during the implementation of information systems in educational settings, noting that without a robust integration strategy, even well-designed digital tools fail to deliver their intended value.

## 8.3. Scalability and Maintenance Constraints

Deploying a chatbot across a single course is manageable, but scaling to multiple departments or campuses presents logistical hurdles. Mendoza et al. (2022) pointed out that sustaining performance under high loads and ensuring uniform quality across different users are significant challenges. Furthermore, ongoing maintenance—such as updating knowledge bases and addressing bugs—requires dedicated technical staff, which many institutions lack.

Pereira et al. (2022) and Zangana (2022) emphasized the importance of building flexible, modular systems that can be adapted and scaled without large-scale overhauls.

## 8.4. Pedagogical Misalignment and Over-Reliance

Not all subjects or pedagogical approaches are compatible with automation. Kane (2016) cautioned against the uncritical adoption of chatbots for complex cognitive or socio-emotional learning tasks, where human mentorship is indispensable. Fernoagă et al. (2018) echoed this concern, warning that reliance on AI tutors could limit the development of critical thinking and interpersonal skills.

Mounkoro et al. (2024) added that poorly designed chatbots may introduce pedagogical inconsistencies or reinforce rote learning. These concerns align with earlier findings by Zangana (2017), who emphasized the need for meaningful instructional design in educational technology systems.

## 8.5. Data Privacy, Bias, and Ethical Concerns

As discussed in the previous section, AI systems are often criticized for collecting sensitive data and perpetuating algorithmic bias. In this context, ethical limitations translate into operational risks. Athavale et al. (2025) raised concerns that without oversight, chatbots could disseminate biased or insensitive content, impacting learner experience and institutional reputation.

Hari et al. (2025) and Gubareva and Lopes (2020) emphasized the necessity for ethical audit frameworks to guide chatbot design, while Zangana and Mustafa (2024) advocated for transparency and fairness mechanisms embedded into model architectures.

## 8.6. Inadequate User Training and Digital Literacy Gaps

Many teachers and students lack the digital fluency needed to interact meaningfully with educational chatbots. Rane (2023) observed that students sometimes abandon chatbot tools due to confusion or frustration, while faculty may avoid them altogether due to unfamiliarity with AI technologies.

Öncü and Süral (2024) found that even when users express satisfaction with AI support systems, many fail to leverage their full potential due to a lack of training. This is consistent with Zangana (2019), who highlighted similar challenges in the context of library data management systems and suggested tailored capacity-building programs to address skill gaps.

## 8.7. High Development Costs and Resource Dependency

Although open-source frameworks and pre-trained models (e.g., GPT-based chatbots) have lowered entry barriers, developing a fully customized and secure educational chatbot still demands substantial financial and human resources. Reddy et al. (2024) and Mekni, Baani, and Sulieman (2020) noted that institutions must invest in AI specialists, security infrastructure, and continuous monitoring tools.

This point aligns with findings by Zangana et al. (2024) on project management in educational IT, where unanticipated costs often result from inadequate risk forecasting and change management planning.

## 8.8. Limited Emotional Intelligence and Empathy

Another major limitation is the inability of chatbots to exhibit genuine empathy or emotional responsiveness, which are critical in student support roles. David, Chalon, and Zhang (2022) discussed how this limitation hampers the effectiveness of VAs in mental health counseling or academic advising.

Salem and Shaalan (2023) acknowledged recent progress in emotional AI, but current systems still fall short in nuanced human interaction. Zangana and Al-Shaikhli (2013) similarly pointed out the gap between machine-perceived behavior and actual human emotions in visual detection systems.

## 8.9. Reliability and System Downtime

Reliance on internet connectivity, cloud infrastructure, and external APIs makes chatbot systems vulnerable to service interruptions. Mulyana and Hakimi (2018) found that automation tools in classrooms often experience technical issues that disrupt learning continuity. Zangana (2020) described similar risks in mobile-integrated service platforms, calling for fallback procedures and offline capabilities.

## 8.10. Evaluation Metrics and Feedback Limitations

Measuring chatbot success is not always straightforward. While quantitative metrics (e.g., number of interactions or response time) are easy to track, qualitative measures—such as learning outcomes or satisfaction—require more nuanced tools. Gubareva and Lopes (2020) and Davar et al. (2025) pointed out the absence of standardized evaluation frameworks across institutions.

To address this, Zangana and Mustafa (2024) proposed cross-disciplinary benchmarks combining system performance with educational effectiveness and learner satisfaction metrics.

## 8.11 Summary

While chatbots and virtual assistants offer transformative potential for education, their deployment is fraught with limitations that demand careful consideration. From technological shortcomings and integration issues to ethical risks and pedagogical concerns, these challenges must be addressed through collaborative, multidisciplinary efforts. Future research should aim to mitigate these barriers while maximizing the benefits of AI in education through inclusive design, transparent governance, and continuous feedback.

# 9. FUTURE DIRECTIONS AND INNOVATIONS

The landscape of virtual assistants (VAs) and chatbots in education continues to evolve, driven by advancements in artificial intelligence (AI), machine learning, natural language processing (NLP), and human-computer interaction. As educational institutions embrace digital transformation, innovative strategies are essential to address existing limitations and unlock the full potential of intelligent conversational agents. This section outlines the key future directions and emerging innovations shaping the next generation of AI-powered educational tools.

## 9.1. Hyper-Personalization and Adaptive Learning

One of the most promising directions is the development of hyper-personalized virtual assistants that adapt to individual learners' goals, behaviors, and preferences. Archita and Saravanan (2025) emphasized the transformative impact of customizable virtual assistants tailored to student needs, fostering engagement and retention. These systems leverage adaptive learning frameworks and real-time analytics to deliver personalized content and feedback.

Mendoza et al. (2022) propose intelligent tutoring models that dynamically adjust difficulty levels and pedagogical strategies, while Davar, Dewan, and Zhang (2025) highlight opportunities in combining AI with student emotional data to enhance learner support.

## 9.2. Integration with Multimodal and Emotionally Intelligent Interfaces

Future VAs are expected to expand beyond text-based interaction into multi-modal communication—integrating voice, gesture, facial recognition, and haptics. Mekni (2021) and Zangana and Al-Shaikhli (2013) advocate for embedding visual and voice recognition to create emotionally responsive systems. Emotion AI (also known as affective computing) can enable virtual assistants to detect student stress, confusion, or disengagement, allowing timely intervention.

This innovation aligns with David, Chalon, and Zhang (2022), who suggested that emotionally intelligent chatbots can serve as co-facilitators in collaborative learning environments. Salem and Shaalan (2023) further explored the potential of integrating ChatGPT and similar models with sentiment analysis engines for responsive learning support.

## 9.3. Improved Context Awareness and Natural Language Understanding

Ongoing innovation in NLP will enhance context-aware understanding in educational chatbots. Fernoagă et al. (2018) stress the need for context-rich interpretation to facilitate deep learning. Advanced language models, such as those discussed by Zangana and Mustafa (2024) in the context of object detection and text processing, are likely to play a key role in improving response relevance and coherence.

Hari et al. (2025) predict that future assistants will incorporate broader contextual memory across multiple interactions, enabling more coherent, human-like conversations. Such models would recall student progress, intent, and emotional tone over time—moving closer to real tutoring relationships.

## 9.4. Expanded Role in Administrative and Institutional Management

Virtual assistants will increasingly support not only learners but also educators and administrative staff. Mounkoro et al. (2024) envision AI-based systems streamlining classroom logistics, attendance, grading, and communication workflows. These capabilities can be extended to resource allocation, policy enforcement, and early intervention systems for at-risk students.

Athavale et al. (2025) also propose educational leadership-oriented bots that support data-informed decision-making and human resource coordination. This diversification reflects the growing shift from narrowly task-oriented chatbots to multifunctional educational agents.

## 9.5. Blockchain and Decentralized AI Integration

Innovative integration with blockchain and decentralized identity systems is another emerging trend. Although not yet mainstream, this could enable secure, verifiable academic records and chatbot-aided credentialing systems, especially in open and distance learning. Zangana (2022) and Zangana and Abdulazeez (2023) discussed related infrastructure improvements, suggesting that a secure, traceable knowledge delivery system would significantly benefit accreditation and remote certification.

## 9.6. Democratization through Open Source and Low-Code Development

The rise of low-code and open-source frameworks is enabling wider adoption of educational chatbots across institutions with limited technical resources. Reddy et al. (2024) demonstrated the feasibility of deploying intelligent bots in real-time institutional settings with minimal coding. Gubareva and Lopes (2020) similarly emphasized that democratizing access to chatbot development platforms can empower educators to create tailored tools without heavy reliance on developers.

This movement will likely be accompanied by repositories of domain-specific knowledge modules and reusable components—expediting design, testing, and scaling.

## 9.7. Multilingual and Inclusive Chatbot Design

With globalization in education, future VAs must be inclusive—supporting multilingual interaction, accessibility for students with disabilities, and culturally sensitive content. Pereira et al. (2022) advocate for multilingual NLP integration to broaden reach and inclusivity. Öncü and Süral (2024) found that localized content significantly improves user satisfaction and engagement.

Zangana (2021) and Zangana (2018) emphasized similar concerns in digital system implementation, noting the importance of localization and user-centered design for diverse learning environments.

## 9.8. Integration with Entrepreneurial and Creative Ecosystems

Beyond traditional education, chatbots are poised to support entrepreneurial learning and ideation processes. Zreik (2024) explored the integration of AI assistants into innovation hubs, helping users generate and refine business ideas. Such tools could be extended to hackathons, incubators, and startup courses, where rapid feedback and creative dialogue are essential.

## 9.9. Enhanced Evaluation and Self-Regulated Learning Support

Virtual assistants can play a greater role in formative and summative assessment. Rane (2023) suggested that future VAs could monitor student performance, suggest learning paths, and promote metacognitive awareness. This aligns with Zangana and Mustafa (2024), who advocate for hybrid models combining real-time assessment with adaptive instruction.

Self-regulated learning, supported by reminders, nudges, and performance summaries, could empower students to manage their time and goals autonomously—especially in blended or remote settings.

## 9.10. Holistic Ecosystems and Longitudinal Data Integration

Future innovations will likely center on unifying disparate educational services into cohesive ecosystems. Kyrylenko (2024) emphasized the potential for integrated platforms that merge tutoring, support, and content delivery into seamless experiences. Zangana (2019) noted that longitudinal data from such systems could fuel predictive analytics, guiding institutional strategy and learner intervention.

As data from VAs accumulate, institutions will gain deeper insights into learner behavior and curriculum performance—providing a foundation for continuous improvement and innovation.

## 9.11 Summary

The future of chatbots and virtual assistants in education lies in continuous refinement and bold innovation. From emotionally intelligent tutoring and administrative automation to blockchain-backed learning records and entrepreneurial idea generation, the possibilities are vast. Realizing these potentials requires collaboration among educators, developers, policymakers, and learners to ensure these systems are ethical, inclusive, and pedagogically sound.

Emerging work by Mekni, Baani, and Sulieman (2020), Mulyana and Hakimi (2018), and Reyes et al. (2020) underscores the importance of robust system architecture and iterative design. Meanwhile, foundational research by Zangana et al. (2024) and Kane (2016) provides the framework to embed these innovations into institutional practice with clarity and sustainability.

The adoption of chatbots in education has followed a distinct timeline of innovation and implementation. Figure 6 outlines key milestones and anticipated future developments based on current trends and technological trajectories.

*Figure 6. Timeline of Educational Chatbot Evolution*

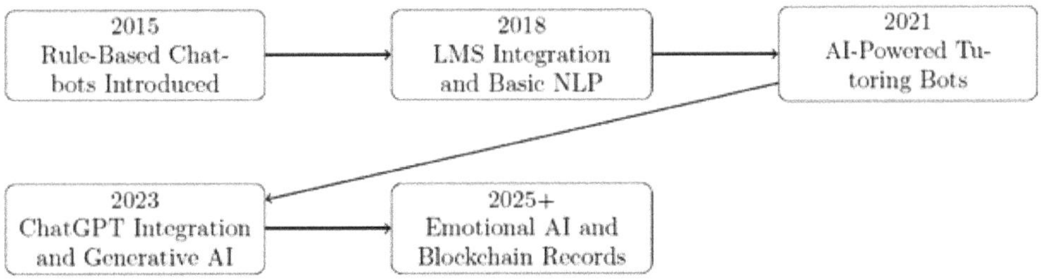


## 10. CONCLUSION

This chapter has explored the multifaceted role of chatbots and virtual assistants in educational settings, highlighting their transformative potential as well as the significant challenges and limitations they face. AI-powered conversational agents are increasingly being adopted to enhance learning experiences, improve administrative workflows, and support educators and students alike. The benefits of these technologies include increased accessibility, personalized learning, and automation of routine tasks, which collectively contribute to more efficient and engaging educational environments.

However, as thoroughly discussed, the adoption of chatbots is not without hurdles. Technical limitations such as contextual understanding and integration issues, ethical and privacy concerns, as well as pedagogical misalignments, continue to pose risks to their effective implementation. Additionally, challenges related to scalability, user training, and emotional intelligence underline the necessity for continuous improvement and careful design tailored to diverse educational contexts.

Looking forward, the future of educational chatbots lies in overcoming these limitations through advances in adaptive learning, emotional intelligence, multimodal interaction, and integration with institutional systems. Innovations in AI will foster hyper-personalized, context-aware, and inclusive tools that not only support cognitive learning but also address social and emotional dimensions. Collaboration between educators, developers, and policymakers will be crucial to ensure these technologies are deployed ethically, responsibly, and effectively.

In conclusion, while chatbots and virtual assistants present exciting opportunities to revolutionize education, realizing their full potential demands a balanced approach that addresses current challenges and embraces innovation with a learner-centric and ethical mindset. Continued research, robust implementation strategies, and ongoing evaluation will be essential to harness the benefits of AI-driven conversational agents and to shape the future of education in a sustainable and inclusive manner.

## REFERENCES


Archita, S., & Saravanan, S. (2025, April). Enhancing Student Learning with a Customizable Virtual Assistant. In *2025 3rd International Conference on Advancements in Electrical, Electronics, Communication, Computing and Automation (ICAECA)* (pp. 1-7). IEEE.

Athavale, V. A., Selvakumar, P., Poorani, S., Anand, T., & Rathore, D. S. (2025). Designing chatbots for educational leadership. *Chatbots in Educational Leadership and Management*, 181-204.

Davar, N. F., Dewan, M. A. A., & Zhang, X. (2025). AI chatbots in education: Challenges and opportunities. *Information (Basel), 16*(3), 235. DOI: 10.3390/info16030235

David, B., Chalon, R., & Zhang, X. (2022, September). Virtual assistants (chatbots) as help to teachers in collaborative learning environment. In *International Conference on Interactive Collaborative Learning* (pp. 135-146). Cham: Springer International Publishing.

Fernoagă, V., Stelea, G. A., Gavrilă, C., & Sandu, F. (2018). Intelligent Education Assistant Powered by Chatbots. *eLearning & Software for Education, 2.*

Gubareva, R., & Lopes, R. P. (2020). Virtual Assistants for Learning: A Systematic Literature Review. *CSEDU*, (1), 97–103. DOI: 10.5220/0009417600970103

Hari, D., Zemljak, D., Kerneža, M., Kurbus, N., Krabonja, M. V., & Flogie, A. (2025). CONVERSATIONAL ASSISTANTS IN EDUCATION: ADVANTAGES, CHALLENGES, AND OPPORTUNITIES FOR THE FUTURE. *INTED2025 Proceedings*, 6675-6683.

Kane, D. A. (2016). The role of chatbots in teaching and learning. *E-learning and the academic library: Essays on innovative initiatives, 131*, 131-147.

Kyrylenko, Y. (2024). Chatbots and virtual assistants vs. human agents in IT customer support.

Mekni, M. (2021). An artificial intelligence based virtual assistant using conversational agents. *Journal of Software Engineering and Applications, 14*(9), 455–473. DOI: 10.4236/jsea.2021.149027

Mekni, M., Baani, Z., & Sulieman, D. (2020, January). A smart virtual assistant for students. In *Proceedings of the 3rd international conference on applications of intelligent systems* (pp. 1-6).

Mendoza, S., Sánchez-Adame, L. M., Urquiza-Yllescas, J. F., González-Beltrán, B. A., & Decouchant, D. (2022). A model to develop chatbots for assisting the teaching and learning process. *Sensors (Basel), 22*(15), 5532. DOI: 10.3390/s22155532 PMID: 35898035

Mounkoro, I., Uberas, A. D., Cadelina, F. A., Saleem, M. U., Maryam, S., Almagharbeh, W. T., ... & Hidayatallah, Z. (2024). Integrating AI in Classroom Management: Improving Educational Efficiency and Teacher Workflows.

Mulyana, E., & Hakimi, R. (2018, July). Bringing automation to the classroom: A chatOps-based approach. In *2018 4th International Conference on Wireless and Telematics (ICWT)* (pp. 1-6). IEEE. DOI: 10.1109/ICWT.2018.8527810

Öncü, S. E., & Süral, İ. (2024). Leveraging AI for Enhanced Support: Satisfaction Levels of Users Utilizing Virtual Assistant in Open Education. *Asian Journal of Distance Education, 19*(1).

Pereira, R., Reis, A., Barroso, J., Sousa, J., & Pinto, T. (2022, August). Virtual assistants applications in education. In *International conference on technology and innovation in learning, teaching and education* (pp. 468-480). Cham: Springer Nature Switzerland.

Rane, N. (2023). Chatbot-enhanced teaching and learning: Implementation strategies, challenges, and the role of ChatGPT in education. *Challenges, and the Role of ChatGPT in Education (July 21, 2023).*

Reddy, N. S., Chaitanya, N. P., Varshitha, P. S., Varma, R. C., Reddy, P. K., & Dandu, J. (2024, August). Intelligent Chatbot For Educational Institutions. In *2024 7th International Conference on Circuit Power and Computing Technologies (ICCPCT)* (Vol. 1, pp. 1337-1343). IEEE. DOI: 10.1109/ICCPCT61902.2024.10673214

Reyes, R., Garza, D., Garrido, L., Cueva, V., & Ramírez Uresti, J. (2020). *Virtual assistants in education: model, implementation, and results. Novus2020.* Available at ResearchGate.

Salem, M., & Shaalan, K. (2023, December). ChatGPT: Advancing Education with Virtual Assistants. In *International Conference on Business Intelligence and Information Technology* (pp. 283-293). Singapore: Springer Nature Singapore.

Zangana, H. M. (2015). A New Skin Color Based Face Detection Algorithm by Combining Three Color Model Algorithms. *IOSR J. Comput. Eng, 17*, 06-125.

Zangana, H. M. (2017). A new algorithm for shape detection. *IOSR Journal of Computer Engineering (IOSR-JCE), 19*(3), 71-76.

Zangana, H. M. (2017). Library Data Quality Maturity (IIUM as a Case Study). *IOSR Journal of Computer Engineering, 19*(March), 29. DOI: 10.9790/0661-1902033844

Zangana, H. M. (2017). Watermarking System Using LSB. *IOSR Journal of Computer Engineering, 19*(3), 75–79. DOI: 10.9790/0661-1903027579

Zangana, H. M. (2018). Design an information management system for a pharmacy. *International Journal of Advanced Research in Computer and Communication Engineering*, *7*(10), 52–55. DOI: 10.17148/IJARCCE.2018.71012

Zangana, H. M. (2018). Developing Data Warehouse for Student Information System (IIUM as a Case Study). *International Organization of Scientific Research, 20*(1), 09-14.

Zangana, H. M. (2018). Implementing a System for Recognizing Optical Characters.

Zangana, H. M. (2019). Issues of Data Management in the Library: A Case Study.

Zangana, H. M. (2019). ITD Data Quality Maturity (A Case Study). *International Journal Of Engineering And Computer Science, 8*(10).

Zangana, H. M. (2020). Mobile Device Integration in IIUM Service. *International Journal (Toronto, Ont.)*, *8*(5).

Zangana, H. M. (2021). The Global Finical Crisis from an Islamic Point Of View. *Qubahan Academic Journal*, *1*(2), 55–59. DOI: 10.48161/qaj.v1n2a39

Zangana, H. M. (2022). Creating a Community-Based Disaster Management System. *Academic Journal of Nawroz University*, *11*(4), 234–244. DOI: 10.25007/ajnu.v11n4a1485

Zangana, H. M. (2022). Implementing New Interactive Video Learning System for IIUM. *Academic Journal of Nawroz University*, *11*(2), 23–29. DOI: 10.25007/ajnu.v11n2a1281

Zangana, H. M. (2022). Improving The Web Services for Remittance Company: Express Remit as a Case Study. *Academic Journal of Nawroz University (AJNU), 11*(3).

Zangana, H. M., & Abdulazeez, A. M. (2023). Developed Clustering Algorithms for Engineering Applications: A Review. *International Journal of Informatics* [IN-JIISCOM]. *Information System and Computer Engineering*, *4*(2), 147–169.

Zangana, H. M., & Al-Shaikhli, I. F. (2013). A new algorithm for human face detection using skin color tone. *IOSR Journal of Computer Engineering*, *11*(6), 31–38. DOI: 10.9790/0661-1163138

Zangana, H. M., Bazeed, S. M. S., Ali, N. Y., & Abdullah, D. T. (2024). Navigating Project Change: A Comprehensive Review of Change Management Strategies and Practices. *Indonesian Journal of Education and Social Sciences*, *3*(2), 166–179. DOI: 10.56916/ijess.v3i2.735

Zangana, H. M., & Mustafa, F. M. (2024). From Classical to Deep Learning: A Systematic Review of Image Denoising Techniques. *Jurnal Ilmiah Computer Science*, *3*(1), 50–65. DOI: 10.58602/jics.v3i1.36

Zangana, H. M., & Mustafa, F. M. (2024). Review of Hybrid Denoising Approaches in Face Recognition: Bridging Wavelet Transform and Deep Learning. *The Indonesian Journal of Computer Science*, *13*(4). Advance online publication. DOI: 10.33022/ijcs.v13i4.4209

Zangana, H. M., & Mustafa, F. M. (2024). Surveying the Landscape: A Comprehensive Review of Object Detection Algorithms and Advancements. *Jurnal Ilmiah Computer Science*, *3*(1), 1–15. DOI: 10.58602/jics.v3i1.29

Zreik, M. (2024). Harnessing AI for entrepreneurial idea generation: Navigating the new frontier. In *Generating Entrepreneurial Ideas With AI* (pp. 1–18). IGI Global Scientific Publishing. DOI: 10.4018/979-8-3693-3498-0.ch001

# Chapter 6
# Automated Feedback Systems for Enhancing Teacher Self-Assessment

**Luay Albtosh**
https://orcid.org/0009-0009-0338-9123
*Capitol Technology University, USA & Houston Community College, USA*

**Rindah Febriana Suryawati**
*Universitas Airlangga, Indonesia*

## ABSTRACT

*The integration of Artificial Intelligence (AI) in education has paved the way for more personalized and scalable professional development opportunities. One significant innovation in this space is the use of automated feedback systems to support teacher self-assessment. These systems leverage machine learning algorithms, natural language processing, and data analytics to provide timely, evidence-based feedback to educators, helping them reflect on their instructional practices, classroom interactions, and professional growth areas. This chapter explores the theoretical foundations, design principles, and practical implementations of automated feedback systems in educational settings. It also examines the benefits and limitations of these technologies, considering ethical, technical, and pedagogical dimensions. Through a review of existing platforms, case studies, and emerging trends, this chapter highlights how AI-driven feedback tools can enhance self-regulation, foster continuous improvement, and contribute to a culture of reflective practice among educators.*

DOI: 10.4018/979-8-3373-5951-9.ch006

## 1. INTRODUCTION

In the evolving landscape of education, continuous teacher development has emerged as a cornerstone of effective pedagogy. Central to this professional growth is self-assessment—the ability of educators to critically reflect on their teaching practices, student engagement, and instructional outcomes. Traditionally, self-assessment has relied on subjective reflection, peer observations, or occasional administrative reviews. However, with the advent of artificial intelligence (AI) and automated technologies, educators now have access to sophisticated feedback systems that can provide timely, objective, and personalized evaluations of their instructional performance (Ng, 2016; Nieminen, Asikainen, & Rämö, 2021).

Automated feedback systems harness machine learning, natural language processing, and multimodal analytics to offer actionable insights, enabling educators to engage in real-time reflective practices (Buckingham Shum et al., 2023; Žerovnik, 2024). These systems align well with models of self-regulated learning, fostering autonomy and self-efficacy among teachers. For example, Almutawa (2023) proposed a conceptual framework for integrating automated feedback into instructor self-assessment, emphasizing AI's capacity to support reflective decision-making and instructional refinement.

The emergence of these systems is driven by a convergence of technological advancements and pedagogical demands. Studies have shown their effectiveness in both language learning (Khasawneh, 2024; Evenddy, 2024; Li & Kim, 2024) and STEM education (Araujo et al., 2025; Barczak et al., 2023; Marchisio et al., 2018), where educators must continually adjust content delivery to match evolving learner needs. In particular, retrieval-augmented and context-aware feedback mechanisms, such as those developed by Martinez-Romo et al. (2025), highlight how AI can simulate meaningful human-like feedback based on a vast array of educational data.

Automated assessment systems are not limited to academic content. For instance, Dimitriadou and Lanitis (2025) evaluated body language assessment systems that use computer vision and behavioral analytics to support self-evaluation in teacher training. Similarly, Hsia et al. (2025) introduced AI-supported self-assessment in physical education, demonstrating how non-textual data like physical motion and gesture can be processed for feedback.

AI-driven tools also offer significant promise for feedback organization in intelligent learning environments (Kerimbayev et al., 2024). These systems are built on computational models capable of analyzing teacher behavior, student interactions, and assessment patterns, generating reports that inform instructional strategies. Nunes et al. (2022) affirmed that automated writing evaluation systems have improved accuracy and consistency in educational settings, a feature that is now being extended to teacher professional development.

From a human-centric perspective, the success of these systems relies on how well they are integrated into teachers' workflows. Žerovnik (2024) emphasizes usability as a critical component of effectiveness, noting that overwhelming interfaces or irrelevant feedback can hinder adoption. To that end, research by Hooda et al. (2022) and Seifert and Feliks (2019) shows that well-designed systems not only provide feedback but also serve as catalysts for self-improvement and instructional redesign.

Personalized feedback remains a critical theme in the literature. Belcadhi (2016) explored semantic web-based systems that tailor feedback to individual learning paths, while Darvishi et al. (2022) proposed models integrating AI-assisted peer feedback to refine educational judgment. These innovations build on early efforts to embed adaptability and context into educational technologies, providing a more learner- and teacher-centered approach.

Real-world applications of automated feedback are being demonstrated across diverse educational domains. Pando Cerra et al. (2023) showcased how interactive self-assessment tools in CAD education boosted engagement and comprehension. Similarly, Khasawneh (2024) and Liu et al. (2025) illustrated the benefits of AI-based pronunciation and language assessment tools that help educators and students alike develop metacognitive awareness.

Technological underpinnings of these systems are supported by foundational work in AI, including object detection (Zangana & Mustafa, 2024), clustering (Zangana & Abdulazeez, 2023), skin color detection (Zangana & Al-Shaikhli, 2013), and shape recognition (Zangana, 2017). These computational techniques enable feedback systems to analyze complex visual, textual, and behavioral data—a necessity for multimodal assessment environments (Zangana, 2015; 2018; 2020).

Furthermore, the scalability of AI systems provides the potential to democratize access to high-quality feedback. Martinez-Romo et al. (2025) and Shivshankar and Acharya (2025) argue that generative AI models can close the feedback gap in large classes and remote education, where human feedback is often limited. Zreik (2024) added that AI's potential for idea generation and reflective discourse could be a game-changer in entrepreneurial and interdisciplinary education, including teacher training.

Lastly, successful implementation depends on the alignment of system design with educational objectives. Rhode, Richter, and Miller (2017) developed frameworks for personalized professional development based on self-assessment. Their work complements current efforts to leverage AI not just for monitoring, but also for mentoring and empowering educators toward sustainable professional growth (Zangana et al., 2024; Zangana, 2025).

In summary, the integration of automated feedback systems into teacher self-assessment marks a transformative shift in professional development. By combining cognitive theory, computational sophistication, and reflective pedagogy, these systems offer an unprecedented opportunity to enhance teaching quality at scale—supporting a culture of continuous improvement and innovation in education.

## 2. THEORETICAL FOUNDATIONS OF SELF-ASSESSMENT AND FEEDBACK

Self-assessment is central to lifelong learning and reflective teaching practice. Theoretically grounded in metacognitive regulation and formative learning principles, self-assessment empowers teachers to reflect critically on their pedagogical decisions, classroom behavior, and student interactions. Feedback, particularly when timely, relevant, and actionable, is a foundational element of the self-assessment process, helping educators identify both strengths and areas for development (Ng, 2016; Nieminen, Asikainen, & Rämö, 2021).

Automated feedback systems, powered by artificial intelligence (AI), expand the traditional understanding of feedback by enabling continuous, data-informed reflection. These systems draw from theories of self-regulated learning and formative assessment to offer scalable and personalized insights (Buckingham Shum et al., 2023; Žerovnik, 2024). Through AI-supported mechanisms, teachers receive individualized, real-time commentary on their performance, which supports autonomy and growth.

Belcadhi (2016) emphasizes the role of the semantic web in personalizing feedback for lifelong learners. Semantic technologies allow AI systems to analyze user behavior and generate context-aware feedback that supports deeper learning. In line with this, Darvishi et al. (2022) argue that integrating AI with peer feedback mechanisms enhances the accuracy and usefulness of formative assessments. These tools not only streamline the feedback process but also elevate its pedagogical value by embedding instructional guidance in the workflow.

Research by Almutawa (2023) introduces a comprehensive framework that links automated feedback with instructor self-assessment, grounded in educational psychology. The system he proposed aligns machine-generated insights with teachers' cognitive and emotional appraisal, promoting reflection through design thinking and AI-supported analytics. Similarly, Zreik (2024) points out that feedback systems leveraging AI can reinforce teacher autonomy and professional identity by simulating coaching-like experiences through adaptive interfaces.

The connection between feedback and self-assessment becomes particularly significant in technical domains. Araujo et al. (2025) and Barczak et al. (2023) demonstrated how AI can assist educators in assessing algorithmic and data structure knowledge, enhancing both student learning and the instructors' capacity to evaluate their own teaching effectiveness. These insights further validate the broader theory that automated tools serve as cognitive partners in professional development (Marchisio et al., 2018).

Studies by Dimitriadou and Lanitis (2025) and Hsia et al. (2025) expand the boundaries of automated feedback to include multimodal input, such as body language and physical skill assessment, supported by machine vision. These models, underpinned by embodied cognition theory, demonstrate how AI can foster awareness of non-verbal communication in teaching—an essential but often overlooked aspect of self-assessment.

Another vital theoretical perspective stems from self-efficacy and self-regulation frameworks. Li and Kim (2024) observed that English language teachers using automated feedback tools often perceived them as supportive "peers," suggesting that such systems nurture intrinsic motivation and learner agency. This aligns with the work of Liu et al. (2025), who found that automated corrective feedback mechanisms improved learners' self-regulation in pronunciation practice—an effect transferable to teacher training scenarios.

AI feedback systems also align with social constructivist approaches when combined with collaborative learning environments. Seifert and Feliks (2019) highlighted how online self- and peer-assessment promoted assessment literacy among pre-service teachers, a point reinforced by Hooda et al. (2022), who discussed the role of AI in scaling such feedback affordances across higher education.

The literature also shows the importance of feedback accuracy, credibility, and adaptability. Martinez-Romo et al. (2025) introduced a retrieval-augmented feedback system that bridges generative AI with educational repositories, providing contextualized feedback that reflects subject-specific standards. This design supports the personalization and scaffolding principles central to Vygotsky's zone of proximal development (ZPD).

Recent studies by Kerimbayev et al. (2024) and Shivshankar and Acharya (2025) affirm that intelligent learning systems must be designed to support meaningful teacher agency. Feedback mechanisms should not only diagnose teaching behavior but also guide reflection and transformation. As Pando Cerra et al. (2023) demonstrate through CAD education, graphical and interactive feedback tools can enhance educators' engagement with self-assessment activities, especially in STEM contexts.

From an instructional design perspective, systems described by Khasawneh (2024) and Nunes et al. (2022) show how AI-driven platforms can incorporate models of writing and language evaluation to scaffold reflection. These platforms are especially useful in tertiary and language education settings, where feedback needs to be nuanced and discipline-specific.

The necessity of system usability and user experience is also evident. Žerovnik (2024) stressed that feedback systems should not overwhelm the user but rather facilitate intuitive, actionable reflection. This insight is consistent with findings from Rhode, Richter, and Miller (2017), who designed a self-assessment framework that emphasizes accessibility and teacher buy-in. Additionally, Evenddy (2024) reinforces the significance of culturally responsive feedback systems, especially in diverse educational environments.

Lastly, foundational technologies underlying feedback tools—such as image analysis (Zangana, 2015, 2017a), skin detection (Zangana & Al-Shaikhli, 2013), optical character recognition (Zangana, 2018), and clustering (Zangana & Abdulazeez, 2023)—contribute to the robust development of AI frameworks that can interpret complex inputs from multimodal teaching environments. Such innovations are foundational to expanding the scope and quality of feedback mechanisms.

The following diagram models the reflective learning cycle supported by automated feedback systems, showing how feedback drives ongoing self-assessment and instructional adjustment.

*Figure 1. AI-Supported Reflective Learning Cycle*

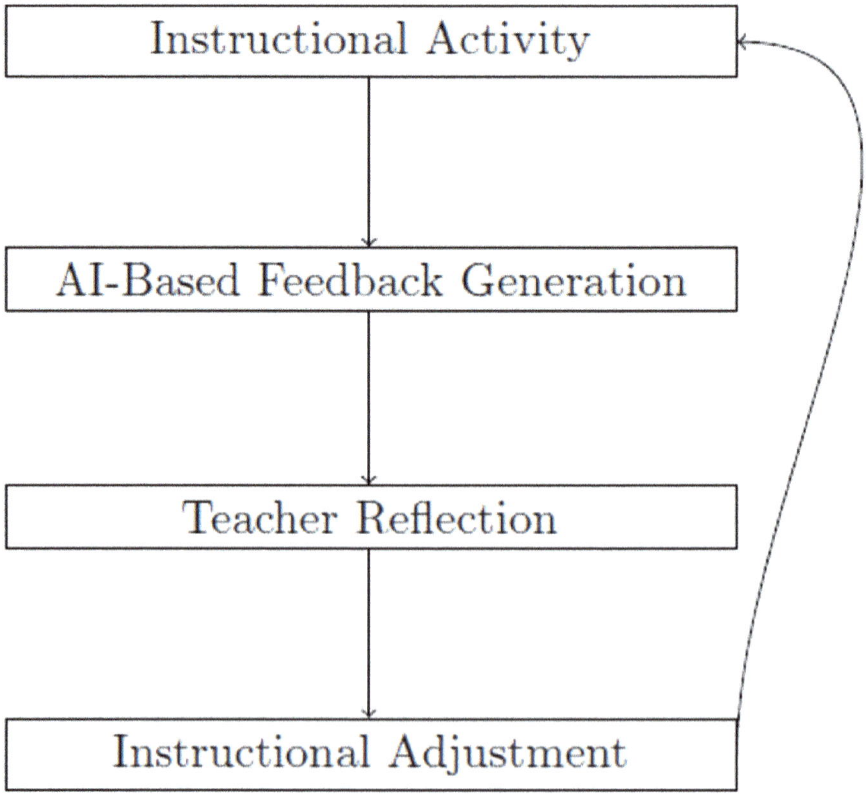

In conclusion, the theoretical foundation for automated feedback systems in teacher self-assessment lies at the intersection of metacognition, self-regulation, feedback literacy, and AI design. This integration offers transformative possibilities for professional growth, provided that ethical design, pedagogical alignment, and user-centric development remain core priorities (Zangana et al., 2025; Zangana & Mustafa, 2024).

## 3. AI AND AUTOMATED FEEDBACK TECHNOLOGIES

Artificial Intelligence (AI) has emerged as a transformative force in education, enabling the development of automated feedback systems that empower teachers to engage in meaningful, data-driven self-assessment. These technologies combine machine learning, natural language processing (NLP), computer vision, and knowledge representation techniques to deliver timely, personalized, and actionable feedback to educators across a variety of domains (Shivshankar & Acharya, 2025; Hooda et al., 2022).

Automated feedback systems work by analyzing inputs such as audio recordings, video lectures, text documents, or student evaluations, and then generating constructive feedback based on predefined pedagogical models or adaptive algorithms (Martinez-Romo et al., 2025). For instance, Almutawa (2023) introduced a framework that facilitates instructor self-assessment by integrating intelligent feedback generation into a continuous learning loop, emphasizing alignment with personal teaching goals and reflective cycles.

One key area where AI-based feedback has shown effectiveness is in programming education. Barczak et al. (2023) and Araujo et al. (2025) developed systems that provide real-time, formative feedback on data structures and algorithms, not only benefiting students but also enabling instructors to identify instructional blind spots. These systems rely heavily on natural language understanding and code analysis, allowing educators to evaluate the precision of their teaching in technical domains.

In the broader scope of STEM and interactive learning, Marchisio et al. (2018) demonstrated an automatic assessment model that combines formative assessment principles with real-time feedback, fostering both student learning and instructor reflection. Similarly, Pando Cerra et al. (2023) showed how AI can enhance design-based learning through graphical feedback tools in CAD education—tools which can also be utilized for teacher training and feedback in visually intensive domains.

Language education has also benefited significantly from AI-driven feedback tools. Evenddy (2024) investigated AI's role in language learning, highlighting its effectiveness in grammar correction, pronunciation evaluation, and communication enhancement. Khasawneh (2024) developed an AI-driven model for language proficiency assessment, integrating intelligent feedback loops that promote reflective self-assessment for both learners and instructors. Liu et al. (2025) reported improved self-regulated learning and motivation when learners used peer-assessment systems driven by automated corrective feedback—systems with potential to support teacher self-evaluation as well.

AI-supported feedback mechanisms extend beyond verbal or textual input to include multimodal data such as gesture, facial expression, and body language. Dimitriadou and Lanitis (2025) evaluated a body-language assessment system that analyzed non-verbal cues in teaching simulations using AI, offering insights into classroom presence and affective communication. Likewise, Hsia et al. (2025) demonstrated the application of AI in physical education, using reflection-promoting mechanisms to deliver automatic feedback on physical skills—potentially adaptable for evaluating teacher movement, gesture, and classroom engagement.

Another crucial component of effective feedback is personalization. Belcadhi (2016) emphasized the importance of semantic web technologies in tailoring feedback to individual needs and learning contexts, a principle adopted by many adaptive learning systems. These systems leverage ontologies and metadata to provide feedback that aligns with both the user's behavior and professional learning trajectory. This idea is echoed by Martinez-Romo et al. (2025), who applied generative AI and retrieval-augmented models to produce feedback contextualized to specific instructional settings.

Feedback quality is equally important. Buckingham Shum et al. (2023) analyzed the use of automated feedback tools from the perspective of teacher feedback literacy, emphasizing that quality feedback must be meaningful, actionable, and context-aware. Darvishi et al. (2022) proposed a model that incorporates AI assistance into peer feedback training to improve accuracy and relevance, an approach that is particularly valuable in teacher education programs.

These systems do not function in isolation but are often embedded within intelligent learning systems that structure and deliver feedback. Kerimbayev et al. (2024) discussed the organizational principles of feedback within intelligent learning platforms, highlighting the role of structured data, analytics dashboards, and continuous updates for supporting professional growth. Žerovnik (2024) further emphasized usability and user-centered design, noting that feedback systems must balance complexity and simplicity to support self-regulation.

Li and Kim (2024) explored the emotional and relational dynamics of AI feedback systems, suggesting that learners often anthropomorphize these tools and view them as supportive partners. In higher education, this sense of "digital companionship" fosters a safe environment for self-reflection and self-improvement—an aspect that is transferable to teacher self-assessment as well.

Moreover, AI-powered tools are beginning to support collaborative learning environments, offering opportunities for peer-based reflection and joint feedback sessions. Seifert and Feliks (2019) explored how online peer-assessment enhances pre-service teachers' feedback capabilities, while Ng (2016) found that wiki-based self- and peer-assessment nurtures self-regulated learning. Integrating these practices with AI can scale such capabilities, allowing teachers to engage with professional learning communities while receiving real-time feedback.

The technical infrastructure of these systems relies on foundational AI algorithms. Face and skin detection techniques (Zangana, 2015; Zangana & Al-Shaikhli, 2013), shape recognition algorithms (Zangana, 2017), optical character recognition (Zangana, 2018), and clustering techniques (Zangana & Abdulazeez, 2023) have all contributed to the backend processing capabilities of feedback platforms. Zangana and Mustafa (2024) provide a comprehensive review of object detection and image denoising approaches that support AI's role in visual and spatial assessments.

The design of AI-driven feedback platforms also demands robust data architecture. Zangana (2018) proposed a student information data warehouse system that facilitates data extraction for reflective analytics. Similarly, Zangana (2017, 2019) discussed information maturity and data quality frameworks, which are essential for ensuring that feedback systems are both reliable and trustworthy. Zangana et al. (2024) extend this concept to the domain of educational change management, where feedback mechanisms must adapt to institutional shifts and reforms.

Finally, AI's role in enabling entrepreneurial thinking in education is addressed by Zreik (2024), who envisions feedback systems as tools for creative ideation and exploration. In the context of teacher development, such systems could be designed to inspire innovative pedagogical approaches and experimentation through safe, low-risk feedback loops.

The following flowchart illustrates the general architecture of an AI-powered feedback system for teacher self-assessment, highlighting the flow from data input to actionable insights.

*Figure 2. Architecture of an AI-Powered Feedback System*

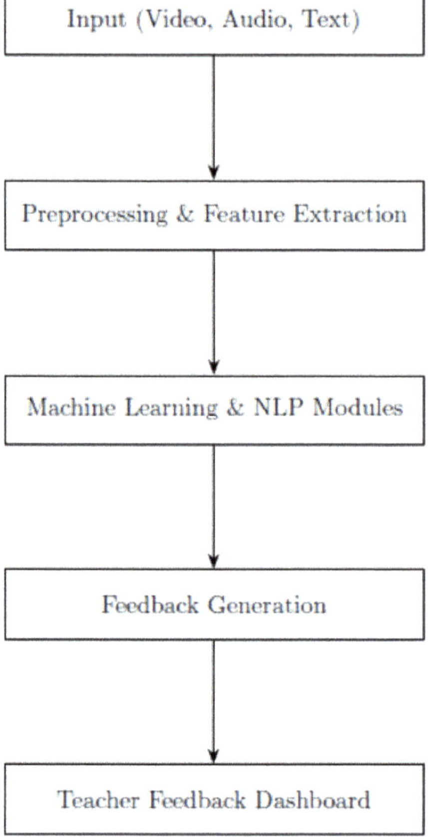


In summary, AI and automated feedback technologies offer scalable, intelligent, and adaptive solutions for enhancing teacher self-assessment. Their design and implementation rest on a confluence of advanced computational models, pedagogical theory, and user-centered design. When thoughtfully integrated, these systems have the potential to revolutionize reflective practice and elevate teaching quality across diverse educational contexts.

# 4. TYPES OF FEEDBACK IN AI-SUPPORTED SELF-ASSESSMENT

In the domain of AI-supported teacher self-assessment, feedback can take multiple forms, each fulfilling distinct pedagogical purposes. These variations include differences in **timing** (formative vs. summative), **format** (textual, visual, or multimodal), and **interactivity** (static vs. dynamic). Each type of feedback influences how educators perceive and act upon the input, shaping their engagement with professional reflection and instructional refinement (Buckingham Shum et al., 2023; Žerovnik, 2024).

## 4.1. Formative Feedback

Formative feedback is continuous and developmental, designed to support teaching improvement throughout the instructional process. It is the cornerstone of reflective teaching practices and is most effective when delivered in real time or near-real time. AI-powered platforms, such as those discussed by Araujo et al. (2025) and Marchisio et al. (2018), offer formative feedback by evaluating teachers' explanations, pacing, or assessment design during lesson planning or delivery. These systems help educators modify their teaching strategies while they are still in progress, supporting iterative refinement.

## 4.2. Summative Feedback

Summative feedback typically evaluates teacher performance after the completion of a teaching cycle, unit, or course. AI technologies can generate summative reports using data collected throughout instructional activities. These include automated evaluations of teaching videos, voice recordings, lesson plans, or classroom engagement patterns. Systems developed by Barczak et al. (2023) and Dimitriadou and Lanitis (2025) provide end-of-course feedback on aspects such as clarity, enthusiasm, and nonverbal communication, summarizing teacher effectiveness over time.

## 4.3. Corrective Feedback

Corrective feedback highlights specific errors or areas of concern, often with suggestions for improvement. In teaching contexts, it might address issues such as misaligned assessment tasks, lack of engagement strategies, or limited differentiation. Liu et al. (2025) and Evenddy (2024) show how AI systems provide corrective feedback in language teaching, a model that can be extended to teacher speech analysis and instructional clarity. Such feedback enhances precision and ensures actionable responses.

## 4.4. Reflective Feedback

Reflective feedback is metacognitive, encouraging teachers to engage in deeper thinking about their teaching philosophy, decisions, and classroom dynamics. Li and Kim (2024) observed that teachers often perceive AI-generated reflective prompts as conversational or even motivational. Systems like those by Almutawa (2023) and Martinez-Romo et al. (2025) embed reflective triggers within dashboards, encouraging educators to connect data with professional goals and internal benchmarks.

## 4.5. Predictive Feedback

Predictive feedback uses trend analysis and learning analytics to forecast outcomes or suggest future improvements. Hooda et al. (2022) and Kerimbayev et al. (2024) describe how intelligent learning systems can predict teaching challenges based on behavioral data, thereby helping educators plan interventions in advance. Predictive insights help educators prioritize areas that may affect student learning or engagement in the near future.

## 4.6. Visual and Graphical Feedback

AI platforms often include visualizations such as heat maps, timelines, emotion charts, and interaction graphs. These formats can illustrate patterns in classroom discourse, student engagement, or gesture dynamics. For instance, Dimitriadou and Lanitis (2025) and Pando Cerra et al. (2023) utilized graphical tools to present physical performance metrics and spatial teaching strategies. These visuals offer intuitive pathways for interpreting complex teaching behaviors.

## 4.7. Peer-Based Feedback Enhanced by AI

Peer feedback systems, augmented with AI, provide a hybrid model of human and machine insight. Darvishi et al. (2022) and Seifert and Feliks (2019) emphasize how AI can guide peer reviewers to offer more precise and constructive comments. These systems are particularly valuable in teacher training environments, where collaborative reflection is a key component of development.

## 4.8. Gamified or Interactive Feedback

Some AI systems use gamification elements such as badges, progress bars, or scenario-based learning to deliver feedback. Hsia et al. (2025) and Nunes et al. (2022) describe the benefits of interactive, simulation-based environments for language and skill training. These techniques enhance motivation and engagement while supporting critical thinking and self-evaluation.

To understand the relative emphasis placed on each feedback type in educational applications, the bar chart below visualizes the reported usage frequencies of major AI-supported feedback types.

*Figure 3. Usage Frequency of AI-Supported Feedback Types*

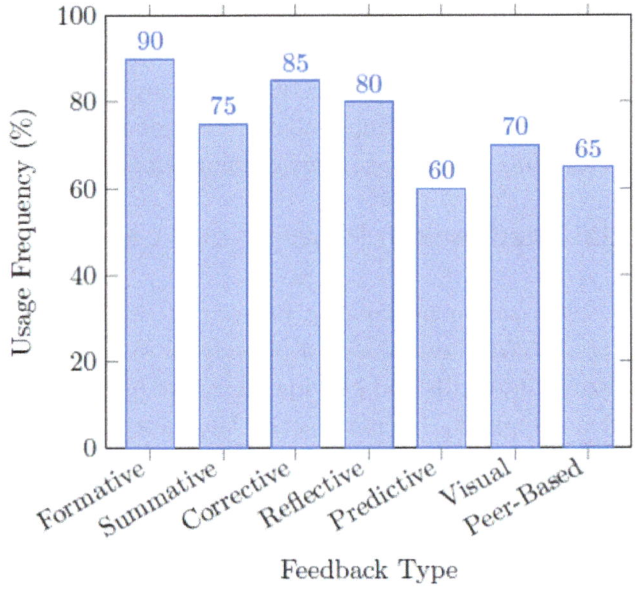


## 5. CASE STUDIES AND APPLICATIONS

Real-world implementations of AI-driven feedback systems offer compelling evidence of their transformative impact on teacher self-assessment. This section explores diverse case studies across educational contexts, highlighting how automated feedback mechanisms are enhancing reflection, teaching quality, and professional development.

## 5.1. Instructor Self-Assessment Frameworks

Almutawa (2023) presented a comprehensive framework for an automated feedback system aimed at supporting instructor self-assessment. The system emphasized integration with reflective cycles, allowing teachers to receive structured feedback based on recorded lessons, which they could analyze and iterate upon. This approach facilitated personalized development by aligning feedback with individual teaching goals.

## 5.2. Programming Education and Algorithm Analysis

In computer science education, particularly in programming and algorithm instruction, AI has enabled automated formative assessment at scale. Araujo et al. (2025) and Barczak et al. (2023) implemented AI systems that provided real-time feedback to both students and instructors. The systems highlighted the effectiveness of teaching data structures and algorithms by identifying gaps in content delivery and cognitive engagement. These implementations demonstrated that instructors could refine their teaching based on system-generated analytics.

## 5.3. Multimodal Feedback in Physical and Language Education

AI-supported self-assessment has also been effectively deployed in physical education. Hsia et al. (2025) introduced a physical skill auto-assessment system using AI to analyze motor skills and provide reflective prompts. Dimitriadou and Lanitis (2025) further applied AI to assess body language in instructional contexts, offering insights into non-verbal communication—a critical element often overlooked in traditional feedback.

Similarly, in language learning, Evenddy (2024), Khasawneh (2024), and Liu et al. (2025) demonstrated AI tools that evaluated pronunciation, grammar, and fluency. Teachers using these systems could monitor their language instruction quality, adjust strategies, and support student needs more effectively.

## 5.4. Semantic Feedback and Personalization

Belcadhi (2016) explored personalized feedback systems in lifelong learning using semantic web technologies. These systems allowed feedback to be tailored to each educator's teaching history and goals. Martinez-Romo et al. (2025) and Hooda et al. (2022) similarly applied AI to create adaptive learning environments, integrating generative AI and predictive analytics to offer contextual, individualized feedback.

## 5.5. Peer and Collaborative Feedback Systems

Peer-based feedback systems enhanced with AI are particularly impactful in teacher education. Darvishi et al. (2022) and Seifert and Feliks (2019) introduced platforms that guide student-teachers in providing and receiving quality feedback. Ng (2016) implemented a wiki-based self- and peer-assessment system, fostering self-regulated learning. These systems showed that collaborative AI-enhanced feedback not only benefits individuals but also builds communities of reflective practice.

## 5.6. Feedback in Design and STEM Contexts

In STEM education, Marchisio et al. (2018) and Pando Cerra et al. (2023) developed automatic feedback systems for design-based learning and CAD pedagogy. These systems used interactive and graphical tools to visualize feedback, helping educators interpret complex performance metrics. Such models are also adaptable for teacher training in visually intensive disciplines.

## 5.7. Professional Development and Instructional Change

Rhode et al. (2017) examined how self-assessment tools embedded in professional development courses enabled educators to design personalized learning plans. These findings were echoed by Kerimbayev et al. (2024), who illustrated how feedback in intelligent learning systems supports large-scale instructional change.

Shivshankar and Acharya (2025) emphasized that AI technologies should be embedded within institutional culture to ensure adoption and sustained impact. Zreik (2024) added a forward-looking view, noting that AI feedback tools can foster entrepreneurial thinking by encouraging risk-taking and innovation in pedagogy.

## 5.8. Systems Infrastructure and Algorithmic Foundations

AI feedback systems rely on robust technical infrastructures. Zangana and colleagues contributed foundational algorithms in face detection (2013, 2015), shape recognition (2017), data warehousing (2018), image compression (2025), and cybersecurity (Zangana et al., 2025), which underpin feedback analytics and system performance. These technologies ensure scalability, reliability, and responsiveness in real-time feedback delivery.

## 5.9. Feedback Literacy and Usability

Buckingham Shum et al. (2023) and Žerovnik (2024) highlighted that system effectiveness also depends on user interface design and teacher feedback literacy. Systems must be intuitive, transparent, and empower educators to interpret feedback constructively.

## 5.10. Evaluation and Systematic Reviews

Nunes et al. (2022) conducted a systematic review demonstrating the effectiveness of automated feedback in school settings. Nieminen et al. (2021) contrasted formative and summative self-assessment approaches, concluding that formative, feedback-rich models promoted deeper learning and greater self-efficacy.

These case studies collectively demonstrate that AI-powered feedback systems are not one-size-fits-all solutions but rather adaptable tools that can be customized to meet the specific needs of different teaching contexts. By leveraging advances in algorithm design, data management, and user-centered design, these systems are reshaping how teachers evaluate and improve their practice.

# 6. BENEFITS TO TEACHERS AND INSTITUTIONS

Automated feedback systems (AFSs) offer transformative benefits for both individual educators and educational institutions by promoting efficiency, precision, self-regulation, and professional development. These systems are increasingly integrated into teacher workflows, enhancing reflection, streamlining assessment, and promoting institutional accountability and innovation.

## 6.1. Enhanced Teacher Reflection and Professional Growth

AFSs facilitate reflective practice by providing timely, personalized, and data-driven feedback. This empowers teachers to evaluate their instructional strategies and identify areas for improvement (Almutawa, 2023). Through structured self-assessment, teachers gain actionable insights, enhancing pedagogical awareness and professional development (Ng, 2016; Rhode, Richter, & Miller, 2017). Such tools support the development of teacher feedback literacy, which is critical for interpreting and responding to automated inputs (Buckingham Shum et al., 2023).

## 6.2. Personalized and Continuous Self-Assessment

Personalized feedback generated by AFSs supports adaptive learning for instructors, allowing for nuanced assessments tailored to teaching context and style (Belcadhi, 2016). Systems such as those proposed by Martinez-Romo et al. (2025) and Araujo et al. (2025) provide retrieval-augmented, formative feedback, helping educators to iteratively reflect and improve instructional delivery in algorithm-intensive courses. These capabilities also strengthen motivation and self-efficacy among teachers (Nieminen, Asikainen, & Rämö, 2021).

## 6.3. Improved Assessment Quality and Consistency

By automating parts of the feedback loop, institutions can maintain consistency in evaluation and reduce subjectivity in teacher reviews. This is particularly beneficial in large-scale settings where managing individualized feedback is resource-intensive (Barczak et al., 2023). Dimitriadou and Lanitis (2025) demonstrated that even non-verbal teaching performance, such as body language, could be evaluated reliably through AI-based assessments, adding a new dimension to teacher evaluations.

## 6.4. Institutional Efficiency and Data-Driven Decision Making

From an institutional perspective, AFSs promote streamlined evaluation processes and efficient use of resources. Administrators can monitor aggregate performance trends, detect gaps in teaching strategies, and prioritize professional development efforts (Zangana, 2017, 2018, 2019). Systems leveraging data warehouses and intelligent reporting tools, such as those discussed by Zangana (2018), enable institutions to enhance data-driven policy and decision-making.

## 6.5. Scalable Support for Teacher Development

AFSs offer scalability in supporting faculty across different departments and campuses. For example, the feedback model proposed by Marchisio et al. (2018) for STEM disciplines has shown potential for replication across other domains. Similarly, the intelligent systems described by Kerimbayev et al. (2024) emphasize the organizational advantage of centralized feedback mechanisms that can be tailored and deployed across diverse educational contexts.

## 6.6. Support for Diverse Learning and Teaching Contexts

AFSs are adaptable across various disciplines, including language instruction (Khasawneh, 2024; Liu et al., 2025; Evenddy, 2024), physical education (Hsia et al., 2025), and computer-aided design (Pando Cerra et al., 2023). These systems accommodate subject-specific criteria while maintaining universal frameworks for feedback, thus aligning institutional goals with discipline-specific needs.

## 6.7. Promotion of a Culture of Continuous Improvement

AFSs foster a culture where feedback is not an endpoint but part of a continuous improvement cycle. Teachers become co-designers of their professional development journeys, leveraging AI-driven insights to guide their actions (Li & Kim, 2024; Darvishi et al., 2022). Institutions benefit as well, as these systems embed reflective practice and performance optimization into the core of their educational mission (Shivshankar & Acharya, 2025).

This Venn diagram displays the overlapping and unique benefits of automated feedback systems for teachers and educational institutions, emphasizing areas of mutual value.

*Figure 4. Overlapping Benefits of AFSs for Teachers and Institutions*

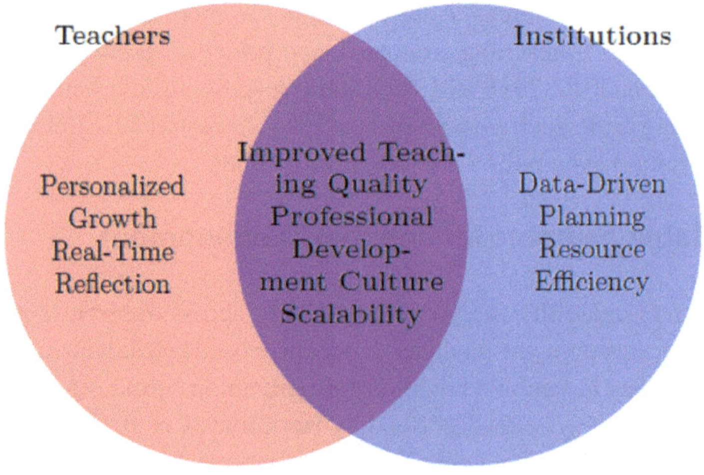

## 6.8. Robust Support for Online and Hybrid Learning Models

As education increasingly shifts toward hybrid and online models, AFSs provide essential support in virtual environments. Automated tools help maintain engagement, ensure performance tracking, and deliver meaningful feedback asynchronously (Hooda et al., 2022; Žerovnik, 2024). For example, the systems developed by Zangana and colleagues (2020, 2022) for interactive video-based learning enhance self-paced teacher training and monitoring.

# 7. CHALLENGES AND LIMITATIONS

Despite the significant promise and advancements of automated feedback systems (AFSs) and AI-driven assessment tools in education, their adoption and effectiveness face several important challenges and limitations. These issues range from technical constraints to pedagogical concerns and institutional readiness, which must be addressed to realize their full potential.

## 7.1. Technical and Algorithmic Limitations

Automated systems often struggle with the complexity and nuance of educational tasks. For example, Barczak et al. (2023) note that programming course assessments face challenges in accurately evaluating creative problem-solving and coding style beyond mere correctness. Similarly, Dimitriadou and Lanitis (2025) highlight limitations in automated body language assessment, where contextual interpretation and cultural differences complicate AI evaluation.

Moreover, many AFSs rely on predefined rubrics and may lack adaptability to diverse teaching approaches or learner contexts (Belcadhi, 2016; Kerimbayev et al., 2024). Generative AI models, while promising (Martinez-Romo et al., 2025; Araujo et al., 2025), require extensive data and tuning to avoid errors or bias, posing technical barriers for implementation.

## 7.2. Quality and Reliability of Feedback

The quality of automated feedback can vary significantly. Nunes et al. (2022) found mixed effectiveness in automated writing evaluation systems, with some tools providing surface-level comments insufficient for deep learning. Similarly, Liu et al. (2025) report that automated peer feedback systems may sometimes reduce motivation if feedback is perceived as generic or inaccurate.

Ensuring feedback is constructive, specific, and actionable remains a major challenge. Hooda et al. (2022) stress that AI systems must be carefully designed to avoid reinforcing misconceptions or misinterpretations. The balance between automated and human input is critical to maintain feedback literacy among users (Buckingham Shum et al., 2023).

## 7.3. User Acceptance and Teacher Feedback Literacy

Teachers' readiness to engage with and trust automated feedback tools varies widely. Li and Kim (2024) describe how some educators and learners perceive AFSs as impersonal or limiting, impacting their willingness to integrate these systems into their practice. Training and support are essential, as Darvishi et al. (2022) demonstrate that AI-assisted peer feedback quality improves with self-monitoring and scaffolding.

Furthermore, Buckingham Shum et al. (2023) emphasize the need for teacher feedback literacy — the skills to interpret, critically evaluate, and effectively use automated feedback. Without these competencies, adoption may falter or lead to misapplication.

## 7.4. Ethical and Privacy Concerns

The use of AI in feedback raises ethical issues around data privacy, consent, and transparency (Shivshankar & Acharya, 2025). Dimitriadou and Lanitis (2025) point to potential biases in body language analysis, while Khasawneh (2024) discusses challenges in balancing data-driven insights with learner confidentiality.

Institutions must navigate regulatory requirements and ensure responsible data governance, which adds complexity to deploying these systems (Zangana, Mohammed, & Husain, 2025).

## 7.5. Contextual and Cultural Limitations

Automated feedback systems often lack sensitivity to cultural, linguistic, or contextual factors influencing learning and teaching (Evenddy, 2024; Khasawneh, 2024). For instance, Li and Kim (2024) note that English language learners may interpret automated feedback differently depending on their cultural background and proficiency level.

These limitations challenge the universal applicability of AFSs and call for more adaptable, context-aware solutions (Hsia et al., 2025).

## 7.6. Resource and Infrastructure Constraints

Implementing advanced AI-driven feedback systems requires substantial technological infrastructure and ongoing maintenance (Kerimbayev et al., 2024; Hooda et al., 2022). Many institutions face barriers in funding, technical expertise, or integration with legacy systems (Zangana, 2018; Zangana & Mustafa, 2024).

Moreover, Marchisio et al. (2018) highlight that STEM-focused AFSs, though effective in some environments, may demand high initial investment and training that can limit scalability.

## 7.7. Risk of Over-Reliance on Automation

While automation offers efficiency, over-reliance can lead to reduced human judgment and diminished critical reflection. Nieminen, Asikainen, and Rämö (2021) warn that formative feedback's educational value depends on its integration with reflective practices, which can be undermined if educators or learners depend excessively on automated outputs.

Seifert and Feliks (2019) also caution that online self-assessment and peer-assessment require balanced human moderation to avoid misjudgments.

In summary, while automated feedback and AI-driven assessment systems provide substantial benefits, their challenges and limitations necessitate careful design, ongoing evaluation, and human-in-the-loop approaches to ensure quality, equity, and ethical compliance.

# 8. ETHICAL AND PEDAGOGICAL CONSIDERATIONS

The deployment of automated feedback systems (AFSs) and AI-driven assessment tools in education presents both ethical and pedagogical challenges that educators and institutions must thoughtfully address to ensure responsible, effective, and equitable use.

## 8.1. Ethical Concerns: Privacy, Transparency, and Bias

One of the foremost ethical issues revolves around data privacy and the transparency of AI systems. Many AFSs collect sensitive information about learners and educators, including performance data and sometimes nonverbal cues (Dimitriadou

& Lanitis, 2025). Ensuring that this data is securely managed and that users are fully informed about how their data is used is essential (Shivshankar & Acharya, 2025).

Bias embedded in AI algorithms can perpetuate inequities. For example, Khasawneh (2024) highlights how language proficiency assessment models may not equally represent all dialects or cultural variations, potentially disadvantaging certain learner groups. Similarly, Dimitriadou and Lanitis (2025) caution about biases in body language recognition systems that may misinterpret gestures based on cultural contexts.

Ethical frameworks and regulatory compliance must guide AI adoption to promote fairness, accountability, and inclusivity (Kerimbayev et al., 2024; Zangana, Mohammed, & Husain, 2025).

## 8.2. Pedagogical Alignment and Feedback Quality

Automated feedback must align with sound pedagogical principles to support meaningful learning. Belcadhi (2016) and Marchisio et al. (2018) emphasize that feedback should be personalized, timely, and formative to foster self-regulated learning and deep understanding.

However, as Nunes et al. (2022) review, many automated writing evaluation systems offer superficial feedback that may fail to advance higher-order thinking. Ensuring that AI systems provide actionable, context-aware feedback remains a critical pedagogical challenge (Hooda et al., 2022; Li & Kim, 2024).

The integration of AI should complement, not replace, human judgment. Buckingham Shum et al. (2023) argue that teachers need to develop feedback literacy to interpret and enhance AI-generated comments effectively, ensuring that pedagogical intent is preserved.

## 8.3. Supporting Teacher and Learner Agency

AFSs should empower users rather than diminish agency. Ng (2016) and Darvishi et al. (2022) illustrate that self- and peer-assessment processes foster self-regulation and deeper engagement when supported by AI scaffolding.

Automated tools that adapt to learners' goals and preferences—such as those discussed by Martinez-Romo et al. (2025) and Araujo et al. (2025)—help maintain motivation and personalize learning pathways. Conversely, rigid, non-transparent systems risk alienating users or promoting over-reliance (Li & Kim, 2024).

## 8.4. Inclusivity and Accessibility

Pedagogical fairness requires AFSs to be inclusive and accessible across diverse learner profiles. Evenddy (2024) and Hsia et al. (2025) show that AI systems tailored for language learners or physical education students must accommodate different abilities, languages, and cultural backgrounds to avoid exclusion.

Moreover, technological infrastructure and digital literacy vary widely; equitable access is an ongoing concern (Kerimbayev et al., 2024).

## 8.5. Transparency and Explainability

Users—both teachers and learners—need clear explanations of how automated feedback is generated. Transparency fosters trust and supports critical evaluation of AI suggestions (Buckingham Shum et al., 2023; Shivshankar & Acharya, 2025).

Systems with opaque decision-making can lead to confusion, misinterpretation, or blind acceptance of feedback, undermining pedagogical goals.

## 8.6. Ethical Use of AI in Teacher Self-Assessment

AI-supported instructor self-assessment systems, like those developed by Almutawa (2023), provide opportunities for reflective practice but raise questions about surveillance and autonomy. Ensuring that teachers retain control over their data and how it informs evaluations is paramount.

## 8.7. Balancing Automation with Human Interaction

While AI can augment feedback provision, human interaction remains crucial for emotional support, contextual judgment, and fostering motivation (Rhode, Richter, & Miller, 2017; Seifert & Feliks, 2019). The ethical pedagogical approach embraces a hybrid model where AI assists but educators guide.

To ensure responsible implementation, AFSs should be guided by layered design principles incorporating ethical, pedagogical, and user-centered elements, as illustrated in the model below.

*Figure 5. Layered Ethical and Pedagogical Framework for Designing AFSs*

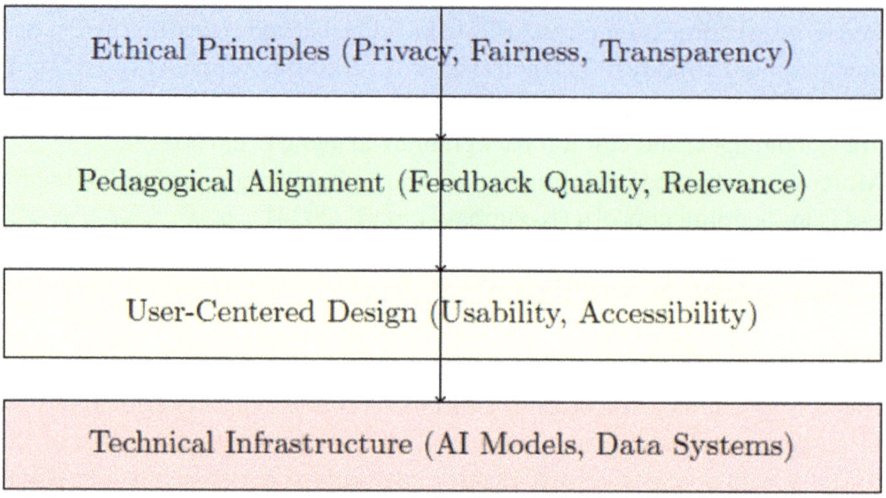


In summary, ethical and pedagogical considerations for AI-driven automated feedback systems demand a balanced approach emphasizing transparency, fairness, inclusivity, and support for human agency. Thoughtful design and continuous evaluation are essential to harness AI's benefits while mitigating risks.

## 9. FUTURE RESEARCH AND DEVELOPMENT DIRECTIONS

The rapid evolution of automated feedback systems (AFSs) and AI-driven assessment tools offers promising opportunities, yet also exposes several gaps and challenges that future research and development must address to optimize educational impact and ethical deployment.

### 9.1. Enhancing Feedback Personalization and Adaptivity

Despite advances in automated feedback, personalization remains an ongoing research priority. Belcadhi (2016) emphasized the role of semantic web technologies for tailoring feedback to lifelong learners' contexts. Future work should deepen adaptive mechanisms that dynamically respond to learners' evolving skills, motivation, and preferences (Martinez-Romo et al., 2025; Araujo et al., 2025). The integration of multimodal data, including body language or speech, as explored by Dimitriadou and Lanitis (2025) and Hsia et al. (2025), offers a rich avenue for more nuanced feedback systems that reflect learners' holistic performance.

## 9.2. Improving AI Transparency, Explainability, and Trust

Building on Buckingham Shum et al. (2023), there is a critical need to enhance the transparency and explainability of AI-generated feedback to foster user trust and promote feedback literacy among educators and learners. Research should focus on developing interfaces that clearly communicate the rationale behind AI assessments and suggest actionable insights, enabling users to critically engage with feedback rather than passively accept it (Shivshankar & Acharya, 2025).

## 9.3. Ethical Frameworks and Bias Mitigation

The ethical concerns surrounding AI bias, data privacy, and fairness require continued attention. Khasawneh (2024) and Kerimbayev et al. (2024) urge the development of robust ethical frameworks and algorithmic fairness auditing tools to ensure inclusivity, especially for marginalized learner groups. Future research should explore bias detection and mitigation strategies specifically tailored to educational contexts, along with transparent data governance models that protect user privacy (Zangana, Mohammed, & Husain, 2025).

## 9.4. Hybrid Human-AI Feedback Models

While automation offers scalability and consistency, fully replacing human judgment is neither feasible nor desirable. As highlighted by Rhode, Richter, and Miller (2017) and Ng (2016), future development should investigate hybrid models where AI tools augment teacher and peer feedback rather than substitute it. This includes AI systems that support teacher decision-making, scaffold peer assessment quality (Darvishi et al., 2022), and facilitate reflective self-assessment processes (Almutawa, 2023).

## 9.5. Cross-Disciplinary and Multimodal Assessment Approaches

Emerging trends emphasize assessing complex skills across disciplines and modalities. For instance, Barczak et al. (2023) demonstrated automated assessment in programming courses, while Pando Cerra et al. (2023) explored self-assessment graphical tools in engineering education. Future R&D should expand multimodal assessment capabilities—integrating textual, visual, auditory, and kinesthetic data—to capture comprehensive learner performance in STEM, language learning, physical education, and creative domains (Evenddy, 2024; Hsia et al., 2025).

## 9.6. Scaling AI Solutions for Diverse Educational Contexts

Many current AI feedback tools are tested in controlled or higher education environments. There is an urgent need to adapt and scale these systems for K-12, vocational training, and lifelong learning settings globally, considering local languages, cultures, and infrastructure constraints (Nunes et al., 2022; Khasawneh, 2024). Research into low-resource AI models and offline-capable systems will be pivotal for equitable educational access.

## 9.7. Fostering Self-Regulated Learning and Motivation

Future developments should leverage AI to support metacognitive skills and motivation, crucial for lifelong learning. Liu et al. (2025) and Li and Kim (2024) showed promising effects of automated corrective feedback on self-regulation and motivation. Enhancing feedback systems to provide prompts that encourage reflection, goal-setting, and strategy adjustment could significantly improve learning outcomes (Nieminen, Asikainen, & Rämö, 2021; Žerovnik, 2024).

## 9.8. Integration with Broader Educational Technologies

Integration of AI-driven feedback with other educational technologies, such as Learning Management Systems (LMS) and virtual/augmented reality, presents exciting future possibilities (Kerimbayev et al., 2024). Such ecosystems can deliver continuous, context-aware feedback that supports immersive and personalized learning experiences.

In conclusion, future research and development in AI-based automated feedback systems must pursue personalized, transparent, ethical, and multimodal solutions that synergize with human expertise and diverse educational contexts. Addressing these directions promises to transform assessment practices and empower learners and educators alike.

# 10. CONCLUSION

Automated feedback systems and AI-driven assessment technologies have emerged as transformative tools in education, offering unprecedented opportunities to enhance teaching and learning processes. This chapter has explored their multifaceted benefits, including timely, personalized feedback that supports student self-regulation, motivation, and deeper engagement with course content. Additionally, these systems hold promise for alleviating teacher workload and enabling scalable, consistent assessment across diverse educational settings.

However, the adoption of these technologies also brings significant ethical and pedagogical considerations. Ensuring transparency, fairness, and inclusivity in AI algorithms is essential to prevent bias and protect learner privacy. Moreover, the quality and contextual relevance of automated feedback must align with sound pedagogical principles to truly support meaningful learning rather than merely providing superficial evaluation. The crucial role of educators in interpreting, supplementing, and guiding AI-generated feedback underscores that these technologies are best employed as tools that augment—not replace—human judgment and interaction.

Looking ahead, ongoing research and development should prioritize adaptive, multimodal, and explainable AI feedback systems that empower both learners and teachers. Equally important is the establishment of ethical frameworks and robust data governance to ensure responsible use, particularly in diverse cultural and resource contexts. Hybrid human-AI feedback models hold great promise for balancing efficiency with the nuanced understanding required for effective education.

In sum, the integration of automated feedback and AI assessment systems represents a dynamic frontier in educational innovation. When thoughtfully designed and ethically implemented, these technologies can enrich learning experiences, foster equity, and support lifelong learning in a rapidly evolving educational landscape.

## REFERENCES


Almutawa, A. (2023). *An Automated Feedback System Framework to Facilitate Instructor Self-Assessment* (Doctoral dissertation, University of Guelph).

Araujo, L., Lopez-Ostenero, F., Plaza, L., & Martinez-Romo, J. (2025). Automated Formative Feedback for Algorithm and Data Structure Self-Assessment. *Electronics (Basel)*, *14*(5), 1034. DOI: 10.3390/electronics14051034

Barczak, A. L., Mathrani, A., Han, B., & Reyes, N. H. (2023). Automated assessment system for programming courses: A case study for teaching data structures and algorithms. *Educational Technology Research and Development*, *71*(6), 2365–2388. DOI: 10.1007/s11423-023-10277-2

Belcadhi, L. C. (2016). Personalized feedback for self assessment in lifelong learning environments based on semantic web. *Computers in Human Behavior*, *55*, 562–570. DOI: 10.1016/j.chb.2015.07.042

Buckingham Shum, S., Lim, L. A., Boud, D., Bearman, M., & Dawson, P. (2023). A comparative analysis of the skilled use of automated feedback tools through the lens of teacher feedback literacy. *International Journal of Educational Technology in Higher Education*, *20*(1), 40. DOI: 10.1186/s41239-023-00410-9

Darvishi, A., Khosravi, H., Abdi, S., Sadiq, S., & Gašević, D. (2022, June). Incorporating training, self-monitoring and AI-assistance to improve peer feedback quality. In *Proceedings of the ninth ACM conference on learning@ scale* (pp. 35-47). DOI: 10.1145/3491140.3528265

Dimitriadou, E., & Lanitis, A. (2025). Evaluating the impact of an automated body language assessment system. *Education and Information Technologies*, *30*(3), 3509–3539. DOI: 10.1007/s10639-024-12931-5

Evenddy, S. S. (2024). Investigating AI's Automated Feedback in English Language Learning. *Foreign Language Instruction Probe*, *3*(1), 76–87. DOI: 10.54213/flip.v3i1.401

Hooda, M., Rana, C., Dahiya, O., Rizwan, A., & Hossain, M. S. (2022). Artificial intelligence for assessment and feedback to enhance student success in higher education. *Mathematical Problems in Engineering*, *2022*(1), 5215722. DOI: 10.1155/2022/5215722

Hsia, L. H., Hwang, G. J., Lin, Y. N., & Hwang, J. P. (2025). Artificial intelligence-supported physical education during the pandemic: A physical skill auto-assessment and feedback approach based on a reflection-promoting mechanism. *Educational Technology Research and Development*, •••, 1–22. DOI: 10.1007/s11423-025-10452-7

Kerimbayev, N., Adamova, K., Jotsov, V., Shadiev, R., Umirzakova, Z., & Nurymova, A. (2024, August). Organization of Feedback in the Intelligent Learning Systems. In *2024 IEEE 12th International Conference on Intelligent Systems (IS)* (pp. 1-7). IEEE. DOI: 10.1109/IS61756.2024.10705178

Khasawneh, D. M. A. S. K. (2024). Improving the learning of language proficiency at tertiary education level through AI-driven assessment models and automated feedback systems. *Migration Letters : An International Journal of Migration Studies*, *21*(2), 712–726.

Li, L., & Kim, M. (2024). It is like a friend to me: Critical usage of automated feedback systems by self-regulating English learners in higher education. *Australasian Journal of Educational Technology*, *40*(1), 1–18. DOI: 10.14742/ajet.8821

Liu, C. C., Hwang, G. J., Yu, P., Tu, Y. F., & Wang, Y. (2025). Effects of an automated corrective feedback-based peer assessment approach on students' learning achievement, motivation, and self-regulated learning conceptions in foreign language pronunciation. *Educational Technology Research and Development*, •••, 1–22. DOI: 10.1007/s11423-025-10484-z

Marchisio, M., Barana, A., Fioravera, M., Rabellino, S., & Conte, A. (2018, July). A model of formative automatic assessment and interactive feedback for STEM. In *2018 ieee 42nd annual computer software and applications conference (compsac)* (Vol. 1, pp. 1016-1025). IEEE. DOI: 10.1109/COMPSAC.2018.00178

Martinez-Romo, J., Araujo, L., Plaza, L., & López-Ostenero, F. (2025, April). Generative AI for Education: A Retrieval-Augmented System for Effective Feedback in Self-Assessment. In *2025 IEEE Global Engineering Education Conference (EDUCON)* (pp. 1-9). IEEE. DOI: 10.1109/EDUCON62633.2025.11016446

Ng, E. M. (2016). Fostering pre-service teachers' self-regulated learning through self-and peer assessment of wiki projects. *Computers & Education*, *98*, 180–191. DOI: 10.1016/j.compedu.2016.03.015

Nieminen, J. H., Asikainen, H., & Rämö, J. (2021). Promoting deep approach to learning and self-efficacy by changing the purpose of self-assessment: A comparison of summative and formative models. *Studies in Higher Education*, *46*(7), 1296–1311. DOI: 10.1080/03075079.2019.1688282

Nunes, A., Cordeiro, C., Limpo, T., & Castro, S. L. (2022). Effectiveness of automated writing evaluation systems in school settings: A systematic review of studies from 2000 to 2020. *Journal of Computer Assisted Learning*, *38*(2), 599–620. DOI: 10.1111/jcal.12635

Pando Cerra, P., Fernández Álvarez, H., Busto Parra, B., & Castaño Busón, S. (2023). Boosting computer-aided design pedagogy using interactive self-assessment graphical tools. *Computer Applications in Engineering Education*, *31*(1), 26–46. DOI: 10.1002/cae.22569

Rhode, J., Richter, S., & Miller, T. (2017). Designing personalized online teaching professional development through self-assessment. *TechTrends*, *61*(5), 444–451. DOI: 10.1007/s11528-017-0211-3

Seifert, T., & Feliks, O. (2019). Online self-assessment and peer-assessment as a tool to enhance student-teachers' assessment skills. *Assessment & Evaluation in Higher Education*, *44*(2), 169–185. DOI: 10.1080/02602938.2018.1487023

Shivshankar, S., & Acharya, N. (2025). AI in assessment and feedback. In *Next-generation AI methodologies in education* (pp. 119–146). IGI Global Scientific Publishing.

Zangana, H. M. (2015). A New Skin Color Based Face Detection Algorithm by Combining Three Color Model Algorithms. *IOSR J. Comput. Eng, 17*, 06-125.

Zangana, H. M. (2017). A new algorithm for shape detection. *IOSR Journal of Computer Engineering (IOSR-JCE), 19*(3), 71-76.

Zangana, H. M. (2017). Library Data Quality Maturity (IIUM as a Case Study). *IOSR Journal of Computer Engineering*, *19*(March), 29. DOI: 10.9790/0661-1902033844

Zangana, H. M. (2017). Watermarking System Using LSB. *IOSR Journal of Computer Engineering*, *19*(3), 75–79. DOI: 10.9790/0661-1903027579

Zangana, H. M. (2018). Design an information management system for a pharmacy. *International Journal of Advanced Research in Computer and Communication Engineering*, *7*(10), 52–55. DOI: 10.17148/IJARCCE.2018.71012

Zangana, H. M. (2018). Developing Data Warehouse for Student Information System (IIUM as a Case Study). *International Organization of Scientific Research, 20*(1), 09-14.

Zangana, H. M. (2018). Implementing a System for Recognizing Optical Characters.

Zangana, H. M. (2019). Issues of Data Management in the Library: A Case Study.

Zangana, H. M. (2019). ITD Data Quality Maturity (A Case Study). *International Journal Of Engineering And Computer Science, 8*(10).

Zangana, H. M. (2020). Mobile Device Integration in IIUM Service. *International Journal (Toronto, Ont.), 8*(5).

Zangana, H. M. (2021). The Global Finical Crisis from an Islamic Point Of View. *Qubahan Academic Journal, 1*(2), 55–59. DOI: 10.48161/qaj.v1n2a39

Zangana, H. M. (2022). Creating a Community-Based Disaster Management System. *Academic Journal of Nawroz University, 11*(4), 234–244. DOI: 10.25007/ajnu.v11n4a1485

Zangana, H. M. (2022). Implementing New Interactive Video Learning System for IIUM. *Academic Journal of Nawroz University, 11*(2), 23–29. DOI: 10.25007/ajnu.v11n2a1281

Zangana, H. M. (2022). Improving The Web Services for Remittance Company: Express Remit as a Case Study. *Academic Journal of Nawroz University (AJNU), 11*(3).

Zangana, H. M. (2025). Design and Implementation of a Novel Parallel Algorithm for Efficient Image Compression in High-Performance Computing. *EAI Endorsed Transactions on AI and Robotics, 4*. Advance online publication. DOI: 10.4108/airo.7832

Zangana, H. M., & Abdulazeez, A. M. (2023). Developed Clustering Algorithms for Engineering Applications: A Review. *International Journal of Informatics* [IN-JIISCOM]. *Information System and Computer Engineering, 4*(2), 147–169.

Zangana, H. M., & Al-Shaikhli, I. F. (2013). A new algorithm for human face detection using skin color tone. *IOSR Journal of Computer Engineering, 11*(6), 31–38. DOI: 10.9790/0661-1163138

Zangana, H. M., Bazeed, S. M. S., Ali, N. Y., & Abdullah, D. T. (2024). Navigating Project Change: A Comprehensive Review of Change Management Strategies and Practices. *Indonesian Journal of Education and Social Sciences, 3*(2), 166–179. DOI: 10.56916/ijess.v3i2.735

Zangana, H. M., Mohammed, H. S., & Husain, M. M. (2025). Addressing insider threats: The human factor in cybersecurity for financial institutions. *Journal of Innovation Information Technology and Application, 7*(1), 88–96. DOI: 10.35970/jinita.v7i1.2686

Zangana, H. M., & Mustafa, F. M. (2024). From Classical to Deep Learning: A Systematic Review of Image Denoising Techniques. *Jurnal Ilmiah Computer Science, 3*(1), 50–65. DOI: 10.58602/jics.v3i1.36

Zangana, H. M., & Mustafa, F. M. (2024). Review of Hybrid Denoising Approaches in Face Recognition: Bridging Wavelet Transform and Deep Learning. *The Indonesian Journal of Computer Science, 13*(4). Advance online publication. DOI: 10.33022/ijcs.v13i4.4209

Zangana, H. M., & Mustafa, F. M. (2024). Surveying the Landscape: A Comprehensive Review of Object Detection Algorithms and Advancements. *Jurnal Ilmiah Computer Science, 3*(1), 1–15. DOI: 10.58602/jics.v3i1.29

Žerovnik, A. (2024). Technology-Enhanced Feedback System Usability in the Context of Self-Regulation Promotion. *Education Sciences, 14*(9), 948. DOI: 10.3390/educsci14090948

Zreik, M. (2024). Harnessing AI for entrepreneurial idea generation: Navigating the new frontier. In *Generating Entrepreneurial Ideas With AI* (pp. 1–18). IGI Global Scientific Publishing. DOI: 10.4018/979-8-3693-3498-0.ch001

# Chapter 7
# Sociological Perspectives on AI Integration in Teacher Development:
## Equity, Identity, and Institutional Change

**Rozhan A. Muhyadeen**
https://orcid.org/0009-0009-3367-6983
*University of Duhok, Iraq*

## ABSTRACT

*This chapter explores the sociological dimensions of integrating artificial intelligence (AI) into teacher development, focusing on the critical intersections of equity, professional identity, and institutional change. As AI technologies increasingly influence educational practices, it becomes imperative to examine how these tools shape the experiences of educators across diverse social and institutional contexts. Drawing on key sociological theories, the chapter analyzes how AI-mediated development opportunities may either reinforce or disrupt existing power structures, professional hierarchies, and systemic inequalities. It also considers how teachers negotiate their professional identities within AI-infused environments and how institutions respond to such technological shifts. The discussion is grounded in current literature and case studies that highlight both the promise and the challenges of sociotechnical transformation in teacher support systems.*

DOI: 10.4018/979-8-3373-5951-9.ch007

# 1. INTRODUCTION

The rapid integration of artificial intelligence (AI) into educational environments has fundamentally transformed the landscape of teacher development, creating both new possibilities and complex challenges. While AI-powered tools—such as personalized learning systems, predictive analytics, and virtual assistants—have shown the potential to enhance instructional design and support (Ayeni et al., 2024; Jin et al., 2024), their impact must be interrogated through a sociological lens that attends to the structural, cultural, and identity-based dynamics of educational institutions.

Historically, sociologists of education have emphasized that schools are not merely neutral spaces for knowledge transmission but are embedded in broader systems of power and inequality (SWARGIARY, 2025; Ray, 2019). As such, the integration of AI into teacher development cannot be disentangled from questions of equity, access, and institutional change (Pedro et al., 2019; Grab, 2025). Culturally responsive teaching, inclusive pedagogies, and critical engagement with digital tools are central to ensuring that AI does not exacerbate existing disparities but instead contributes to transformative educational practices (Murtiningsih & Sujito, 2024; Monahan et al., 2024).

Sociological inquiry into AI in education calls for attention to the ways AI-mediated systems reproduce or disrupt traditional hierarchies. For example, research shows that women and marginalized educators in STEM often face implicit bias in academia, and such biases may become encoded in AI algorithms unless explicitly addressed (Casad et al., 2021; Peer Mohamed, 2024). In parallel, the professional identities of teachers are being reshaped by AI technologies that challenge conventional notions of expertise and autonomy (Lan, 2024; Moradi-Kelayeh, 2025). These shifts intersect with broader organizational dynamics, where AI is influencing not only classroom interactions but also institutional decision-making and faculty development models (Steinert, 2025; Halmo, 2025).

From a change management perspective, the introduction of AI in educational contexts necessitates careful navigation of institutional cultures and power relations. Theories of organizational change underscore the importance of contingency, leadership, and stakeholder engagement in successful transformation (Battilana & Casciaro, 2012; Palmer et al., 2016). As educational institutions adapt to technological innovations, they must balance efficiency with critical reflection and sustainability (Stouten et al., 2018; Benn et al., 2014). Faculty development programs and teacher training initiatives, therefore, must go beyond technical proficiency to include critical reflection on ethics, justice, and identity (Kohli et al., 2021; Quan et al., 2019).

Moreover, teacher development cannot be separated from broader educational policy and institutional structures. Recent research has emphasized the need to examine how AI integration intersects with racialized and gendered organizational logics

(Ray, 2019; Rajesh, 2024), the shaping of campus culture (Museus & Jayakumar, 2012), and responses to global disruptions such as COVID-19 (Sá & Serpa, 2020). AI adoption in teacher development is thus both a technical and a sociopolitical process that requires collaborative efforts among educators, policymakers, and technologists (Shani et al., 2025; Kalashnikova et al., 2025).

Another critical dimension is how sociology itself is taught within teacher education programs. Some studies indicate a growing disconnection between student-teachers and the sociological foundations of education, raising concerns about whether future educators are equipped to critically engage with the systemic consequences of AI (Brennan & Canny, 2023). To foster a truly inclusive and ethical AI integration, teacher education must reaffirm the value of sociological thinking and develop spaces for epistemic agency and critical engagement (Blackmore, 2013; Mac Fadden et al., 2024).

In sum, this chapter argues that the integration of AI into teacher development should not be viewed merely as a matter of adopting new technologies. Instead, it must be approached as a transformative sociological process that engages with questions of identity, equity, and institutional change. By bridging theories of organizational change, sociological critiques of inequality, and contemporary developments in educational technology, we aim to offer a comprehensive framework for understanding the implications of AI for teacher development in both local and global contexts.

## 2. THEORETICAL FRAMEWORK

Understanding the integration of AI in teacher development through a sociological lens requires robust theoretical grounding. This section explores key sociological theories—Bourdieu's Theory of Practice, Foucault's Power/Knowledge, and Critical Theory—to frame the analysis of how equity, identity, agency, and institutional culture are shaped and reshaped in AI-enhanced educational contexts.

### 2.1 Bourdieu's Theory of Practice

Pierre Bourdieu's framework, particularly the interrelation of habitus, field, and capital, provides a foundational lens to analyze how AI technologies influence teacher development. *Habitus* refers to the dispositions and internalized norms teachers acquire through socialization, shaping how they respond to AI tools and reforms. *Field* represents the structured space of educational institutions where power relations and professional hierarchies are enacted. *Capital*—be it cultural, social, or technological—serves as a resource that determines one's positioning within this field.

For instance, teachers with high digital capital may more readily integrate AI tools, while others—particularly from underserved communities—might face exclusion from professional advancement (Ayeni et al., 2024; Kalashnikova et al., 2025). The field of teacher education is itself undergoing reconfiguration as AI reshapes what is valued, who holds expertise, and how professional identities are cultivated (Lan, 2024; Grab, 2025).

## 2.2 Foucault's Power/Knowledge

Michel Foucault's concept of power/knowledge reveals how AI is not merely a neutral set of tools but part of a broader apparatus of control, categorization, and normalization. AI systems produce and reproduce certain knowledge regimes, privileging efficiency, datafication, and quantifiable outcomes, often at the expense of context-specific pedagogical judgment (Pedro et al., 2019; Jin et al., 2024).

AI-infused systems in education—such as predictive analytics or behavior-monitoring algorithms—can subtly shift authority from teachers to machines, embedding surveillance logics into institutional life (Halmo, 2025; Padua, 2025). These dynamics reflect broader struggles over epistemic power and raise critical questions about who defines "good teaching" and "effective development" in AI-mediated contexts (Monahan et al., 2024; Peer Mohamed, 2024).

## 2.3 Critical Theory and Structuration

Critical Theory offers tools to interrogate how technological innovations may entrench or disrupt existing social inequities. In the context of AI and education, this approach compels us to ask: who benefits, who is excluded, and what systemic biases are embedded in algorithmic logic? As Casad et al. (2021) and Kohli et al. (2021) argue, AI risks amplifying gendered and racialized inequities unless development is grounded in justice-oriented frameworks.

Structuration Theory, particularly as developed by Anthony Giddens, is also relevant, emphasizing the recursive relationship between human agency and institutional structures. Teachers are not passive recipients of AI; they actively negotiate, resist, or co-create the norms surrounding its use. This tension between agency and structure is evident in how educators adopt, adapt, or challenge AI-driven reforms (Palmer et al., 2016; Quan et al., 2019; Moradi-Kelayeh, 2025).

## 2.4 Defining Key Concepts

### 2.4.1 Equity

In this context, *equity* refers to fair and just access to opportunities, resources, and support for all educators, regardless of their background. Equity-focused AI implementation recognizes disparities in access to technology, training, and influence within institutional cultures (Sullivan et al., 2015; Murtiningsih & Sujito, 2024; Mac Fadden et al., 2024). Grab (2025) emphasizes that culturally responsive AI must actively counteract digital divides and support marginalized voices in higher education.

### 2.4.2 Identity

*Professional identity* is shaped through interactions between individuals and their institutional and sociocultural environments. AI alters how identity is performed and perceived, introducing new tensions between traditional roles and data-driven responsibilities (Lan, 2024; Rajesh, 2024). Identity formation also intersects with broader questions of gender, race, and power, especially in relation to STEM fields and underrepresented groups (Casad et al., 2021; Brennan & Canny, 2023).

### 2.4.3 Agency

*Agency* refers to the capacity of educators to act independently, make choices, and influence their environments. AI technologies may either constrain or enhance agency, depending on how they are deployed and who controls their use (Blackmore, 2013; Monahan et al., 2024). Educators' epistemic agency is especially critical when confronting systems that embed normative assumptions about what constitutes effective teaching or successful outcomes (Steinert, 2025; Mishra et al., 2024).

## 2.5 Institutional Culture

*Institutional culture* encompasses the norms, values, and practices that define organizational life. As AI becomes embedded in education systems, it transforms not only pedagogy but also professional development, governance, and leadership models (Museus & Jayakumar, 2012; Liu, 2025). Institutional resistance or openness to AI often reflects deeper cultural values around hierarchy, innovation, and knowledge production (Shani et al., 2025; Stouten et al., 2018; Benn et al., 2014).

In sum, these sociological theories and conceptual tools provide a framework for critically assessing the implications of AI integration in teacher development. They highlight the need to view AI not simply as a technical innovation but as a cultural and political force embedded in institutional structures and social relations. Future sections of this chapter will apply these frameworks to explore specific domains of equity, identity negotiation, and organizational transformation in educational systems.

## 3. AI AND TEACHER IDENTITY

Artificial Intelligence (AI) is reshaping not only the pedagogical tools teachers use but also how they perceive themselves and are perceived within educational systems. Teacher identity—traditionally grounded in relational, instructional, and moral dimensions—is increasingly influenced by AI-driven expectations for efficiency, data interpretation, and technological fluency (Lan, 2024; Mishra, Oster, & Henriksen, 2024). This section explores how the integration of AI into teacher development affects professional identity, especially in relation to equity, power, and institutional transformation.

### 3.1 Reconfiguring the Teacher's Role

AI alters the landscape of teaching by shifting traditional roles from knowledge delivery to technology-facilitated mentorship, data analysis, and adaptive instruction. With the rise of intelligent tutoring systems and predictive analytics, teachers are expected to interpret real-time data and modify their strategies accordingly (Ayeni et al., 2024; Jin, Goyal, & Rajawat, 2024). As a result, the boundaries between pedagogy and technology management are increasingly blurred, challenging teachers' professional self-understanding and requiring new forms of identity negotiation (Halmo, 2025; Moradi-Kelayeh, 2025).

However, this transformation is not evenly experienced. Teachers from different backgrounds, disciplines, or institutional types encounter varying degrees of support, autonomy, and inclusion. As Blackmore (2013) argues from a feminist critical perspective, structural inequalities—particularly related to gender and power—may be reinforced rather than disrupted by technological reforms. Casad et al. (2021) further show that female educators in STEM, for instance, often face underrepresentation and marginalization in AI-centric environments, complicating the narrative of universal progress through technology.

## 3.2 Tensions Between Humanism and Algorithmic Norms

The incorporation of AI into educational decision-making introduces tensions between the humanistic values that traditionally guide teacher identity—such as empathy, ethical reflection, and relational care—and the algorithmic logics of optimization, efficiency, and standardization. This dichotomy raises important ethical and pedagogical questions: What happens to a teacher's sense of agency when recommendations from AI systems override professional judgment? How do data-driven evaluations reshape self-perceptions of teaching effectiveness?

Peer Mohamed (2024) and Monahan, MacCormac, and Minogue (2024) emphasize the epistemic risks associated with AI-enhanced environments, especially when implicit biases embedded in algorithms go unchallenged. These technologies may inadvertently marginalize teachers whose values or pedagogical practices do not align with dominant digital norms. Padua (2025) highlights the need for cultivating a *digital culture* that centers human values and critical awareness in teacher development, rather than uncritically adopting technological solutions.

## 3.3 Intersectionality and Identity Formation

Teacher identity is shaped at the intersection of race, class, gender, and institutional positioning. Kohli et al. (2021) and Ray (2019) underscore the need to understand how AI interacts with the racialized and gendered structures of educational institutions. Teachers of color, for instance, may experience dual pressures: navigating underrepresentation in digital reform initiatives while being positioned as "change agents" for culturally responsive teaching (Grab, 2025; Rajesh, 2024).

Such intersectional dynamics require educational institutions to go beyond surface-level equity claims and invest in meaningful, context-aware faculty development (Steinert, 2025; Museus & Jayakumar, 2012). Murtiningsih and Sujito (2024) advocate for inclusive pedagogies that address intergenerational and sociotechnical justice, enabling teachers to engage with AI in ways that affirm rather than erase their identities.

## 3.4 Agency and Resistance in AI Integration

Despite structural constraints, teachers are not passive recipients of AI. Instead, they exercise professional agency by critically engaging with, resisting, or adapting technologies to align with their values and pedagogical goals (Lan, 2024; Quan et al., 2019). Mishra et al. (2024) suggest that AI's integration presents both short-term adaptations and long-term shifts in what counts as legitimate teacher knowledge and expertise.

Institutional support for such agency is crucial. Palmer, Dunford, and Buchanan (2016) and Battilana and Casciaro (2012) emphasize the importance of organizational structures that empower change agents within complex systems. Without systemic alignment between values, policies, and technologies, teachers' identities can become fragmented, particularly when institutional mandates are in conflict with educators' epistemologies and lived experiences (Liu, 2025; Sullivan, Artiles, & Hernandez-Saca, 2015).

## 3.5 Sociological Implications of Identity Shifts

From a sociological perspective, the ongoing transformation of teacher identity through AI is embedded in broader questions about cultural capital, organizational norms, and institutional change. Brennan and Canny (2023) raise concerns about student-teachers' disengagement from the sociology of education, warning that critical awareness is diminishing in favor of technocratic compliance. Kalashnikova et al. (2025) argue for the integration of sociological tools and digital competence in professional training, ensuring that future educators are equipped to question, not just implement, AI systems.

These identity shifts are not isolated; they reflect deeper sociotechnical processes and organizational cultures that influence how change unfolds (Stouten, Rousseau, & De Cremer, 2018; Benn, Edwards, & Williams, 2014). Shani et al. (2025) note that successful innovation in teacher development depends on aligning cultural narratives, leadership practices, and inclusive participation strategies.

## 3.6 Summary

The integration of AI into teacher development is reconfiguring how educators define themselves, relate to their institutions, and engage with their students. While AI offers new opportunities for personalization and growth, it also introduces challenges to teacher identity, autonomy, and equity. To navigate this evolving landscape, it is essential to cultivate spaces for critical reflection, foster inclusive institutional cultures, and prioritize teacher agency in the face of algorithmic change.

The following conceptual diagram summarizes the key forces influencing teacher identity in AI-enhanced environments. It illustrates the dynamic interplay among sociotechnical systems, institutional power, and intersectional identity formation—highlighting how AI mediates roles, agency, and professional values.

*Figure 1. Framework for AI's Sociological Impact on Teacher Identity*

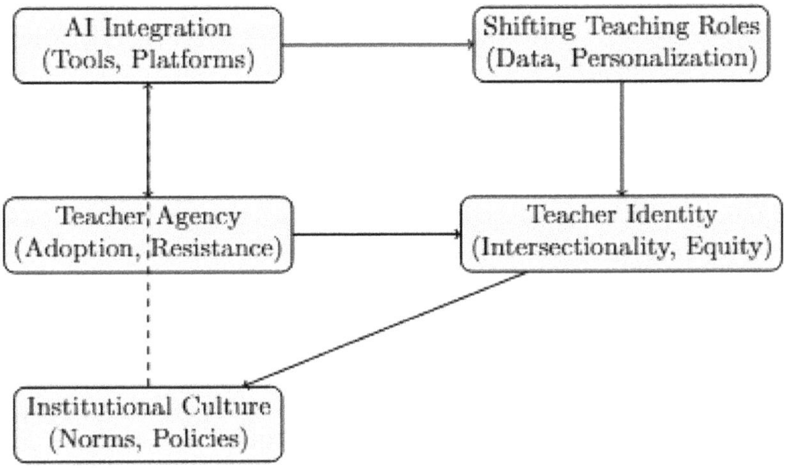


## 4. EQUITY AND ACCESS

The integration of Artificial Intelligence (AI) into education promises a revolution in how teachers are supported, evaluated, and developed. However, without an intentional and critical approach, AI may exacerbate rather than alleviate pre-existing inequalities in educational systems. Equity and access in AI-enhanced teacher development must be understood through multiple sociological lenses—highlighting how systemic privilege, structural bias, and institutional cultures intersect with technological design and deployment.

### 4.1 Digital Divides and the Unequal Landscape of AI Access

The promise of AI as a personalized and scalable tool for teacher development often obscures stark inequalities in access to the required infrastructure, digital literacy, and institutional support. As Ayeni et al. (2024) observe, the benefits of AI are disproportionately experienced by those in well-resourced schools and higher education institutions, leaving teachers in underfunded or rural contexts at a systemic disadvantage. Mac Fadden, García-Alonso, and López Meneses (2024) reinforce this concern, showing that AI adoption in education follows existing digital inequality patterns, with marginalized populations often excluded from meaningful engagement.

This technological stratification reflects broader organizational inequalities. As Blackmore (2013) and Liu (2025) note, issues of race, gender, and class are deeply embedded in educational structures and shape how change is enacted. Schools serving historically marginalized communities may lack the political and economic capital to acquire or maintain cutting-edge AI systems. Even when access is achieved, the lack of culturally responsive design may render such tools ineffective or alienating for teachers of color and linguistically diverse educators (Kohli et al., 2021; Grab, 2025).

## 4.2 Bias in Algorithms and Structural Inequity

Beyond questions of access lies a deeper issue: the risk that AI systems encode and perpetuate existing structural biases. Algorithms trained on biased datasets can reproduce racial, gendered, and class-based disparities in educational evaluations, teacher feedback, and professional development recommendations. Ray's (2019) theory of racialized organizations provides a framework for understanding how institutions—despite appearing neutral—embed racialized assumptions that are now being operationalized in digital systems.

Casad et al. (2021) offer evidence from STEM fields that women and minoritized faculty are systematically undervalued by performance metrics, a trend that AI could automate at scale. Peer Mohamed (2024) warns that without clear ethical oversight, AI may amplify implicit biases, especially in language-based learning environments. Monahan, MacCormac, and Minogue (2024) similarly highlight the epistemic risks of opaque algorithms, urging that bias mitigation strategies be embedded within AI development and implementation.

## 4.3 Access to Data, Voice, and Decision-Making

Equity also concerns **who gets to shape AI systems** and whether educators have a voice in their development, deployment, and refinement. Mishra, Oster, and Henriksen (2024) argue that teachers' knowledge must inform the design of AI tools to ensure alignment with classroom realities. However, teachers often remain on the periphery of AI innovation, particularly those from historically excluded backgrounds. Kohli et al. (2021) emphasize the importance of "critical professional development" that positions teachers as leaders in equity-focused, tech-enhanced environments.

Organizational culture plays a crucial role here. Museus and Jayakumar (2012) stress that inclusive campus cultures must enable teachers—especially from minoritized groups—to participate meaningfully in technology governance. Without this, AI adoption becomes a top-down process, reinforcing feelings of disempowerment and exclusion. Brennan and Canny (2023) show that even student-teachers disengage from critical sociological reflection when the institutional emphasis is solely on compliance and efficiency, which AI systems can unwittingly reinforce.

## 4.4 Institutional and Organizational Enablers of Equity

Addressing these inequities requires more than technical fixes; it demands organizational transformation. Palmer, Dunford, and Buchanan (2016) and Battilana and Casciaro (2012) argue that structural change depends on cultivating networks of change agents within institutions. Faculty development programs—when inclusive and participatory—can foster awareness, equity, and resilience in AI transitions (Steinert, 2025). Halmo (2025) demonstrates that human-centered academic advising models can use AI to support equity, but only when embedded in intentional organizational reform.

Stouten, Rousseau, and De Cremer (2018) further stress that successful change must integrate both management practice and scholarly insights. Murtiningsih and Sujito (2024) add a critical lens by calling for intergenerational justice, suggesting that equity is not only about present-day access but about ensuring sustainable and inclusive systems for future teachers.

Rajesh (2024) takes this even further by critiquing how dominant AI discourses erase identities that do not conform to normative scripts. Equity in AI-enhanced teacher development therefore must include cultural recognition and validation of diverse ways of knowing, teaching, and being.

## 4.5 Designing for Inclusive Participation

The design of AI tools must incorporate the needs and experiences of all educators, especially those who have been traditionally marginalized. Kalashnikova et al. (2025) advocate for integrating ICT competencies in teacher education with sociological awareness to ensure meaningful participation in digital transitions. Padua (2025) calls for cultivating a digital culture grounded in justice, participation, and pedagogical agency.

Pedro et al. (2019) caution that the promise of AI for sustainable development will only be realized if inclusion and equity are made explicit in policy and practice. Sá and Serpa (2020) view the COVID-19 pandemic as a potential turning point—an opportunity to reimagine education through digital equity and sustainable practice.

Finally, Benn, Edwards, and Williams (2014) emphasize that sustainable change requires not just technology but new ways of thinking about leadership, culture, and systemic inclusion. This involves creating institutional ecosystems that are adaptive, participatory, and justice-oriented—traits essential for equitable AI integration in teacher development.

## 4.6 Summary

Equity and access in AI-mediated teacher development go far beyond distributing tools or installing infrastructure. They demand a structural, ethical, and cultural reckoning with the values, norms, and biases embedded within educational institutions and technological systems. Only by centering marginalized voices, confronting systemic inequality, and designing inclusive and participatory AI systems can education live up to the transformative potential of artificial intelligence.

To visualize the complexity of equitable AI adoption in education, the following diagram maps three key dimensions—Access, Representation, and Participation—alongside structural enablers and constraints. It demonstrates how equity challenges transcend technical infrastructure and extend into design, leadership, and voice.

*Figure 2. Dimensions of Equity in AI-Mediated Teacher Development*

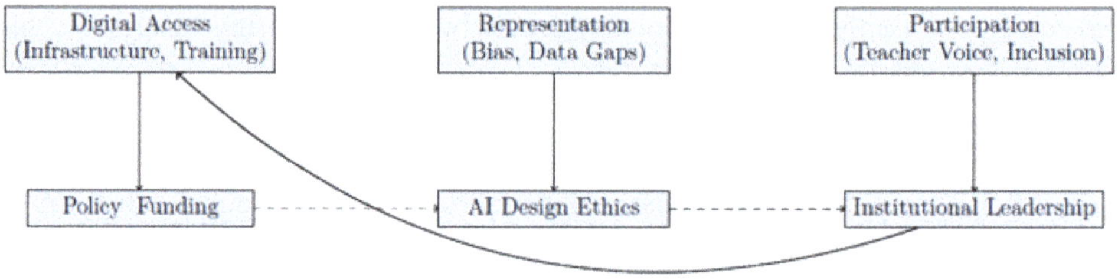


# 5. INSTITUTIONAL AND CULTURAL CHANGE

The integration of artificial intelligence (AI) in teacher development demands more than technological adoption; it requires a fundamental shift in institutional cultures, leadership ideologies, and organizational practices. AI disrupts traditional educational norms by introducing new frameworks of authority, expertise, and decision-making. As educational systems incorporate AI to enhance teacher evaluation, development, and support, questions surrounding institutional resistance, cultural adaptation, and sustainable change become increasingly critical.

## 5.1 Institutional Cultures and the Sociotechnical Paradigm Shift

Educational institutions are embedded within complex cultural ecosystems that shape how technological innovations are received and implemented. Padua (2025) emphasizes that successful AI integration depends not only on technological readiness but also on cultivating a digital culture rooted in pedagogical values and social justice. Similarly, Sá and Serpa (2020) argue that crises such as the COVID-19 pandemic offer opportunities for higher education institutions to reimagine teaching through more flexible, sustainable, and inclusive models.

The incorporation of AI technologies into teacher development challenges the dominant institutional logics that have historically privileged human judgment, seniority-based leadership, and bureaucratic hierarchies. According to Pedro, Subosa, Rivas, and Valverde (2019), the tension between traditional educational structures and emerging digital logics can create organizational inertia unless aligned with strategic change management practices.

Stouten, Rousseau, and De Cremer (2018) suggest that successful organizational change hinges on integrating scholarly insights with management practices that address resistance, enable participation, and foster shared vision. This includes rethinking leadership structures, performance incentives, and professional development programs to accommodate the fluidity and complexity of AI-enhanced teaching.

## 5.2 The Role of Organizational Change Agents

Change agents play a vital role in bridging the gap between innovation and institutional adaptation. Battilana and Casciaro (2012) present a contingency theory of organizational change in which the success of change agents depends on the nature of their social networks and their strategic positioning within power structures. In the context of AI integration, educators, technology specialists, and institutional leaders must collaborate to reshape organizational norms and narratives.

Halmo (2025) documents how predictive analytics in academic advising can facilitate personalized student support, but only when organizational conditions—such as inclusive leadership and data literacy—are met. Similarly, Lan (2024) highlights the tensions teachers face in reconciling their professional identities with AI-enhanced training environments. These tensions require institutional mechanisms that validate teacher agency and cultivate a culture of continuous, critical learning.

Benn, Edwards, and Williams (2014) stress that sustainable organizational change requires shared ownership of goals, long-term vision, and the embedding of values such as equity, transparency, and inclusion. The presence of change agents who can model and scaffold these transformations is crucial in building institutional capacity for innovation.

## 5.3 Leadership, Equity, and Institutional Power

Institutional change is deeply intertwined with questions of power, representation, and justice. Blackmore (2013) draws from feminist critical theory to critique how leadership discourses often marginalize women and racialized educators, particularly in technology-focused reforms. Casad et al. (2021) further highlight how academic institutions frequently reinforce gender inequality, with AI-based performance metrics potentially perpetuating these inequities unless they are deliberately audited for bias.

Kohli et al. (2021) propose that leadership for racial justice must be embedded within professional development programs that empower teachers of color as change agents. In AI-enabled environments, this means designing systems that not only recognize but center diverse perspectives in policy, design, and implementation.

Museus and Jayakumar (2012) argue for cultivating inclusive campus cultures where all educators feel empowered to contribute to institutional innovation. This cultural shift involves challenging dominant ideologies, transforming hiring practices, and ensuring equitable access to leadership pipelines in both digital and organizational domains.

## 5.4 Cultural Resistance and Epistemic Agency

Resistance to institutional change is often rooted in cultural concerns about autonomy, values, and trust. Monahan, MacCormac, and Minogue (2024) stress the importance of fostering epistemic agency, wherein educators are positioned as active agents in shaping AI systems, rather than passive implementers. Their findings show that when teachers are given opportunities to question and co-design AI tools, resistance diminishes and ownership increases.

Brennan and Canny (2023) also reveal that teacher candidates may disengage from critical sociological thinking when institutional norms favor conformity over inquiry. Therefore, fostering a reflective institutional culture—where questioning is normalized and sociological perspectives are valued—is essential for cultural transformation.

Mishra, Oster, and Henriksen (2024) call for a shift in educational research to bridge short- and long-term views on teacher development in the age of generative AI. They argue that institutions must create environments that balance rapid technological shifts with the enduring values of pedagogical reflection, ethical engagement, and inclusivity.

## 5.5 Towards a Participatory Institutional Ethos

Cultural change in institutions involves redefining who gets to participate in conversations about educational reform. Kalashnikova et al. (2025) emphasize the importance of equipping future educators with both digital competencies and sociological literacy to engage critically with AI-driven systems. Grab (2025) further demonstrates that AI can enhance culturally responsive teaching—but only when institutional contexts support reflection, dialogue, and co-creation.

Institutional change also requires a reevaluation of success metrics. Traditional indicators of teacher performance, often tied to standardized outcomes, must evolve to incorporate values such as collaboration, innovation, and equity (Ayeni et al., 2024). Institutions must foster spaces for experimentation and learning, recognizing that cultural transformation is non-linear, relational, and context-dependent (Palmer, Dunford, & Buchanan, 2016).

Rajesh (2024) contends that true transformation in AI education lies "beyond identities"—in challenging essentialist assumptions and allowing for fluid, intersectional engagements with knowledge and selfhood. Institutional change, therefore, must be epistemologically pluralistic, culturally inclusive, and ethically grounded.

## 5.6 Summary

Institutional and cultural change in the era of AI is not simply about adopting new tools—it is about reimagining the values, relationships, and structures that shape teacher development. By empowering change agents, fostering inclusive leadership, and cultivating cultures of reflection and participation, educational institutions can harness AI not as a force of disruption, but as a catalyst for justice-oriented transformation.

# 6. ETHICAL AND SOCIAL IMPLICATIONS

The integration of artificial intelligence (AI) into teacher development offers transformative potential, but it also presents a constellation of ethical and social implications that must be critically examined. From concerns about surveillance and algorithmic bias to issues of teacher agency and social justice, AI-driven initiatives risk reproducing and amplifying existing educational inequalities if implemented without ethical foresight and sociological reflection. This section explores the moral tensions, systemic risks, and responsibilities associated with AI in teacher development through the lens of educational ethics, social theory, and organizational change.

## 6.1 Bias, Transparency, and Algorithmic Ethics

One of the most pressing ethical concerns is the potential for AI systems to encode and perpetuate systemic biases. As AI tools rely on historical data and opaque algorithms, they risk reproducing racial, gendered, and class-based disparities that are already entrenched in education systems. Ray (2019) highlights how racialized organizational structures frame decision-making processes, and these same structures are embedded in the datasets used to train AI models. Without intentional design and oversight, AI may further marginalize underrepresented teachers through biased feedback, evaluation, or support systems.

Peer Mohamed (2024) underscores the ethical risks of using AI in language education, where cultural assumptions, linguistic norms, and implicit power dynamics may be embedded in automated learning environments. Similarly, Monahan, MacCormac, and Minogue (2024) argue that mitigating bias requires cultivating "epistemic agency"—ensuring that educators are active participants in critiquing and shaping the technologies they are expected to use.

Casad et al. (2021) warn that gender disparities, particularly in STEM and academic evaluation, can be exacerbated by AI-driven decision-making unless there is transparency in how algorithms assess performance and potential. AI systems must therefore be subjected to rigorous auditing and ethical scrutiny, especially when they are used to make high-stakes decisions about teacher performance or professional growth.

## 6.2 Surveillance, Autonomy, and Professional Integrity

AI systems are often employed to monitor teaching practices, classroom engagement, and even emotional expressions of educators and learners. While these applications may offer data for continuous improvement, they also raise ethical concerns regarding autonomy, consent, and surveillance. Moradi-Kelayeh (2025) describes how teachers increasingly navigate digital environments that track and evaluate their interactions, sometimes without clear communication or the opportunity to challenge findings.

Jin, Goyal, and Rajawat (2024) caution that AI's informational power must be used to enhance, not replace, human judgment in educational settings. Ethical integration requires that teacher data be treated with dignity and confidentiality and that educators retain agency over how their data is used. Mishra, Oster, and Henriksen (2024) advocate for balancing short-term technological gains with long-term ethical considerations that support human-centered professional growth.

The tension between innovation and autonomy is particularly salient in organizational contexts where institutional expectations may conflict with professional values. Blackmore (2013) explores how feminist perspectives on leadership highlight the emotional labor and relational ethics often overlooked in data-driven systems. When AI prioritizes efficiency over empathy, it risks dehumanizing the teacher's role and undervaluing contextual, affective, and relational dimensions of education.

## 6.3 Social Justice and Inclusive Design

AI implementation must address the broader sociocultural and political context of teacher development. Kohli et al. (2021) emphasize that racial justice must be central to any professional development model—especially in AI-mediated environments—by designing systems that uplift the voices and needs of teachers of color. Brennan and Canny (2023) reinforce this by noting that sociology's role in teacher education should not be marginalized, particularly when social dynamics are embedded in technological design.

Grab (2025) shows how AI can support culturally responsive teaching when designed in partnership with educators and grounded in equity frameworks. However, this potential is undermined if AI tools are created without critical pedagogical input. Inclusive design also involves acknowledging intersectional barriers faced by educators, as discussed by Rajesh (2024), who critiques how AI systems often erase the nuanced identities of those at the margins.

Liu (2025) adds that leadership must actively confront the sociological dynamics of inequality in schools to ensure that AI does not further segregate access to resources, opportunities, or support. Equity-oriented AI must be intentionally crafted and contextually deployed within organizational cultures that value diversity, justice, and belonging.

## 6.4 Responsibility, Policy, and Organizational Ethics

Institutions bear a significant responsibility in guiding ethical AI adoption. Benn, Edwards, and Williams (2014) argue that ethical organizational change requires sustainability, transparency, and accountability. This is echoed by Pedro et al. (2019), who contend that AI in education must be aligned with the UN's Sustainable Development Goals to ensure that technological innovation contributes to broader societal well-being.

Steinert (2025) suggests that faculty development programs can serve as ethical training grounds for AI literacy and critical engagement. Yet for such programs to be effective, they must be embedded in institutional cultures that prioritize reflexivity, inclusivity, and collaborative leadership (Museus & Jayakumar, 2012; Palmer, Dunford, & Buchanan, 2016).

The role of change agents is also critical. Battilana and Casciaro (2012) stress that transformative change requires individuals and networks who can challenge dominant logics and advocate for ethical alternatives. Halmo (2025) illustrates how predictive analytics can be implemented ethically through participatory leadership and human-centered design principles.

Furthermore, Shani, Noumair, Zandee, and Coghlan (2025) assert that ethical organizational development is iterative and must evolve with constant feedback from diverse stakeholders. This approach aligns with Stouten, Rousseau, and De Cremer's (2018) call to integrate scholarly and practical knowledge to ensure AI's ethical alignment with organizational goals.

## 6.5 Ethics of Access and Global Implications

Access to AI tools is itself an ethical concern. Ayeni et al. (2024) reveal how disparities in infrastructure, funding, and digital skills create uneven landscapes of AI adoption. Kalashnikova et al. (2025) argue that digital training must be paired with sociological sensitivity to ensure all educators can engage meaningfully with AI. Without addressing such inequities, AI risks becoming a vehicle for further stratification.

Sullivan, Artiles, and Hernandez-Saca (2015) point out that systemic educational inequities, including those in special education, demand structural interventions—not just technological fixes. SWARGIARY (2025) emphasizes that sociological education must train future teachers to navigate these complexities, including the ethical tensions that arise in AI-mediated teaching environments.

Finally, Murtiningsih and Sujito (2024) highlight the need for intergenerational justice in the ethical evaluation of AI: how today's technological decisions shape the future of equitable and inclusive pedagogy. Institutions must weigh not only immediate benefits but also the long-term social consequences of AI adoption in teacher development.

## 6.6 Summary

AI's integration into teacher development is not ethically neutral. It reconfigures relationships of power, knowledge, and responsibility across institutional, cultural, and social contexts. Addressing its ethical and social implications requires a comprehensive framework rooted in justice, transparency, inclusivity, and human dignity. Only through deliberate design, participatory governance, and sustained ethical reflection can AI serve as a tool for equity rather than oppression in educational systems.

The cyclical diagram below outlines the ethical governance model proposed in this chapter. It integrates data transparency, teacher voice, inclusive design, and bias auditing as recurring stages in responsible AI implementation within teacher development systems.

*Figure 3. Ethical Governance Cycle for AI in Teacher Development*

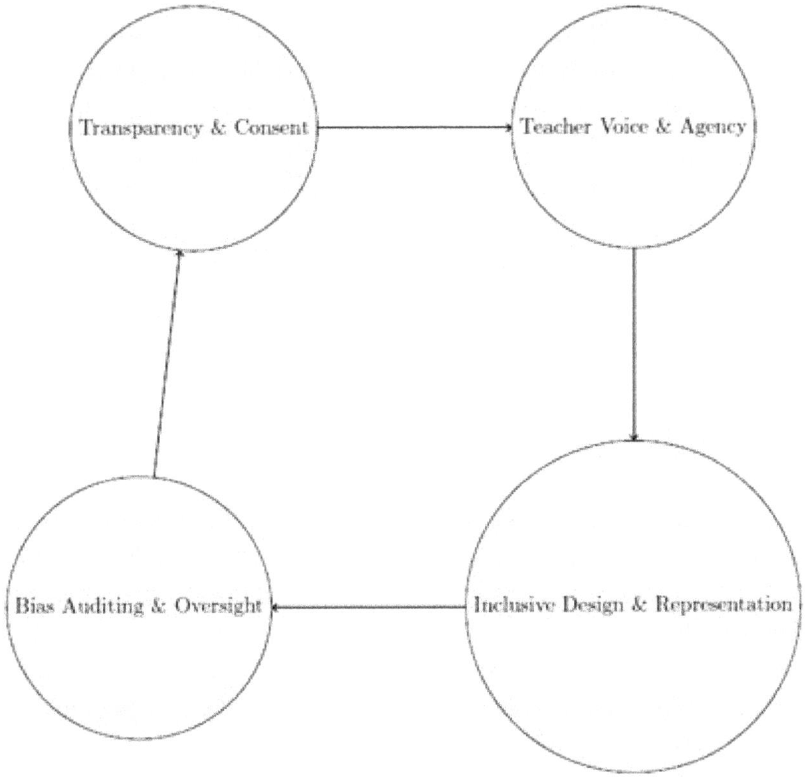


## 7. POLICY AND PRACTICE RECOMMENDATIONS

The sociological analysis of AI integration into teacher development underscores the need for forward-looking, equitable, and ethically grounded policies. As AI becomes increasingly embedded in educational systems, policymakers, educational leaders, and institutions must align their practices with principles of justice, inclusivity, and sustainability. Drawing upon organizational change theory, digital equity literature, and critical pedagogy, this section outlines actionable recommendations that address the institutional, pedagogical, and sociocultural dimensions of AI-enhanced teacher development.

## 7.1. Establish Equity-Centered AI Policies in Education

Policymakers must prioritize digital equity and inclusion by ensuring that AI tools are accessible and responsive to the needs of diverse teacher populations. Mac Fadden, García-Alonso, and López Meneses (2024) emphasize that sociologically informed policy should address digital divides, including disparities in infrastructure, skills, and representation. Similarly, Ayeni et al. (2024) highlight that AI-driven personalization must not be implemented at the cost of reinforcing socioeconomic stratification.

In response, governments and institutions should create national frameworks for AI in education that embed equity assessments and cultural responsiveness as key evaluation metrics (Grab, 2025; Kohli et al., 2021). AI systems should be audited for bias and re-trained regularly to reflect shifting demographic and pedagogical realities (Peer Mohamed, 2024; Ray, 2019).

## 7.2. Advance Ethical Governance and Transparency in Educational AI

Transparent data governance and ethical oversight mechanisms must accompany the deployment of AI technologies in teacher development. Padua (2025) argues for the establishment of a "digital culture of accountability" where educators are informed and empowered to understand how their data is used. Institutions should publish AI use policies, require informed consent, and provide opt-out mechanisms.

Organizational leaders, as outlined by Benn, Edwards, and Williams (2014), must ensure that AI is used not only for efficiency but also to uphold the ethical responsibilities of education as a public good. Institutional policies should draw from organizational development frameworks (Stouten, Rousseau, & De Cremer, 2018; Shani et al., 2025) that balance innovation with inclusivity, reflexivity, and transparency.

## 7.3. Cultivate Teacher Agency and Professional Identity

Educational policies should foster environments in which teachers can engage critically and constructively with AI technologies. Lan (2024) demonstrates how teacher identity evolves in response to AI-enhanced professional development; thus, training programs should include critical AI literacy that helps educators shape—not just use—emerging technologies.

Faculty development models should be reimagined to promote participatory learning, interdisciplinary dialogue, and identity-affirming practices (Steinert, 2025; Quan et al., 2019). Policies must also empower teachers of color, women, and those in marginalized communities by acknowledging intersectional challenges in AI-mediated environments (Casad et al., 2021; Blackmore, 2013).

### 7.4. Promote Interdisciplinary and Sociological Integration in Training

Incorporating sociological perspectives into teacher training is essential to navigating the social impacts of AI. Brennan and Canny (2023) critique the marginalization of sociology in initial teacher education programs. To rectify this, teacher education curricula should explicitly integrate sociology of education, AI ethics, and critical pedagogy.

Training modules must reflect the complexity of organizational change (Palmer, Dunford, & Buchanan, 2016), especially where AI intersects with institutional culture. As Museus and Jayakumar (2012) suggest, cultivating inclusive campus cultures requires aligning professional development with institutional missions of justice and transformation.

### 7.5. Institutionalize Culturally Responsive AI Practices

At the school and university level, institutions must design AI-supported systems that reflect local cultural, linguistic, and pedagogical realities. Murtiningsih and Sujito (2024) argue that future-ready education must be grounded in inclusive pedagogies and intergenerational justice. AI tools should therefore be customizable to accommodate regional values, indigenous knowledge systems, and diverse epistemologies (Rajesh, 2024).

Institutions should consult with diverse teacher groups, community leaders, and sociologists during AI implementation to ensure relevance and responsiveness. Kalashnikova et al. (2025) emphasize the value of including sociological expertise in digital training programs to close cultural gaps and avoid standardization pitfalls.

## 7.6. Embed AI Ethics into Leadership and Organizational Change Models

Educational leaders must model ethical engagement with AI and support structural changes that promote fair access and responsible use. Battilana and Casciaro (2012) emphasize the importance of change agents in institutional transformation. Leadership development programs should include components on AI ethics, organizational justice, and social impact assessments.

Halmo (2025) demonstrates that academic advising systems using predictive analytics can succeed only when they are supported by collaborative, human-centered organizational strategies. This reinforces the findings of Liu (2025), who illustrates how equitable leadership practices shape school success under technological transition.

## 7.7. Encourage Research-Practice Partnerships for AI Innovation

Ongoing research-practice partnerships are essential to inform evidence-based policies that evolve with AI technologies. Mishra, Oster, and Henriksen (2024) advocate for bridging short-term AI applications with long-term educational research. Public-private collaborations should include not only tech developers and policymakers but also sociologists, educators, and critical theorists.

Pedro et al. (2019) recommend that national education plans treat AI as a driver of sustainable development, aligning technological innovation with broader social goals. Policies should fund community-driven innovation hubs and cross-sectoral research that centers teachers as co-creators of AI tools (Moradi-Kelayeh, 2025).

## 7.8. Redesign Evaluation Systems for AI-Enhanced Pedagogy

Traditional models of teacher evaluation are inadequate for AI-enhanced learning environments. Jin, Goyal, and Rajawat (2024) argue that AI reshapes the informational landscape of higher education, demanding new metrics for performance, engagement, and effectiveness. Evaluation policies must evolve to consider collaborative learning, emotional intelligence, digital competence, and cultural relevance.

Sullivan, Artiles, and Hernandez-Saca (2015) further suggest that systemic inequities in evaluation can be addressed through ecologically grounded, multilevel policy reforms. AI must be positioned not as a neutral observer but as a socially embedded actor in teacher appraisal processes.

## 7.9. Institutionalize Reflexivity and Bias Mitigation in AI Design

AI deployment must be accompanied by institutional practices that continually examine and mitigate implicit biases. Monahan, MacCormac, and Minogue (2024) call for strategies that empower educators to identify, critique, and resist algorithmic assumptions. Schools and universities should require bias testing, inclusive design standards, and stakeholder feedback loops in AI procurement and development.

Such reflexivity also aligns with the sociological imperative to view AI not as a static tool, but as part of broader organizational and cultural ecosystems (SWARGIARY, 2025). Embedding continuous evaluation and user-led design processes can help institutions adapt to evolving ethical and pedagogical challenges.

## 7.10 Summary

Policy and practice must move beyond technical efficiency to confront the sociological and ethical realities of AI integration in teacher development. Grounded in equity, inclusion, and critical reflection, these recommendations aim to foster a future where AI serves as a transformative ally rather than a disruptive force. Implementing such changes demands cross-disciplinary collaboration, sustained investment in teacher voice and identity, and a shared commitment to educational justice.

# 8. CONCLUSION

As artificial intelligence increasingly permeates educational systems, its integration into teacher development presents a profound opportunity—and challenge—for institutional transformation. Through a sociological lens, this chapter has explored how AI is reshaping teacher identity, equity, and institutional practices. Rather than viewing AI solely as a technological advancement, it must be recognized as a socially embedded force that both reflects and reconfigures existing power dynamics, professional norms, and cultural values.

The interplay between teacher identity and AI-enhanced learning environments demands more than technical adaptation. As Lan (2024) and Grab (2025) argue, teacher development must consider the tensions, motivations, and aspirations that arise when educators engage with emerging technologies. AI's capacity to personalize learning, enhance feedback, and analyze pedagogical patterns is significant, yet it must not overshadow the human-centered and context-specific nature of teaching (Ayeni et al., 2024; Mishra et al., 2024).

Ethically, the deployment of AI in professional development necessitates critical interrogation of bias, surveillance, and consent. As highlighted by Peer Mohamed (2024) and Monahan et al. (2024), educators require the skills and institutional support to engage with AI ethically, responsibly, and reflectively. Equity must not be a peripheral goal but a central pillar—addressing systemic inequalities, digital access, and culturally responsive pedagogies (Kohli et al., 2021; Casad et al., 2021).

Institutionally, successful integration of AI in teacher development will depend on robust leadership, inclusive governance, and sustainable organizational change models (Battilana & Casciaro, 2012; Palmer et al., 2016; Benn et al., 2014). Policies and practices must prioritize reflexivity, cultural sensitivity, and the co-construction of knowledge with teachers as active participants in shaping the future of AI in education (Mac Fadden et al., 2024; Museus & Jayakumar, 2012).

Furthermore, sociological engagement should not be treated as an afterthought but as a critical foundation for designing, evaluating, and scaling AI systems in teacher education. As SWARGIARY (2025) emphasizes, educational sociology provides essential tools for examining how institutions, identities, and inequalities intersect with technological change. Embedding this perspective across teacher training programs and policy initiatives is vital to ensuring that AI contributes to—not detracts from—the goals of justice, empowerment, and inclusive learning.

Ultimately, the promise of AI in teacher development lies not only in its computational capacity but in our collective willingness to integrate it thoughtfully, ethically, and sociologically. If guided by principles of equity, identity affirmation, and institutional transformation, AI can support a more just and reflective teaching profession—one that is as committed to human dignity as it is to innovation.

## REFERENCES


Ayeni, O. O., Al Hamad, N. M., Chisom, O. N., Osawaru, B., & Adewusi, O. E. (2024). AI in education: A review of personalized learning and educational technology. *GSC Advanced Research and Reviews*, *18*(2), 261–271. DOI: 10.30574/gscarr.2024.18.2.0062

Battilana, J., & Casciaro, T. (2012). Change agents, networks, and institutions: A contingency theory of organizational change. *Academy of Management Journal*, *55*(2), 381–398. DOI: 10.5465/amj.2009.0891

Benn, S., Edwards, M., & Williams, T. (2014). *Organizational change for corporate sustainability*. Routledge. DOI: 10.4324/9781315819181

Blackmore, J. (2013). A feminist critical perspective on educational leadership. *International Journal of Leadership in Education*, *16*(2), 139–154. DOI: 10.1080/13603124.2012.754057

Brennan, A., & Canny, A. (2023). Problematising Irish student-teachers'(dis) engagement with sociology of education in initial teacher education programmes. *Teaching and Teacher Education*, *130*, 104173. DOI: 10.1016/j.tate.2023.104173

Casad, B. J., Franks, J. E., Garasky, C. E., Kittleman, M. M., Roesler, A. C., Hall, D. Y., & Petzel, Z. W. (2021). Gender inequality in academia: Problems and solutions for women faculty in STEM. *Journal of Neuroscience Research*, *99*(1), 13–23. DOI: 10.1002/jnr.24631 PMID: 33103281

Grab, M. O. (2025). Teaching for Equity: An Exploration of AI's Role in Culturally Responsive Teaching in Higher Education Settings. *Innovative Higher Education*, •••, 1–22. DOI: 10.1007/s10755-025-09801-4

Halmo, H. (2025). *Human-Centered, Tech-Enabled: Scaling Academic Advising in Higher Education Through Predictive Analytics and Organizational Change an Innovation Study* (Doctoral dissertation, New York University).

Jin, Z., Goyal, S. B., & Rajawat, A. S. (2024). The informational role of artificial intelligence in higher education in the New era. *Procedia Computer Science*, *235*, 1008–1023. DOI: 10.1016/j.procs.2024.04.096

Kalashnikova, L. V., Lobanova, A. S., Hrabovets, I. V., Chernous, L. S., Chorna, V. A., & Davydenko, Y. O. (2025, March). Modern information and communication technologies in professional training of sociology students: Evolving needs and significance in the digital age. In *CTE Workshop Proceedings* (Vol. 12, pp. 381-398). DOI: 10.55056/cte.922

Kohli, R., Pizarro, M., Garcia, L. G., Kelly, L., Espinoza, M., & Cordova, J. (2021). Critical professional development and the racial justice leadership possibilities of teachers of colour in K-12 schools. *Professional Development in Education*, *47*(1), 89–101. DOI: 10.1080/19415257.2020.1814387

Lan, Y. (2024). Through tensions to identity-based motivations: Exploring teacher professional identity in Artificial Intelligence-enhanced teacher training. *Teaching and Teacher Education*, *151*, 104736. DOI: 10.1016/j.tate.2024.104736

Liu, S. (2025). Navigating Equality in Schools: The Sociological Impact of Leadership on Student Success. *Education and Urban Society*, *57*(3), 245–298. DOI: 10.1177/00131245241304404

Mac Fadden, I., García-Alonso, E. M., & López Meneses, E. (2024). Science Mapping of AI as an Educational Tool Exploring Digital Inequalities: A Sociological Perspective. *Multimodal Technologies and Interaction*, *8*(12), 106. DOI: 10.3390/mti8120106

Mishra, P., Oster, N., & Henriksen, D. (2024). Generative AI, teacher knowledge and educational research: Bridging short-and long-term perspectives. *TechTrends*, *68*(2), 205–210. DOI: 10.1007/s11528-024-00938-1

Monahan, R., MacCormac, A., & Minogue, J. (2024, July). Fostering Epistemic Agency: Strategies for Mitigating Implicit Bias in AI-Enhanced Education. In *EdMedia+ Innovate Learning* (pp. 1011-1025). Association for the Advancement of Computing in Education (AACE).

Moradi-Kelayeh, N. (2025). *From Chalkboard to Chatbots: The Integration of Artificial Influence on Pedagogical Practices* (Master's thesis, Harvard University).

Murtiningsih, S., & Sujito, A. (2024). Reimagining the future of education: Inclusive pedagogies, critical intergenerational justice, and technological disruption. *Policy Futures in Education*, •••, 14782103251341406.

Museus, S. D., & Jayakumar, U. M. (2012). Creating campus cultures. *Routledge, 10*, 9780203832417.

Padua, D. (2025). Artificial intelligence and quality education: The need for digital culture in teaching. *Journal of Educational* [ECPS Journal]. *Cultural and Psychological Studies*, (30), 181–193.

Palmer, I., Dunford, R., & Buchanan, D. (2016). *EBOOK: Managing Organizational Change: A Multiple Perspectives Approach (ISE).* McGraw Hill.

Pedro, F., Subosa, M., Rivas, A., & Valverde, P. (2019). Artificial intelligence in education: Challenges and opportunities for sustainable development.

Peer Mohamed, M. S. (2024). *Exploring ethical dimensions of AI-enhanced language education: A literature perspective*. Technology in Language Teaching & Learning.

Quan, T., Bracho, C. A., Wilkerson, M., & Clark, M. (2019). Empowerment and transformation: Integrating teacher identity, activism, and criticality across three teacher education programs. *Review of Education, Pedagogy & Cultural Studies*, *41*(4-5), 218–251. DOI: 10.1080/10714413.2019.1684162

Rajesh, R. (2024). *ARTIFICIAL INTELLIGENCE: BEYOND IDENTITIES. Routledge Handbook of Gender*. Culture, and Development in India.

Ray, V. (2019). A theory of racialized organizations. *American Sociological Review*, *84*(1), 26–53. DOI: 10.1177/0003122418822335

Sá, M. J., & Serpa, S. (2020). The COVID-19 pandemic as an opportunity to foster the sustainable development of teaching in higher education. *Sustainability (Basel)*, *12*(20), 8525. DOI: 10.3390/su12208525

Shani, A. B., Noumair, D. A., Zandee, D. P., & Coghlan, D. (Eds.). (2025). *Research in organizational change and development*. Emerald Publishing Limited. DOI: 10.1108/S0897-3016202531

Steinert, Y. (2025). Faculty development: core concepts and principles. *Faculty development in the health professions: A focus on research and practice*, 3-28.

Stouten, J., Rousseau, D. M., & De Cremer, D. (2018). Successful organizational change: Integrating the management practice and scholarly literatures. *The Academy of Management Annals*, *12*(2), 752–788. DOI: 10.5465/annals.2016.0095

Sullivan, A. L., Artiles, A. J., & Hernandez-Saca, D. I. (2015). Addressing special education inequity through systemic change: Contributions of ecologically based organizational consultation. *Journal of Educational & Psychological Consultation*, *25*(2-3), 129–147. DOI: 10.1080/10474412.2014.929969

SWARGIARY. K. (2025). *Educational Sociology: Theory, Practice, and Contemporary Challenges*. ERA, US.

# Chapter 8
# Ethical and Legal Frameworks for the Responsible Use of Generative AI in Scientific Research and Intellectual Property Protection

**Rismawati Rismawati**
https://orcid.org/0000-0001-8046-6764
*Universitas Muhammadiyah Palopo, Indonesia*

**Faradila Hasan**
https://orcid.org/0000-0002-7297-9313
*Institut Agama Islam Negeri Manado, Indonesia*

**Anny Widiasmara**
*Universitas PGRI Madiun, Indonesia*

**Muhammad Tahmid Nur**
*Institut Agama Islam Negeri Palopo, Indonesia*

**Ramakant Amar Navghare**
https://orcid.org/0000-0001-8458-0724
*Changu Kana Thakur Arts, Commerce, and Science College, New Panvel, India*

## ABSTRACT

*This chapter investigates the revolutionary impact of generative AI on scientific*

DOI: 10.4018/979-8-3373-5951-9.ch008

*research, while rigorously analyzing its ethical and legal ramifications. It examines how AI technologies disrupt conventional research procedures and introduce new issues in authorship, data protection, permission, and intellectual property. Utilizing bioethical principles—autonomy, fairness, beneficence, and non-maleficence—it delineates frameworks for the ethical application of AI. The book emphasizes governance frameworks, institutional ethical guidelines, algorithmic assessment, and deficiencies in patent and copyright legislation. Priority is given to cultivating AI ethics literacy and developing responsible AI from the beginning. This paper presents strategic directions for a globally cohesive, transparent, and inclusive AI research ecosystem that maintains scientific integrity and public trust through a comprehensive, interdisciplinary approach*

## 1. INTRODUCTION

### 1.1 A New Paradigm in AI-Driven Scientific Research

#### 1.1.1 The Transformation of Research Methodologies through Generative AI

The swift progress of generative artificial intelligence (AI) has significantly transformed the epistemological and methodological framework of scientific inquiry (Wong, 2024). Traditionally, the scientific method depended significantly on manual literature review, hypothesis development, experimental verification, and iterative analysis. Generative AI models, namely large language models (LLMs) and generative adversarial networks (GANs), are currently used to expedite, automate, and improve multiple phases of research production (Sengar et al., 2024; Wagner et al., 2021). This technological disruption establishes a new paradigm in which AI functions not merely as a passive analytical instrument but as an active collaborator in the generation of scientific knowledge.

A fundamental shift transpires during the initial phases of research design. Generative AI can swiftly assimilate extensive scientific material, pinpoint knowledge deficiencies, and propose innovative possibilities. In contrast to conventional databases, these AI systems function through pattern recognition and semantic comprehension, enabling researchers to formulate research questions based on multidimensional data. This feature significantly alleviates the cognitive burden on researchers, facilitating a more integrative and interdisciplinary method of knowledge generation.

Moreover, generative AI is essential in data simulation, modeling, and visualization. In domains including materials science, genetics, and climate modeling, AI algorithms can produce synthetic data that replicates real-world complexity, hence improving the resilience and scalability of experimental frameworks (Bhuyan et al., 2025; Bolick & Silva, 2023; Hadid et al., 2024). AI aids in formulating experimental protocols, forecasting results, and enhancing resource distribution, all of which enhance research efficiency and accelerate innovation. Nonetheless, these improvements also provoke methodological apprehensions over data authenticity, repeatability, and transparency.

The incorporation of generative AI into research methodologies, notwithstanding its benefits, engenders epistemic uncertainty around authorship, accountability, and interpretability. The conventional standards of peer review and replicability are being questioned by results produced collaboratively with non-human agents. Consequently, researchers and institutions must evolve by creating methodological frameworks that authenticate AI-assisted results and guarantee adherence to ethical and scientific standards (Hosseini et al., 2023). The generative AI possesses the capacity to democratize research, improve accuracy, and stimulate creativity across various fields. Nevertheless, achieving these advantages necessitates a critical examination of the evolution of research methodology in the AI era, alongside the implementation of ethical and regulatory protections to uphold scientific integrity, authorship transparency, and public confidence. Figure 1 below presents a conceptual framework illustrating the ethical foundations and governance components necessary for the responsible use of generative AI in scientific research:

*Figure 1. Framework Diagram: Ethical AI in Scientific Research*

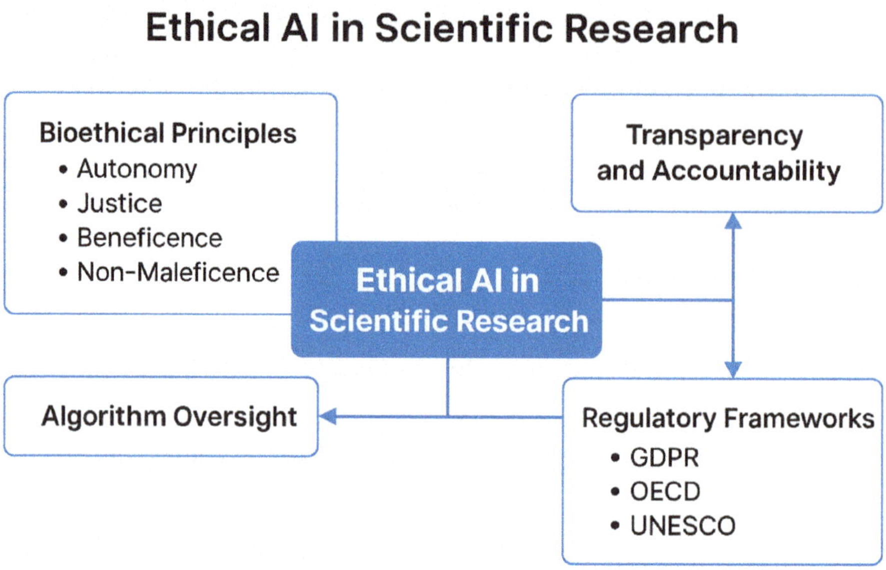


### 1.1.2 Generative AI in Scientific Discovery and Knowledge Production

Generative Artificial Intelligence (AI) has evolved as a transformative entity in the modern realm of scientific discovery and knowledge creation (Antwi et al., 2024; Cheng & Wu, 2024; Chetwynd, 2024). Generative AI systems, utilizing deep learning architectures such as GPT, BERT, and transformer-based neural networks, have transcended auxiliary roles like data processing and statistical modeling. They are now adept at autonomously generating hypotheses, simulating intricate systems, and drafting initial research findings. These advancements signify a notable transformation in the conceptualization, generation, and dissemination of scientific knowledge. Figure 2 illustrates a typical AI-enhanced scientific research workflow, detailing the integration of generative AI tools from hypothesis formulation to knowledge dissemination.

*Figure 2. Flowchart: AI-Driven Scientific Research Process*

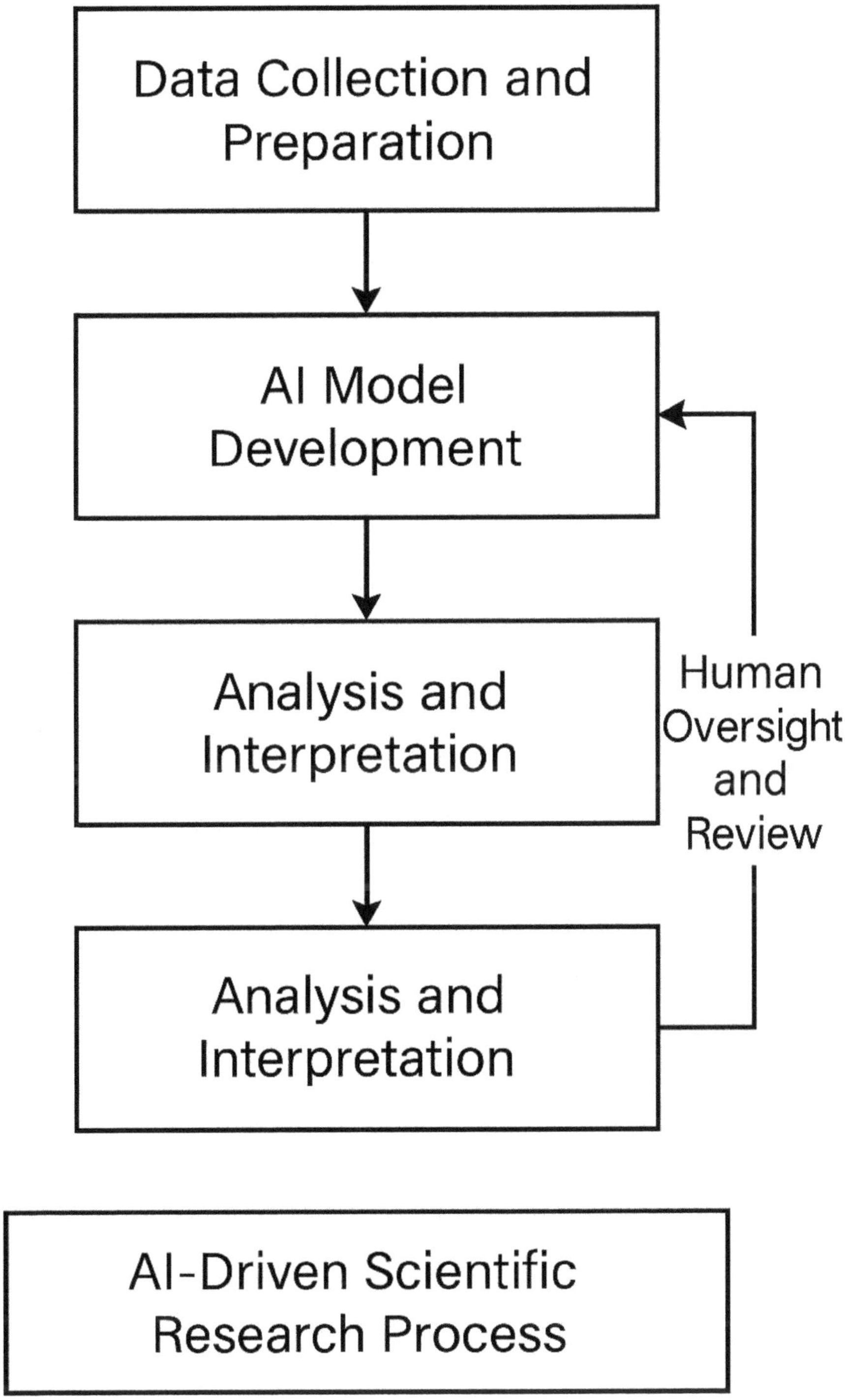

Generative AI's significant contribution is its ability to reveal concealed patterns and produce innovative insights from complex and unstructured data. In fields including computational biology, materials science, and quantum physics, generative models can accurately predict protein structures, create chemical compounds, or mimic particle behaviors (Bian & Xie, 2021; Hashmi et al., 2020). This feature not only expedites discovery but also enables researchers to investigate problems that were previously insurmountable due to computational or theoretical constraints.

Moreover, generative AI techniques are progressively used to co-author literature evaluations, plan experiments, and develop theoretical frameworks. They obscure the distinctions between tool and collaborator (Elbadawi et al., 2024; O'Toole & Horvát, 2024). These tools can aid scientists in progressively honing their research focus by providing alternate interpretations, recommending experimental variables, and proposing explanations derived from real-time literature analysis. This enhancement enhances human creativity and facilitates multidisciplinary integration on an unparalleled scale.

Nonetheless, these developments provoke significant epistemological inquiries. Who is the creator of AI-generated insights? Can the outputs of generative models be regarded as original contributions? What methods are in place to guarantee the verifiability of AI-generated outcomes? These inquiries are especially urgent in a time when scientific products must be transparent, reproducible, and subjected to peer validation. In the absence of strong methodological and ethical frameworks, generative AI may lead to epistemic opacity, obscuring the logic and origin of knowledge (Chetwynd, 2024).

Furthermore, dependence on generative AI may create biases inherent in the training data, thereby perpetuating erroneous scientific narratives or reinforcing historical disparities in research priorities. Consequently, although the incorporation of generative AI into knowledge creation presents significant potential, it necessitates governance through rigorous examination, ethical supervision, and legal protections that maintain the principles of rigor, integrity, and equity in scientific endeavors.

### 1.1.3 Ethical Concerns on Validity and Authority of AI-Assisted Knowledge

As generative AI becomes more integrated into scientific investigation, essential ethical issues arise concerning the legitimacy, reliability, and authority of AI-generated knowledge. Although these tools possess the capacity to transform research by improving efficiency and revealing novel insights, they simultaneously contest entrenched standards of scientific rigor, peer validation, and epistemic accountability.

A significant ethical issue is in the lack of transparency of generative AI systems. In contrast to conventional approaches that depend on explicitly defined processes for hypothesis testing and data interpretation, generative AI typically operates as a "black box," generating outputs without complete transparency in its reasoning (Ning et al., 2024; Pavlik, 2023; Xu & Shuttleworth, 2023). The absence of interpretability compromises the principle of scientific reproducibility, which is fundamental to credible knowledge production. If researchers cannot ascertain how an AI model reached a result or insight, the credibility of that output is called into doubt, particularly in critical domains such as medical diagnostics, climate science, or pharmacogenomics.

Another ethical quandary pertains to the assignment of epistemic authority to robots. As AI-generated outputs grow increasingly sophisticated and human-like, the inclination to accept these results without scrutiny may escalate. This highlights the concern of algorithmic over-reliance, wherein researchers place undue trust in AI-generated recommendations without sufficient examination (Klingbeil et al., 2024; Lepri et al., 2021; Steyvers & Kumar, 2023). In this process, scientific inquiry may transition from a contemplative, human-centric practice to a passive, machine-directed approach, thus undermining human agency and accountability in research.

Moreover, authorship and intellectual property are becoming increasingly unclear in AI-assisted endeavors. Should a generative model that substantially aids in a literature review, formulates hypotheses, or proposes research paths be recognized as a co-author or regarded solely as a tool? Many ethical and academic standards have not yet addressed this subtlety, resulting in ambiguity regarding the attribution of intellectual credit and accountability.

Bias in training data poses an additional ethical dilemma. Generative AI systems acquire knowledge from pre-existing datasets, which may have historical, cultural, or disciplinary biases. When these biases are ingrained in AI-generated outputs, they can perpetuate systemic injustices and alter scientific narratives, frequently without the researcher's cognizance. To resolve these difficulties, the establishment of transparent AI design, stringent validation methods, and comprehensive ethical monitoring is necessary. The future of AI in research relies on its capabilities and our collaborative commitment to maintaining honesty, accountability, and epistemic justice among fast advancing technologies.

# 2. BACKGROUND

## 2.1 Ethical Principles for the Use of Generative AI in Research

### 2.1.1 Core Bioethical Principles: Autonomy, Justice, Beneficence, and Non-Maleficence for the Responsible Use of Generative AI in Scientific Research

The incorporation of generative AI into scientific study offers both significant prospects and intricate ethical dilemmas. To guarantee its responsible implementation, it is essential to ground AI deployment in the established bioethical concepts of autonomy, justice, beneficence, and non-maleficence. The four pillars of medical ethics are increasingly pertinent in directing AI applications in wider scientific contexts, especially with human beings, data sensitivity, and intellectual property (Abujaber & Nashwan, 2024; Hain, 2020).

Autonomy underscores the entitlement of individuals—whether study participants, data suppliers, or researchers—to make informed, voluntary decisions concerning their participation in AI-assisted research. When generative AI processes personal or human subject data, it is imperative that people are thoroughly informed about the utilization of AI, the processing of their data, and the potential ramifications of AI-generated interpretations. Moreover, honoring researcher autonomy requires preserving human oversight during crucial decision-making phases, guaranteeing that AI does not usurp the intellectual agency of scientists.

Justice necessitates the fair allocation of the advantages and disadvantages of AI-driven research. AI models developed using datasets that disproportionately reflect specific regions, groups, or epistemologies may sustain systemic prejudice, marginalize underrepresented communities, or exacerbate existing discrepancies in scientific knowledge (Campbell & Koffi, 2024; Uddin et al., 2024). Ethical AI must be inclusive, encompassing different datasets, open-access research methodologies, and equitable representation in scientific discoveries and intellectual credit.

Beneficence requires that AI be utilized to promote well-being, facilitate scientific advancement, and increase results. In research settings, generative AI must not only be efficient but also facilitate the creation of information that serves societal interests. The application of AI should focus on fostering positive, socially significant outcomes, whether through the enhancement of diagnostic instruments, the acceleration of pharmaceutical development, or the improvement of instructional materials.

Non-maleficence, or the principle of "do no harm," necessitates the careful deployment of AI systems to prevent unexpected repercussions. These may encompass data breaches, misinterpretation of AI outputs, continuation of inaccuracies, or misuse of AI-generated information. Researchers must implement safeguards, validation processes, and error-correction mechanisms to alleviate such hazards.

These ethical principles collectively offer a normative framework for the proper incorporation of generative AI in scientific endeavors. Incorporating them into research procedures, funding policies, and institutional governance frameworks is essential for ensuring that technological progress is consistent with human dignity, equity, and social accountability.

### 2.1.2 Transparency, Explainability, and Accountability of AI Algorithms for the Responsible Use of Generative AI in Scientific Research

As generative AI systems become essential to scientific research, establishing openness, explainability, and accountability is crucial for maintaining the integrity and credibility of knowledge production (Ganguly et al., 2025). The three interconnected ethical pillars are the foundation of responsible AI governance, especially in research areas where algorithmic decisions significantly impact scientific validity, public trust, and intellectual property rights.

Transparency denotes the clarity with which AI systems, their training data, and decision-making procedures are conveyed to stakeholders. In scientific research, openness must include comprehensive documentation of the development of generative AI models, the datasets utilized for training, and the assumptions inherent in their algorithms. (D'Souza et al., 2024) In the absence of this transparency, researchers and reviewers cannot effectively assess the validity and dependability of AI-generated results. Insufficient transparency might impede reproducibility, a fundamental principle of the scientific method. Furthermore, in legal and ethical frameworks, openness is crucial for resolving issues related to authorship, data origin, and possible exploitation.

Explainability is predicated on transparency, requiring AI systems to reveal their processes in a manner comprehensible to human users. Explainable AI (XAI) allows researchers to comprehend the reasoning, justification, and causal connections that inform AI-generated results. In intricate domains like genetics, climate science, or synthetic drug creation, researchers must be capable of delineating the process by which an AI formulated a hypothesis or proposal. This interpretability is essential for cultivating confidence, enabling peer review, and guaranteeing that AI conclusions may be contested, amended, or dismissed when required.

Accountability guarantees that human agents—developers, researchers, or institutions—retain ethical and legal responsibility for the outcomes and repercussions of AI systems. Assigning scientific responsibilities to AI does not relieve human researchers of their supervisory duties (Hermann & Hermann, 2021; Uddin, 2023).

Accountability necessitates explicit processes for assessing AI-generated outputs, designating responsibility in instances of errors or harm, and establishing redress methods for impacted parties. Institutions must establish governance frameworks that delineate explicit responsibilities, ensure compliance, and maintain ethical standards throughout all phases of AI-assisted research. Incorporating openness, explainability, and accountability into generative AI applications is imperative, not optional. These principles protect the epistemic integrity of science and reinforce the ethical obligation of researchers to act ethically in an age of algorithmic enhancement.

### 2.1.3 Informed Consent and Human Data Protection in AI-Based Research

As generative AI becomes integral to scientific research, especially in areas involving human beings or sensitive personal data, the ethical requirements of informed consent and data security grow more intricate yet essential (Ganguly et al., 2025; Ning et al., 2024). These concepts, grounded in human rights and bioethics, are essential for maintaining individual autonomy and trust in research. The magnitude, velocity, and opacity of AI systems create new vulnerabilities that undermine traditional consent and data governance frameworks.

Informed consent typically denotes the voluntary assent of a participant to engage in research, based on a comprehensive understanding of the research's aim, methodologies, dangers, and data utilization (Andreotta et al., 2021; D'Souza et al., 2024; Zhou & Gattinger, 2024). In AI research, participants may be oblivious to the utilization of their data beyond the initial parameters, particularly when data are extracted from online platforms or repurposed across other studies using generative models. Moreover, the intricacy of AI algorithms frequently complicates researchers' ability to thoroughly elucidate potential downstream use of data, so compromising the fundamental principle of "informed" consent.

Consent methods must advance to address these concerns. Dynamic consent models, which allow participants to modify their preferences over time, and tiered consent frameworks, providing more detailed control over data utilization, are becoming vital. Transparency in the construction of AI models and data processing pipelines is essential to facilitate the advancement of consent procedures.

Simultaneously, data protection must be strengthened to avert misuse, breaches, and unauthorized inferences. Generative AI systems can reconstitute sensitive information from anonymised datasets, a danger referred to as re-identification. This requires strong protections such as data minimization, differential privacy, encryption, and stringent access controls. Adherence to data protection legislation, including the General Data Protection Regulation (GDPR), constitutes both a legal need and an ethical necessity for preserving public trust.

Furthermore, when generative AI systems are trained on extensive datasets containing identifiable or biometric information, the potential for data commodification and exploitation escalates. Researchers and institutions must guarantee ethical data stewardship by establishing transparent data governance standards and ethical review processes that encompass both the technical and social aspects of data utilization. The maintaining informed consent and safeguarding human data in AI-driven research is not only a procedural obligation—it is an ethical commitment to dignity, autonomy, and fairness in the contemporary scientific landscape.

## 3. MAIN FOCUS OF THE CHAPTER

### 3.1 Legal Dimensions of Intellectual Property in AI-Driven Science

#### 3.1.1 Legal Status of AI-Generated Scientific Outputs

The rise of generative AI technologies in scientific research has initiated significant legal discussions on the ownership, authorship, and safeguarding of AI-generated outputs (Miernicki & Ng, 2020; Watiktinnakorn et al., 2023). As artificial intelligence systems progressively assist in or independently generate scientific writings, models, visualizations, and discoveries, current intellectual property (IP) rules encounter difficulties in classifying, protecting, and attributing these outputs. The primary legal inquiry is: Who possesses the rights to the creations of the machine? In most jurisdictions, existing legal frameworks render intellectual property rights—such as copyright and patent protections—intrinsically human-centric. They are based on the concepts of creativity, originality, and inventiveness originating from human cognition (Harahap & Hamid, 2020; Watiktinnakorn et al., 2023; Wen & Tong, 2023). As a result, AI-generated scientific results devoid of significant human contribution may not be eligible for protection under conventional intellectual property frameworks. The United States protection Office and the European Union Intellectual Property Office have routinely rejected protection for works generated exclusively by machines, underscoring the necessity of human authorship.

Nonetheless, the necessity for human authorship becomes progressively contentious in research settings where generative AI plays a substantial role in the conceptualization, drafting, or analysis of scientific endeavors. In these circumstances, distinguishing the boundaries between human and machine contributions is frequently unclear. This complicates the determination of authorship attribution, licensing rights, and academic recognition, especially in multi-author collaborations where AI is regarded as a "co-pilot" in the knowledge production process

(Al-Sharieh, 2021; Chen et al., 2023; Khosrowi et al., 2024; Watiktinnakorn et al., 2023; Woudenberg et al., 2024).

Patent law faces analogous tensions. Although ideas resulting from AI-generated simulations or automated design procedures may qualify for patents, uncertainties persist regarding the status of inventors and responsibility. The lack of legal personhood for AI systems prevents them from being designated as inventors, hence complicating ownership assertions for AI-assisted ideas, particularly when no individual has a decisive involvement.

To tackle these difficulties, certain countries are initiating the examination of hybrid legal frameworks that acknowledge AI-assisted creations and suggest a "human-in-the-loop" criterion, wherein minimal human involvement may be adequate to preserve legal protection. Some proponents support the creation of totally new intellectual property categories specifically designed for autonomous systems (Llorca et al., 2023; Picht & Thouvenin, 2023). In scientific research, elucidating the legal status of AI-generated outputs is crucial for safeguarding innovation and maintaining the ethical principles of transparency, accountability, and academic integrity within a progressively automated research environment.

### 3.1.2 AI, Plagiarism, and the Redefinition of Originality

The use of generative AI into scientific research has significantly altered conventional notions of plagiarism and originality. As AI tools, including large language models (LLMs) and image generators, increasingly assist in manuscript drafting, literature summarization, and dataset generation, the distinctions between inspiration, reproduction, and intellectual theft have become increasingly ambiguous (Fyfe, 2022; Hutson, 2024; Tan & Maravilla, 2024). This convergence necessitates a reevaluation of the definitions of originality and the mechanisms for detecting and regulating plagiarism within an AI-mediated research context. Table 1 presents a comparative overview of human-authored, AI-generated, and hybrid research outputs across key dimensions including authorship eligibility, transparency, accountability, and intellectual property rights.

*Figure 3. Comparison Table: Human vs AI Authorship vs Hybrid Output*

**Comparison of Human vs. AI Authorship vs. Hybrid Output in Scientific Research**

| | Cretivitivy Source | AI-Generated Output | Hybrid (Human + AI) |
|---|---|---|---|
| Creativity Source | Intellectual contribution and original thinking | Pattern-based generation with pre-trainedd data | With human ag lentit/y AI-augmented generain |
| Authorship Eligibility* | Recognized by academic and legal | Legal vacuum ("black-box" algorithms) | Debated - attribution often considered solely -al 'human |
| Transparency and Expiainability | Fuily transparent, but research process et | No personal respoensability or llability to assigned | Shared responsibility but difficult to delineateate |
| Accountability | Generally reproducible | May difter due to stochascic non-deterministic output | Varies, depends on current research methods |
| Ethical Over sight | Glear framework within guidelines and IRB | Ethically underdeveloped | Shared frameworks, but additional AI-specific review |
| Plagiarism Risk | Minimal risk if properly attributabie | Typically unintentional, but high risk, especially if it ot tet or acknowledged | Higher risk if AI output R properly cited-and attributed |
| Submission and Publication | Academic standards | Typlcally unintentional but high risk, especially if ot | Debated under current copyright/patent laws |
| Submission and Publication | Follows academic standards | Typically not accepted under current copyright/at laws | R Debated under current copyright/patent la |

Transcribed by accumulating clear current standards R = Debated under current copyrightpatent laws

Plagiarism fundamentally constitutes the unauthorized appropriation of another's intellectual work. In traditional academic practice, this entails replicating text, concepts, or data without appropriate citation. When an AI model produces information that closely resembles existing literature—either literally or paraphrased—without citing the original source, it raises concerns about potential unintended plagiarism. AI systems, trained on extensive collections of existing human work, frequently reproduce learning structures, terminologies, or individual words, which may infringe against the intellectual property rights of original writers.

Furthermore, artificial intelligence complicates the identification of plagiarism. Conventional methods identify direct matches in published databases, whereas AI-generated content can create seemingly original writing that discreetly reconfigures previous material. This type of "algorithmic plagiarism" may elude discovery while simultaneously violating the moral and legal rights of the original inventors (Guan et al., 2020; Hutson, 2024; Xue et al., 2023). Consequently, academics and organizations must implement advanced plagiarism detection techniques that can recognize semantic similarities and conceptual duplication.

Concurrently, the concept of originality is undergoing redefinition. In academic study, originality involves the generation of novel knowledge or viewpoints through human intellect. Nonetheless, if a significant fraction of a study result is produced by AI, can it still be considered "original"? Does originality now encompass prompt engineering, curation, or the creative guidance offered by the researcher to the AI system?

Academic institutions and publishers must establish explicit guidelines for the ethical utilization of AI in content creation, encompassing disclosure mandates, authorship attribution policies, and acceptable limits for AI-generated contributions (Antwi et al., 2024; Chen et al., 2023; Ganguly et al., 2025; Hosseini et al., 2023). Ensuring transparency in the utilization of AI tools and upholding stringent citation standards is crucial for preserving scholarly integrity and confidence. In the expanding digital context, upholding ethical clarity regarding plagiarism and originality is essential for preserving the legitimacy of scientific research and safeguarding intellectual property.

### 3.1.3 AI and Patent Law: Innovation, Attribution, and Liability

The emergence of generative AI in scientific research has profoundly altered the processes of technological discovery and innovation. AI algorithms already facilitate medicine development, materials design, and product engineering by producing innovative outputs that may qualify for patent protection. These advancements, however, prompt significant inquiries concerning the attribution of inventorship, the ownership of AI-assisted discoveries, and the distribution of legal liability—matters that current patent law frameworks insufficiently address (Miernicki & Ng, 2020).

In most national and international legal frameworks, a patent can alone be awarded to a human inventor, as legal personality is essential for possessing and enforcing patent rights. This notion presents difficulties when an invention is autonomously or semi-autonomously produced by AI systems without direct human involvement (Basha & Thoti, 2024). Should the AI be recognized as the inventor? Who is legally recognized as the inventor—the programmer, the AI operator, or the business financing the research? The ambiguity in determining inventorship jeopardizes the enforcement of patents and the fair allocation of rights and benefits arising from AI-generated discoveries.

A further issue pertains to the standards of innovation and non-obviousness, which are critical factors for patentability. Generative AI can produce outputs by reconfiguring existing information in seemingly innovative manners, however these are statistically generated from extensive datasets (Basha & Thoti, 2024; Booyse & Scheepers, 2023; Jackson et al., 2024). Legal examiners must determine whether such outputs satisfy the criteria of human creativity or are simply algorithmic byproducts. This ambiguity necessitates the establishment of revised evaluating criteria capable of effectively differentiating between machine-generated simulations and authentic creative advancements.

Liability constitutes an additional legal boundary. When an AI-assisted creation inflicts harm—such as a defective medical device or erroneous engineering blueprint—attributing accountability becomes intricate. When the AI plays a substantial role in the innovation and no human can be distinctly recognized as the principal inventor, legal ambiguities arise over the assignment of civil or criminal liability. Policymakers and legal experts are already examining ideas of "shared liability" and "developer responsibility" to address these concerns.

To accommodate these changing circumstances, legal regimes may need to explore hybrid models of patent law that acknowledge AI-assisted discoveries while maintaining legal accountability and incentives for innovation. This need global discourse and regulatory anticipation to guarantee that patent law stays congruent with the technical evolution of AI-driven science.

# 4. SOLUTIONS AND RECOMMENDATIONS

## 4.1 Institutional Policies and Governance Models for Ethical AI Use

### 4.1.1 Institutional Codes of Conduct on AI Use in Research

With the rising integration of generative AI in scientific research, academic and research institutions must formulate formal codes of conduct to ensure its ethical, responsible, and transparent application (Akintayo et al., 2024; Antwi et al., 2024; Ganguly et al., 2025). Institutional governance is crucial for ensuring that AI technologies enhance, rather than compromise, scientific integrity, academic freedom, and public confidence in research results.

A code of conduct establishes a systematic framework for governing the integration of AI inside research workflows, encompassing data collecting, analysis, hypothesis creation, and dissemination. These standards delineate permissible bounds, elucidate researcher obligations, and reinforce shared principles such as transparency, responsibility, and equity. Without institutional monitoring, the utilization of AI may become uneven, opaque, and susceptible to ethical violations or inadvertent exploitation.

Essential components of an institutional AI code of conduct must encompass disclosure protocols, mandating researchers to delineate the circumstances and methodologies of AI tool utilization in their endeavors, especially regarding content development, data interpretation, and publication. This guarantees transparency in authorship attribution and methodological rigor, essential for upholding scientific credibility (Booyse & Scheepers, 2023; Hosseini et al., 2023; Kumar, 2025).

Furthermore, institutions must implement training and capacity-building initiatives to provide academics, students, and research personnel with the ethical understanding and technical proficiency required for the responsible use of AI. This encompasses instruction on data privacy, algorithmic bias, reproducibility, and the constraints of AI systems. Ethical AI literacy must be incorporated into research ethics training and institutional review board (IRB) procedures. Oversight tools, including specialized AI ethics committees or the broadening of current research ethics boards, are crucial. These entities can evaluate AI-related plans, examine adherence to institutional and legal requirements, and offer counsel in intricate issues concerning human data, intellectual property, or dual-use dangers.

Institutional rules must be flexible and routinely evaluated in light of advancing technical capabilities, regulatory changes, and shifting social values. An inflexible or too prescriptive methodology may obstruct innovation and neglect to mitigate developing hazards. By formalizing ethical standards for AI utilization in research, universities and research institutions can cultivate a culture of responsible innovation, safeguard the rights of participants and stakeholders, and enhance the validity of AI-facilitated scientific investigation. These norms of conduct fundamentally establish a basis for sustainable and ethically robust research ecosystems in the era of artificial intelligence.

### 4.1.2 Algorithmic Auditing and International Compliance

With the increasing prominence of generative AI in scientific research, the ethical implementation necessitates comprehensive algorithmic auditing mechanisms and adherence to international legal frameworks (Koshiyama et al., 2024; Mökander, 2023; Murikah et al., 2024). In the absence of regular control, the opacity and intricacy of AI algorithms may lead to biased outcomes, unverifiable conclusions, and breaches of data protection regulations. Algorithmic auditing—an evaluative procedure aimed at assessing fairness, accountability, and compliance—has emerged as a vital element of institutional governance in AI-assisted research settings.

Algorithmic auditing denotes the evaluation of AI models, both internally and externally, to verify their operational efficacy and adherence to ethical, legal, and institutional standards. In scientific research, auditing must span the full AI lifecycle, including data sourcing, model training, output generation, and real-world application. Institutions must mandate the documenting of algorithmic judgments, data provenance, and model assumptions to identify any biases, inaccuracy, or misuse.

Audits fulfill multiple ethical objectives. Initially, they improve transparency and reproducibility, allowing peers, reviewers, and stakeholders to assess the validity of AI-generated results. Secondly, they maintain accountability by determining who is responsible for supervising algorithmic results and ensuring that research techniques conform to stated ethical commitments (Ajiga et al., 2024; Badmus et al., 2024). Third, they advocate for remedial measures when AI systems yield detrimental or erroneous outcomes, such as racially skewed datasets or inaccurate medical forecasts. Figure 4 presents a risk matrix identifying key ethical risks associated with the use of generative AI in scientific research, highlighting both the likelihood and potential impact of each risk dimension.

*Figure 4. Risk Matrix*

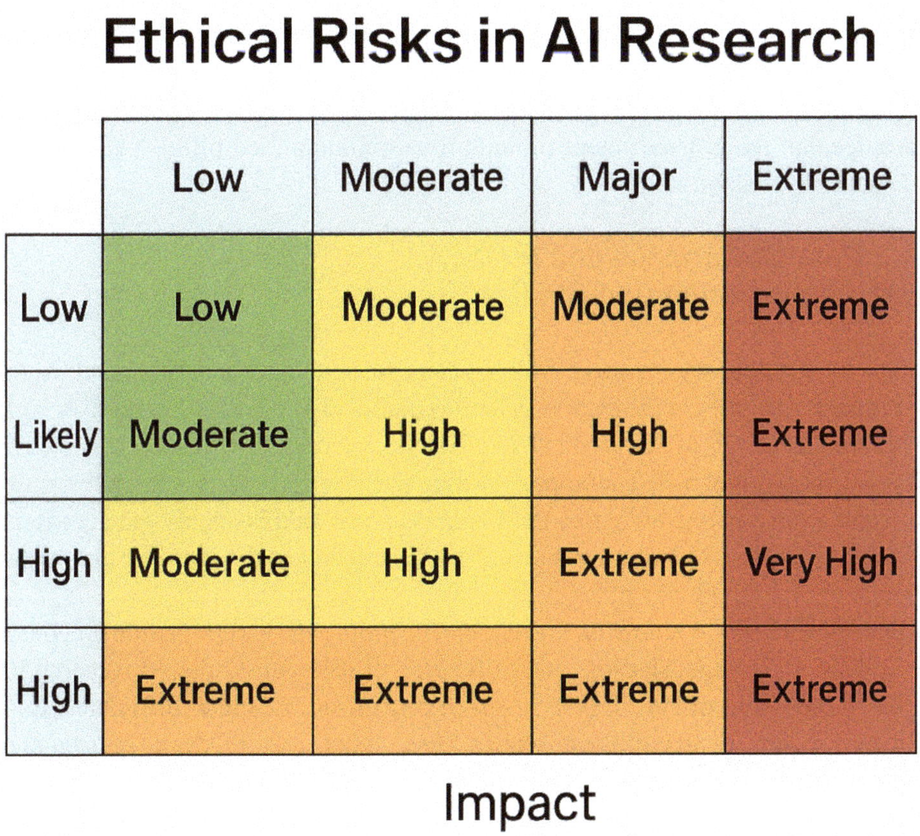


Simultaneously, institutions must synchronize AI utilization with global compliance norms, including the EU General Data Protection Regulation (GDPR), the OECD AI Principles, UNESCO's Recommendation on the Ethics of Artificial Intelligence, and forthcoming AI-specific legislation such as the EU AI Act. These frameworks underscore the principles of human oversight, data minimization, risk management, and algorithmic explainability, all of which are pertinent to scientific contexts (Badmus et al., 2024; Booyse & Scheepers, 2023; Chen et al., 2023; Dignum, 2022).

Compliance must not be merely reactive or superficial. Research institutions must incorporate compliance requirements into proposal assessments, funding standards, publication procedures, and review board directives. Neglecting to comply may result in reputational harm, legal repercussions, and public skepticism. The algorithmic auditing and regulatory compliance must operate in conjunction. Institutions must not solely depend on researcher discretion or voluntary ethics; they must have enforceable policies and an auditing framework (-, 2024; Anamol et al., 2023; Antwi et al., 2024; Marcellis-Warin et al., 2022; Oduro et al., 2022). By integrating these procedures into institutional governance, research institutions may guarantee that AI-assisted scientific initiatives maintain credibility, legal integrity, and social responsibility.

### 4.1.3 Data Governance and Privacy Protection in AI-Assisted Studies

The integration of generative AI into scientific research necessitates robust data governance and privacy protection systems (Batool et al., 2025; Campbell & Koffi, 2024; Ning et al., 2024; Ye et al., 2024). AI systems rely significantly on extensive datasets, many of which encompass personal, sensitive, or private information. Inadequate governance increases the likelihood of data misuse, illegal access, and ethical violations, which may compromise the integrity of the research process and infringe upon individual rights.

Data governance encompasses the policies, protocols, and standards that dictate the collection, storage, sharing, and utilization of data across the AI research lifecycle. In the realm of AI-assisted research, organizations must formulate explicit policies for data ownership, consent, access rights, and lifecycle management. These protocols must guarantee that data use corresponds with the designated study objective, honors participant autonomy, and averts function creep—where data is repurposed for unexpected applications without further consent (Akintayo et al., 2024; Herington et al., 2023; Rossi & Lenzini, 2020).

A robust data governance framework incorporates data classification systems that ascertain the sensitivity levels of various datasets and implement suitable security protocols. Identifiable health data and genetic information require more stringent protections than anonymised aggregate data. Institutions must adopt data minimization principles by gathering only the data essential to achieve the research aims.

Privacy protection is particularly difficult with generative AI models, which might deduce sensitive information from ostensibly anonymous data. Re-identification concerns, wherein individuals can be traced from de-identified datasets, require sophisticated privacy-preserving methodologies, including differential privacy, federated learning, encryption, and stringent access controls. Furthermore, AI's ability to generate new material from pre-existing datasets prompts concerns around the secondary utilization of data and the possibility of privacy infringements. Researchers must disclose to participants the intended use of their data, including its potential application in training generative models that may produce synthetic or derivative content.

Adherence to international standards, including the General Data Protection Regulation (GDPR), the California Consumer Privacy Act (CCPA), and various national data protection statutes, is imperative (Badmus et al., 2024; Chen et al., 2023; Ionescu & Dıaconı a, 2023; Mbah, 2024). Institutional review boards (IRBs) and data protection officers (DPOs) must interact with AI ethics committees to evaluate risks and ensure compliance. The strong data governance and privacy protection are not merely legal requirements; they are ethical necessities that enhance trust, integrity, and responsibility inside the AI-driven scientific ecosystem.

## 5. STRATEGIC RECOMMENDATIONS AND FUTURE DIRECTIONS

### 5.1 Toward a Global Framework for Ethical AI in Science

The swift incorporation of generative AI into scientific research highlights the pressing necessity for a universal ethical framework that surpasses national borders and institutional barriers (Kadri et al., 2024; Lasker, 2024). Although various nations and organizations have advanced in formulating AI ethics guidelines, the disjointed character of these initiatives poses problems of inconsistency, loopholes, and ethical relativism. A cohesive, internationally acknowledged framework is needed to guarantee that the application of AI in science complies with common norms of transparency, fairness, accountability, and respect for human rights. Figure 4 maps key global regulatory frameworks on AI, illustrating the fragmented yet emerging landscape of international compliance relevant to scientific research and intellectual property.

*Figure 5. Policy Mapping: Global Regulatory Landscape*

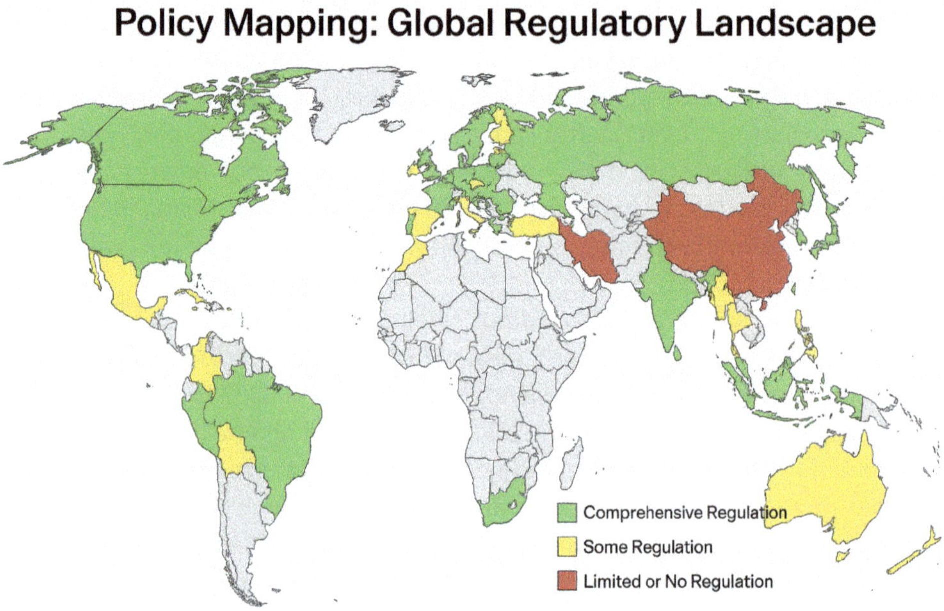


Numerous international organizations have established solid groundwork. The OECD AI Principles promote human-centric ideals, resilience, and transparency. The UNESCO Recommendation on the Ethics of Artificial Intelligence underscores the importance of inclusive, sustainable, and rights-oriented governance of AI. Concurrently, the EU AI Act presents one of the most thorough legislative frameworks for risk classification and compliance methods (Akintayo et al., 2024; Campbell & Koffi, 2024; Díaz-Rodríguez et al., 2023). Nonetheless, these frameworks require alignment and enhancement to address the distinct ethical dilemmas presented by generative AI in research, namely with authorship, consent, intellectual property, and data protection.

A worldwide framework must integrate minimal ethical norms relevant to all scientific disciplines and localities. These standards must encompass mandates for algorithmic transparency, AI explainability, data governance, equitable access to AI technologies, and informed consent in research involving human subjects (Abu-jaber & Nashwan, 2024; Norori et al., 2021; Radanliev, 2025). Additionally, they must require cross-institutional oversight mechanisms, such as international review boards or compliance consortia, to ensure adherence and address ethical disputes.

Furthermore, compatibility is essential. Ethical and legal standards must be flexible across many legal systems while preserving a fundamental set of common values (Gurgu et al., 2020). Mutual recognition agreements could streamline ethical approvals for cross-border joint research, guaranteeing uniformity while preserving local sovereignty and regulatory autonomy.

The framework must additionally facilitate capacity-building, especially in low- and middle-income nations that may lack the technical infrastructure or legal acumen necessary for the implementation of advanced AI governance. This encompasses worldwide investment in education, digital infrastructure, and the democratization of artificial intelligence technologies.

A global ethical AI framework must be dynamic and inclusive, evolving with technological progress and shaped by contributions from a variety of stakeholders, including scientists, ethicists, policymakers, civil society, and impacted communities. A global framework can promote coherence, accountability, and collective ethical responsibility, ensuring that AI promotes, rather than undermines, the validity, inclusivity, and integrity of scientific research globally (Akintayo et al., 2024; Erdélyi & Goldsmith, 2022).

## 5.2 Responsible AI by Design for Scientific Communities

As generative AI becomes a fundamental instrument in scientific research, it is imperative to ensure its responsible development and deployment by design to uphold ethical norms, scientific rigor, and social accountability (Antwi et al., 2024; Badmus et al., 2024; Díaz-Rodríguez et al., 2023). "Responsible AI by Design" denotes the deliberate incorporation of ethical, legal, and social factors across the whole lifecycle of AI systems—from conception and model creation to implementation and governance—rather than regarding these issues as mere afterthoughts or external limitations.

For scientific communities, the integration of responsible AI by design commences with the incorporation of ethical concepts directly into the architecture of AI systems. This encompasses algorithmic openness, equity in training data, strategies to alleviate bias, and human oversight procedures (Ajiga et al., 2024; Akintayo et al., 2024; Booyse & Scheepers, 2023). Researchers and developers must foresee and address potential harms—such as output misinterpretation, re-identification of anonymised data, or algorithmic bias—prior to the deployment of these systems in practical research settings.

The design of auditable and explainable systems is equally significant. Scientific research relies on replicability, peer validation, and methodological transparency (Ajiga et al., 2024; Lepri et al., 2021). Consequently, AI systems employed in research must yield interpretable outcomes, allow users to track the derivation of findings, and facilitate comprehensive documentation. This is particularly crucial in fields such as healthcare, environmental science, and social policy, where judgments derived from AI outputs can have substantial ethical and societal ramifications.

Responsible AI necessitates collaborative, interdisciplinary contributions during the design phase. Ethical AI systems get advantages from the collaborative knowledge of computer scientists, ethicists, legal academics, domain-specific researchers, and impacted communities (Akintayo et al., 2024; Dignum, 2022; Rawas, 2024; Uddin, 2023). Incorporating different perspectives bolsters the validity and relevance of AI models, ensuring they align with real-world complexities and value-sensitive design objectives.

Moreover, scientific institutions and funding organizations ought to advocate for responsible design via incentive frameworks and governance systems. This may entail mandating AI ethics impact evaluations in grant applications, promoting open-source and repeatable model development, and instituting review boards to supervise responsible innovation processes. Responsible AI by design enables scientific communities to fully utilize generative AI while upholding human dignity, promoting inclusive knowledge advancement, and strengthening public faith in research. It asserts that ethical design is not a constraint, but rather a cornerstone of scientific achievement in the era of AI.

## 5.3 Fostering AI Ethics Literacy Among Researchers and Academics

In the era of generative artificial intelligence, cultivating AI ethics literacy among researchers and academics is imperative; it is a fundamental prerequisite for responsible and equitable scientific investigation (Chen et al., 2023; Khan, 2024; Nguyen, 2025). As AI technologies integrate into study design, data analysis, and knowledge dissemination, scholars must have both technical proficiency and a comprehensive awareness of the ethical, legal, and societal ramifications of AI implementation in their disciplines.

AI ethics literacy denotes the capacity to critically analyze the ethical aspects of AI systems, encompassing concerns such as bias, transparency, accountability, data protection, intellectual property, and the wider socio-technical ramifications of AI-generated knowledge (Akintayo et al., 2024; Antwi et al., 2024; Booyse & Scheepers, 2023). It necessitates deeper awareness; it entails the development of ethical reasoning, transdisciplinary sensitivity, and the practical abilities essential for executing responsible AI practices.

To integrate AI ethics literacy into the scientific community, institutions must establish organized educational programs across all tiers of academic training, from undergraduate curricula to doctorate supervision and faculty development (Antwi et al., 2024; Hutson, 2024; Yang et al., 2025). Ethics must not be restricted to philosophy departments or regarded as a supplementary subject; instead, it should be incorporated into STEM education as an essential element of research design, methodology, and innovative practices.

Workshops, seminars, and case-based learning modules that confront real-world ethical challenges in AI research can promote critical thought and contextual awareness. Subjects such as consent in big data analytics, attribution in AI-generated publications, and algorithmic harms in predictive modeling necessitate exploration through interdisciplinary dialogue and active learning methodologies (Akintayo et al., 2024; Al-Zahrani, 2024; Bleher & Braun, 2023; Borenstein & Howard, 2020; Kajiwara & Kawabata, 2024; Kazim & Koshiyama, 2021; Lepri et al., 2021; Vargas, 2024).

Furthermore, institutions should facilitate continuous professional growth via certification programs, collaborative research on AI ethics, and incentives for ethical research practices. Ethical literacy must be evident in institutional regulations, peer review standards, and funding criteria to guarantee that researchers are responsible to ethical principles in their utilization of AI. In a worldwide and digitally mediated research environment, promoting AI ethics literacy entails advocating for cultural and epistemic diversity in the comprehension and application of ethical frameworks. Involving scholars from the Global South, indigenous communities, and underprivileged groups guarantees that AI development embodies diverse values and prevents the perpetuation of past inequalities. By fostering AI ethics literacy, scientific communities can establish a robust culture of critical engagement, moral accountability, and ethical innovation—preserving the credibility and humanity of research in the age of AI.

## 6. CONCLUSION

The advent of generative AI signifies a pivotal development in the realm of scientific inquiry and innovation. Although new technologies provide unparalleled prospects for expediting discovery, automating analysis, and enhancing human creativity, their integration also poses significant ethical, legal, and institutional concerns. This chapter illustrates that the ethical application of generative AI in research necessitates a fundamental transformation in our definitions of originality, responsibility, authorship, and data integrity within scientific frameworks.

Fundamental ethical principles—namely autonomy, justice, beneficence, and non-maleficence—should be integral to the design and implementation of AI systems. Institutions must formulate adaptive policies, establish codes of conduct, and implement algorithmic auditing procedures that ensure transparency, equity, and privacy protection. The establishment of legal frameworks that elucidate the status of AI-generated outputs inside intellectual property systems, especially regarding inventorship and copyright, is equally crucial.

Moreover, cultivating AI ethics literacy among researchers and scholars is essential for navigating this swiftly advancing domain. Education and capacity building will guarantee that ethical awareness transcends mere compliance checklists and becomes an integral aspect of scientific culture. Researchers must be enabled to utilize AI technologies proficiently while also critically examining their ramifications and designing AI systems that conform to overarching societal ideals.

A cohesive global framework—anchored in common ethical principles, inclusive governance, and interdisciplinary cooperation—is urgently required to guarantee coherence and equity in AI-driven science. The appropriate integration of generative AI transcends mere technical or regulatory challenges; it constitutes a moral obligation. Integrating ethical and legal awareness into all phases of scientific endeavors allows us to maximize the promise of AI while preserving the fundamental values that underpin reliable and inclusive scientific research.

## REFERENCES


Abujaber, A. A., & Nashwan, A. J. (2024). Ethical framework for artificial intelligence in healthcare research: A path to integrity. *World Journal of Methodology*, *14*(3). Advance online publication. DOI: 10.5662/wjm.v14.i3.94071 PMID: 39310239

Ajiga, D. I., Ndubuisi, N. L., Asuzu, O. F., Owolabi, O. R., Tubokirifuruar, T. S., & Adeleye, R. A. (2024). Ai-Driven Predictive Analytics In Retail: A Review Of Emerging Trends And Customer Engagement Strategies [Review Of Ai-Driven Predictive Analytics In Retail: A Review Of Emerging Trends And Customer Engagement Strategies. International Journal of Management & Entrepreneurship Research, 6(2), 307. Fair East Publishers. https://doi.org/DOI: 10.51594/ijmer.v6i2.772

Akintayo, T. A., Paul, C., Queenet, M. C., Nnadiekwe, O. A., Victoria, S. S., David, F. B., Joel, O. O., Agada, O. I., Ngozi, E. R., Arinze, U. U., Ojemerenvhie, G. A., Oluwadamilola, A. A., Nnamani, C. C., & Olayinka, U. W. (2024). Transforming Data Analytics with AI for Informed Decision-Making. *International Journal of Education Management and Technology*, *2*(3), 196–215. DOI: 10.58578/ijemt.v2i3.3812

Al-Sharieh, S. (2021). The intellectual property road to the knowledge economy: Remarks on the readiness of the UAE Copyright Act to drive AI innovation. *Law, Innovation and Technology*, *13*(1), 141–166. DOI: 10.1080/17579961.2021.1898312

Al-Zahrani, A. M. (2024). Unveiling the shadows: Beyond the hype of AI in education. *Heliyon*, *10*(9), e30696. Advance online publication. DOI: 10.1016/j.heliyon.2024.e30696 PMID: 38737255

Anamol, S., Anjaneyulu, A., & Aseem, M. R. (2023). Utilizing AI to predict and mitigate financial risks in banking and investment sectors. *International Journal of Science and Research Archive*, *10*(1), 1098–1104. DOI: 10.30574/ijsra.2023.10.1.0701

Andreotta, A. J., Kirkham, N., & Rizzi, M. (2021). AI, big data, and the future of consent. *AI & Society*, *37*(4), 1715–1728. DOI: 10.1007/s00146-021-01262-5 PMID: 34483498

Antwi, B. O., Adelakun, B. O., & Eziefule, A. O.Bernard Owusu AntwiBeatrice Oyinkansola AdelakunAugustine Obinna Eziefule. (2024). Transforming Financial Reporting with AI: Enhancing Accuracy and Timeliness. *International Journal of Advanced Economics*, *6*(6), 205–223. DOI: 10.51594/ijae.v6i6.1229

Badmus, O., Rajput, S., Arogundade, J. B., & Williams, M. H. (2024). AI-driven business analytics and decision making. *World Journal of Advanced Research and Reviews*, *24*(1), 616–633. DOI: 10.30574/wjarr.2024.24.1.3093

Basha, Mrs. N. R. Dr. H. S. A., & Thoti, K. K. (. (2024). AI-powered Recruitment and Employee Selection: Evaluating Bias and Fairness in Hiring Practices. [EEL]. *European Economic Letters*, *14*(1), 827. DOI: 10.52783/eel.v14i1.1107

Batool, A., Zowghi, D., & Bano, M. (2025). AI governance: A systematic literature review. *AI and Ethics*, *5*(3), 3265–3279. Advance online publication. DOI: 10.1007/s43681-024-00653-w

Bhuyan, S. S., Sateesh, V., Mukul, N., Galvankar, A., Mahmood, A., Nauman, M., Rai, A., Bordoloi, K., Basu, U., & Samuel, J. (2025). Generative Artificial Intelligence Use in Healthcare: Opportunities for Clinical Excellence and Administrative Efficiency. *Journal of Medical Systems*, *49*(1), 10. Advance online publication. DOI: 10.1007/s10916-024-02136-1 PMID: 39820845

Bian, Y., & Xie, X. (2021). Generative chemistry: drug discovery with deep learning generative models [Review of Generative chemistry: drug discovery with deep learning generative models]. Journal of Molecular Modeling, 27(3). Springer Science+Business Media. https://doi.org/DOI: 10.1007/s00894-021-04674-8

Bleher, H., & Braun, M. (2023). Reflections on Putting AI Ethics into Practice: How Three AI Ethics Approaches Conceptualize Theory and Practice. *Science and Engineering Ethics*, *29*(3), 21. Advance online publication. DOI: 10.1007/s11948-023-00443-3 PMID: 37237246

Bolick, A. D., & da Silva, R. L. (2023). Exploring Artificial Intelligence Tools and Their Potential Impact to Instructional Design Workflows and Organizational Systems. *TechTrends*, *68*(1), 91–100. DOI: 10.1007/s11528-023-00894-2

Booyse, D., & Scheepers, C. B. (2023). Barriers to adopting automated organisational decision-making through the use of artificial intelligence. *Management Research Review*, *47*(1), 64–85. DOI: 10.1108/MRR-09-2021-0701

Borenstein, J., & Howard, A. (2020). Emerging challenges in AI and the need for AI ethics education. *AI and Ethics*, *1*(1), 61–65. DOI: 10.1007/s43681-020-00002-7 PMID: 38624388

Campbell, J., & Koffi, B. A. (2024). The Role of AI-powered financial analytics in shaping economic policy: A new era for risk management and national growth in the United States. *World Journal of Advanced Research and Reviews*, *23*(3), 2816–2825. DOI: 10.30574/wjarr.2024.23.3.2963

Chen, B., Wu, Z., & Zhao, R. (2023). From fiction to fact: The growing role of generative AI in business and finance. *Journal of Chinese Economic and Business Studies*, *21*(4), 471–496. DOI: 10.1080/14765284.2023.2245279

Cheng, K., & Wu, H. (2024, April 18). Policy framework for the utilization of generative AI. In Critical Care (Vol. 28, Issue 1). BioMed Central. https://doi.org/DOI: 10.1186/s13054-024-04917-z

Chetwynd, E. (2024). Ethical Use of Artificial Intelligence for Scientific Writing: Current Trends. *Journal of Human Lactation*, *40*(2), 211–215. DOI: 10.1177/08903344241235160 PMID: 38482810

D'Souza, R., Mathew, M., Mishra, V., & Surapaneni, K. M. (2024). Twelve tips for addressing ethical concerns in the implementation of artificial intelligence in medical education. *Medical Education Online*, *29*(1), 2330250. Advance online publication. DOI: 10.1080/10872981.2024.2330250 PMID: 38566608

de Marcellis-Warin, N., Marty, F., Thelisson, E., & Warin, T. (2022). Artificial intelligence and consumer manipulations: From consumer's counter algorithms to firm's self-regulation tools. *AI and Ethics*, *2*(2), 259–268. DOI: 10.1007/s43681-022-00149-5

Díaz-Rodríguez, N., Ser, J. D., Coeckelbergh, M., de Prado, M. L., Herrera-Viedma, E., & Herrera, F. (2023). Connecting the dots in trustworthy Artificial Intelligence: From AI principles, ethics, and key requirements to responsible AI systems and regulation. *Information Fusion*, *99*, 101896. DOI: 10.1016/j.inffus.2023.101896

Dignum, V. (2022). Responsible Artificial Intelligence: Recommendations and Lessons Learned. In Social and cultural studies of robots and AI (p. 195). Springer International Publishing. https://doi.org/DOI: 10.1007/978-3-031-08215-3_9

Elbadawi, M., Li, H., Basit, A. W., & Gaisford, S. (2024). The role of artificial intelligence in generating original scientific research. *International Journal of Pharmaceutics*, *652*, 123741. DOI: 10.1016/j.ijpharm.2023.123741 PMID: 38181989

Erdélyi, O. J., & Goldsmith, J. (2022). Regulating artificial intelligence: Proposal for a global solution. *Government Information Quarterly*, *39*(4), 101748. DOI: 10.1016/j.giq.2022.101748

Fyfe, P. (2022). How to cheat on your final paper: Assigning AI for student writing. *AI & Society*, *38*(4), 1395–1405. DOI: 10.1007/s00146-022-01397-z

Ganguly, A., Johri, A., Ali, A., & McDonald, N. (2025). Generative artificial intelligence for academic research: Evidence from guidance issued for researchers by higher education institutions in the United States. *AI and Ethics*, *5*(4), 3917–3933. Advance online publication. DOI: 10.1007/s43681-025-00688-7

Guan, C., Mou, J., & Jiang, Z. (2020). Artificial intelligence innovation in education: A twenty-year data-driven historical analysis. *International Journal of Innovation Studies*, *4*(4), 134–147. DOI: 10.1016/j.ijis.2020.09.001

Gurgu, E., Bucea-Manea- oni , R., Avram, L. G., & Simion, V. (2020). Applicability of the ethics management tools in Romanian academia. *Independent Journal of Management & Production*, *11*(7), 2709–2732. DOI: 10.14807/ijmp.v11i7.1205

Hadid, A., Chakraborty, T., & Busby, D. (2024). When geoscience meets generative AI and large language models: Foundations, trends, and future challenges. *Expert Systems: International Journal of Knowledge Engineering and Neural Networks*, *41*(10), e13654. Advance online publication. DOI: 10.1111/exsy.13654

Hain, R. (2020). Principles and ethics in medicine. *Medicine (Abingdon)*, *48*(10), 631–633. DOI: 10.1016/j.mpmed.2020.07.009

Harahap, H., & Hamid, A. (2020). Analysis of The Importance of Omnibus Law "Cipta Karya" in Indonesia. [IJSRM]. *International Journal of Scientific Research and Management*, *8*(8), 236–250. DOI: 10.18535/ijsrm/v8i08.lla01

Hashmi, M. F., Ashish, B. K. K., Keskar, A. G., Bokde, N. D., & Geem, Z. W. (2020). FashionFit: Analysis of Mapping 3D Pose and Neural Body Fit for Custom Virtual Try-On. *IEEE Access : Practical Innovations, Open Solutions*, *8*, 91603–91615. DOI: 10.1109/ACCESS.2020.2993574

Herington, J., Connelly, K., & Illes, J. (2023). Ethical Imperatives for Working With Diverse Populations in Digital Research. *Journal of Medical Internet Research*, *25*, e47884. Advance online publication. DOI: 10.2196/47884 PMID: 37721792

Hermann, E., & Hermann, G. (2021). Artificial intelligence in research and development for sustainability: The centrality of explicability and research data management. *AI and Ethics*, *2*(1), 29–33. DOI: 10.1007/s43681-021-00114-8

Hosseini, M., Rasmussen, L. M., & Resnik, D. B. (2023). Using AI to write scholarly publications. *Accountability in Research*, *31*(7), 715–723. DOI: 10.1080/08989621.2023.2168535 PMID: 36697395

Hosseini, M., Resnik, D. B., & Holmes, K. (2023). The ethics of disclosing the use of artificial intelligence tools in writing scholarly manuscripts. *Research Ethics*, *19*(4), 449–465. DOI: 10.1177/17470161231180449 PMID: 39749232

Hutson, J. (2024). Rethinking Plagiarism in the Era of Generative AI. *Journal of International Communication*, *4*(1). Advance online publication. DOI: 10.54963/jic.v4i1.220

Ionescu, S.-A., & Dıaconı a, V. (2023). Transforming Financial Decision-Making: The Interplay of AI, Cloud Computing and Advanced Data Management Technologies. *International Journal of Computers, Communications & Control, 18*(6). Advance online publication. DOI: 10.15837/ijccc.2023.6.5735

Jackson, I., Ivanov, D., Dolgui, A., & Namdar, J. (2024). Generative artificial intelligence in supply chain and operations management: A capability-based framework for analysis and implementation. *International Journal of Production Research, 62*(17), 6120–6145. DOI: 10.1080/00207543.2024.2309309

Kadri, S., Dorri, N., Osaiweran, M., Garyali, P., & Petkovic, M. (2024). *Scientific Peer Review in an Era of Artificial Intelligence*., DOI: 10.1007/978-981-97-4060-4_23

Kajiwara, Y., & Kawabata, K. (2024). AI literacy for ethical use of chatbot: Will students accept AI ethics? *Computers and Education Artificial Intelligence, 6*, 100251. DOI: 10.1016/j.caeai.2024.100251

Kazim, E., & Koshiyama, A. (2021). A high-level overview of AI ethics [Review of A high-level overview of AI ethics]. Patterns, 2(9), 100314. Elsevier BV. https://doi.org/DOI: 10.1016/j.patter.2021.100314

Khan, Z. R. (2024). Ethics of Artificial Intelligence in Academia. In *Springer international handbooks of education* (p. 1551). Springer Nature., DOI: 10.1007/978-3-031-54144-5_188

Khosrowi, D., Finn, F., & Clark, E. (2024). Engaging the many-hands problem of generative-AI outputs: A framework for attributing credit. *AI and Ethics*. Advance online publication. DOI: 10.1007/s43681-024-00440-7

Klingbeil, A., Grützner, C., & Schreck, P. (2024). Trust and reliance on AI — An experimental study on the extent and costs of overreliance on AI. *Computers in Human Behavior, 160*, 108352. DOI: 10.1016/j.chb.2024.108352

Koshiyama, A., Kazim, E., Treleaven, P., Rai, P., Szpruch, Ł., Pavey, G., Ahamat, G., Leutner, F., Goebel, R., Knight, A. W., Adams, J., Hitrova, C., Barnett, J., Nachev, P., Barber, D., Chamorro-Premuzic, T., Klemmer, K., Gregorovic, M., Khan, S., & Chatterjee, S. (2024). Towards algorithm auditing: Managing legal, ethical and technological risks of AI, ML and associated algorithms. *Royal Society Open Science, 11*(5), 230859. Advance online publication. DOI: 10.1098/rsos.230859 PMID: 39076787

Kumar, C. R. (2025). AI-Powered Recruitment: Transforming Talent Acquisition in the Digital Age. *Journal of Informatics Education and Research, 5*(1). Advance online publication. DOI: 10.52783/jier.v5i1.2166

Lasker, A. (2024). Exploring Ethical Considerations In Generative AI. *International Journal of Advanced Research, 12*(4), 531–535. DOI: 10.21474/IJAR01/18578

Lepri, B., Oliver, N., & Pentland, A. (2021). Ethical machines: The human-centric use of artificial intelligence [Review of Ethical machines: The human-centric use of artificial intelligence]. iScience, 24(3), 102249. Cell Press. https://doi.org/DOI: 10.1016/j.isci.2021.102249

Llorca, D. F., Charisi, V., Hamon, R., Sánchez, I., & Gómez, E. (2023). Liability Regimes in the Age of AI: A Use-Case Driven Analysis of the Burden of Proof. *Journal of Artificial Intelligence Research, 76*, 613–644. DOI: 10.1613/jair.1.14565

Mbah, G. O.Geraldine O Mbah. (2024). Data privacy in the era of AI: Navigating regulatory landscapes for global businesses. *International Journal of Science and Research Archive, 13*(2), 2040–2058. DOI: 10.30574/ijsra.2024.13.2.2396

Miernicki, M., & Ng, I. (2020). Artificial intelligence and moral rights. *AI & Society, 36*(1), 319–329. DOI: 10.1007/s00146-020-01027-6

Mökander, J. (2023). Auditing of AI: Legal, Ethical and Technical Approaches. *Digital Society : Ethics, Socio-Legal and Governance of Digital Technology, 2*(3), 49. Advance online publication. DOI: 10.1007/s44206-023-00074-y

Murikah, W., Nthenge, J. K., & Musyoka, F. M. (2024). Bias and ethics of AI systems applied in auditing - A systematic review [Review of Bias and ethics of AI systems applied in auditing - A systematic review]. Scientific African, 25. Elsevier BV. https://doi.org/DOI: 10.1016/j.sciaf.2024.e02281

Nguyen, V. (2025). The Use of Generative AI Tools in Higher Education: Ethical and Pedagogical Principles. *Journal of Academic Ethics*. Advance online publication. DOI: 10.1007/s10805-025-09607-1

Norori, N., Hu, Q., Aellen, F. M., Faraci, F. D., & Tzovara, A. (2021). Addressing bias in big data and AI for health care: A call for open science [Review of Addressing bias in big data and AI for health care: A call for open science]. Patterns, 2(10), 100347. Elsevier BV. https://doi.org/DOI: 10.1016/j.patter.2021.100347

O'Toole, K., & Horvát, E.-Á. (2024). Extending human creativity with AI. *Journal of Creativity, 34*(2), 100080. DOI: 10.1016/j.yjoc.2024.100080

Oduro, S., Moss, E., & Metcalf, J. (2022). Obligations to assess: Recent trends in AI accountability regulations [Review of Obligations to assess: Recent trends in AI accountability regulations]. Patterns, 3(11), 100608. Elsevier BV. https://doi.org/DOI: 10.1016/j.patter.2022.100608

Pavlik, J. V. (2023). Collaborating With ChatGPT: Considering the Implications of Generative Artificial Intelligence for Journalism and Media Education. *Journalism & Mass Communication Educator, 78*(1), 84–93. DOI: 10.1177/10776958221149577

Picht, P. G., & Thouvenin, F. (2023). AI and IP: Theory to Policy and Back Again – Policy and Research Recommendations at the Intersection of Artificial Intelligence and Intellectual Property. *IIC; International Review of Industrial Property and Copyright Law, 54*(6), 916–940. DOI: 10.1007/s40319-023-01344-5

Radanliev, P. (2025). AI Ethics: Integrating Transparency, Fairness, and Privacy in AI Development. *Applied Artificial Intelligence, 39*(1), 2463722. Advance online publication. DOI: 10.1080/08839514.2025.2463722

Rawas, S. (2024). AI: The future of humanity. *Discover Artificial Intelligence, 4*(1), 25. Advance online publication. DOI: 10.1007/s44163-024-00118-3

Rossi, A., & Lenzini, G. (2020). Transparency by design in data-informed research: A collection of information design patterns. *Computer Law & Security Review, 37*, 105402. DOI: 10.1016/j.clsr.2020.105402

Sengar, S. S., Hasan, A. B., Kumar, S., & Carroll, F. (2024). Generative artificial intelligence: a systematic review and applications [Review of Generative artificial intelligence: a systematic review and applications]. Multimedia Tools and Applications. Springer Science+Business Media. https://doi.org/DOI: 10.1007/s11042-024-20016-1

Steyvers, M., & Kumar, A. (2023). Three Challenges for AI-Assisted Decision-Making. *Perspectives on Psychological Science, 19*(5), 722–734. DOI: 10.1177/17456916231181102 PMID: 37439761

Tan, M. J. T., & Maravilla, N. M. A. T. (2024). Shaping integrity: Why generative artificial intelligence does not have to undermine education. *Frontiers in Artificial Intelligence, 7*, 1471224. Advance online publication. DOI: 10.3389/frai.2024.1471224 PMID: 39512399

Uddin, A. S. M. A. (2023). The Era of AI: Upholding Ethical Leadership. *Open Journal of Leadership, 12*(4), 400–417. DOI: 10.4236/ojl.2023.124019

Uddin, M. Z., Jamal, M. Z. U., Umair, M., Khader, M., & Kumar, M. U. (2024). AI-Powered financial modeling and valuation analysis: Unleashing data-driven insights. *International Journal of Multidisciplinary Research and Growth Evaluation, 5*(2), 626–629. DOI: 10.54660/.IJMRGE.2024.5.2.626-629 van Woudenberg, R., Ranalli, C., & Bracker, D. (2024). Authorship and ChatGPT: A Conservative View. *Philosophy & Technology*, *37*(1), 34. Advance online publication. DOI: 10.1007/s13347-024-00715-1 PMID: 38419827

Vargas, N. C. (2024). Exploiting the margin: How capitalism fuels AI at the expense of minoritized groups. *AI and Ethics*. Advance online publication. DOI: 10.1007/s43681-024-00502-w

Wagner, G., Lukyanenko, R., & Paré, G. (2021). Artificial intelligence and the conduct of literature reviews. *Journal of Information Technology*, *37*(2), 209–226. DOI: 10.1177/02683962211048201

Watiktinnakorn, C., Seesai, J., & Kerdvibulvech, C. (2023). Blurring the lines: How AI is redefining artistic ownership and copyright. *Discover Artificial Intelligence*, *3*(1), 37. Advance online publication. DOI: 10.1007/s44163-023-00088-y

Wen, Z., & Tong, D. (2023). Analysis of the Legal Subject Status of Artificial Intelligence. *Beijing Law Review*, *14*(1), 74–86. DOI: 10.4236/blr.2023.141004

Wong, W. K. O. (2024). The sudden disruptive rise of generative artificial intelligence? An evaluation of their impact on higher education and the global workplace. *Journal of Open Innovation*, *10*(2), 100278. DOI: 10.1016/j.joitmc.2024.100278

Xu, H., & Shuttleworth, K. M. J. (2023). Medical artificial intelligence and the black box problem: A view based on the ethical principle of "do no harm.". *Intelligent Medicine*, *4*(1), 52–57. DOI: 10.1016/j.imed.2023.08.001

Xue, B., Green, R., & Zhang, M. (2023). Artificial Intelligence in New Zealand: applications and innovation. In Journal of the Royal Society of New Zealand (Vol. 53, Issue 1, p. 1). Taylor & Francis. https://doi.org/DOI: 10.1080/03036758.2023.2170165

Yang, Y., Zhang, Y., Sun, D., He, W., & Wei, Y. (2025). Navigating the landscape of AI literacy education: Insights from a decade of research (2014–2024). *Humanities & Social Sciences Communications*, *12*(1), 374. Advance online publication. DOI: 10.1057/s41599-025-04583-8

Ye, X., Yan, Y., Li, J., & Jiang, B. (2024). Privacy and personal data risk governance for generative artificial intelligence: A Chinese perspective. *Telecommunications Policy*, *102851*(10), 102851. Advance online publication. DOI: 10.1016/j.telpol.2024.102851

Zhou, K. R., & Gattinger, G. (2024). The Evolving Regulatory Paradigm of AI in MedTech: A Review of Perspectives and Where We Are Today [Review of The Evolving Regulatory Paradigm of AI in MedTech: A Review of Perspectives and Where We Are Today]. Therapeutic Innovation & Regulatory Science, 58(3), 456. Springer Science+Business Media. https://doi.org/DOI: 10.1007/s43441-024-00628-3

# Chapter 9
# AI as a Co-Teacher:
## Designing Symbiotic Human-AI Classroom Partnerships

**Shubhanshi**
https://orcid.org/0009-0001-2755-7605
*SHUATS Naini, Prayagraj, India*

## ABSTRACT

*This chapter critically examines AI co-teaching models that position artificial intelligence as a collaborative partner rather than a pedagogical replacement. It presents the Complementary Strengths Model and Teacher-in-the-Loop (TiTL) framework, highlighting role division between AI's analytical capabilities and teachers' emotional and instructional leadership. Implementation strategies across co-planning, co-instruction, and co-assessment are discussed using case studies and workflow models. Ethical issues such as bias, teacher autonomy, and trust via explainable AI (XAI) are addressed with practical guidance. The chapter also explores challenges like emotional AI's cultural risks and limited research from Global South contexts. Recommendations for educators, developers, and policymakers stress AI literacy, participatory co-design, and inclusive policy. It concludes by advocating interdisciplinary collaboration to create equitable, transparent, and culturally responsive AI-augmented education systems.*

## INTRODUCTION

The integration of Artificial Intelligence (AI) into educational ecosystems represents one of the most transformative shifts in contemporary pedagogy. Over the past few decades, AI has evolved from rudimentary intelligent tutoring systems to complex, adaptive learning platforms that now actively co-participate in instructional

DOI: 10.4018/979-8-3373-5951-9.ch009

delivery (Luckin et al., 2016). Despite this progression, the collaborative dynamics between AI systems and human teachers remain underexplored and, in some cases, poorly defined. This chapter investigates the theoretical and empirical contours of AI co-teaching frameworks, emphasizing the necessity of maintaining human pedagogical agency within technologically mediated classrooms. To establish the relevance and direction of this inquiry, this section provides a historical overview of AI's educational applications, identifies persistent gaps in teacher-AI partnerships, articulates specific research questions, and presents a structured roadmap for the chapter.

## Background

### Historical Evolution of AI in Education

The application of Artificial Intelligence (AI) in educational contexts has undergone significant transformation since its inception. In the 1970s and 1980s, early implementations such as Computer-Assisted Instruction (CAI) and Intelligent Tutoring Systems (ITS) primarily relied on rule-based decision trees and offered limited personalization (Anderson et al., 1990). These systems conceptualized learners as passive recipients of instruction, with minimal responsiveness to individual learning trajectories or socio-emotional factors.

During the 1990s and early 2000s, the field advanced toward adaptive learning technologies that employed more sophisticated algorithms to tailor instructional content based on real-time student performance (VanLehn, 2006). However, AI's pedagogical function remained narrowly defined, largely focusing on content sequencing, while human teachers operated outside the AI-driven feedback mechanisms.

In the past decade, AI applications in education have expanded significantly with the integration of learning analytics, natural language processing (NLP), and machine learning (ML), enabling systems to interpret student engagement, conceptual understanding, and affective states (Holmes et al., 2019). These tools now hold the potential to co-facilitate classroom instruction, introducing new questions regarding role delineation, ethical use, and accountability. Despite these technological gains, many educational AI systems continue to prioritize automation of tasks such as assessment, content delivery, and classroom administration, often marginalizing the relational and adaptive dimensions that are central to effective pedagogy (Luckin et al., 2016).

This developmental trajectory—from automation to potential co-teaching—is illustrated in Figure 1, which maps the historical evolution of AI roles in educational environments.

*Figure 1. AI in Education Evolution*

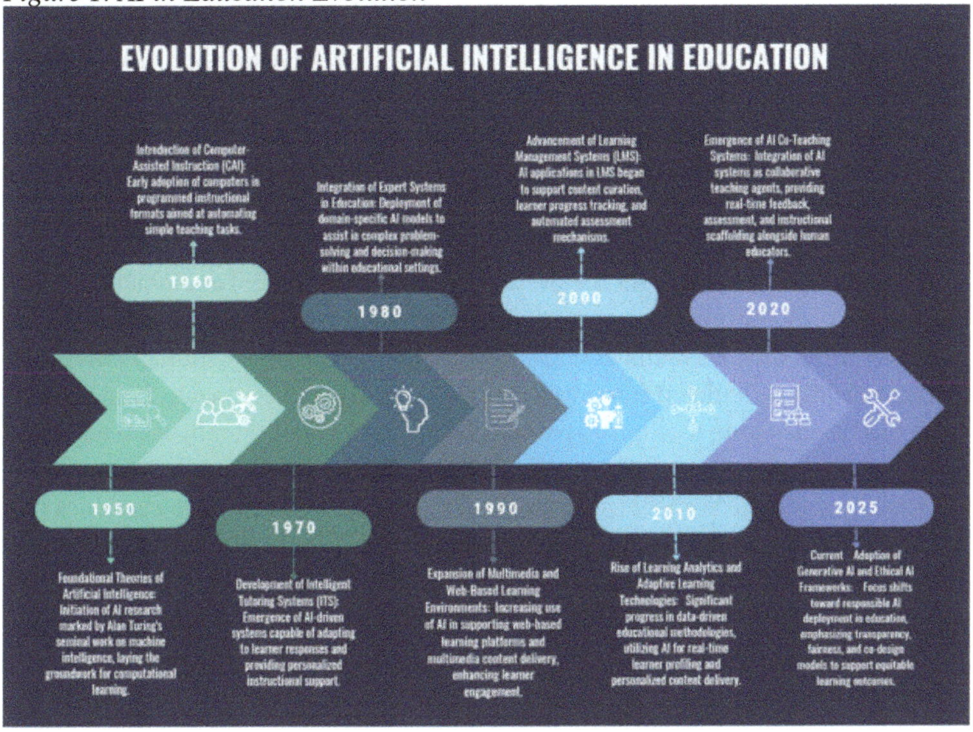


## Current Gaps in Teacher-AI Partnerships

Recent scholarship suggests that the growing integration of Artificial Intelligence (AI) in educational settings is predominantly oriented toward enhancing operational efficiency and expanding scalability, often at the expense of fostering meaningful teacher-AI collaboration (Zawacki-Richter et al., 2019). Most AI-driven educational systems are engineered for autonomous functioning, with limited design considerations for incorporating real-time teacher input or enabling joint pedagogical decision-making.

This automation-centric approach introduces several critical challenges:

**System opacity**. Many AI applications in education operate as opaque "black boxes," offering limited transparency regarding how decisions or recommendations are generated, thereby constraining teachers' ability to interrogate or contextualize AI outputs (Miller, 2019).

**Lack of cultural sensitivity**. These systems frequently apply generalized learning models that inadequately reflect diverse cultural, linguistic, and contextual learner profiles, leading to potential bias and exclusion (Buolamwini & Gebru, 2018).

**Diminished professional agency**. As AI-generated suggestions gain prominence, educators may perceive a reduction in their pedagogical autonomy, with algorithmic logic superseding instructional judgment (Perrotta et al., 2021).

These limitations highlight the pressing need for theoretical and practical models that not only leverage the computational strengths of AI but also safeguard the cognitive, affective, and ethical capacities uniquely offered by human educators. Without clearly articulated frameworks for cooperative engagement, there is a tangible risk of relegating teachers to passive supervisory roles, thereby weakening the relational dynamics that underpin effective teaching and learning.

To respond to these concerns, this chapter presents and critically examines two interrelated frameworks—the Complementary Strengths Model and the Teacher-in-the-Loop (TiTL) framework—both of which promote collaborative, transparent, and culturally responsive partnerships between human teachers and AI systems.

## Objectives

This chapter is guided by a set of research questions aimed at systematically exploring the theoretical, practical, and ethical dimensions of AI co-teaching partnerships:

### Research Questions

1. How can the division of labour between AI systems and human teachers be optimized to enhance both learning outcomes and teacher satisfaction?
2. What design features are necessary in AI systems to support transparent, accountable, and culturally sensitive teacher-AI collaborations?
3. How do existing AI co-teaching models address (or fail to address) student trust and cultural bias within diverse educational settings?
4. What are the long-term implications of embedding AI in instructional practices for teacher autonomy, pedagogical equity, and student agency?

These research questions provide a scaffolding for examining both the theoretical models and the practical interventions that can support sustainable and equitable teacher-AI partnerships.

## Chapter Roadmap

This chapter critically examines the evolving integration of Artificial Intelligence (AI) as a co-teacher within contemporary educational settings, with an emphasis on designing effective and ethical human–AI classroom partnerships. The chapter begins with the Introduction, which traces the historical trajectory of AI in education and articulates the chapter's central objectives and research questions.

The Literature Review synthesizes foundational theories, including the Complementary Strengths Model and the Teacher-in-the-Loop (TiTL) framework, while highlighting significant research gaps concerning cultural bias in AI systems and the dynamics of student trust.

The Conceptual Frameworks section presents a structured classification of AI co-teaching roles, delineates the division of cognitive and affective responsibilities between human teachers and AI systems, and introduces practical instruments such as ethical decision-making checklists and implementation flowcharts. Subsequently, the Implementation Models section outlines operational strategies for co-planning, co-instruction, and co-assessment, supported by empirical case studies and illustrative figures. The chapter then explores the Ethical and Professional Implications, focusing on bias mitigation, safeguarding teacher agency, and fostering trust through explainable AI.

The Recommendations section offers stakeholder-specific guidance for educators, developers, and policymakers. The chapter concludes with Future Directions and a final synthesis, advocating for interdisciplinary collaboration in building equitable, culturally responsive AI-enhanced classrooms.

## LITERATURE REVIEW

The emergence of Artificial Intelligence (AI) in educational contexts has generated extensive theoretical and empirical interest in recent years. This section synthesizes foundational frameworks underpinning AI co-teaching and identifies persistent research gaps concerning cultural biases and student trust in AI-mediated learning environments. The review is structured into two primary subsections: theoretical foundations and research gaps, each critically analysing existing models, empirical findings, and their implications for future inquiry.

## Theoretical Foundations

### Complementary Strengths Model (CSM)

The Complementary Strengths Model (CSM) conceptualizes AI co-teaching as a symbiotic partnership in which artificial intelligence and human educators collaboratively harness their respective strengths to enhance learning outcomes. Rather than viewing AI as a substitute for teachers, this model emphasizes its role as a co-facilitator—where the computational accuracy and data-processing capabilities of AI systems augment, rather than replace, the educator's capacity for social, emotional, and ethical judgment (Holmes et al., 2023). Figure 2 presents a role-division flowchart within this model, outlining the distinct yet interdependent responsibilities shared between AI tools and human instructors.

*Figure 2. Role-Division Flowchart in Complementary Strengths Model*

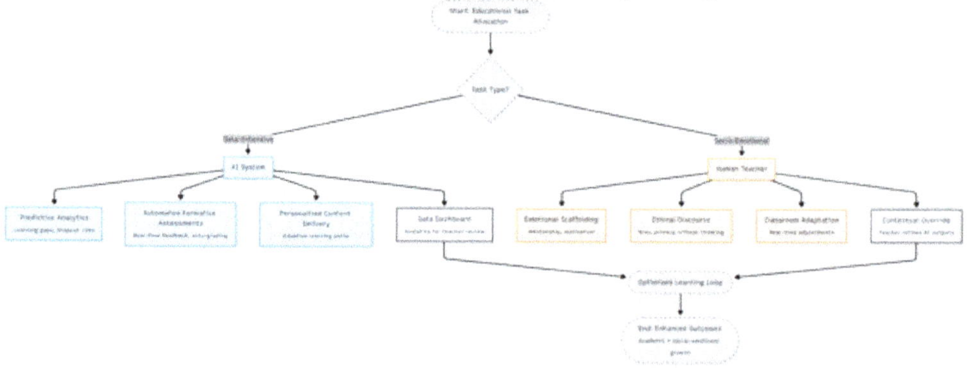

The Complementary Strengths Model (CSM) is theoretically grounded in socio-constructivist learning paradigms, particularly Vygotsky's (1978) concept of the zone of proximal development (ZPD), wherein the human teacher orchestrates the learning environment while AI functions as a scaffolding agent to support and extend student learning. Within this framework, AI augments instructional processes by offering real-time data analysis and adaptive feedback, while the teacher remains central to interpreting context and guiding moral and emotional development. Empirical research supports this synergistic arrangement; studies by Johnson et al. (2021) and Lee and Park (2022) demonstrate that AI's capacity to process extensive datasets enhances teachers' decision-making and responsiveness to student needs.

Importantly, CSM also addresses the issue of explainability in AI. By mandating transparent, interpretable algorithmic operations, the model ensures that teachers can understand and articulate how AI recommendations are generated, thereby reinforcing pedagogical accountability and reducing overreliance on opaque "black box" systems (Miller, 2019). Furthermore, CSM embeds ethical safeguards, cautioning against the delegation of value-laden responsibilities—such as grading qualitative assignments or managing sensitive classroom discussions—to algorithmic agents.

A distinctive feature of CSM is its proposed iterative feedback loop, wherein AI systems adapt based on teacher interventions, and teachers, in turn, refine their instructional strategies using AI-generated insights. This reciprocal learning dynamic creates a continuous professional development cycle for both human and machine actors (Chen et al., 2020). Unlike fully autonomous AI tools, the CSM prioritizes ongoing human oversight, making it particularly well-suited for culturally diverse and ethically nuanced educational contexts.

## Teacher-in-the-Loop (TiTL) Framework

The Teacher-in-the-Loop (TiTL) framework builds upon and extends the foundational principles of the Complementary Strengths Model (CSM), offering a paradigm in which structured human oversight is embedded throughout AI-mediated decision-making in educational contexts. Unlike fully autonomous systems that function with minimal human input, TiTL formalizes the teacher's active role at critical decision points, reinforcing pedagogical relevance and ethical alignment in classroom applications (Amershi et al., 2014). This embedded human presence ensures that contextual nuances—such as socio-emotional dynamics, cultural sensitivity, and ethical accountability—are integrated into instructional processes, which purely algorithmic systems often neglect.

As detailed in Table 1, the TiTL framework differs significantly from autonomous AI systems across a spectrum of operational parameters, including decision-making authority, override mechanisms, system transparency, ethical safeguards, and adaptability to classroom context. In TiTL-based systems, teachers retain the final decision-making power, can adjust or reject AI-generated suggestions in real time, and interpret data through the lens of pedagogical and cultural knowledge—thereby fostering greater trust among students and enhancing instructional quality.

*Table 1. Comparative Analysis of Teacher-in-the-Loop (TiTL) vs. Autonomous AI in Classroom Management*

| Parameter | Teacher-in-the-Loop (TiTL) AI | Autonomous AI |
|---|---|---|
| Decision Authority | Final decision-making authority remains with the human teacher. | AI executes decisions independently, often without human input. |
| Override Capability | Teachers can override, adjust, or reject AI-generated recommendations in real time. | Override mechanisms are limited or non-existent. |
| System Transparency | AI decision-making pathways are explainable and visible to the teacher. | Decision processes are typically opaque or non-interpretable. |
| Ethical Safeguards | Human oversight ensures strong ethical accountability and value alignment. | Increased ethical risks due to lack of immediate human supervision. |
| Student Trust | Higher levels of trust due to teacher-mediated AI interactions. | Reduced trust if AI actions are perceived as arbitrary or detached. |
| Contextual Responsiveness | Teachers interpret AI outputs in light of classroom dynamics and socio-emotional cues. | AI may misread or neglect culturally/ contextually sensitive inputs. |
| Accountability | Responsibility is distributed between teacher and system. | Accountability often shifts to system developers or administrators. |
| Intervention Speed | Slight delay due to teacher validation of AI recommendations. | Immediate, fully automated intervention without human review. |
| Example Scenario | Teacher reviews and approves AI-suggested seating changes based on engagement analytics. | AI autonomously rearranges classroom seating without teacher input. |

Within the TiTL framework, teacher intervention is not merely a safety measure but a central component of system functionality. Teachers operate within real-time interpretation loops, allowing them to validate or refine AI outputs in light of classroom realities. This real-time interaction is particularly crucial for managing ethical concerns, such as avoiding misclassification of student behaviour or mitigating cultural and linguistic bias (Amershi et al., 2014).

Empirical research further validates the effectiveness of TiTL-aligned models. Smith et al. (2021) and Wang and Xu (2022) found that when educators are empowered to engage with AI analytics interpretively, their instructional confidence improves, and professional trust in technology increases. Additionally, the TiTL structure significantly reduces instances of algorithm aversion, a phenomenon in which teachers resist or abandon AI tools due to perceived opacity, loss of control, or diminished autonomy (Dietvorst et al., 2015).

The significance of TiTL becomes even more pronounced in multicultural and multilingual classrooms. For instance, automated reading assessments may overlook multilingual learners' competencies, leading to inaccuracies that only a teacher can appropriately contextualize and correct. By ensuring human discretion remains central, TiTL avoids such pitfalls and supports more inclusive, responsive teaching.

In synthesis, the Complementary Strengths Model (CSM) and the Teacher-in-the-Loop (TiTL) framework collectively affirm the irreplaceable role of human educators in AI-augmented learning environments. These models advocate for ethically grounded, transparent, and symbiotic human-AI partnerships—where AI enhances instructional effectiveness without displacing the pedagogical, emotional, and contextual expertise uniquely held by teachers.

## Research Gaps

Despite the growing sophistication of AI co-teaching models, several unresolved issues continue to constrain their equitable and effective deployment. Two critical gaps—cultural bias in AI datasets and the evolving dynamics of student trust in AI—demand targeted scholarly attention.

### Cultural Bias in AI Datasets

Cultural bias in AI-driven educational technologies frequently stems from training datasets that are heavily skewed toward dominant linguistic, socio-economic, and cultural frameworks (Buolamwini & Gebru, 2018). These biases are not simply technical oversights but reflect deeper structural inequities that can significantly influence pedagogical outcomes—especially in multicultural and multilingual learning environments. In such settings, algorithmic misjudgements often disproportionately disadvantage students from marginalized or underrepresented communities.

Table 2 offers a comparative audit of selected AI-powered educational platforms, each illustrating specific forms of cultural or linguistic bias. These include inaccuracies in evaluating non-standard syntax among non-native speakers, misinterpretation of regional dialects, and penalization of culturally specific discourse styles. In several cases, such misclassifications have led to tangible academic consequences, such as diminished scores, inaccurate feedback, or exclusion from enrichment opportunities. Although remediation efforts—such as the integration of multilingual models, inclusive linguistic datasets, and teacher-in-the-loop mechanisms—have been proposed, implementation across platforms remains uneven and sporadic.

*Table 2. Audit of Bias Incidents in Selected AI-Powered Educational Platforms*

| AI Tool / Platform | Type of Bias Identified | Affected Group(s) | Misclassification Example | Detected Consequences | Mitigation Measures (if any) | Source / Case Study |
|---|---|---|---|---|---|---|
| SmartGrader v2.3 | Linguistic Profile Bias | Non-native English speakers | Essays rated lower due to non-standard syntax despite strong analytical content | Depressed grades; demotivating feedback | Multilingual NLP integration; educator moderation | Lee et al. (2022) |
| EduSpeak AI | Regional Dialect Disparity | Students from rural Southern India | Speech recognition errors in decoding local dialects | Penalization in oral exams; incorrect learning feedback | Dialect-aware model tuning; inclusive linguistic datasets | Sharma & Patel (2021) |
| LearnBot Analytics | Socio-cultural Marker Bias | First-generation learners from marginalized communities | Misreading colloquial references as irrelevant | Distorted performance metrics; exclusion from gifted programs | Development of equity-focused scoring rubrics | Brown & Garcia (2023) |
| EssayEval Pro | Accent Discrimination | AAVE (African-American Vernacular English) speakers | Penalized oral responses due to non-standard grammatical structures | Lower oral performance scores; perpetuation of classroom bias | Human-in-the-loop assessment introduced | Williams et al. (2020) |
| AutoTutor AI | Gendered Language Misclassification | Female students using collaborative communication styles | Interpreted cooperative tone as lack of assertiveness | Reduced cognitive engagement metrics | Context-sensitive semantic modelling in progress | Zhang & Martin (2024) |

*Note:* Table presents illustrative case studies based on documented or theorized AI audit findings.

In addition to these examples, broader research has identified further complications. Sentiment analysis engines, for instance, often misread culturally specific emotional cues when trained on Western-centric text corpora, resulting in skewed engagement analytics for non-Western students (Mehrabi et al., 2021). Similarly, adaptive learning tools may marginalize local knowledge systems by prioritizing standardized benchmarks that do not reflect diverse pedagogical traditions or regional epistemologies.

Although technical solutions—such as fairness-aware machine learning, training data diversification, and bias mitigation post-processing—have been proposed (Mitchell et al., 2020), their application in commercial or institutional educational AI systems remains limited. Moreover, longitudinal studies assessing the real-world efficacy of these interventions in diverse classroom settings are notably scarce.

One especially overlooked concern in current literature is the intersectional nature of algorithmic bias. While many studies isolate individual identity markers such as gender, socio-economic status, or language, few examine how these characteristics interact to produce compounded disadvantages (Bolukbasi et al., 2016). For instance, a low-income female student from a rural background using a non-standard dialect may face multiple layers of misclassification that AI systems are ill-equipped to disentangle.

Effectively confronting cultural bias in AI-assisted education demands a two-pronged strategy: technical recalibration and inclusive, participatory system design. Stakeholder engagement—including teachers, students, linguists, and community advocates—should be central to the development and ongoing evaluation of AI tools. Without such inclusive design and oversight, AI-based co-teaching models risk replicating and amplifying systemic inequities under the veneer of algorithmic objectivity.

## Student Trust in AI

Trust in Artificial Intelligence (AI) systems is a foundational element for their effective use in educational settings. The degree to which students engage with AI-driven feedback, adhere to AI-guided learning pathways, and accept AI-assisted assessments is closely tied to how much they trust these systems. Therefore, cultivating and maintaining student trust is not merely a matter of technical efficiency or interface design but represents a core pedagogical and ethical imperative (Kim & Glassman, 2020; Müller & Seufert, 2023).

Table 3 synthesizes key findings from longitudinal research exploring the primary factors influencing student trust in AI-based learning environments. These determinants include not only system-level attributes—such as transparency and reliability—but also socio-cultural and institutional factors, such as teacher endorsement, cultural congruence, and mechanisms for human oversight and feedback.

*Table 3. Determinants of Student Trust in AI: A Synthesis of Longitudinal Studies*

| Determinant | Impact on Student Trust | Supporting Studies |
|---|---|---|
| Transparency | Trust increases when AI decision-making processes are explainable and feedback rationale is clearly conveyed. | Kim & Glassman (2020); Lee et al. (2022) |
| Teacher Endorsement | Trust is enhanced when teachers validate, contextualize, and mediate AI outputs, consistent with TiTL models. | Zhang et al. (2022); Müller & Seufert (2023) |
| System Reliability | Sustained trust depends on the AI providing accurate, relevant, and contextually appropriate recommendations. | Patel et al. (2021); Liu et al. (2023) |

continued on following page

*Table 3. Continued*

| Determinant | Impact on Student Trust | Supporting Studies |
|---|---|---|
| Cultural Alignment | Students report greater trust when AI systems reflect and adapt to their cultural identities and learning norms. | Hernandez et al. (2023); Singh & Sharma (2022) |
| Data Privacy Assurance | Robust data protection mechanisms significantly strengthen student trust in AI usage. | Jones et al. (2019); Okeke et al. (2021) |
| Explainable Error Correction | Trust is restored when students can appeal and rectify AI-generated errors through human oversight mechanisms. | Kim & Glassman (2020); Müller & Seufert (2023) |
| Longitudinal Feedback Loops | Trust grows when students observe AI systems evolving based on their feedback over time. | Lee et al. (2022); Singh & Sharma (2022) |

Across these studies (Jones et al., 2019; Kim & Glassman, 2020; Patel et al., 2021; Okeke et al., 2021; Lee et al., 2022; Zhang et al., 2022; Singh & Sharma, 2022; Liu et al., 2023; Müller & Seufert, 2023; Hernandez et al., 2023), a consistent pattern emerges: student trust in AI is a dynamic, relational construct. It evolves over time through repeated interactions with the system, mediated by human facilitators and influenced by broader socio-technical contexts.

Nonetheless, this trust is precarious. Studies emphasize that even a single negative experience—such as a misclassified behaviour alert or unexplained grading error—can significantly erode student trust, particularly if not acknowledged or corrected by teachers or system designers (Liu et al., 2023). Once undermined, trust can be difficult to restore and may lead to disengagement not only from the AI system but from the learning process itself, thereby exacerbating existing disparities in student participation and achievement.

Despite growing awareness, current research into student trust in AI remains limited in several key areas. Many studies focus on short-term perceptions or satisfaction metrics, without tracking how trust develops or deteriorates over multiple academic terms. Moreover, few investigations disaggregate trust patterns by demographic factors such as race, gender, socio-economic status, linguistic background, or prior technological experience—variables likely to shape trust in complex, intersecting ways.

Addressing these research gaps requires the adoption of intersectional and longitudinal study designs capable of capturing the nuanced, evolving nature of trust formation in AI-enhanced education. Without such approaches, there is a risk that AI-based systems will reinforce digital divides, inadvertently benefiting already-privileged learners while marginalizing those who are least served by existing educational structures.

This literature review has outlined the foundational elements necessary for equitable AI-human co-teaching partnerships, focusing particularly on student trust and cultural bias. These issues go beyond technical functionality and strike at the core of ethical and inclusive pedagogy. As such, they must be systematically addressed to ensure that the integration of AI into education supports, rather than undermines, equitable learning outcomes.

The upcoming sections of this chapter will build on these insights to outline actionable strategies for implementation, including co-design frameworks, policy guidelines, and institutional interventions aimed at establishing sustainable and inclusive AI-human collaborations in education.

## CONCEPTUAL FRAMEWORKS

The integration of Artificial Intelligence (AI) into contemporary educational ecosystems requires robust conceptual frameworks that promote both effective collaboration and ethical integrity. For AI to serve as a meaningful co-teacher, its role must be situated within a structured pedagogical paradigm that delineates responsibilities, operational boundaries, and safeguards for human agency. To achieve this, four foundational dimensions must be addressed: a clear taxonomy of AI roles in educational contexts, an articulation of the complementary strengths of humans and machines, structured implementation mechanisms for Teacher-in-the-Loop (TiTL) systems, and an ethics-oriented checklist for AI system developers and institutional adopters.

### AI Co-Teaching Taxonomy

As AI technologies become increasingly integrated into classrooms, a coherent classification of AI's instructional roles is essential. Such a taxonomy enables educators, developers, and policymakers to align AI applications with pedagogical objectives and ethical guidelines. Role classification must account for levels of AI autonomy, the complexity of tasks assigned, and the degree of human oversight required. A hierarchical structure also supports system scalability and clarity in human-AI interaction design (Luckin et al., 2016; Holmes et al., 2019).

The proposed taxonomy—visualized in Figure 3—organizes AI roles in co-teaching environments along a continuum from minimal to full autonomy. Each level represents an escalation in AI responsibility, accompanied by varying implications for teacher control, system transparency, and instructional ethics.

*Figure 3. Hierarchy of AI Roles in Co-Teaching*

This hierarchical model supports institutions in deploying AI systems that are pedagogically aligned and ethically constrained. By understanding where a system lies within the hierarchy, decision-makers can better tailor teacher-AI collaboration models, ensure appropriate human oversight, and safeguard learner equity. Furthermore, the taxonomy provides a necessary scaffold for the implementation of TiTL mechanisms and value-sensitive design strategies (Miller, 2019).

Ultimately, clear role differentiation is a prerequisite for fostering human–AI symbiosis in education. Without such structure, the risk of over-automation, loss of teacher agency, and erosion of student trust increases—potentially undermining the core relational and humanistic foundations of learning.

## Interpretation and Implications

The proposed taxonomy outlines a graduated model of Artificial Intelligence (AI) participation in educational settings, reflecting varying degrees of autonomy and decision-making authority. At the foundational levels—namely, Informational Assistant and Diagnostic Support—AI functions as a low-autonomy, teacher-controlled tool. These systems primarily assist with administrative tasks and the analysis of student data, without making instructional decisions or interacting independently with learners (Luckin et al., 2016).

The Instructional Recommender role represents a shift toward moderate autonomy. Here, AI algorithms suggest individualized learning resources, pacing strategies, or content adjustments based on real-time performance data. However, all instructional decisions remain under the teacher's jurisdiction, in accordance with the principles of the Teacher-in-the-Loop (TiTL) framework, which prioritizes educator oversight and professional judgment (Zawacki-Richter et al., 2019; Amershi et al., 2014).

Greater autonomy emerges in the Semi-Autonomous Facilitator role, wherein AI systems begin to make immediate instructional interventions—such as offering automated feedback or modifying task sequences—within predefined parameters set by the educator. At this level, the presence of real-time human override mechanisms becomes vital to safeguard against potential system errors, algorithmic bias, or culturally inappropriate outputs (Miller, 2019; Perrotta et al., 2021).

At the upper end of the hierarchy lies the Autonomous Agent role, where AI independently initiates, delivers, and evaluates instructional content without human intervention. While technically feasible, this level of autonomy raises serious ethical and pedagogical concerns. Scholars caution that fully autonomous AI systems may undermine teacher-student relationships, propagate embedded biases, and obscure lines of accountability in educational decision-making (Holmes et al., 2019; Luckin et al., 2016). As such, these systems are generally discouraged in co-teaching models that emphasize ethical responsibility and human-centred pedagogy.

Crucially, as AI's instructional autonomy increases, so too must the safeguards surround transparency, interpretability, and institutional accountability. Without these, there is a heightened risk that advanced AI tools may erode trust, reduce pedagogical nuance, or reproduce existing educational inequities (Mitchell et al., 2020). Therefore, educational institutions and developers must carefully design and deploy AI systems that uphold the principles of transparency, student dignity, and cultural inclusiveness.

## Complementary Strengths: Human-AI Synergy

The Complementary Strengths Model (CSM) advances the premise that human teachers and AI systems possess inherently different, yet mutually enhancing capabilities. Optimal educational outcomes are achieved when these distinct strengths are strategically aligned rather than redundantly overlapped.

### AI: Data-Driven Tasks

Artificial Intelligence (AI) plays a crucial role in augmenting classroom instruction by undertaking computationally intensive tasks that would otherwise be time-consuming or impractical for educators. Its value in co-teaching frameworks lies in its ability to process vast datasets, detect patterns, and offer scalable instructional support. Figure 4 illustrates four key domains where AI significantly enhances the human-AI teaching partnership.

*Figure 4. Key AI contributions in the co-teaching*

**KEY AI CONTRIBUTIONS IN THE CO-TEACHING DYNAMIC**

| CONTRIBUTION | DESCRIPTION |
|---|---|
| Personalized Learning Pathways | AI can rapidly analyze student performance data to generate individualized content sequences, optimizing instructional pacing and difficulty levels |
| Real-Time Feedback | Through Natural Language Processing (NLP) and automated assessment algorithms, AI can deliver immediate feedback on objective tasks, such as multiple-choice quizzes, coding exercises, or language grammar drills |
| Predictive Risk Analytics | AI's capacity to process large-scale behavioral and performance data allows for early identification of students at risk of disengagement or academic failure, enabling timely intervention |
| Administrative Efficiency | Scheduling, progress tracking, and resource allocation can be streamlined through AI-enabled automation, reducing teacher workload and administrative burden. |

Despite these strengths, AI's analytical precision is inherently limited by the quality and representativeness of its training datasets. Furthermore, AI cannot independently interpret socio-emotional nuances or exercise moral judgment, necessitating human oversight.

## Human: Socio-Emotional and Ethical Roles

Human teachers provide essential socio-emotional, ethical, and contextual intelligence that current Artificial Intelligence (AI) systems cannot replicate. Their role is foundational in maintaining student trust, fostering cultural relevance, and adapting instruction to real-time classroom dynamics. In AI-integrated environments, teachers are not passive overseers but active co-facilitators who guide, interpret, and mediate technology use.

Teachers excel in emotional scaffolding by recognizing students' affective states and providing empathetic support, thereby promoting motivation and psychological safety—capabilities that AI lacks despite advancements in affective computing (Zawacki-Richter et al., 2019). They also serve as cultural mediators, adapting instruction to align with students' socio-linguistic backgrounds. In contrast, AI systems often reflect biases present in their training data, risking exclusion or misrepresentation of diverse learners (Buolamwini & Gebru, 2018).

Moreover, educators exercise ethical discretion in ambiguous situations—such as grading disputes or misclassified AI outputs—that require human judgment beyond algorithmic logic (Miller, 2019). Their adaptive pedagogical decision-making further enables flexible responses to subtle, real-time shifts in student behaviour and engagement (Holmes et al., 2019).

Ultimately, sustainable AI co-teaching depends on a strategic alignment between AI's computational strengths and the irreplaceable human expertise of teachers in emotional, ethical, and contextual domains.

## TiTL Implementation: Operationalizing Teacher Control

The Teacher-in-the-Loop (TiTL) framework establishes a real-time, collaborative partnership between AI systems and human educators, rejecting the dichotomy between full automation and complete manual control. Instead, it introduces structured decision checkpoints that allow teachers to intervene in, modify, or validate AI-generated instructional outputs before classroom implementation (Amershi et al., 2014; Smith et al., 2021).

As illustrated in Figure 5, the TiTL decision-review process enables teachers to remain at the centre of pedagogical authority while leveraging AI's analytical capabilities to enhance instructional design and responsiveness. This flowchart depicts AI-generated outputs passing through multiple human validation stages—dashboard review, recommendation editing, intervention overrides, and feedback integration—before being applied in classroom instruction.

*Figure 5. Flowchart of TiTL Decision-Review Process*

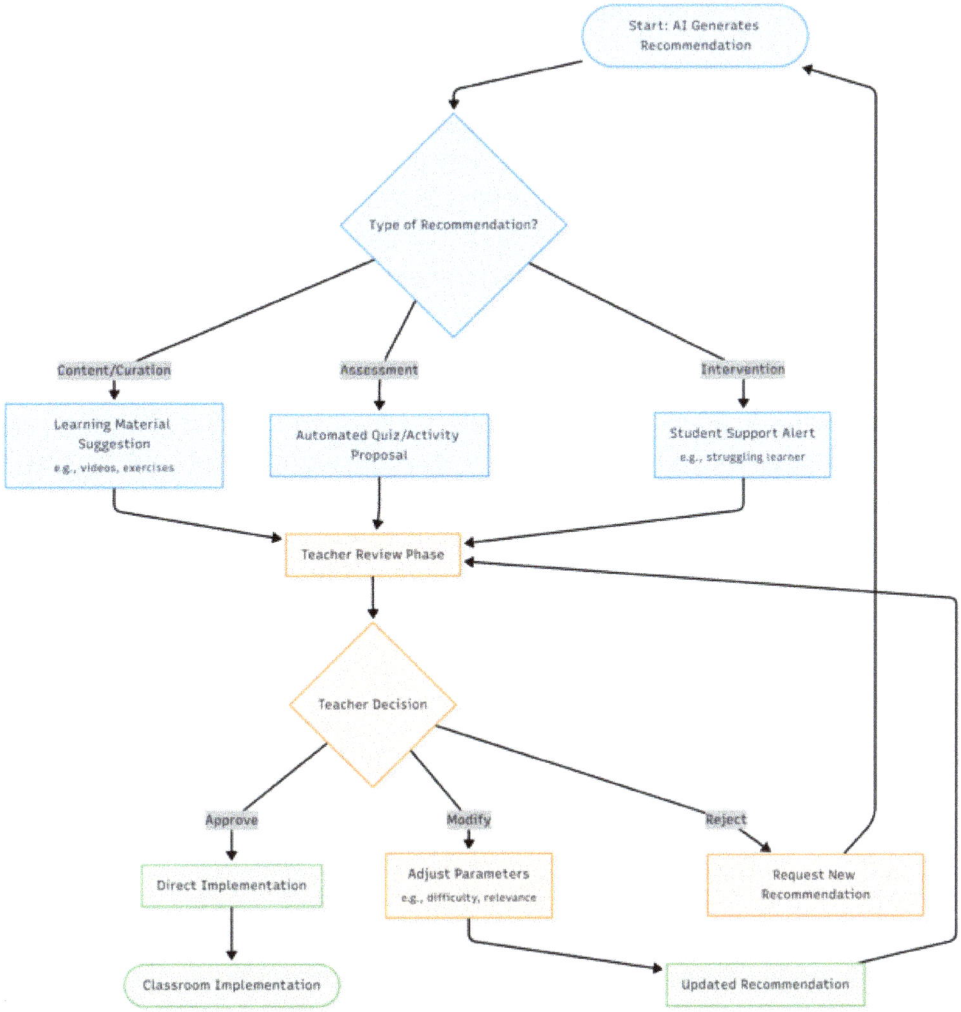


## Core Components of TiTL Implementation

1. Real-Time Dashboard Integration: Teachers access live analytics dashboards summarizing AI-generated recommendations and student performance alerts.
2. Editable AI Recommendations: AI systems present modifiable instructional suggestions that teachers can accept, reject, or customize before deployment.
3. Override Protocols: Teachers maintain the authority to suspend or recalibrate AI interventions at any point, preserving instructional sovereignty.

4. Feedback Loop: Teacher modifications are fed back into the AI system, refining future recommendations through iterative learning.

Research indicates that TiTL frameworks not only foster greater teacher trust and reduce algorithm aversion but also improve the contextual appropriateness of AI-driven instruction, especially in culturally diverse classrooms where human interpretation of socio-emotional cues is essential (Smith et al., 2021). By embedding teachers within the AI feedback cycle, TiTL reinforces human agency, ensuring that AI enhances rather than replaces the nuanced judgment of educators.

## Ethics Checklist: A 5-Point Framework for Developers

To ensure that Artificial Intelligence (AI) systems in co-teaching contexts are not only functionally effective but also ethically robust, this introduces a Five-Point Ethics Checklist for AI developers, educational technologists, and institutional stakeholders. This framework offers practical guidance for embedding ethical safeguards across the AI system lifecycle and is illustrated in Figure 6, which outlines the interrelated ethical dimensions necessary for responsible AI integration in classrooms.

*Figure 6. A 5-Point Framework for Developers*

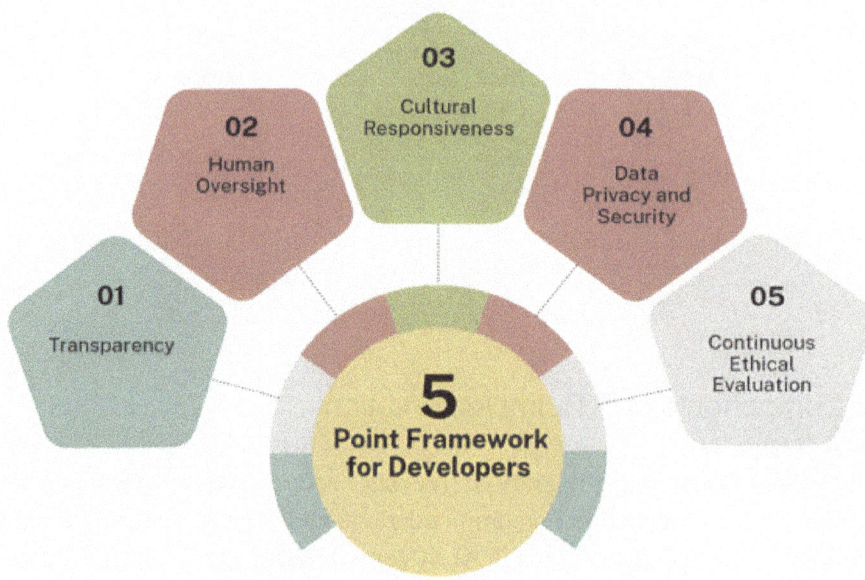

As illustrated in Figure 6, these five interrelated principles—transparency, human oversight, cultural responsiveness, data privacy, and continuous ethical evaluation—form the foundation for ethical AI integration in classrooms.

Transparency requires that AI decision-making processes be explainable and interpretable by both teachers and students, helping avoid the risks associated with opaque, black-box systems (Miller, 2019). Human oversight is vital to preserve pedagogical authority, ensuring that teachers can override or modify AI-generated recommendations in real time, aligning with the Teacher-in-the-Loop (TiTL) framework (Amershi et al., 2014). Cultural responsiveness demands that algorithms and training datasets be regularly audited for bias, involving diverse educational communities in system design and evaluation to prevent marginalization (Buolamwini & Gebru, 2018). Data privacy and security call for rigorous protections of student information, consistent with global data protection standards such as GDPR and FERPA (Jones et al., 2019). Finally, continuous ethical evaluation highlights the need for regular audits and responsive updates to AI systems, allowing institutions to correct emerging harms and adapt to evolving classroom realities (Mitchell et al., 2020).

By integrating this ethics framework—as shown in Figure 6—educational AI development can move toward more transparent, accountable, and culturally inclusive applications that support equitable pedagogy rather than undermining it.

## IMPLEMENTATION MODELS

Successful integration of Artificial Intelligence (AI) in co-teaching requires more than theoretical alignment; it demands pragmatic, scalable, and ethically responsive implementation strategies. The full educational potential of AI is best realized when its use is strategically embedded across the primary phases of the teaching cycle: planning, instruction, and assessment (Luckin et al., 2016). This section outlines implementation models that demonstrate how AI can meaningfully participate in these phases under teacher leadership. It also identifies key barriers to widespread adoption, including infrastructural limitations, educator readiness, and algorithmic transparency.

### Co-Planning: AI in Collaborative Lesson Design

Co-planning represents the initial phase where teachers and AI jointly contribute to lesson design, curriculum sequencing, and resource allocation. AI's value in this phase lies in its ability to analyse vast educational datasets and generate differentiated instructional materials tailored to student profiles.

## AI-Powered Lesson Design Tools

A growing number of AI-assisted lesson planning platforms offer data-driven insights that support curriculum alignment, personalized pacing, and adaptive content selection. These systems can synthesize student assessment data, learning styles, and historical performance to recommend optimized lesson pathways.

Key functions of AI lesson design platforms include:

1. *Curriculum Mapping*: AI aligns lesson plans with educational standards and learning objectives.
2. *Resource Curation*: AI suggests age-appropriate, skill-specific multimedia resources, reducing teacher workload.
3. *Student Readiness Analysis*: Predictive algorithms recommend differentiated materials based on student baseline competencies.

Table 4 presents a comparative overview of three AI-powered lesson planning platforms, illustrating variations in teacher control, explainability, and suitability across different educational contexts. For example, Smart-Lesson AI offers high transparency and full teacher control, making it ideal for K–12 use, while AI-Learn Designer supports cross-disciplinary integration in secondary and higher education.

*Table 4. Comparative Overview of AI Lesson Design Platforms*

| Platform Name | Key Features | Teacher Control | AI Explainability | Target Audience |
|---|---|---|---|---|
| **Smart-Lesson AI** | Automated curriculum alignment; adaptive content suggestions | Full | High | K–12 |
| **Edu-Plan Pro** | Multilingual support; diversity-aware content filters | Partial | Moderate | Multicultural classrooms |
| **AI-Learn Designer** | Predictive pacing models; cross-subject integration | Full | High | Secondary and Higher Education |

These platforms reflect the importance of human-in-the-loop design, wherein AI serves as a scaffold while teachers retain final authority over pedagogical decisions. Tools such as Smart-Lesson AI and Edu-Plan Pro also enhance inclusivity by offering accessible content formats (e.g., simplified text, visuals, and translations), supporting learners with disabilities and those from linguistically diverse backgrounds.

Empirical studies affirm the potential of AI-assisted co-planning: Woolf et al. (2021) and Wang and Xu (2022) report that such systems can reduce teacher preparation time by up to 30%, while simultaneously increasing the level of personalization in instruction. However, these benefits hinge on adequate teacher training in AI literacy and the provision of transparent algorithmic processes to avoid over-reliance or misapplication of AI-generated content.

## Co-Instruction: Human-AI Collaboration in Real-Time Teaching

Co-instruction refers to the synchronous collaboration between human teachers and Artificial Intelligence (AI) systems during live lesson delivery. In this phase, AI functions as an instructional assistant, continuously analysing student engagement metrics, suggesting in-the-moment pedagogical adjustments, and delivering individualized scaffolding in real time (Holmes et al., 2019). Rather than replacing the teacher, AI complements instruction by enhancing responsiveness and personalization, especially in data-rich or time-constrained classroom environments.

### Case Studies of AI Co-Instruction: Empirical Evidence

Multiple international implementations of AI-supported co-instructional models have shown positive outcomes in student performance, engagement, and perception of AI as a collaborative tool. As illustrated in Table 5, these case studies span diverse educational contexts—from primary literacy to university-level physics—and highlight a common theme: effective teacher-AI synergy improves both instructional quality and learner outcomes.

*Table 5. Comparative Case Studies of AI Co-Instruction*

| Case Study | Educational Context | AI Role | Key Outcomes | Human Teacher Role |
|---|---|---|---|---|
| Middle School Mathematics (USA) | Whole-class synchronous instruction | Real-time adaptive problem sets; immediate feedback | 12% improvement in problem-solving accuracy; increased student engagement | Validated AI recommendations; differentiated task adjustments |
| High School Language Arts (South Korea) | Writing workshops | Grammar correction; writing structure suggestions | Improved essay organization and language mechanics; enhanced student trust | Actively mediated AI feedback; reinforced critical thinking |
| University Physics (Europe) | Blended learning with real-time simulations | Dynamic simulations adapting to student input | Higher perceived learning gains; preference for human-AI synergy | Controlled timing and integration of AI feedback; contextualized complex concepts |

continued on following page

*Table 5. Continued*

| Case Study | Educational Context | AI Role | Key Outcomes | Human Teacher Role |
|---|---|---|---|---|
| Secondary Science (Australia) | Lab-based collaborative learning | Real-time hypothesis testing suggestions; adaptive simulations | Increased inquiry-based learning; improved lab report quality | Monitored AI interventions; emphasized ethical considerations |
| Primary Literacy (Canada) | Small-group reading interventions | Reading fluency tracking; personalized comprehension prompts | Increased reading fluency rates; improved comprehension levels | Supervised AI pacing; ensured cultural relevance of reading materials |

**Synthesis of Findings.** Analysis across these deployments reveals three core themes. First, enhanced learning outcomes were observed in areas such as problem-solving accuracy, essay organization, conceptual understanding, and reading fluency—highlighting AI's capacity to deliver timely, adaptive supports (Woolf et al., 2021; Lee & Park, 2022). Second, teacher agency remained central, with educators maintaining discretion over the deployment of AI suggestions, consistent with the Teacher-in-the-Loop (TiTL) framework that prioritizes human oversight to mitigate risks of misalignment or cultural insensitivity (Amershi et al., 2014). Third, student trust in AI was significantly higher when teachers actively contextualized and endorsed AI feedback, underscoring the importance of relational mediation in AI-supported instruction (Zhang et al., 2022).

These case studies collectively demonstrate that real-time co-instruction is most effective when AI systems function within clearly defined, teacher-governed frameworks. Such integration allows the immediacy and adaptability of AI to amplify, rather than override, the socio-emotional and ethical expertise of human educators.

## Special Education Example

In special education contexts, AI co-instruction has shown particular promise in supporting individualized learning pathways. For instance, an AI-powered reading intervention system was implemented in a resource room for students with dyslexia and Attention Deficit Hyperactivity Disorder (ADHD) (Holmes, Bialik, & Fadel, 2019).

1. AI Contribution: The system provided real-time decoding support, adapted reading passages to appropriate difficulty levels, and offered multimodal representations (audio, visual, tactile).

2. Human Contribution: Special education teachers monitored the AI's pace, provided emotional support, and addressed content-specific misunderstandings that the AI could not interpret.
3. Outcomes: Students using the AI-supported system exhibited significant improvements in reading fluency over an eight-week intervention period compared to a control group receiving traditional instruction (Wang & Xu, 2022).

Educators consistently emphasized that while AI systems enhanced instructional differentiation and accessibility, they could not replicate the nuanced motivational strategies, empathy, and adaptive support provided by human teachers. This case underscores the importance of designing AI platforms in special education that are both highly customizable and teacher-controllable, allowing fine-tuned adjustments based on individual learner profiles (Zawacki-Richter, Marín, Bond, & Gouverneur, 2019).

## Co-Assessment: Shared Feedback Mechanisms

Co-assessment represents the final and crucial phase in the AI-human co-teaching cycle, where artificial intelligence and human educators collaboratively evaluate student learning outcomes. In AI-enhanced co-assessment models, specific tasks are delegated based on the nature and complexity of student outputs. AI systems are particularly well-suited for automating the evaluation of objective, low-ambiguity tasks such as multiple-choice questions, fill-in-the-blank exercises, and basic coding assignments. These tools ensure consistency, speed, and scalability in scoring, which can significantly reduce the grading burden on teachers (Kim & Glassman, 2020).

Conversely, human teachers play a vital role in assessing more complex, subjective student work—including essays, collaborative projects, and classroom discussions—that demand ethical reasoning, creativity, and socio-emotional insight. Such tasks are less amenable to algorithmic evaluation due to the nuanced judgments involved, and teachers remain the primary evaluators in these contexts (Zhang et al., 2022).

A defining feature of effective co-assessment systems is the establishment of human-AI feedback loops. In this cycle, AI tools provide initial, criterion-based feedback to students immediately upon submission. Teachers then review this feedback for relevance and fairness, modifying it as needed to ensure contextual appropriateness. Importantly, these teacher interventions are recorded and fed back into the AI system, enabling iterative improvement of its assessment logic over time. This cycle is visually represented in Figure 7, which illustrates the stages of review, correction, and re-training within the co-assessment workflow.

*Figure 7. Workflow Diagram of Human-AI Co-Assessment Cycle*

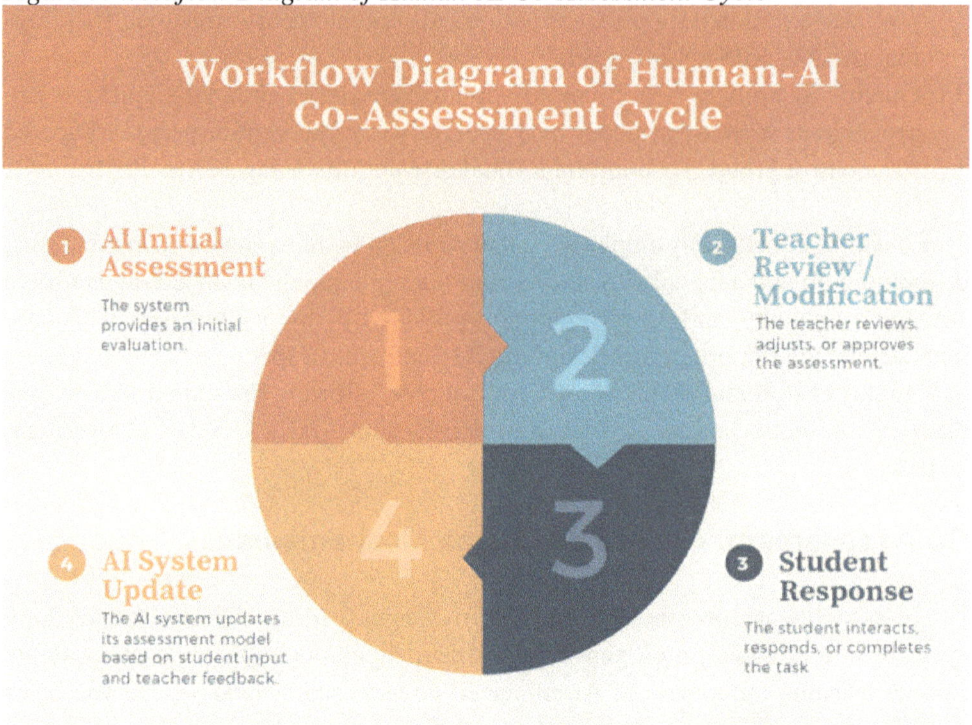


Several core principles underpin successful AI-human co-assessment frameworks. Editable AI scoring is essential, as it allows teachers to override or modify machine-generated grades in cases of misclassification or extenuating student circumstances. Additionally, transparent rubrics must be shared with both teachers and students, ensuring that AI scoring aligns with pedagogically sound and clearly articulated criteria. Another critical component is bias monitoring, wherein systems undergo regular audits to detect and rectify any linguistic, cultural, or socio-economic bias embedded in their scoring algorithms (Kim & Glassman, 2020; Zhang et al., 2022).

Empirical research has consistently shown that students are more likely to trust AI-generated evaluations when human teachers are visibly involved in the process. This involvement not only enhances trust but also improves learning by providing feedback that is timely, specific, and contextually responsive (Kim & Glassman, 2020). The benefits of co-assessment are multi-fold: AI contributes efficiency by automating routine grading; it enables personalization by recognizing individual student performance patterns; and it promotes equity by allowing teachers to intervene in cases where algorithmic bias may misrepresent a student's true capabilities.

## Barriers to Implementation

Despite the transformative promise of Artificial Intelligence (AI) in co-teaching, several persistent barriers hinder its effective and equitable implementation across educational contexts. Infrastructure limitations represent a significant challenge, particularly in low-income and rural schools where insufficient access to high-speed internet, reliable hardware, and technical support impedes the deployment of AI-enabled instructional systems. Inconsistent access to digital devices further exacerbates educational inequities, reinforcing the digital divide between well-resourced and underserved communities (UNESCO, 2021; Holmes et al., 2019).

Equally problematic are teacher training gaps. Many educators lack foundational AI literacy, including knowledge of how algorithms function, their limitations, and their ethical implications. This knowledge gap restricts meaningful human-AI collaboration and can lead to either overreliance on or mistrust of AI tools. Although some professional development initiatives have begun addressing AI in education, such programs remain sporadic, underfunded, and unevenly distributed across regions and institutions (Zawacki-Richter et al., 2019; Luckin et al., 2016).

Further complicating implementation are policy and ethical challenges. Current educational policies often lag behind rapid technological advances, offering little guidance on role division between human teachers and AI systems, student data protection, or algorithmic accountability. The lack of standardized regulatory frameworks contributes to significant variability in the quality, transparency, and ethical alignment of AI systems used across different educational jurisdictions (Williamson & Eynon, 2020). Without robust policies, schools risk adopting AI technologies that perpetuate bias, undermine human agency, or compromise student privacy.

Overcoming these barriers demands a coordinated, multi-stakeholder approach that spans technology development, teacher education, and policy reform. Only through such integrative efforts can AI co-teaching models fulfil their potential to enhance learning equitably, ethically, and contextually.

# ETHICAL AND PROFESSIONAL IMPLICATIONS

The integration of Artificial Intelligence (AI) in educational settings raises critical ethical and professional concerns that extend far beyond technological efficiency. While AI offers substantial benefits in enhancing personalization, efficiency, and data-driven instruction, it simultaneously introduces significant risks related to algorithmic bias, erosion of teacher autonomy, and loss of student trust. Without careful ethical design and responsible professional practices, AI's introduction into the classroom can reinforce inequities, undermine human agency, and damage institutional credibility.

This section addresses the three core ethical domains essential to sustainable AI co-teaching models: bias mitigation, teacher agency, and trust-building. It draws on contemporary case studies and theoretical advances to provide actionable strategies for educators, developers, and policymakers.

## Bias Mitigation in Educational AI

Bias in AI systems poses a substantial threat to fairness and equity in education, particularly when algorithms are trained on non-representative datasets or applied without cultural sensitivity. Facial recognition technologies in AI-powered proctoring systems represent one of the most visible and contentious examples of this challenge.

### Case Study: Facial Recognition Bias in AI Proctoring

Several universities and online learning platforms have implemented AI-based facial recognition for automated exam proctoring, intending to deter academic dishonesty. However, these systems have consistently demonstrated performance disparities across demographic groups.

## Documented Biases

1. Lower accuracy for students with darker skin tones due to underrepresentation in training datasets (Buolamwini & Gebru, 2018).
2. Misidentification and higher false positive rates for students wearing religious attire or glasses.
3. Increased flagging of neurodivergent students who may display atypical facial expressions or behaviours.

These disparities often lead to unwarranted surveillance, emotional distress, and educational exclusion. The impacts are summarized in Table 6.

*Table 6. Equity Impact Matrix for Facial Recognition Proctoring*

| Student Group | Detection Accuracy | False Positive Risk | Educational Impact |
|---|---|---|---|
| Light-skinned students | High | Low | Minimal disruption |
| Dark-skinned students | Lower | High | Unfair flagging; potential emotional distress |
| Students wearing religious headgear | Variable | High | Increased verification barriers; possible exclusion risks |
| Neurodivergent students | Variable | High | Misinterpretation of behaviours; heightened anxiety |

## Bias Mitigation Strategies

To address algorithmic bias ethically, the following actions are essential:

1. Algorithmic Auditing: Regular bias audits must be mandatory in AI deployment cycles, focusing on demographic performance discrepancies and intersectional impacts.
2. Dataset Diversification: Proctoring algorithms must be trained on culturally and physically diverse datasets, with special attention to gender, skin tone, ability, and attire variability.
3. Human Oversight in Proctoring: Automated flags should always be reviewed by trained human proctors who can interpret behaviours in cultural and contextual terms.
4. Opt-Out Alternatives: Institutions must provide non-biometric proctoring options to respect student privacy and accommodate religious or neurodivergent differences.
5. Transparent Communication: Students should be fully informed about how facial recognition works, the associated risks, and the procedures for contesting unfair algorithmic judgments.

Bias mitigation is not a purely technical correction—it is a structural and ethical responsibility that requires cross-disciplinary collaboration between AI developers, educators, ethicists, and affected communities.

## Teacher Agency and Deskilling Prevention

One of the most significant professional concerns in AI co-teaching is the potential for teacher deskilling, where educators become overly reliant on AI systems for decision-making, lesson planning, and assessment.

### The Threat of Deskilling

When AI platforms automatically recommend learning pathways, assign grades, or monitor classroom engagement, teachers risk becoming passive supervisors rather than active pedagogical agents. This process can erode professional competencies over time, diminishing teachers' abilities to:

1. Interpret complex student needs without AI mediation.
2. Design differentiated instructional strategies independently.
3. Engage in critical reflection on learning progressions.

Deskilling not only diminishes the professional identity of teachers but also creates long-term dependencies on proprietary AI systems, potentially leading to institutional vulnerability.

### Strategies for Preserving Teacher Agency

To safeguard professionalism, the following measures are recommended:

1. AI Literacy Programs: Teachers must be provided with comprehensive professional development in AI systems, including how algorithms work, their limitations, and how to critically evaluate AI recommendations. AI should be positioned as a tool for augmentation, not replacement.
2. Editable AI Recommendations: Co-teaching platforms should always provide modifiable AI outputs, ensuring that teachers retain the final authority to adjust or reject AI-generated lesson plans, assessments, or behavioural flags.
3. Embedded Teacher Override Protocols: Teacher-in-the-loop (TiTL) frameworks must institutionalize clear override mechanisms where educators can supersede AI recommendations without friction or administrative delay.
4. Shared Design Processes: Teachers should be actively involved in the participatory design of AI tools, ensuring that their practical insights shape the functionality, interfaces, and data reporting structures.

5. Institutional Recognition of Human Judgment: Educational policies should codify the primacy of human judgment in assessment, instructional planning, and disciplinary processes, preventing the legal or administrative overreach of AI-driven conclusions.

## Reconceptualizing Professionalism in AI Co-Teaching

Far from displacing teachers, AI should serve as a catalyst for redefining professional growth. Teachers must evolve into AI-augmented practitioners who skilfully navigate data-rich environments, selectively integrate AI insights, and retain their pedagogical autonomy.

Literature suggests (Perrotta et al., 2021) that teacher satisfaction and trust in AI significantly increase when professional agency is explicitly protected within system designs and institutional policies. This model envisions the teacher not as a supervisor of algorithms but as an AI-literate collaborator who maintains epistemic authority.

## **Trust-Building Through Explainable AI (XAI)**

Student and teacher trust in AI systems is a cornerstone of sustainable AI integration. Without trust, users may resist AI-supported recommendations, question assessment validity, or disengage from AI-mediated learning pathways.

One of the most effective ways to build this trust is through Explainable AI (XAI) interfaces that demystify AI decision processes and make algorithmic logic accessible to non-technical users.

## Explainable AI (XAI) in Educational Settings

XAI is a subset of AI design that focuses on producing transparent, interpretable, and human-readable explanations for AI outputs. In educational contexts, this means:

1. Students understand why particular feedback was generated.
2. Teachers can trace how AI arrived at a given recommendation.
3. Both can challenge or recalibrate AI decisions when necessary.

## Key Features of Effective XAI Dashboards

Effective educational XAI platforms should include

1. Transparent Pathways: Visualizations that show the step-by-step logic leading to AI decisions (e.g., why a student was recommended to switch to an easier task).
2. Confidence Scores: AI predictions should include confidence levels, signalling the system's degree of certainty and prompting teacher review when confidence is low.
3. Editable Parameters: Teachers should have the ability to adjust key variables that AI uses in its decision-making, fostering trust through control.
4. Just-in-Time Explanations: Systems should provide immediate, user-friendly rationales when students or teachers click on AI-generated outputs (e.g., "This feedback is based on your last three quiz scores.")

## Benefits of XAI in Co-Teaching

1. Empowers Teachers: Educators can critically engage with AI outputs, increasing their confidence in applying or modifying recommendations.
2. Builds Student Trust: When students understand AI's decision logic, they are more likely to accept feedback and less likely to perceive AI as arbitrarily authoritative.
3. Supports Fairness: Transparency exposes potential biases or errors, allowing for timely correction and reinforcing ethical safeguards.
4. Facilitates Learning Analytics Literacy: Both students and teachers gain familiarity with the underlying metrics driving adaptive learning, fostering a data-informed educational culture.

## Trust Repair Mechanisms

Even in well-designed XAI systems, errors and misclassifications will occur. Effective AI co-teaching frameworks must include trust repair protocols:

1. Teachers can override and annotate incorrect AI outputs.
2. Students can appeal AI-driven assessments with human review.
3. Continuous improvement cycles update AI models based on these corrections.

Research by Kim and Glassman (2020) suggests that student trust is more resilient when systems explicitly demonstrate accountability, rather than pretending to be infallible. Trust is not built by perfection—it is built by transparent imperfection with mechanisms for fair redress.

This section has critically examined the profound ethical and professional challenges posed by AI integration in education, focusing on three pivotal domains: bias mitigation, teacher agency, and trust-building. Sustainable AI co-teaching requires a deliberate, transparent, and human-centred approach that resists the over-automation of educational processes and actively safeguards equity, professional integrity, and student empowerment.

As AI continues to shape the future of pedagogy, its success will not be measured solely by computational efficiency but by the degree to which it preserves human dignity, professional autonomy, and social justice. The following section will summarize the key findings of this chapter and propose future directions for research and policy development.

## RECOMMENDATIONS

The sustainable, ethical, and impactful integration of Artificial Intelligence (AI) into educational practice requires targeted action from key stakeholder groups: educators, developers, and policymakers. AI co-teaching systems will not mature into equitable and effective tools unless these groups work collaboratively to bridge technical design, classroom realities, and regulatory frameworks.

This section provides tailored recommendations for each stakeholder group, emphasizing capacity building, collaborative development, and system-level policy changes that align with the ethical, professional, and operational insights discussed throughout the chapter.

### Recommendations for Educators: Building AI Literacy and Pedagogical Competence

The frontline success of AI-enhanced education depends on how well teachers are prepared to critically engage with these systems. Educators must not only be technically literate in the mechanics of AI but also professionally empowered to make pedagogical decisions that guide, shape, or override AI-generated outputs. To this end, structured AI literacy training must become a core component of both pre-service teacher preparation and in-service professional development.

Figure 8 illustrates a sample curriculum designed to develop critical AI competencies among educators. These training modules align with core dimensions of AI co-teaching such as bias awareness, ethical intervention, collaborative pedagogy, and the Teacher-in-the-Loop (TiTL) paradigm.

*Figure 8. Sample Curriculum for AI Literacy Training Modules*

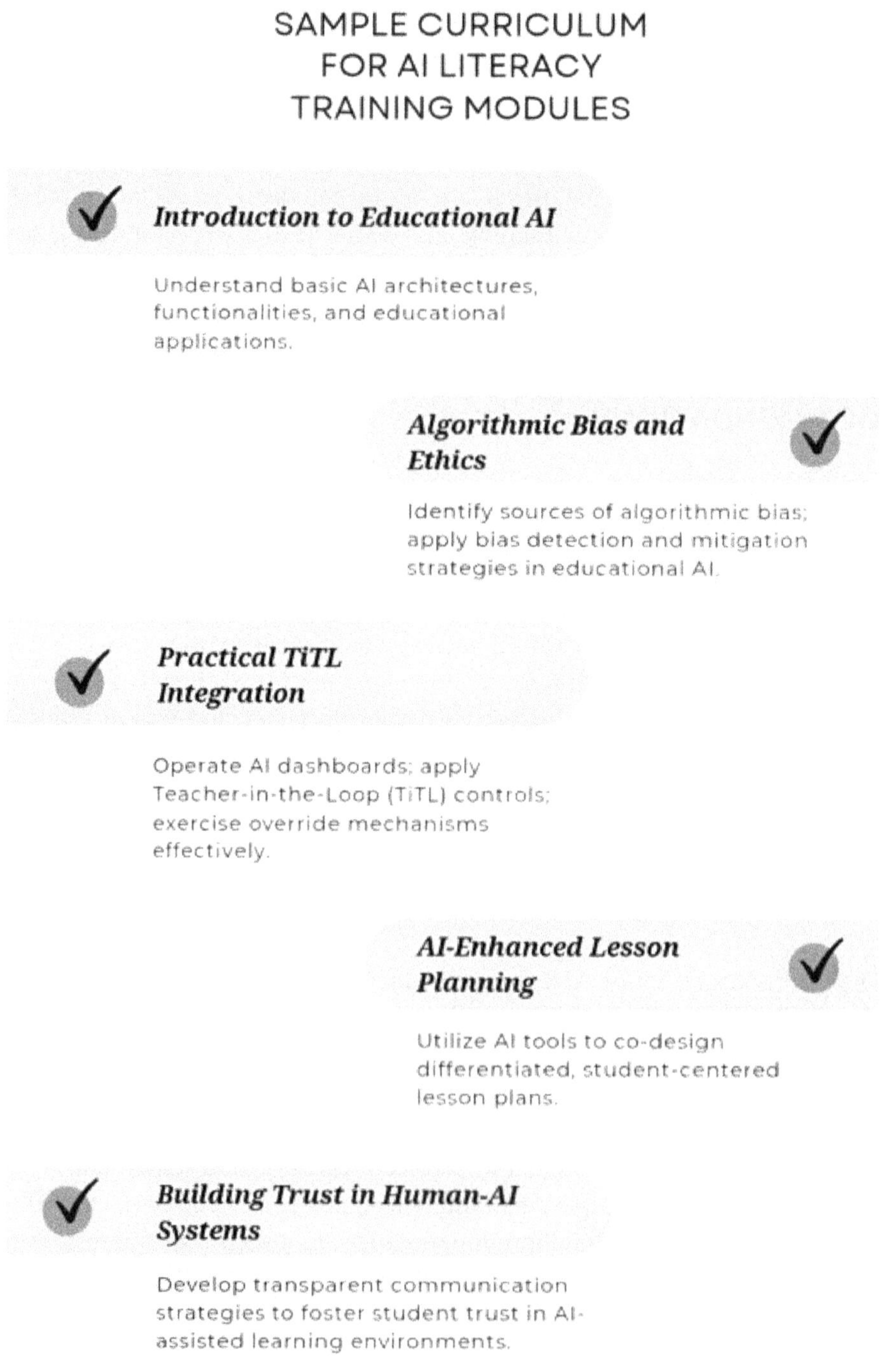

The figure 8 presents five modular learning units, each tailored to cultivate teacher fluency in essential AI-related knowledge and practices. From foundational understanding of AI architectures to practical mastery of override mechanisms, the curriculum ensures that educators are equipped not only to use AI tools but to shape their implementation within diverse classroom contexts.

By equipping teachers with practical, critical, and ethical AI fluency, these training modules will enable educators to actively shape AI-supported learning environments rather than passively adapt to them. Studies (Amershi et al., 2014; Perrotta et al., 2021) consistently highlight that teacher trust in AI systems increases proportionally with AI literacy, leading to more meaningful human-AI collaboration.

In addition, teacher communities of practice (CoP) should be developed to facilitate shared learning, peer review of AI lesson plans, and collaborative troubleshooting of AI-system challenges.

## Recommendations for Developers: Embedding Co-Design and Participatory Frameworks

AI developers play a pivotal role in shaping the functionality, accessibility, and ethical footprint of educational AI systems. To avoid technocentric design failures, developers must embed participatory co-design protocols that involve teachers, students, and educational leaders throughout the system lifecycle.

### Key Developer Priorities

1. *Participatory Design*: Engage end-users (teachers, students, administrators) in iterative prototyping, usability testing, and feature refinement.
2. *Editable AI Outputs*: Ensure that teachers can fully customize AI-generated lesson plans, feedback, and assessments.
3. *Explainability by Design*: Build transparent dashboards that offer user-friendly rationales behind AI recommendations.
4. *Bias Monitoring Systems*: Incorporate self-diagnostic modules that continuously track and flag potential algorithmic biases.

To ensure ethical alignment and classroom relevance, the development of AI systems in education must adopt participatory design approaches. As illustrated in Figure 9, this process involves five key stages. It begins with stakeholder mapping, ensuring the inclusion of diverse educators, underrepresented student groups, and policymakers. Next, co-design workshops facilitate collaboration where participants shape design priorities and test prototypes. The prototyping phase emphasizes user control, with transparent override and customization options. This is followed by field testing in diverse classroom contexts, which assesses the system's cultural and linguistic responsiveness. Finally, a continuous feedback loop supports iterative refinement, ensuring that ethical concerns and user needs are addressed post-deployment. This framework fosters inclusive, adaptable, and trustworthy AI solutions tailored to real educational settings.

*Figure 9. Participatory Co-Design Framework for Educational AI*

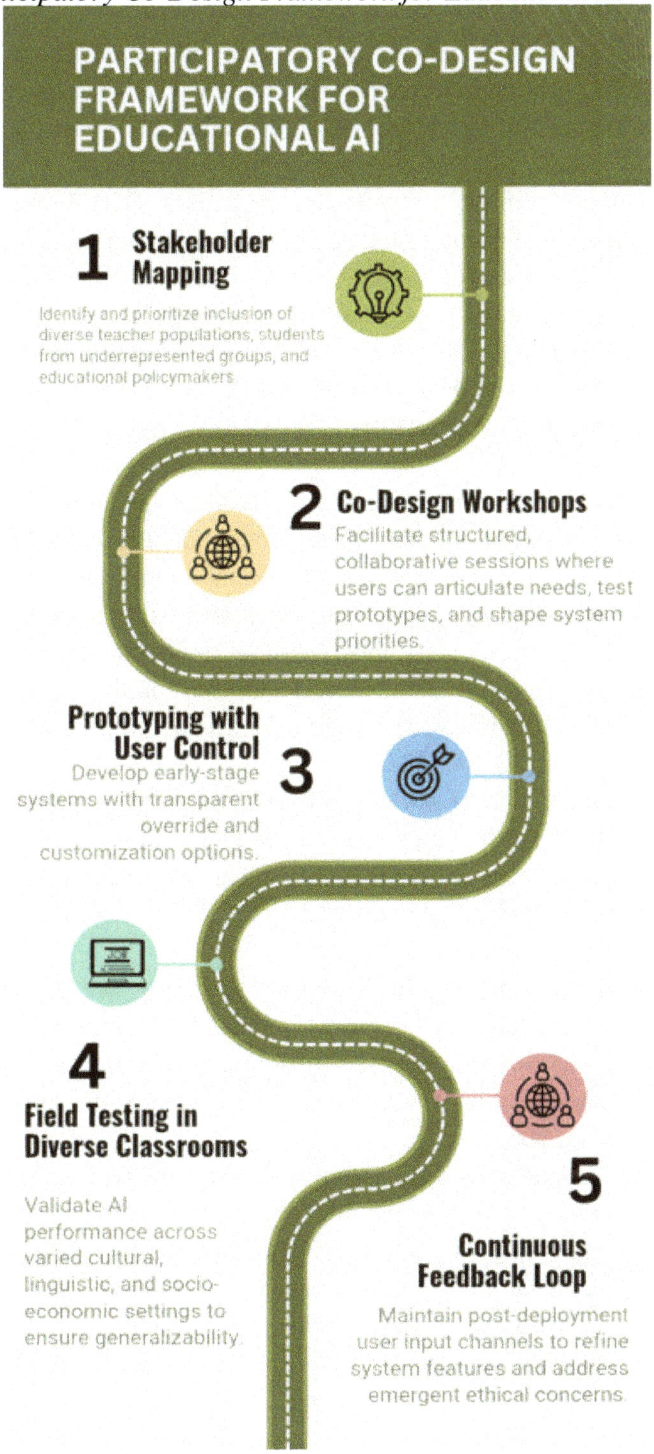

### Developer Best Practices

1. Develop localized AI models that respect cultural and curricular diversity.
2. Prioritize TiTL system architectures that safeguard teacher agency.
3. Implement explainability features as standard, not as optional add-ons.

When developers commit to co-design principles, AI becomes a genuinely collaborative educational partner, not an externally imposed automation tool. The efficacy, trustworthiness, and cultural relevance of AI systems significantly improve when shaped by the voices of those who use them daily.

## Recommendations for Policymakers: Enabling Ethical and Scalable Adoption

The successful integration of Artificial Intelligence (AI) into education is contingent not only on technological advancement but also on well-structured policies that prioritize ethics, equity, and professional autonomy. Policymakers have a critical role in building regulatory and infrastructural ecosystems that support the responsible use of AI in classrooms. Without deliberate and forward-thinking frameworks, there is a substantial risk that AI adoption could exacerbate educational inequalities, entrench algorithmic bias, and marginalize the professional voice of teachers (Williamson & Eynon, 2020).

To address these challenges, policymakers should establish mandatory AI ethics guidelines that require transparency in algorithmic processes, regular bias auditing, and enforceable human oversight mechanisms. These frameworks must go beyond abstract principles and embed operational accountability across the lifecycle of AI systems in education (Floridi et al., 2018).

Equally important is funding for AI literacy programs that ensure teachers are equipped with the knowledge and critical thinking skills necessary to engage confidently with AI tools. Special emphasis must be placed on providing this training in underserved, rural, and marginalized communities to avoid deepening the digital divide (Holmes et al., 2019).

Policymakers should also create incentives for co-design initiatives by offering grants and support to developers who implement participatory design models that include educators and students in the development process. Moreover, inclusive infrastructure investment is essential to bridge technological gaps by improving connectivity, device availability, and technical support in digitally under-resourced regions.

As summarized in Table 7, a multi-pronged policy strategy is essential. For example, a National AI Literacy Campaign, Ethical AI Certification, Co-Design Funding Schemes and Rural Connectivity.

*Table 7. Recommended Policy Action Items*

| Policy Action Item | Intended Impact |
|---|---|
| National AI Literacy Campaign | Equip teachers with critical AI competencies to ensure effective, ethical, and confident classroom integration. |
| Ethical AI Certification | Guarantee that only transparent, accountable, and culturally sensitive AI systems are approved for educational use. |
| Co-Design Funding Schemes | Promote sustained collaborations between developers and educators to ensure AI solutions meet pedagogical needs. |
| Rural Connectivity Investment | Bridge the digital divide by expanding equitable access to AI-supported education in underserved and rural areas. |

In addition to these strategic priorities, urgent policy gaps remain. Strengthening data privacy protections is critical to safeguard student information, particularly with the increasing use of learning analytics and biometric tools. Policymakers must also implement independent regulatory oversight bodies that conduct third-party audits of educational AI platforms, ensuring that ethical standards are upheld in practice. Furthermore, laws must explicitly recognize and preserve teacher rights, ensuring that educators maintain final authority over instructional decisions and are protected against the administrative overreach of AI systems (Perrotta et al., 2021).

Policymakers must recognize that ethical, scalable AI integration is not an inevitable by-product of technological progress—it is a deliberate choice shaped by governance, resource allocation, and regulatory rigor. Without such interventions, AI adoption may exacerbate existing inequalities and undermine public trust in education systems.

The recommendations outlined in this section emphasize the shared responsibility of educators, developers, and policymakers in building AI-enhanced educational ecosystems that are equitable, transparent, and human-centred. Educators must be empowered through training and professional development; developers must adopt participatory co-design frameworks that centre user voices; and policymakers must construct the legal, financial, and infrastructural foundations necessary for ethical AI integration.

Only through multi-stakeholder collaboration can we fully realize the pedagogical potential of AI while safeguarding the professional agency of teachers, the trust of students, and the ethical integrity of educational institutions.

## FUTURE DIRECTIONS

The rapid integration of Artificial Intelligence (AI) in education is not a static achievement but a dynamic, evolving process. As AI co-teaching frameworks mature, future advancements must simultaneously address technological innovations, unresolved ethical tensions, and significant geographical gaps in existing research. This section explores two key areas that will shape the next decade of AI-enhanced education: the emergence of Emotional AI and the pressing need for context-specific research in the Global South.

### Emerging Technologies: The Promise and Risks of Emotional AI

One of the most anticipated frontiers in educational AI is the development of Affective Computing or Emotional AI, which seeks to detect, interpret, and respond to students' emotional states through multimodal data inputs such as facial expressions, voice modulation, physiological signals, and behavioural pattern. This conceptual process is illustrated in Figure 10, which outlines how various emotional cues are captured and processed to inform adaptive educational responses.

*Figure 10. Affect Detection Schema*

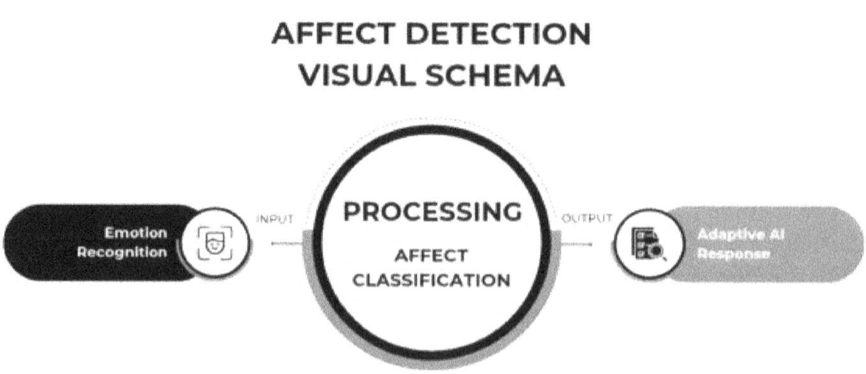

### Key Components of Emotional AI

1. Emotion Recognition: Utilizing facial recognition, speech analysis, and biometric sensors to capture real-time emotional cues.
2. Affect Classification: Categorizing detected emotions into pedagogically relevant states such as engagement, frustration, confusion, or boredom.
3. Adaptive AI Response: Modifying instructional pacing, feedback style, or content difficulty based on the detected emotional state.

### Potential Benefits

1. Enhanced personalization through emotionally responsive feedback loops.
2. Early identification of student disengagement or frustration, enabling timely human or AI intervention.
3. Improved socio-emotional learning integration within AI-mediated environments.

### Ethical and Technical Risks

1. High Risk of Bias: Emotional AI systems often fail to generalize across diverse cultural, racial, and neurodivergent expressions of emotion (Barrett et al., 2019).
2. Data Privacy Concerns: Emotional AI relies on highly sensitive biometric and behavioural data, raising complex questions about informed consent, storage, and potential misuse.
3. Overreach of Surveillance: The expansion of AI into students' emotional lives may erode psychological safety if implemented without robust human oversight and strict ethical governance.

Future research must prioritize the development of culturally responsive affective models, rigorous bias audits, and the design of transparent, opt-in systems that protect student agency. Emotional AI should support, not replace, human socio-emotional interactions and must always operate under teacher supervision within TiTL frameworks.

## Research Needs: Contextual Gaps in the Global South

Current scholarship on AI in education is overwhelmingly concentrated in high-income countries, particularly the United States, China, and Europe. This geographic skew presents a critical research gap regarding the feasibility, ethics, and impact of AI co-teaching in Global South contexts.

## Key Research Priorities for the Global South

1. Infrastructure Realities: Many schools in the Global South face persistent challenges such as limited internet connectivity, unstable electricity supply, and inadequate access to digital devices. AI co-teaching models must be adapted to low-bandwidth, offline-compatible, and mobile-optimized platforms.
2. Cultural Pedagogies: Educational practices in the Global South often involve community-based, oral, and multilingual pedagogies that may not align with Western-centric AI system designs. Research is urgently needed to localize AI learning pathways that respect indigenous knowledge systems and culturally specific ways of learning.
3. Language Diversity: The dominance of English and other high-resource languages in AI datasets excludes a significant portion of learners in the Global South. Future AI models must prioritize the inclusion of underrepresented languages, dialects, and trans-language practices to ensure linguistic equity.
4. Trust and Adoption: Historical legacies of technological marginalization may influence teacher and student trust in AI systems. Investigating local perceptions, barriers to adoption, and culturally resonant trust-building strategies is essential for successful deployment.
5. Ethical Governance: Regulatory environments in many Global South countries lack robust frameworks for AI ethics, student data protection, and algorithmic accountability. Policy research must address how ethical guidelines can be developed and enforced in resource-constrained settings.

Global South-focused research will not only fill a major empirical gap but also enrich the global AI education discourse by challenging the one-size-fits-all assumptions embedded in many existing systems.

As educational AI advances into emotional domains and seeks to expand globally, it must be governed by a commitment to equity, cultural sensitivity, and human agency. The next generation of research and development must deliberately address the systemic risks of emotional surveillance and geographic exclusion.

By prioritizing context-specific design, inclusive linguistic representation, and robust ethical protections, the future of AI co-teaching can be more just, more adaptable, and more universally beneficial.

## CONCLUSION

This chapter has critically examined the transformative potential and complex challenges of integrating Artificial Intelligence (AI) within co-teaching frameworks. Through a detailed exploration of conceptual models, ethical considerations, and implementation strategies, it is evident that AI's role in education must be carefully positioned as a complementary partner, not a replacement for human teachers.

The Complementary Strengths Model and the Teacher-in-the-Loop (TiTL) framework provide practical pathways for balancing AI's computational capabilities with the irreplaceable socio-emotional, cultural, and ethical dimensions of human pedagogy. AI excels at data-driven tasks such as adaptive lesson planning, real-time feedback, and predictive assessment, while teachers retain leadership over complex instructional decisions, emotional support, and value-based judgments. The co-teaching taxonomy, co-planning, co-instruction, and co-assessment models outlined in this chapter demonstrate that effective AI-human collaboration requires transparent, editable, and trust-centred system designs.

However, the successful adoption of AI co-teaching demands vigilant ethical governance. As the discussion of bias, teacher agency, and student trust has shown, AI systems risk perpetuating inequalities, deskilling educators, and eroding learner confidence if not properly regulated. Emotional AI and the expansion of AI into Global South contexts further complicate these dynamics, raising urgent questions about privacy, cultural adaptation, and equitable access.

A key synthesis of this chapter is the recognition that no single discipline can address these challenges in isolation. The future of AI in education requires genuine interdisciplinary collaboration among computer scientists, educational researchers, ethicists, linguists, policymakers, and teachers. Co-design processes, participatory development cycles, and inclusive policy frameworks are essential to ensure that AI systems remain accountable, context-sensitive, and aligned with the diverse realities of global classrooms.

Ultimately, the promise of AI co-teaching can only be realized through shared responsibility and collective stewardship, where all stakeholders actively contribute to building AI-enhanced educational ecosystems that are equitable, transparent, and profoundly human-centred.

## REFERENCES


Amershi, S., Weld, D., Vorvoreanu, M., Fourney, A., Nushi, B., Collisson, P., & Horvitz, E. (2014). Power to the people: The role of humans in interactive machine learning. *AI Magazine*, *35*(4), 105–120. DOI: 10.1609/aimag.v35i4.2513

Anderson, J. R., Boyle, C. F., Farrell, R., & Reiser, B. J. (1990). Cognitive principles in the design of computer tutors. *Cognitive Science*, *14*(2), 179–211. DOI: 10.1207/s15516709cog1402_1

Bolukbasi, T., Chang, K. W., Zou, J. Y., Saligrama, V., & Kalai, A. T. (2016). Man is to computer programmer as woman is to homemaker? Debiasing word embeddings. *Advances in Neural Information Processing Systems*, *29*, 4349–4357.

Brown, A., & Garcia, M. (2023). Socio-cultural bias in AI: Implications for equitable learning analytics. *Journal of Educational Technology Equity*, *5*(1), 45–62.

Buolamwini, J., & Gebru, T. (2018). Gender shades: Intersectional accuracy disparities in commercial gender classification. *Proceedings of the 1st Conference on Fairness, Accountability and Transparency*, 77–91. https://proceedings.mlr.press/v81/buolamwini18a.html

Chen, X., Xie, H., Zou, D., & Hwang, G.-J. (2020). Application and theory gaps during the rise of Artificial Intelligence in Education. *Computers and Education: Artificial Intelligence*, *1*, 100002. DOI: 10.1016/j.caeai.2020.100002

Dietvorst, B. J., Simmons, J. P., & Massey, C. (2015). Algorithm aversion: People erroneously avoid algorithms after seeing them err. *Journal of Experimental Psychology. General*, *144*(1), 114–126. DOI: 10.1037/xge0000033 PMID: 25401381

Holmes, W., Bialik, M., & Fadel, C. (2019). *Artificial Intelligence in education: Promises and implications for teaching and learning*. Center for Curriculum Redesign.

Johnson, M., Kumar, S., & Patel, R. (2021). Enhancing teaching decisions with AI: A study of data-driven interventions in middle school classrooms. *Journal of Educational Computing Research*, *59*(4), 747–768.

Lee, J., & Park, Y. (2022). Teacher-AI collaboration in personalized learning environments: A multi-case study. *Computers & Education*, *182*, 104465. DOI: 10.1016/j.compedu.2022.104465

Lee, S., Chen, Y., & Alvarez, M. (2022). Linguistic equity in automated essay scoring: Challenges and innovations. *Computers & Education*, *187*, 104608. DOI: 10.1016/j.compedu.2022.104608

Luckin, R., Holmes, W., Griffiths, M., & Forcier, L. B. (2016). *Intelligence unleashed: An argument for AI in education*. Pearson Education. https://www.pearson.com/content/dam/one-dot-com/one-dot-com/global/Files/about-pearson/innovation/open-ideas/Intelligence-Unleashed-Publication.pdf

Mehrabi, N., Morstatter, F., Saxena, N., Lerman, K., & Galstyan, A. (2021). A survey on bias and fairness in machine learning. *ACM Computing Surveys*, *54*(6), 1–35. DOI: 10.1145/3457607

Miller, T. (2019). Explanation in artificial intelligence: Insights from the social sciences. *Artificial Intelligence*, *267*, 1–38. DOI: 10.1016/j.artint.2018.07.007

Mitchell, M., Wu, S., Zaldivar, A., Barnes, P., Vasserman, L., Hutchinson, B., & Gebru, T. (2020). Model cards for model reporting. *Proceedings of the Conference on Fairness, Accountability, and Transparency*, 220–229. https://doi.org/DOI: 10.1145/3287560.3287596

Perrotta, C., Selwyn, N., & Cramman, H. (2021). AI and the teaching profession: Navigating the disruption. *Teaching in Higher Education*, *26*(7–8), 1045–1059. DOI: 10.1080/13562517.2021.1928063

Smith, L., Tan, E., & Morris, J. (2021). Teacher trust in AI: A mixed-method study on interpretability and control. *Educational Technology Research and Development*, *69*(3), 1391–1413.

VanLehn, K. (2006). The behavior of tutoring systems. *International Journal of Artificial Intelligence in Education*, *16*(3), 227–265.

Vygotsky, L. S. (1978). *Mind in society: The development of higher psychological processes*. Harvard University Press.

Wang, Q., & Xu, Z. (2022). Human-centered AI in education: Enhancing teacher agency in data-driven classrooms. *Computers & Education*, *183*, 104516. DOI: 10.1016/j.compedu.2022.104516

Zawacki-Richter, O., Marín, V. I., Bond, M., & Gouverneur, F. (2019). Systematic review of research on artificial intelligence applications in higher education – Where are the educators? *International Journal of Educational Technology in Higher Education*, *16*(1), 39. DOI: 10.1186/s41239-019-0171-0

Chapter 10

# AI and the Future of Teacher Certification and Credentialing

**Rebet Keith Jones**
https://orcid.org/0009-0008-0487-1301
*Capitol Technology University, USA*

**Jacquelyn Andrea Jones**
https://orcid.org/0009-0005-4466-8920
*Walden University, USA*

## ABSTRACT

*As education systems worldwide evolve to meet the demands of a dynamic, digitally interconnected society, traditional models of teacher certification and credentialing are being re-examined through the lens of emerging technologies. Artificial Intelligence (AI) offers transformative potential to reshape how educators are assessed, accredited, and continuously supported in their professional journeys. This chapter explores the integration of AI into teacher certification processes, highlighting innovative approaches such as AI-driven performance analytics, adaptive testing, digital portfolios, and blockchain-enabled credentialing systems. It also considers ethical, legal, and practical challenges surrounding bias, transparency, and data privacy. By analyzing current trends and pilot implementations, the chapter envisions a future where AI enhances fairness, efficiency, and personalization in educator certification, fostering a more agile and equitable professional ecosystem.*

DOI: 10.4018/979-8-3373-5951-9.ch010

## 1. INTRODUCTION

The landscape of teacher certification and credentialing is undergoing a profound transformation. As educational demands evolve in response to the Fourth Industrial Revolution (Chaka, 2023), conventional systems of degree-based qualification are increasingly being questioned for their efficiency, relevance, and adaptability. Today's dynamic learning environments require flexible, skill-based, and continuously updated credentials to meet the changing expectations of both educational institutions and labor markets (Díaz et al., 2022; Rachmad, 2025a). Artificial Intelligence (AI) and blockchain technologies are rapidly emerging as disruptive forces in this domain, offering tools that can automate, personalize, and secure certification processes while enabling continuous professional development pathways.

Traditional credentialing systems have long been criticized for being rigid, time-consuming, and insufficiently reflective of individual teacher competencies and contextual classroom realities (Howell et al., 2018). Moreover, the one-size-fits-all approach often overlooks the unique pedagogical contributions of educators. In contrast, AI-enabled micro-credentialing allows for modular, skills-based recognition that can be personalized and validated through real-time data analysis and adaptive learning algorithms (Asrifan et al., 2025; Charles et al., 2025). These systems not only cater to diverse learning trajectories but also provide an agile framework to keep teacher certifications aligned with evolving pedagogical trends and technologies (Jacques et al., 2024; Kumar et al., 2025).

Blockchain technologies add another layer of innovation by ensuring the security, immutability, and portability of digital credentials. Blockchain-based credentialing platforms empower educators to control and share their professional achievements across borders without intermediaries, thereby fostering transparency and trust (Alsobhi et al., 2023; Jirgensons & Kapenieks, 2018; Williams, 2019). This is especially pertinent in a globalized world where teacher mobility and transnational education are on the rise.

Furthermore, micro-credentialing offers a potential solution to the challenge of lifelong learning in teaching professions. AI can power personalized learning pathways that guide educators toward certifications most relevant to their career goals and classroom needs (Shanmughan et al., 2024; Polydoros, 2025). This personalized approach enhances motivation, increases engagement, and leads to better instructional outcomes. It also supports the attainment of Sustainable Development Goals (SDGs) by promoting inclusive and equitable quality education and lifelong learning opportunities (Ironsi & Ironsi, 2025).

Scholars have emphasized that AI and blockchain technologies are not just tools but drivers of systemic reform in education (Elkhodr et al., 2024; Islam & Rihan, 2024; Singh, 2023). Integrating these technologies into credentialing frameworks can redefine the role of teacher preparation programs and elevate accountability, efficiency, and adaptability in teacher licensing (Singh & Ram, 2024; Weiner et al., 2024). However, the transition also raises challenges, including digital inequities, ethical concerns, data privacy issues, and the risk of over-automation (Tuomi et al., 2023; Trajkovski & Hayes, 2025).

While early adopters in countries like Australia, the EU, and parts of Southeast Asia have begun implementing pilot projects (Elkhodr et al., 2024; Ramírez-Montoya et al., 2024), the global implementation of AI-enhanced credentialing remains in its infancy. This chapter aims to examine how AI, blockchain, and digital micro-credentialing are reshaping teacher certification. It investigates technological architectures, policy frameworks, case studies, and pedagogical implications, while also drawing upon foundational research in computer science and information systems (Zangana, 2015; 2017; 2018; 2022; Zangana & Mustafa, 2024).

In doing so, the chapter builds on the synthesis of current literature and recent innovations (Durak & Cankaya, 2024; Rafi, 2025; Zreik, 2024), proposing a forward-looking model for an equitable, intelligent, and globally integrated certification system for educators.

## 2. BACKGROUND: TRADITIONAL CERTIFICATION AND CREDENTIALING MODELS

Traditional teacher certification systems have long served as the primary gateway to formal teaching positions, particularly within national or regional education systems. Rooted in degree-based qualifications, these models typically involve completion of a prescribed set of academic requirements, supervised teaching practice, and standardized assessments administered by credentialing authorities (Howell et al., 2018). While such frameworks have historically ensured consistency and basic teaching competencies, they are increasingly critiqued for their lack of agility in addressing the needs of modern learners and educational environments (Díaz et al., 2022).

Credentialing, in its conventional form, is often a linear process. Teachers obtain university degrees and teaching licenses through accredited institutions and must periodically undergo re-certification to maintain their status. However, this model does not fully reflect the complexity of today's teaching landscape, where educators are expected to demonstrate a broad array of evolving skills, including digital literacy, inclusivity, and real-time adaptability to technology-enhanced pedagogies (Singh & Ram, 2024; Jacques et al., 2024).

Moreover, the static nature of traditional certification processes often fails to account for informal learning, professional development outside degree programs, or niche expertise. This limits the flexibility needed for mid-career transitions and lifelong learning, both of which are increasingly vital in the context of the Fourth Industrial Revolution (Chaka, 2023; Tuomi et al., 2023). According to Rachmad (2025a), the modern workforce—particularly younger generations—are moving toward competence-based hiring models, rendering traditional degrees less relevant in certain sectors.

In response, many scholars and institutions are advocating for more granular, modular forms of certification, such as micro-credentials, which recognize specific skills or competencies in shorter, flexible formats (Durak & Cankaya, 2024; Charles et al., 2025). These alternative credentials are typically more responsive to industry trends and can be accumulated over time to represent comprehensive expertise. Yet, in traditional systems, micro-credentials often lack formal recognition or standardization, limiting their impact within formal education sectors (Ironsi & Ironsi, 2025).

Another critical limitation of conventional models is their susceptibility to inefficiency, duplication, and administrative opacity. Educators may face significant bureaucratic barriers when attempting to transfer certifications across jurisdictions or institutions (Islam & Rihan, 2024). These inefficiencies underscore the need for systems that support portability, trust, and real-time verification of credentials—an area where blockchain technology is increasingly being explored (Jirgensons & Kapenieks, 2018; Williams, 2019).

A systematic review by Alsobhi et al. (2023) highlights how blockchain-based systems can address issues such as fraud, data silos, and credential verification delays by creating immutable, decentralized records. Similarly, Elkhodr et al. (2024) emphasize that blockchain, when integrated with AI, holds promise for transforming credentialing into a more secure, scalable, and transparent process.

However, technology alone cannot fix structural limitations unless accompanied by policy reform and pedagogical rethinking. As Kumar et al. (2025) point out, adaptive AI-based credentialing systems must be designed with fairness, inclusivity, and contextual flexibility in mind. Moreover, institutional readiness, teacher training programs, and stakeholder buy-in are essential for the success of these innovations (Weiner et al., 2024).

These concerns are further echoed in the healthcare and specialized sectors, where traditional credentialing models are now being supplemented—or replaced—by AI-powered assessments and proctoring systems (Krajcer, 2022). Similar shifts are observable in the vocational and professional training sectors, where digital micro-credentials are increasingly recognized as valid indicators of employable skills (Charles et al., 2025).

Furthermore, existing data management systems used in traditional education often lack the interoperability and responsiveness required for real-time learning analytics and credential updates (Zangana, 2017, 2019; Zangana et al., 2024). A move toward integrated data-driven ecosystems, where AI plays a central role, offers a pathway to continuous, performance-based credentialing (Polydoros, 2025; Rafi, 2025).

It is in this context of limitations, critiques, and transformative pressure that alternative approaches such as AI-enhanced micro-credentialing and blockchain-based verification are emerging—not as mere supplements, but as potential replacements for outdated legacy systems (Asrifan et al., 2025; Ramírez-Montoya et al., 2024). These new models not only address traditional shortcomings but also align more effectively with the skills-oriented demands of contemporary education and labor markets (Rachmad, 2025b; Singh, 2023).

To illustrate the structural differences between traditional and AI-enhanced teacher certification models, the following flowchart contrasts key elements of each system.

*Figure 1. Flowchart Comparing Traditional and AI-Enhanced Credentialing Pathways*

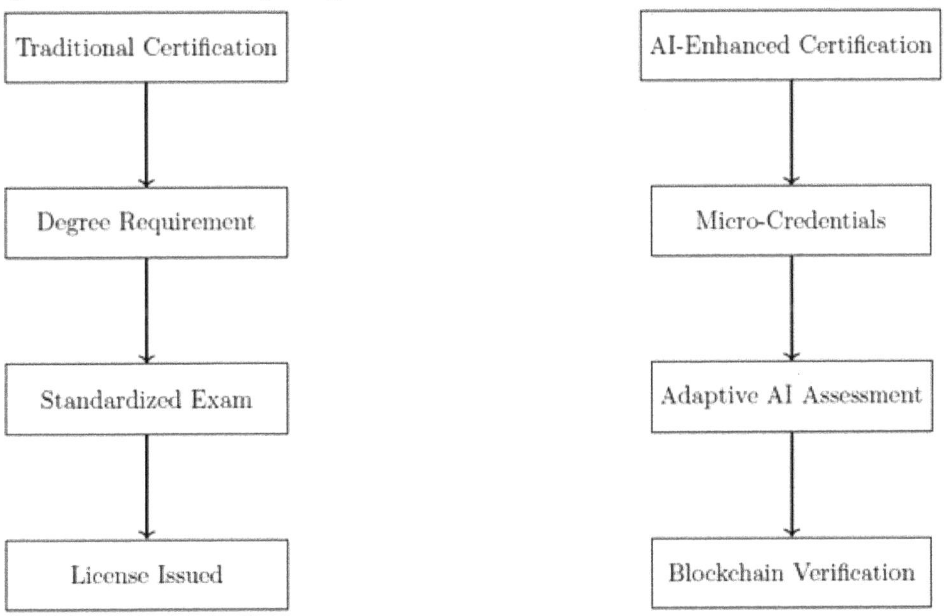


In summary, traditional certification models, while foundational, are increasingly seen as insufficient to meet the evolving requirements of educators and learners in the digital age. This has set the stage for more intelligent, flexible, and decentralized systems that can support the continuous and competency-based development of educators worldwide—an idea this chapter will explore in greater detail through the lenses of AI, blockchain, and micro-credentialing innovations.

## 3. AI TECHNOLOGIES IN ASSESSMENT AND CREDENTIALING

Artificial Intelligence (AI) technologies are rapidly reshaping the landscape of educational assessment and credentialing, introducing automation, adaptability, and precision to traditionally manual and standardized processes. AI's capacity to collect, analyze, and interpret data in real time allows for the creation of personalized, competency-based assessment systems that align more closely with the needs of today's dynamic educational and professional environments (Jacques, Moss, & Garger, 2024; Singh & Ram, 2024).

One of the most transformative applications of AI in education is adaptive assessment systems, which tailor evaluation items to the learner's proficiency level, reducing test anxiety while providing a more accurate measure of skills and knowledge. Such systems are particularly useful in teacher education, where competencies are multi-faceted and context-dependent (Trajkovski & Hayes, 2025). AI can support dynamic item generation, plagiarism detection, and real-time feedback loops, making assessments more reflective of authentic learning experiences (Kumar et al., 2025).

The integration of blockchain with AI further enhances credentialing accuracy and security by ensuring the immutability, transparency, and portability of academic records. Alsobhi et al. (2023) systematically reviewed blockchain-based micro-credentialing systems and emphasized their ability to eliminate fraudulent claims, accelerate verification processes, and decentralize trust in credential issuance. These features are particularly beneficial in teacher certification, where trust and standardization are vital.

AI-driven micro-credentialing platforms—especially those embedded with blockchain—enable modular and evidence-based recognition of teaching competencies (Jirgensons & Kapenieks, 2018; Elkhodr et al., 2024). Educators can now receive credentials for discrete skills, such as digital pedagogy or inclusive classroom management, which are validated through performance analytics and smart contracts (Charles et al., 2025; Polydoros, 2025). These systems allow stakeholders—including education ministries and hiring institutions—to verify the authenticity and relevance of qualifications efficiently.

Moreover, AI technologies play a critical role in real-time data collection and analytics, enabling continuous formative assessment over time rather than relying on one-off summative evaluations. This capability supports personalized learning pathways, where credentials reflect both progress and mastery (Shanmughan et al., 2024). According to Asrifan et al. (2025), AI-enhanced micro-credentials significantly improve education efficiency by aligning learning outcomes with individualized career goals and skills demand.

In professional training and vocational education, AI is already enabling simulations, virtual labs, and scenario-based testing that can assess soft and technical skills in authentic environments. These assessments can be stored as digital badges or micro-credentials, further promoting skill-based certification over traditional degree-based models (Rachmad, 2025a; Díaz et al., 2022).

Another critical area of innovation is AI-supported proctoring, which uses facial recognition, behavioral biometrics, and pattern detection to monitor assessments remotely. This has expanded credentialing access while ensuring academic integrity—especially during and post-COVID-19, when online testing surged (Krajcer, 2022). However, concerns around data privacy, algorithmic bias, and surveillance ethics must be addressed through rigorous policy and technical safeguards (Islam & Rihan, 2024).

From a curriculum development perspective, AI enables the creation of intelligent tutoring systems and automated grading mechanisms, which not only assist learners in real time but also collect evidence for credentialing. These systems leverage natural language processing (NLP) and machine learning algorithms to assess open-ended responses, code snippets, or reflective essays with increasing accuracy (Zangana & Mustafa, 2024a; Singh, 2023).

Furthermore, as educators acquire skills across diverse domains—ranging from AI literacy to social-emotional learning—AI systems can scaffold learning experiences and track mastery through integrated dashboards and learning analytics (Durak & Cankaya, 2024; Ramírez-Montoya et al., 2024). These developments reduce reliance on traditional gatekeeping institutions and promote lifelong learning.

In practice, AI technologies are also enabling automated portfolio assessment. By analyzing teaching artifacts, classroom videos, and student feedback, AI systems can generate comprehensive profiles of educator effectiveness (Weiner et al., 2024). These profiles can then be translated into verified digital credentials, aligned with institutional standards and market expectations (Rafi, 2025).

Moreover, the use of AI in educational assessment intersects meaningfully with global goals, particularly in fostering 21st-century skills and inclusive education. Ironsi and Ironsi (2025) highlight how AI-powered credentialing platforms contribute to sustainable development by ensuring that learners—regardless of geography—have equitable access to validated learning experiences.

Despite these advancements, challenges remain. Many teacher preparation programs are not yet equipped to harness AI's full potential, resulting in a disconnect between available technologies and institutional readiness (Weiner et al., 2024). In addition, ethical considerations such as data ownership, fairness, and the explainability of AI systems must be integrated into implementation strategies (Chaka, 2023; Tuomi et al., 2023).

In conclusion, AI technologies offer a transformative pathway for rethinking assessment and credentialing systems in teacher education. When combined with blockchain, these innovations promise to create transparent, modular, and personalized certification frameworks that are better aligned with modern teaching demands. As the global workforce moves toward competence-driven models, the integration of AI in certification processes becomes not just desirable—but imperative (Rachmad, 2025b; Jacques et al., 2024; Williams, 2019).

## 4. AI-ENHANCED MICRO-CREDENTIALING SYSTEMS

The emergence of AI-enhanced micro-credentialing systems marks a fundamental shift in how educational achievements, particularly in teacher training and professional development, are recognized, verified, and applied. Unlike traditional degree programs that require years to complete and are often rigid in content delivery, micro-credentials allow educators to gain recognition for specific, measurable skills and competencies in a modular, personalized manner (Díaz et al., 2022; Durak & Cankaya, 2024).

AI technologies have added significant momentum to the micro-credentialing movement. Adaptive learning algorithms, natural language processing, machine learning-based assessments, and blockchain-backed verification protocols have collectively transformed micro-credentials into credible, scalable alternatives to traditional certifications (Jacques et al., 2024; Elkhodr et al., 2024). These intelligent systems assess learners' progress in real time and dynamically suggest next steps in learning pathways, thereby creating data-driven, responsive credentialing ecosystems (Asrifan et al., 2025).

One of the most powerful features of AI-enhanced micro-credentialing is personalization. AI systems can tailor credential pathways based on individual learner profiles, career goals, and performance analytics. For instance, in the context of teacher education, AI can suggest competencies in inclusive pedagogy, digital classroom tools, or formative assessment strategies based on classroom performance or professional development engagement (Shanmughan et al., 2024; Singh & Ram, 2024). These capabilities ensure that teacher preparation is aligned not only with standards but with the evolving demands of 21st-century classrooms (Ironsi & Ironsi, 2025).

Moreover, the integration of blockchain with AI addresses one of the most critical issues in credentialing: trust and verification. Blockchain-backed micro-credentials ensure immutability and transparency, making them resistant to fraud and manipulation (Alsobhi et al., 2023; Jirgensons & Kapenieks, 2018). Institutions can issue tamper-proof digital badges stored on distributed ledgers, enabling seamless verification by employers or licensing bodies (Williams, 2019).

AI also plays a vital role in evaluating competencies through advanced analytics. Educators can submit teaching videos, lesson plans, or student feedback for AI-assisted analysis, which can then be used to generate micro-credentials based on observed competencies (Trajkovski & Hayes, 2025; Kumar et al., 2025). These intelligent evaluations reduce subjectivity and increase the granularity of assessment, allowing a more nuanced representation of an educator's skills (Polydoros, 2025).

Vocational and professional training fields have been among the earliest adopters of micro-credentialing systems, especially where rapid upskilling and reskilling are essential (Charles et al., 2025). These systems are now being adapted for use in higher education and K-12 teacher preparation, particularly in areas where traditional certification lags behind technological demands (Weiner et al., 2024; Howell et al., 2018).

Importantly, AI-enhanced micro-credentials are also transforming how skills are recognized in global labor markets. As degree inflation continues and the link between diplomas and job readiness weakens, competence-based hiring practices are gaining traction (Rachmad, 2025a, 2025b). AI-supported micro-credentials, when aligned with labor market analytics, can close the gap between education and employment, particularly for Generation Z and digital-first learners (Rafi, 2025; Singh, 2023).

From a global development perspective, these systems contribute to UN Sustainable Development Goals (SDGs) by promoting access to quality education and inclusive lifelong learning opportunities (Ironsi & Ironsi, 2025). In regions with limited access to formal degrees, AI-enhanced credentials democratize access to professional recognition and career advancement (Islam & Rihan, 2024; Tuomi et al., 2023).

Further, AI-enhanced micro-credentials offer a viable solution to challenges in traditional data management systems. Educational institutions, especially those with legacy infrastructures, face hurdles in credential tracking, quality assurance, and interoperability (Zangana, 2017, 2018, 2019). AI-backed credentialing platforms offer integrated solutions for credential creation, tracking, and secure sharing (Zangana & Abdulazeez, 2023; Zangana et al., 2024).

A study by Ramírez-Montoya et al. (2024) across Latin American universities highlights how AI-powered micro-credentialing fosters complex thinking and interdisciplinary competence development. These capabilities are increasingly relevant in teaching, where hybrid skillsets—combining pedagogy, technology, and emotional intelligence—are essential.

Despite the promise, the implementation of AI-enhanced micro-credentials is not without challenges. Issues include institutional resistance, digital infrastructure gaps, and the need for global standardization frameworks (Chaka, 2023; Elkhodr et al., 2024). Moreover, as AI systems become central to credentialing, ethical concerns regarding algorithmic bias, data privacy, and explainability must be addressed (Islam & Rihan, 2024; Jacques et al., 2024).

However, the momentum toward this model is unmistakable. As outlined by Durak and Cankaya (2024), a growing number of universities and teacher preparation programs are piloting AI-based credentialing platforms, often in partnership with edtech providers. These platforms not only offer stackable credentials but also link them to digital wallets and e-portfolios for lifelong learning and career mobility (Díaz et al., 2022; Zreik, 2024).

In conclusion, AI-enhanced micro-credentialing systems offer a transformative pathway for modernizing teacher certification and professional development. By enabling flexible, personalized, and verifiable recognition of skills, these systems respond directly to the inefficiencies of traditional certification models and the skills demands of the 4IR. As the global education sector continues to embrace AI and blockchain innovations, micro-credentials stand to redefine what it means to be qualified, competent, and prepared to teach in a digital age (Asrifan et al., 2025; Chaka, 2023; Kumar et al., 2025).

The diagram below maps out the core components of an AI-powered micro-credentialing platform, highlighting how technology enables modular, adaptive, and verifiable recognition of teacher skills.

*Figure 2. Architecture of an AI-Enhanced Micro-Credentialing System*

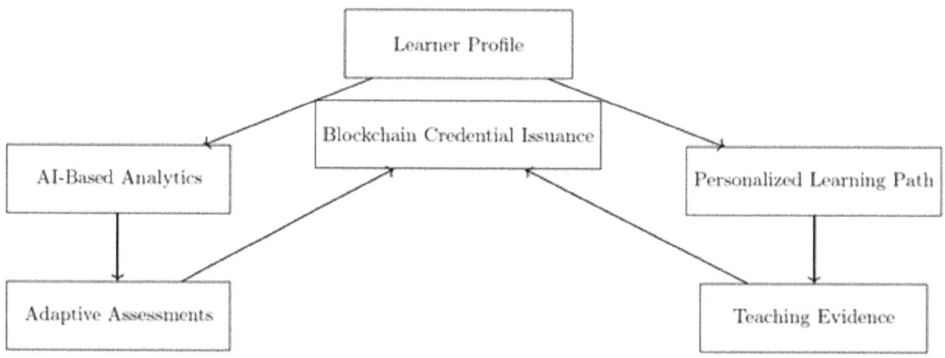

## 5. CASE STUDIES AND PILOT PROGRAMS

The practical application of AI-enhanced micro-credentialing and alternative certification models has gained global momentum. Numerous pilot programs and institutional case studies illustrate how AI, blockchain, and digital credentialing systems are transforming traditional education structures and reshaping teacher training, assessment, and career development pathways.

One notable case is the blockchain-based micro-credentialing systems in higher education institutions, extensively reviewed by Alsobhi et al. (2023). Their study highlighted pilot implementations across Asia, Europe, and North America that leverage blockchain to securely issue, verify, and share teacher credentials. These systems improve transparency, reduce credential fraud, and promote cross-border recognition of qualifications. Notable institutions such as MIT and the University of Melbourne have adopted blockchain for transcript and certificate management.

In Australia, Elkhodr et al. (2024) analyzed national pilot projects that integrate AI and blockchain for future-proofing higher education. These initiatives include partnerships between universities and industry bodies to build credentialing platforms that support lifelong learning, especially in fields like education and nursing. The emphasis is on interoperability, data security, and skill alignment with national workforce frameworks.

In Indonesia, Asrifan et al. (2025) documented a transformative pilot in open education that implemented AI-enhanced micro-credentials to support flexible teacher training. The project showed a 32% increase in training completion rates and improved alignment between learning modules and teaching competencies. AI algorithms were used to assess teaching videos, reflective journals, and peer reviews to generate personalized learning paths and badge-based credentials.

Latin American universities have also advanced pilot programs in AI-enhanced alternative credentialing. Ramírez-Montoya et al. (2024) conducted a comparative study of micro-credentialing frameworks at Mexican and Colombian institutions. Their findings revealed that AI systems used for credential assessment support complex thinking development and multidisciplinary learning—crucial for teacher training in hybrid and online environments.

In mathematics education, Polydoros (2025) reported on a European initiative where AI was used to evaluate learning progress among students with difficulties and to award micro-credentials to teachers who successfully implemented inclusive, adaptive strategies. AI-powered dashboards provided ongoing insights into classroom engagement and instructional effectiveness.

The TVET (Technical and Vocational Education and Training) sector in Southeast Asia has seen rapid adoption of micro-credentialing, especially for teacher trainers. Charles et al. (2025) described a pilot that issued stackable micro-credentials using

AI and blockchain for vocational instructors in Malaysia and the Philippines. The pilot emphasized competency-based certification, offering a flexible alternative to traditional licensure models.

A Middle Eastern pilot, detailed by Kumar et al. (2025), integrated adaptive learning and blockchain to support real-time credentialing in professional education. The system allowed educators to track learners' mastery of AI and pedagogy modules, generating secure digital badges that align with job competencies. This model addressed long-standing issues around fragmented data systems and inconsistent credential validation.

From a global policy perspective, Chaka (2023) and Tuomi et al. (2023) highlighted the role of international collaboration in facilitating pilot programs that bridge AI, blockchain, and credentialing. For example, the European Commission's Digital Education Action Plan supports pilot programs that trial AI-based skills passports and teacher competency recognition across EU states.

In the United States, teacher preparation programs have started experimenting with AI-supported credentialing tools. Weiner et al. (2024) conducted a survey revealing that while adoption is uneven, several universities are incorporating AI tools to assess pre-service teacher portfolios, facilitate reflective feedback, and issue micro-credentials in specific competencies like classroom management or technology integration.

Krajcer (2022) offered a case from medical education, where AI-based proctoring and certification were piloted in cardiovascular medicine training. While the field differs from K-12 education, the infrastructure—using facial recognition, anomaly detection, and adaptive testing—serves as a replicable model for teacher credentialing programs seeking remote assessment solutions.

Pilot programs also explore student-facing impacts. Ironsi and Ironsi (2025) presented evidence from a Nigerian university where AI-driven micro-credential learning environments significantly improved students' critical thinking and digital literacy—both key 21st-century skills. These credentials were integrated into teacher training modules, preparing future educators to facilitate similar outcomes for their own learners.

In a forward-looking pilot by Rachmad (2025a, 2025b), the United Nations Development Programme supported a platform in Southeast Asia that prioritized competence over degrees. The initiative focused on Gen Z learners and pre-service teachers, allowing them to earn stackable micro-credentials in leadership, communication, and AI pedagogy, each backed by AI analysis of performance and verified through blockchain.

Further case studies point to the success of AI-enhanced credentials in bridging skills gaps. Rafi (2025) discussed the use of AI learning analytics to detect deficiencies and recommend targeted micro-courses to teachers at risk of automation-related job loss. These were part of a government-backed initiative to upskill educators in digital environments.

Several pilot programs have also emerged in AI-assisted assessment. Trajkovski and Hayes (2025) presented institutional trials of AI models that autonomously evaluate teaching demonstrations and generate narrative feedback and competency reports. These were tied to micro-credentials issued upon meeting specific performance thresholds.

Singh (2023) and Singh & Ram (2024) highlighted pilot initiatives where AI and Web 3.0 were used in decentralized teacher education platforms. These programs enabled self-paced learning, peer verification, and NFT-based digital credentialing—a futuristic alternative to centralized university degrees.

The success of these pilot programs depends in part on infrastructure and data quality—a challenge explored in several studies by Zangana (2017–2025). His work on library systems, student databases, and video learning systems underscores the need for clean, structured data for AI and blockchain platforms to function effectively. Implementations in Iraq and Malaysia, including interactive learning systems at IIUM, show the feasibility of building credentialing platforms on locally developed digital infrastructure (Zangana & Mustafa, 2024; Zangana & Abdulazeez, 2023).

Moreover, the security and scalability of credentialing systems were examined by Jirgensons and Kapenieks (2018) and Williams (2019), whose work suggests that blockchain-backed AI platforms can ensure long-term viability and trust in digital certifications. These frameworks are increasingly being piloted at scale to replace or augment traditional degree validation processes.

Finally, as noted by Durak & Cankaya (2024), many of these pilot programs are part of broader research and development consortia, bringing together educational institutions, technology providers, and policymakers. These consortia foster shared evaluation frameworks, making it easier to assess the real-world impact of AI-based credentialing systems across institutions and countries.

## 6. BENEFITS OF AI IN CREDENTIALING PROCESSES

Artificial Intelligence (AI) is revolutionizing the landscape of educational credentialing by introducing automation, personalization, security, and efficiency into processes that were traditionally manual, time-consuming, and often unreliable. As the global workforce evolves toward skills-based hiring and lifelong learning, AI-enhanced credentialing systems provide a scalable, accurate, and flexible alternative to conventional models (Díaz et al., 2022; Charles et al., 2025).

## 6.1. Efficiency, Speed, and Scalability

AI enables institutions to streamline credentialing workflows by automating the generation, evaluation, and verification of digital credentials. Machine learning algorithms can rapidly assess student performance across diverse data points—including video submissions, digital portfolios, and simulation results—thereby reducing the administrative burden and increasing the speed of credential issuance (Jacques et al., 2024; Kumar et al., 2025). Asrifan et al. (2025) found that AI-enhanced micro-credentialing in open education platforms significantly improved education efficiency by shortening time-to-certification and increasing learner retention.

AI also supports large-scale deployment, allowing institutions to manage thousands of credentials concurrently. This is especially valuable in professional and vocational education systems, where learners pursue stackable, modular certifications (Charles et al., 2025; Durak & Cankaya, 2024).

## 6.2. Personalization and Adaptive Learning Paths

AI brings dynamic personalization to credentialing through adaptive learning systems. These platforms tailor instructional content, pace, and assessment strategies to individual learners' needs—an advantage particularly beneficial in teacher training (Shanmughan et al., 2024; Singh & Ram, 2024). AI can analyze educators' competencies and suggest micro-credentials aligned with their performance, thereby supporting continuous professional development.

Polydoros (2025) demonstrated how AI-supported systems in mathematics education adapt to learners with cognitive difficulties, thereby offering educators specific credentials based on their capacity to manage diverse learning needs. These individualized pathways enhance engagement and deepen mastery (Ironsi & Ironsi, 2025).

## 6.3. Credibility, Security, and Trust via Blockchain Integration

AI's synergy with blockchain technologies introduces enhanced trust and integrity to credentialing systems. Blockchain ensures immutability and decentralization, while AI verifies competency data and credential criteria (Alsobhi et al., 2023; Jirgensons & Kapenieks, 2018). These systems offer tamper-proof records, real-time validation, and global accessibility, supporting cross-border recognition of qualifications (Islam & Rihan, 2024; Williams, 2019).

In Australia, AI and blockchain integration has already begun reshaping credentialing frameworks by offering secure, interoperable platforms that align with national quality assurance standards (Elkhodr et al., 2024). These systems reduce the need for third-party verification and streamline the mobility of educators across jurisdictions.

## 6.4. Skills-Based Recognition and Workforce Alignment

AI-enhanced credentialing is more granular and competency-focused than traditional degrees. This aligns with emerging HR trends and workforce needs, especially among Gen Z learners who prioritize skills over formal qualifications (Rachmad, 2025a, 2025b). AI can identify job-relevant skills, recommend training modules, and issue verifiable micro-credentials upon mastery, supporting employability and lifelong learning (Rafi, 2025; Singh, 2023).

Krajcer (2022) highlighted how AI systems in cardiovascular medicine credentialing enabled tailored assessment based on real-time simulation performance, providing a model for teacher training programs to adopt domain-specific, skills-oriented evaluations.

## 6.5. Equity and Accessibility

AI democratizes access to credentialing by enabling remote, asynchronous, and on-demand assessments. Learners in remote or underserved areas can pursue verified credentials without the need for traditional, centralized infrastructures (Chaka, 2023; Tuomi et al., 2023). This fosters inclusive education and supports the United Nations Sustainable Development Goals (Ironsi & Ironsi, 2025).

Projects in Latin American universities illustrate how AI-powered micro-credentialing systems foster complex thinking and interdisciplinary learning while reducing barriers to credential access (Ramírez-Montoya et al., 2024). These systems expand opportunities for non-traditional learners and working professionals.

## 6.6. Data-Driven Decision-Making and Continuous Improvement

AI provides real-time analytics that support continuous improvement of credentialing processes. Educators and institutions can use AI-generated dashboards to monitor learner progress, detect gaps, and adjust instructional strategies accordingly (Trajkovski & Hayes, 2025; Jacques et al., 2024). Such insights not only improve learner outcomes but also inform institutional policy and curriculum design (Weiner et al., 2024).

Zangana et al. (2024) emphasized the importance of data quality and system integration in realizing the full potential of AI in education. Earlier work by Zangana (2017–2022) also outlined foundational data architecture strategies essential for deploying scalable AI systems, such as digital repositories, automated feedback loops, and hybrid learning platforms.

## 6.7. Interdisciplinary Applications and Technological Advancement

AI systems in credentialing are inherently interdisciplinary, incorporating advancements in computer vision, natural language processing, and machine learning. Applications range from proctoring systems that use facial detection algorithms (Zangana & Al-Shaikhli, 2013) to intelligent assessment platforms that evaluate reflective writing and teaching videos (Kumar et al., 2025; Singh & Ram, 2024).

The integration of AI in educational platforms also facilitates system automation and quality assurance. As shown by Zangana and Mustafa (2024), hybrid systems using wavelet transforms and deep learning can be repurposed for educational video analysis and behavioral tracking—enabling sophisticated teacher evaluations in real classroom contexts.

Additionally, advanced clustering and image compression algorithms (Zangana, 2025; Zangana & Abdulazeez, 2023) contribute to the design of efficient, real-time AI platforms capable of processing credentialing data at scale and with reduced latency.

## 6.8. Fostering Innovation and Entrepreneurial Thinking

AI-based credentialing fosters innovation by rewarding non-linear, interdisciplinary, and entrepreneurial learning. Zreik (2024) illustrated how AI-driven credentialing in entrepreneurship education supports ideation, creativity, and digital competency—skills equally valuable in teacher training and education leadership.

By validating informal and experiential learning through micro-credentials, AI systems shift the focus from standardized testing to authentic performance assessment, empowering learners to chart their own educational journeys (Durak & Cankaya, 2024; Díaz et al., 2022).

## 6.9 Summary

The benefits of AI in credentialing are multifaceted, addressing challenges across scalability, trust, personalization, and employability. As education systems continue adapting to the demands of the Fourth Industrial Revolution, AI-enhanced credentialing provides a robust foundation for flexible, equitable, and high-quality teacher development. The integration of blockchain, adaptive learning algorithms, and intelligent assessment engines positions AI not just as a tool—but as a transformative force in the global credentialing ecosystem (Chaka, 2023; Alsobhi et al., 2023; Trajkovski & Hayes, 2025).

The following bar chart summarizes the top benefits of integrating AI in credentialing systems as identified in academic and policy literature.

*Figure 3. Perceived Benefits of AI in Teacher Credentialing*

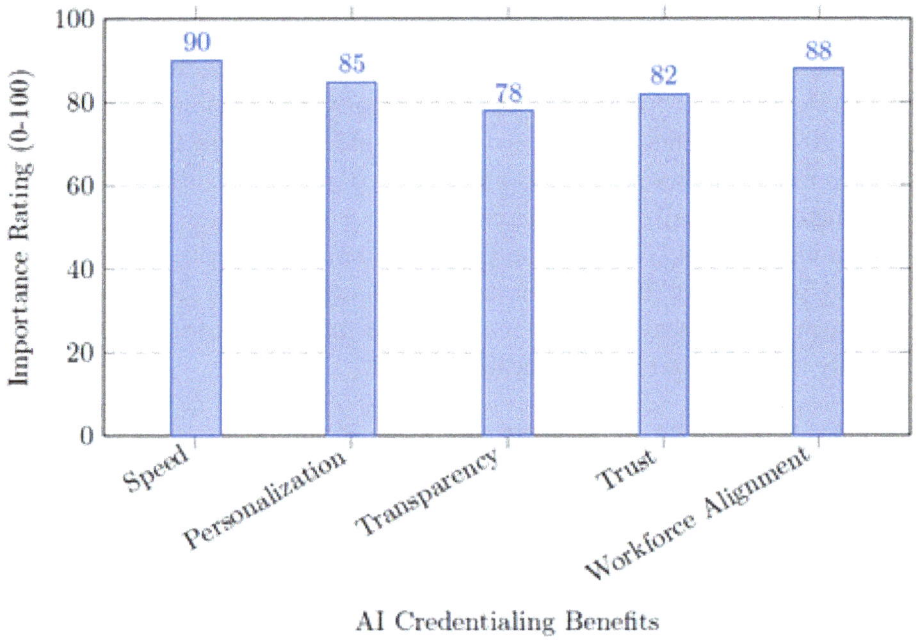


## 7. ETHICAL, LEGAL, AND PRACTICAL CHALLENGES

The integration of Artificial Intelligence (AI) and blockchain technologies into teacher credentialing systems promises transformative benefits, but also raises substantial ethical, legal, and practical concerns. These challenges span from data privacy and algorithmic bias to institutional readiness and equity of access—necessitating critical examination and policy responses before widespread adoption.

## 7.1. Ethical Concerns: Bias, Fairness, and Transparency

One of the most pressing ethical issues in AI-based credentialing is algorithmic bias. AI systems, particularly those used for assessment and certification, may inadvertently reinforce inequalities if trained on unbalanced or culturally narrow datasets (Jacques et al., 2024; Singh & Ram, 2024). As Krajcer (2022) notes, in sensitive fields like medical and teacher education, bias in assessment algorithms can disproportionately affect underrepresented groups.

Furthermore, the opacity of AI decision-making—often referred to as the "black box" problem—limits transparency and challenges the principle of explainability (Chaka, 2023). Students and teachers may not understand how final credentialing decisions are made or what criteria are evaluated, making it difficult to appeal or contest outcomes (Trajkovski & Hayes, 2025).

Shanmughan et al. (2024) raise concerns about personalized learning paths becoming prescriptive, limiting learners' autonomy. Without clear ethical frameworks, such systems may unintentionally narrow rather than expand opportunities, especially in formative teacher education stages.

## 7.2. Legal and Regulatory Challenges: Data Protection and Compliance

Credentialing systems powered by AI and blockchain require handling sensitive personal and academic data, raising serious data protection and legal compliance concerns. As Elkhodr et al. (2024) and Alsobhi et al. (2023) point out, blockchain's immutable nature, while valuable for trust, poses legal conflicts with data erasure rights under laws such as the GDPR.

Additionally, the jurisdictional variance in data protection laws creates challenges for cross-border micro-credentialing (Islam & Rihan, 2024). Institutions working across national lines must reconcile differing standards for data privacy, consent, and storage—often without clear guidance.

The shift toward competency-based education and micro-credentials also exposes gaps in national regulatory frameworks. Williams (2019) notes that existing higher education policies were built around degree programs and are ill-equipped to handle decentralized, stackable credential systems. Díaz et al. (2022) argue for new legal standards that validate alternative credentials without undermining academic quality assurance.

## 7.3. Practical Barriers: Infrastructure, Institutional Resistance, and Readiness

Many institutions lack the technical infrastructure needed to deploy AI and blockchain at scale. According to Zangana (2017–2025), data maturity, system integration, and digital literacy remain core barriers in many educational systems—particularly in developing regions. His work on data warehouses, digital learning systems, and service integration illustrates the foundational digital readiness required for AI-enabled systems to function effectively.

Legacy credentialing systems, often paper-based or poorly digitized, are incompatible with emerging technologies (Zangana, 2018; Zangana & Abdulazeez, 2023). Building secure, interoperable ecosystems requires not only technological upgrades but also organizational change management (Zangana et al., 2024).

Resistance from faculty, administrators, and unions is another barrier. Weiner et al. (2024) found that many teacher preparation programs are hesitant to adopt AI tools, citing fears about job displacement, loss of pedagogical control, and lack of training. Howell et al. (2018) highlighted how middle-level teacher credentialing frameworks are already fragmented, making it difficult to integrate new models without creating confusion or inconsistency.

## 7.4. Security and Trust Concerns in Blockchain Systems

While blockchain is promoted for its tamper-proof records, it also introduces risks related to security, misuse, and unintended permanence. Jirgensons and Kapenieks (2018) point out that storing incorrect or discriminatory data on immutable ledgers could have lifelong implications for learners.

Moreover, credential fraud can shift rather than disappear. Rafi (2025) warned that deepfake technologies and adversarial attacks on AI platforms may exploit vulnerabilities in assessment verification. Zangana, Mohammed, and Husain (2025) reinforce this by emphasizing the human factor in cybersecurity—a dimension often overlooked in technical system design.

## 7.5. Inequity in Access and Global Disparities

AI-based credentialing systems may inadvertently exacerbate educational inequality. As noted by Ironsi and Ironsi (2025), students in low-resource environments may lack the digital tools or internet access needed to participate in AI-enhanced learning environments.

Tuomi et al. (2023) argue that technological innovation outpaces policy inclusivity, leading to "digital winners and losers." This is especially relevant in Latin American and African contexts, where infrastructure gaps persist (Ramírez-Montoya et al., 2024). According to Charles et al. (2025), vocational learners often lack the digital fluency needed to navigate AI-driven platforms without adequate support.

## 7.6. Credential Inflation and Market Saturation

Another risk is credential inflation, where the proliferation of micro-credentials devalues traditional qualifications without necessarily improving quality. As Asrifan et al. (2025) and Durak and Cankaya (2024) warn, the explosion of AI-generated digital badges can confuse employers and reduce trust in the overall credentialing ecosystem. Without standardization, it becomes difficult to compare or verify skills across platforms and regions.

Rachmad (2025a, 2025b) highlights this tension in the labor market, where credentials alone may not guarantee employment unless backed by verified skill demonstration, employer recognition, and ecosystem-wide integration.

## 7.7. Ethical Dilemmas in Surveillance and Proctoring

AI-driven assessment systems often use facial recognition, keystroke tracking, and biometric verification for proctoring purposes (Kumar et al., 2025; Krajcer, 2022). While these tools reduce cheating, they also raise ethical concerns about student surveillance, informed consent, and emotional safety—especially among minors and vulnerable populations.

Zangana and Al-Shaikhli (2013) and Zangana & Mustafa (2024) explored the technical underpinnings of facial recognition and video analysis, noting that these tools must be deployed cautiously in education to avoid misuse or unintentional bias.

## 7.8. Lack of Global Standards and Interoperability

Finally, the absence of global credentialing standards complicates scalability. While AI can streamline skill recognition, its impact is limited without interoperable frameworks and consensus on what credentials represent (Jacques et al., 2024;

Singh, 2023). Kumar et al. (2025) suggest the need for a common skills taxonomy, supported by multilateral agreements and open credentialing consortia.

Blockchain systems further complicate matters due to protocol fragmentation, lack of unified governance, and uncertain scalability (Alsobhi et al., 2023; Elkhodr et al., 2024). Without shared standards, credentials may not be portable across institutions, sectors, or borders.

## 7.9 Summary

The ethical, legal, and practical challenges facing AI-enhanced credentialing systems are complex and interwoven. From algorithmic bias and legal ambiguity to institutional inertia and infrastructure gaps, these barriers must be addressed through inclusive policy design, ethical AI development, and transparent governance structures. Only by confronting these issues can the transformative potential of AI and blockchain in teacher credentialing be realized equitably, securely, and sustainably (Chaka, 2023; Jacques et al., 2024; Trajkovski & Hayes, 2025).

The Venn diagram below categorizes the major concerns surrounding AI-enhanced credentialing into ethical, legal, and practical domains, showing areas of overlap.

*Figure 4. Intersecting Concerns in AI-Based Teacher Certification*

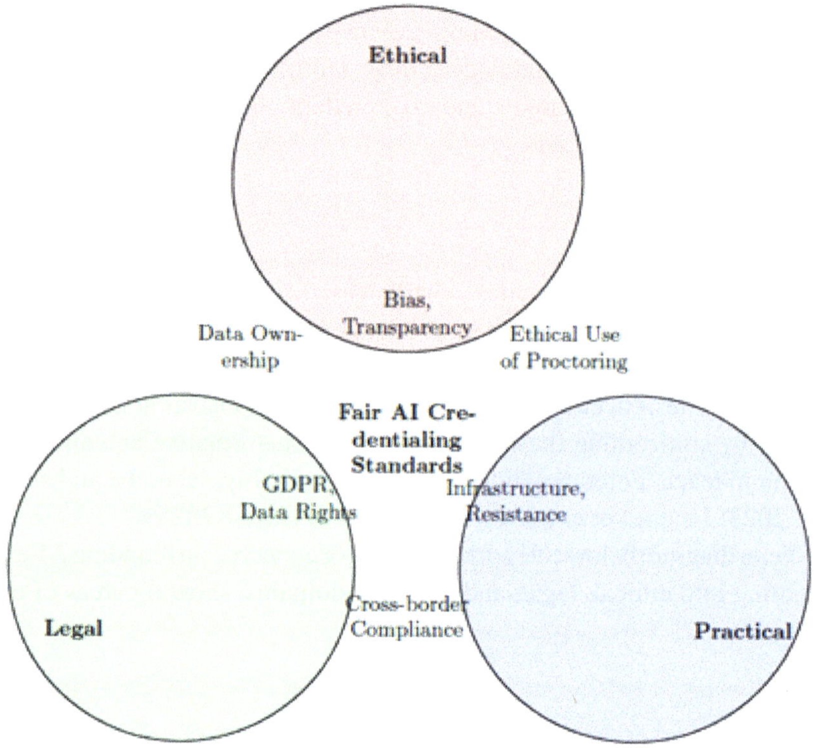


## 8. POLICY IMPLICATIONS AND REGULATORY CONSIDERATIONS

The integration of AI and blockchain technologies into credentialing processes is reshaping traditional education systems, raising profound implications for educational policy, governance, and regulation. As the shift from degree-based learning to skills-based micro-credentialing accelerates, policymakers must address legal gaps, data privacy concerns, institutional readiness, and global standardization to ensure equity, credibility, and scalability in the digital credentialing ecosystem (Díaz et al., 2022; Charles et al., 2025).

## 8.1. Redefining Credential Recognition Policies

Traditional degree structures are increasingly being challenged by micro-credentials that emphasize competency over time-based learning (Durak & Cankaya, 2024). This necessitates a fundamental shift in national qualification frameworks and accreditation policies. As Rachmad (2025a, 2025b) argues, employment markets are moving toward "competence-first" hiring, requiring governments to establish equivalence policies that recognize AI-validated credentials alongside conventional degrees.

To support this shift, Jacques et al. (2024) recommend reworking teacher licensing policies to include performance-based assessments and verified micro-credentials, especially those rooted in real-world teaching competencies.

## 8.2. Standardization and Global Interoperability

One of the most urgent regulatory needs is the standardization of micro-credentials. Without common frameworks, interoperability across institutions, sectors, and countries becomes fragmented. Alsobhi et al. (2023) emphasize that blockchain systems used for credentialing must adopt interoperable schemas and metadata standards to ensure transferability and trust across platforms.

Jirgensons and Kapenieks (2018) further stress that the lack of global credential taxonomies and consensus on credential granularity complicates cross-border recognition. Policymakers must develop international credential registries and digital ID frameworks to allow seamless validation of teacher skills globally.

## 8.3. Legal Compliance: Data Privacy and Security

AI-enhanced credentialing systems involve the processing of sensitive personal, academic, and biometric data, prompting concerns regarding data privacy and sovereignty. Elkhodr et al. (2024) warn that blockchain's immutable nature, while improving trust, may violate data erasure rights under laws such as the GDPR and similar regional acts.

Islam and Rihan (2024) suggest that smart contracts used in AI-driven learning platforms must be legally vetted to comply with data protection and consumer rights. Similarly, Zangana et al. (2025) highlight the necessity of designing secure systems to protect against insider threats and unauthorized data manipulation in education.

Governments and institutions must craft policies that clearly define:

- Who owns the data.
- Who has access.

- What data can be shared and with whom.

This includes updating consent protocols and embedding privacy-by-design principles into all AI-based credentialing platforms (Zangana, 2022; Krajcer, 2022).

## 8.4. Ethical Governance and Accountability

Regulatory frameworks must embed ethical guidelines for AI and blockchain use in credentialing. As Chaka (2023) and Trajkovski and Hayes (2025) argue, these systems must be transparent, auditable, and explainable—especially when used for high-stakes teacher assessments. Issues such as algorithmic bias, black-box evaluations, and automated decision-making require explicit accountability measures.

Policymakers should mandate:

- Regular AI audits.
- Independent impact assessments.
- Clear appeal processes for credential disputes.

Weiner et al. (2024) stress that teacher preparation programs often lack the ethical infrastructure to deploy AI responsibly. To close this gap, public agencies should fund training initiatives, ethics oversight bodies, and policy labs focused on AI in education (Singh & Ram, 2024; Shanmughan et al., 2024).

## 8.5. Institutional Policy Alignment and Change Management

Effective AI policy implementation requires institutional alignment and strategic change management. According to Howell et al. (2018), fragmented teacher credentialing systems present challenges for integrating new technologies unless accompanied by coordinated reforms in licensing, accreditation, and professional development policies.

Zangana et al. (2024) underscore the importance of institutional data quality maturity and digital readiness for supporting AI deployment. Their findings call for government investment in:

- Digital infrastructure modernization.
- Interoperable databases.
- Capacity building in schools of education and certifying bodies.

Such policies must also bridge the urban-rural digital divide and address inequalities in technological access (Ironsi & Ironsi, 2025; Tuomi et al., 2023).

## 8.6. Labor Market Integration and Employer Engagement

To legitimize AI-generated micro-credentials, policymakers must engage employers, professional councils, and industry partners in co-defining credential standards. Rafi (2025) emphasizes the role of public-private partnerships in developing industry-aligned AI learning pathways that mitigate job loss risks.

Rachmad (2025a) further notes that Gen Z career pathways require flexibility and stackability—features AI-based systems can support if officially endorsed by labor ministries and human resources policy agencies.

## 8.7. Technology Procurement, Audit, and Regulation

Given the influx of commercial edtech vendors, regulatory bodies must define procurement and audit standards for AI and blockchain systems in education. Singh (2023) calls for clear guidelines on:

- Vendor compliance with data protection laws.
- Ethical AI certifications.
- Open-source preference policies.

Zangana and Mustafa (2024) recommend that systems involving facial detection or proctoring, such as those used in remote credential assessments, undergo government-approved bias testing and performance audits to protect learner rights.

## 8.8. Sustainable Policy for Developing Contexts

Policymakers in developing nations must tailor regulatory strategies to local contexts. Ramírez-Montoya et al. (2024) illustrate how Latin American universities adopted low-cost, community-based models of AI credentialing aligned with social inclusion goals. Islam and Rihan (2024) advise using AI and blockchain not only for efficiency, but also to democratize access to quality credentials.

Charles et al. (2025) propose vocational policy frameworks that legitimize micro-credentials for informal sector workers, while Kumar et al. (2025) call for mobile-based AI platforms that address infrastructure deficits in low-resource settings.

## 8.9 Summary

As AI and blockchain continue reshaping credentialing models, policymakers must act swiftly to establish robust, equitable, and future-proof regulatory frameworks. This includes defining standards for digital trust, ensuring ethical use of AI, aligning institutional policies, and protecting learner rights. Without coordinated national and international policy efforts, the promise of AI-enhanced credentialing in education may give way to fragmented systems, increased inequality, and lost credibility (Jacques et al., 2024; Alsobhi et al., 2023; Chaka, 2023).

The following layered model outlines a proposed policy framework for implementing AI-based credentialing systems across educational institutions and governments.

*Figure 5. Layered Policy Framework for AI-Driven Teacher Credentialing*

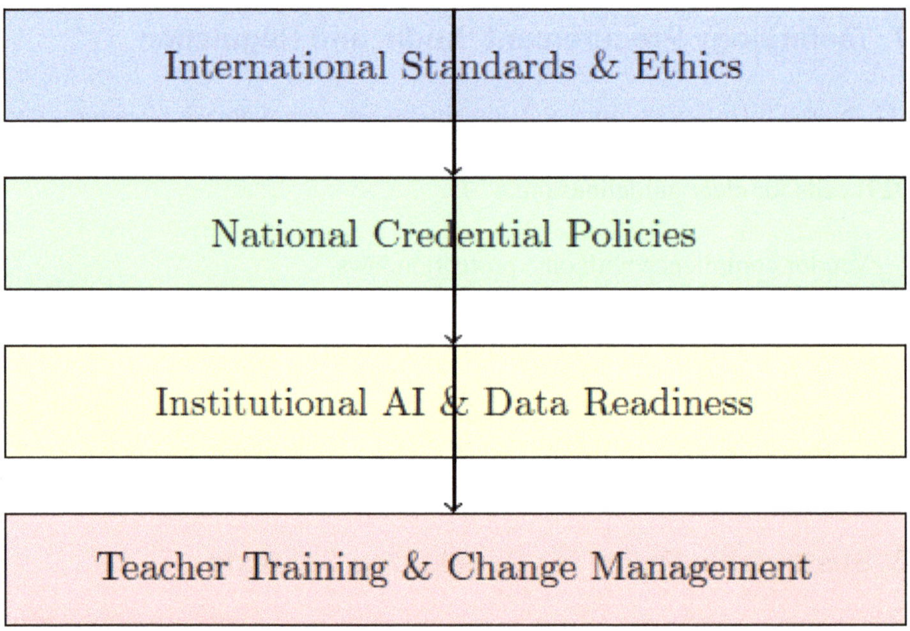


## 9. FUTURE DIRECTIONS AND RESEARCH OPPORTUNITIES

As the integration of AI and blockchain in teacher credentialing accelerates, the future of education stands at a transformative juncture. While present systems emphasize the digitization of credentials and personalized learning, future directions point toward intelligent, secure, and globally interoperable ecosystems that redefine how skills are recognized, validated, and rewarded. This section explores the emergent trends, innovation priorities, and critical research opportunities required to realize the full potential of AI-driven micro-credentialing.

## 9.1. Designing Interoperable, Decentralized Credentialing Architectures

There is a growing need for decentralized micro-credentialing systems that enable learners to own and manage their credentials across institutions and borders. Blockchain offers promising solutions in this regard (Alsobhi et al., 2023; Jirgensons & Kapenieks, 2018). Future research should focus on developing open standards and interoperable protocols that allow credential verification across platforms, reducing fragmentation in the credentialing landscape (Elkhodr et al., 2024).

Kumar et al. (2025) emphasize the role of AI in enabling adaptive credentialing systems that respond to evolving learner profiles, while Durak and Cankaya (2024) call for further exploration of blockchain's role in protecting the integrity of credentials within AI-assisted ecosystems.

## 9.2. AI-Enhanced Competency Mapping and Career Personalization

One of the most exciting future directions lies in the use of AI for personalized learning and career trajectory prediction. Asrifan et al. (2025) note, AI-enhanced micro-credentials can dynamically map learning progress and guide students toward individualized career pathways. This is particularly relevant in addressing the diverse needs of Gen Z learners who seek flexible, modular, and outcome-driven education (Rachmad, 2025a).

Polydoros (2025) suggests applying AI and micro-credentials in specialized domains, such as mathematics education for students with learning difficulties. Similarly, Rafi (2025) proposes designing AI-powered curricula that not only foster personalization but also help prevent mass job displacement in the automation era.

Further research is required to refine AI models that can dynamically recognize skills acquisition, recommend new credentials, and align learners with real-time labor market needs.

## 9.3. Ethical AI and Fair Credentialing Frameworks

As highlighted by Chaka (2023) and Trajkovski and Hayes (2025), ethical AI in education remains under-explored. Future research must investigate transparent and explainable AI algorithms to ensure that credentialing decisions are free from bias, auditable, and fair.

This includes developing governance models for AI accountability, especially in automated assessment, proctoring, and teacher evaluation tools (Krajcer, 2022; Singh & Ram, 2024). Research by Zangana and Al-Shaikhli (2013) and Zangana

& Mustafa (2024) on facial recognition and object detection offers a foundation for improving fairness and accuracy in AI-assisted credential validation.

A key research priority should be the creation of global ethical standards that guide AI and blockchain integration in micro-credentialing, ensuring inclusive, transparent, and equitable access.

## 9.4. Credentialing for Complex Thinking and 21st-Century Skills

A shift toward credentialing for soft skills, complex thinking, and real-world problem-solving is expected. As noted by Ironsi and Ironsi (2025), future learning environments must integrate credentialing models that recognize 21st-century competencies, such as collaboration, digital literacy, and adaptability.

Ramírez-Montoya et al. (2024) recommend using AI to assess "complex thinking" through project-based and peer-reviewed learning models. Jacques et al. (2024) echo this by proposing AI frameworks that measure not just knowledge, but the ability to synthesize and apply it.

Future research could explore alternative assessment models that rely on AI and peer validation to credential problem-solving, civic engagement, and interdisciplinary thinking.

## 9.5. Integration with Workforce and Talent Ecosystems

An important direction is linking AI-powered micro-credentials directly to talent development ecosystems. According to Díaz et al. (2022), as industries prioritize demonstrable skills over degrees, credentialing systems must be integrated with human resource information systems (HRIS) and job market platforms.

Charles et al. (2025) emphasize that vocational and professional training should adopt micro-credentials aligned with specific job tasks. Rachmad (2025b) proposes a new era of HR management focused on competence-first hiring. To support this, future research should investigate automated skill matching, credential portfolios, and digital badges readable by applicant tracking systems (ATS).

Additionally, Zangana, Mohammed, and Husain (2025) argue for stronger attention to cybersecurity in HR credential databases, especially in high-stakes sectors like finance and healthcare.

## 9.6. Teacher Training and Institutional Capacity Building

A key challenge moving forward is preparing institutions—and particularly teacher education programs—for AI-enhanced credentialing. Weiner et al. (2024) find that teacher preparation programs lag in AI integration due to policy inertia and capacity deficits.

Howell et al. (2018) call for revised teacher licensing systems that incorporate competency-based, AI-aided assessments. Singh (2023) advocates for the development of Web 3.0-aligned teacher training platforms that include blockchain and AI competencies.

Research is urgently needed into institutional change strategies, including faculty development, curriculum redesign, and hybrid credential models that blend traditional degrees with stackable micro-credentials (Zangana et al., 2024).

## 9.7. Localization and Equity in Global Credentialing

Future systems must address the global digital divide and avoid creating new forms of exclusion. Islam and Rihan (2024) and Tuomi et al. (2023) argue for contextualized AI and blockchain deployments in the Global South that support localized credentialing frameworks.

Charles et al. (2025) and Ramírez-Montoya et al. (2024) suggest embedding culturally relevant skills and languages into AI credentialing platforms. Further research could focus on multilingual credential taxonomies, offline-friendly mobile platforms, and community-based verification mechanisms.

Zangana (2018, 2020, 2022) underscores the importance of low-cost, scalable digital infrastructure for underserved communities—a critical consideration for equitable deployment.

## 9.8. Emerging Research Areas in Applied AI and Blockchain

Several technical areas remain ripe for innovation:

- **Lightweight, secure blockchain consensus protocols** for education (Zangana, 2025).
- **Explainable AI (XAI)** models for assessment transparency (Trajkovski & Hayes, 2025).
- **Cross-chain credential portability** and inter-institutional sharing (Alsobhi et al., 2023).
- **Edge AI for decentralized proctoring and learning analytics** (Kumar et al., 2025).

- **Integration of generative AI for learner reflection and portfolio compilation** (Zreik, 2024).

Moreover, Zangana & Abdulazeez (2023) suggest adapting engineering-grade clustering algorithms for credential categorization, while Zangana et al. (2024) recommend developing AI-driven change management tools to support institutional transition.

## 9.9 Summary

The future of AI and blockchain in credentialing lies in scalable, ethical, and inclusive systems that empower learners, inform educators, and connect talent to opportunity. As current models evolve, future research must embrace a cross-disciplinary agenda—spanning computer science, education, ethics, public policy, and workforce development. Only through such integration can credentialing systems fulfill their potential in the Fourth Industrial Revolution (Chaka, 2023; Islam & Rihan, 2024; Jacques et al., 2024).

# 10. CONCLUSION

The advent of artificial intelligence and blockchain technologies is fundamentally reshaping teacher certification and credentialing systems. Traditional models, grounded predominantly in degree-based qualifications and static assessments, are evolving into dynamic, competency-focused frameworks that prioritize verified skills, lifelong learning, and adaptability. AI-enhanced micro-credentialing offers unprecedented opportunities to personalize teacher development, increase transparency, and streamline credential verification processes, thus addressing many inefficiencies inherent in legacy systems.

However, realizing this potential requires navigating significant policy, ethical, and technical challenges. As demonstrated, the successful integration of AI and blockchain demands robust regulatory frameworks that safeguard data privacy, promote interoperability, and ensure equitable access for all learners, including those from marginalized communities. Furthermore, transparency and accountability in AI-powered assessments must be prioritized to avoid algorithmic biases and maintain trust in credential validity.

Institutions, policymakers, and educators must collaborate to adapt existing credentialing infrastructures and pedagogical models, fostering digital literacy and AI fluency within teacher preparation programs. Embracing flexible, modular credential pathways can help better align education with evolving workforce needs, particularly in the rapidly changing landscape of the Fourth Industrial Revolution.

Looking forward, research and innovation should continue to focus on ethical AI design, standardization of micro-credential frameworks, and inclusive technology deployment. By thoughtfully harnessing AI and blockchain, the future of teacher certification can become more responsive, efficient, and learner-centered—ultimately empowering educators and enhancing educational outcomes globally.

## REFERENCES


Alsobhi, H. A., Alakhtar, R. A., Ubaid, A., Hussain, O. K., & Hussain, F. K. (2023). Blockchain-based micro-credentialing system in higher education institutions: Systematic literature review. *Knowledge-Based Systems*, *265*, 110238. DOI: 10.1016/j.knosys.2022.110238

Asrifan, A., Sadaruddin, S., Ashar, A., Nonci, J., Setiawan, T., & Erniati, E. (2025). Redefining Learning Pathways: The Impact of AI-Enhanced Micro-Credentials on Education Efficiency. In *Integrating Micro-Credentials With AI in Open Education* (pp. 281-312). IGI Global Scientific Publishing.

Chaka, C. (2023). Fourth industrial revolution—a review of applications, prospects, and challenges for artificial intelligence, robotics and blockchain in higher education. *Research and Practice in Technology Enhanced Learning, 18*, 002-002.

Charles, T., Zoelfakar, S., & Sebastian, S. (2025). Micro-Credentials in Vocational and Professional Training. In *Integrating Micro-Credentials With AI in Open Education* (pp. 217–250). IGI Global Scientific Publishing.

Díaz, M. M. M. B., Lim, J. R., Navia, I. C., & Elzey, K. (2022). A world of transformation: Moving from degrees to skills-based alternative credentials.

Durak, G., & Cankaya, S. (Eds.). (2024). *Integrating Micro-credentials with AI in Open Education*. IGI Global. DOI: 10.4018/979-8-3693-5488-9

Elkhodr, M., Wangsa, K., Gide, E., & Karim, S. (2024). A Systematic Review and Multifaceted Analysis of the Integration of Artificial Intelligence and Blockchain: Shaping the Future of Australian Higher Education. *Future Internet*, *16*(10), 378. DOI: 10.3390/fi16100378

Howell, P. B., Cook, C. M., Miller, N. C., Thompson, N. L., Faulkner, S. A., & Rintamaa, M. F. (2018). The complexities of middle level teacher credentialing: Status report and future directions. *RMLE Online: Research in Middle Level Education*, *41*(4), 1–12. DOI: 10.1080/19404476.2018.1456840

Ironsi, C. S., & Ironsi, S. S. (2025). Efficacy of micro-credential learning environments for developing students' 21st century skills: Toward achieving sustainable development goals. *International Journal of Educational Management*. Advance online publication. DOI: 10.1108/IJEM-07-2024-0379

Islam, M. A., & Rihan, N. M. (2024). AI and Blockchain as sustainable teaching and learning tools to cope with the 4IR. In *Blockchain and AI* (pp. 123–153). CRC Press. DOI: 10.1201/9781003162018-4

Jacques, P. H., Moss, H. K., & Garger, J. (2024). A synthesis of AI in higher education: Shaping the future. *Journal of Behavioral and Applied Management, 24*(2), 103–111. DOI: 10.21818/001c.122146

Jirgensons, M., & Kapenieks, J. (2018). Blockchain and the future of digital learning credential assessment and management. *Journal of teacher education for sustainability, 20*(1), 145-156.

Krajcer, Z. (2022). Artificial intelligence for education, proctoring, and credentialing in cardiovascular medicine. *Texas Heart Institute Journal, 49*(2), e217572. DOI: 10.14503/THIJ-21-7572 PMID: 35481865

Kumar, S., Kameswari, Y. L., Moram, V., & Pasha, M. (2025). Adaptivc Lcarning in Modern Education Systems Leveraged by AI and Blockchain. In *Blockchain and AI in Shaping the Modern Education System* (pp. 44–71). CRC Press. DOI: 10.1201/9781003502739-3

Polydoros, G. V. (2025). Harnessing AI and Digital Tools for Micro-Credentialing in Mathematics Education: Enhancing Learning Outcomes for Students With Learning Difficulties. In *Integrating Micro-Credentials With AI in Open Education* (pp. 195-216). IGI Global Scientific Publishing.

Rachmad, Y. E. (2025). *The Future of Gen Z Careers: Competence and Certification Replacing Degrees*. United Nations Development Programme.

Rachmad, Y. E. (2025). *The New Era of HR Management: Prioritizing Competence Over Degrees*. United Nations Development Programme.

Rafi, M. U. (2025). Fundamentals of AI Learning Curriculum: Preventing Job Losses in the Era of Automation. *Available at SSRN* 5277211. DOI: 10.2139/ssrn.5277211

Ramírez-Montoya, M. S., Quintero Gámez, L., Sanabria-Z, J., & Portuguez-Castro, M. (2024). Exploring complex thinking in latin American universities: Comparative analysis between programs and alternative credentials. *Journal of Latinos and Education, 23*(5), 1744–1765. DOI: 10.1080/15348431.2024.2329671

Shanmughan, P., & Joseph, J. S, B. N., SM, A., CS, A., & Jose, J. (2024, November). The AI revolution in micro-credentialing: personalized learning paths. In *Frontiers in Education* (Vol. 9, p. 1445654). Frontiers Media SA.

Singh, H. (2023). The New Era in Education: Web 3.0. *TAM METİN BİLDİRİ KİTABI*, 78.

Singh, V., & Ram, S. (2024). Impact of artificial intelligence on teacher education. *Shodh Sari-An International Multidisciplinary Journal*, *3*(01), 243–266. DOI: 10.59231/SARI7669

Trajkovski, G., & Hayes, H. (2025). The Future of AI in Educational Assessment. In *AI-Assisted Assessment in Education: Transforming Assessment and Measuring Learning* (pp. 347–380). Springer Nature Switzerland. DOI: 10.1007/978-3-031-88252-4_9

Tuomi, I., Cachia, R., & Villar-Onrubia, D. (2023). *On the futures of technology in education: Emerging trends and policy implications*. Publications Office of the European Union.

Weiner, S., Lake, R., & Rosner, J. (2024). *AI Is Evolving, but Teacher Prep Is Lagging: A First Look at Teacher Preparation Program Responses to AI*. Center on Reinventing Public Education.

Williams, P. (2019). Does competency-based education with blockchain signal a new mission for universities? *Journal of Higher Education Policy and Management*, *41*(1), 104–117. DOI: 10.1080/1360080X.2018.1520491

Zangana, H. M. (2015). A New Skin Color Based Face Detection Algorithm by Combining Three Color Model Algorithms. *IOSR J. Comput. Eng, 17*, 06-125.

Zangana, H. M. (2017). A new algorithm for shape detection. *IOSR Journal of Computer Engineering (IOSR-JCE), 19*(3), 71-76.

Zangana, H. M. (2017). Library Data Quality Maturity (IIUM as a Case Study). *IOSR Journal of Computer Engineering*, *19*(March), 29. DOI: 10.9790/0661-1902033844

Zangana, H. M. (2017). Watermarking System Using LSB. *IOSR Journal of Computer Engineering*, *19*(3), 75–79. DOI: 10.9790/0661-1903027579

Zangana, H. M. (2018). Design an information management system for a pharmacy. *International Journal of Advanced Research in Computer and Communication Engineering*, *7*(10), 52–55. DOI: 10.17148/IJARCCE.2018.71012

Zangana, H. M. (2018). Developing Data Warehouse for Student Information System (IIUM as a Case Study). *International Organization of Scientific Research, 20*(1), 09-14.

Zangana, H. M. (2018). Implementing a System for Recognizing Optical Characters.

Zangana, H. M. (2019). Issues of Data Management in the Library: A Case Study.

Zangana, H. M. (2019). ITD Data Quality Maturity (A Case Study). *International Journal Of Engineering And Computer Science, 8*(10).

Zangana, H. M. (2020). Mobile Device Integration in IIUM Service. *International Journal (Toronto, Ont.), 8*(5).

Zangana, H. M. (2021). The Global Finical Crisis from an Islamic Point Of View. *Qubahan Academic Journal, 1*(2), 55–59. DOI: 10.48161/qaj.v1n2a39

Zangana, H. M. (2022). Creating a Community-Based Disaster Management System. *Academic Journal of Nawroz University, 11*(4), 234–244. DOI: 10.25007/ajnu.v11n4a1485

Zangana, H. M. (2022). Implementing New Interactive Video Learning System for IIUM. *Academic Journal of Nawroz University, 11*(2), 23–29. DOI: 10.25007/ajnu.v11n2a1281

Zangana, H. M. (2022). Improving The Web Services for Remittance Company: Express Remit as a Case Study. *Academic Journal of Nawroz University (AJNU), 11*(3).

Zangana, H. M. (2025). Design and Implementation of a Novel Parallel Algorithm for Efficient Image Compression in High-Performance Computing. *EAI Endorsed Transactions on AI and Robotics, 4*. Advance online publication. DOI: 10.4108/airo.7832

Zangana, H. M., & Abdulazeez, A. M. (2023). Developed Clustering Algorithms for Engineering Applications: A Review. *International Journal of Informatics* [INJIISCOM]. *Information System and Computer Engineering, 4*(2), 147–169.

Zangana, H. M., & Al-Shaikhli, I. F. (2013). A new algorithm for human face detection using skin color tone. *IOSR Journal of Computer Engineering, 11*(6), 31–38. DOI: 10.9790/0661-1163138

Zangana, H. M., Bazeed, S. M. S., Ali, N. Y., & Abdullah, D. T. (2024). Navigating Project Change: A Comprehensive Review of Change Management Strategies and Practices. *Indonesian Journal of Education and Social Sciences, 3*(2), 166–179. DOI: 10.56916/ijess.v3i2.735

Zangana, H. M., Mohammed, H. S., & Husain, M. M. (2025). Addressing insider threats: The human factor in cybersecurity for financial institutions. *Journal of Innovation Information Technology and Application, 7*(1), 88–96. DOI: 10.35970/jinita.v7i1.2686

Zangana, H. M., & Mustafa, F. M. (2024). From Classical to Deep Learning: A Systematic Review of Image Denoising Techniques. *Jurnal Ilmiah Computer Science*, *3*(1), 50–65. DOI: 10.58602/jics.v3i1.36

Zangana, H. M., & Mustafa, F. M. (2024). Review of Hybrid Denoising Approaches in Face Recognition: Bridging Wavelet Transform and Deep Learning. *The Indonesian Journal of Computer Science*, *13*(4). Advance online publication. DOI: 10.33022/ijcs.v13i4.4209

Zangana, H. M., & Mustafa, F. M. (2024). Surveying the Landscape: A Comprehensive Review of Object Detection Algorithms and Advancements. *Jurnal Ilmiah Computer Science*, *3*(1), 1–15. DOI: 10.58602/jics.v3i1.29

Zreik, M. (2024). Harnessing AI for entrepreneurial idea generation: Navigating the new frontier. In *Generating Entrepreneurial Ideas With AI* (pp. 1–18). IGI Global Scientific Publishing. DOI: 10.4018/979-8-3693-3498-0.ch001

# Compilation of References


Abujaber, A. A., & Nashwan, A. J. (2024). Ethical framework for artificial intelligence in healthcare research: A path to integrity. *World Journal of Methodology*, *14*(3). Advance online publication. DOI: 10.5662/wjm.v14.i3.94071 PMID: 39310239

Ajiga, D. I., Ndubuisi, N. L., Asuzu, O. F., Owolabi, O. R., Tubokirifuruar, T. S., & Adeleye, R. A. (2024). Ai-Driven Predictive Analytics In Retail: A Review Of Emerging Trends And Customer Engagement Strategies [Review Of Ai-Driven Predictive Analytics In Retail: A Review Of Emerging Trends And Customer Engagement Strategies. International Journal of Management & Entrepreneurship Research, 6(2), 307. Fair East Publishers. https://doi.org/DOI: 10.51594/ijmer.v6i2.772

Akintayo, T. A., Paul, C., Queenet, M. C., Nnadiekwe, O. A., Victoria, S. S., David, F. B., Joel, O. O., Agada, O. I., Ngozi, E. R., Arinze, U. U., Ojemerenvhie, G. A., Oluwadamilola, A. A., Nnamani, C. C., & Olayinka, U. W. (2024). Transforming Data Analytics with AI for Informed Decision-Making. *International Journal of Education Management and Technology*, *2*(3), 196–215. DOI: 10.58578/ijemt.v2i3.3812

Ali, G., Shah, S., & ElAffendi, M. (2024). Enhancing Cybersecurity Incident Response: AI-Driven Optimization for Strengthened Advance Persistence Threat Detection.

Almehdhar, M., Albaseer, A., Khan, M. A., Abdallah, M., Menouar, H., Al-Kuwari, S., & Al-Fuqaha, A. (2024). Deep learning in the fast lane: A survey on advanced intrusion detection systems for intelligent vehicle networks. *IEEE Open Journal of Vehicular Technology*, *5*, 869–906. DOI: 10.1109/OJVT.2024.3422253

Almutawa, A. (2023). *An Automated Feedback System Framework to Facilitate Instructor Self-Assessment* (Doctoral dissertation, University of Guelph).

Alotaibi, N., Williamson, J., & Khamis, M. (2023). ThermoSecure: Investigating the effectiveness of AI-driven thermal attacks on commonly used computer keyboards. *ACM Transactions on Privacy and Security*, *26*(2), 1–24. DOI: 10.1145/3563693

Al-Sharieh, S. (2021). The intellectual property road to the knowledge economy: Remarks on the readiness of the UAE Copyright Act to drive AI innovation. *Law, Innovation and Technology*, *13*(1), 141–166. DOI: 10.1080/17579961.2021.1898312

Alsobhi, H. A., Alakhtar, R. A., Ubaid, A., Hussain, O. K., & Hussain, F. K. (2023). Blockchain-based micro-credentialing system in higher education institutions: Systematic literature review. *Knowledge-Based Systems*, *265*, 110238. DOI: 10.1016/j.knosys.2022.110238

Al-Zahrani, A. M. (2024). Unveiling the shadows: Beyond the hype of AI in education. *Heliyon*, *10*(9), e30696. Advance online publication. DOI: 10.1016/j.heliyon.2024.e30696 PMID: 38737255

Amershi, S., Weld, D., Vorvoreanu, M., Fourney, A., Nushi, B., Collisson, P., & Horvitz, E. (2014). Power to the people: The role of humans in interactive machine learning. *AI Magazine*, *35*(4), 105–120. DOI: 10.1609/aimag.v35i4.2513

Anamol, S., Anjaneyulu, A., & Aseem, M. R. (2023). Utilizing AI to predict and mitigate financial risks in banking and investment sectors. *International Journal of Science and Research Archive*, *10*(1), 1098–1104. DOI: 10.30574/ijsra.2023.10.1.0701

Anderson, J. R., Boyle, C. F., Farrell, R., & Reiser, B. J. (1990). Cognitive principles in the design of computer tutors. *Cognitive Science*, *14*(2), 179–211. DOI: 10.1207/s15516709cog1402_1

Andreotta, A. J., Kirkham, N., & Rizzi, M. (2021). AI, big data, and the future of consent. *AI & Society*, *37*(4), 1715–1728. DOI: 10.1007/s00146-021-01262-5 PMID: 34483498

Antwi, B. O., Adelakun, B. O., & Eziefule, A. O.Bernard Owusu AntwiBeatrice Oyinkansola AdelakunAugustine Obinna Eziefule. (2024). Transforming Financial Reporting with AI: Enhancing Accuracy and Timeliness. *International Journal of Advanced Economics*, *6*(6), 205–223. DOI: 10.51594/ijae.v6i6.1229

Araujo, L., Lopez-Ostenero, F., Plaza, L., & Martinez-Romo, J. (2025). Automated Formative Feedback for Algorithm and Data Structure Self-Assessment. *Electronics (Basel)*, *14*(5), 1034. DOI: 10.3390/electronics14051034

Archita, S., & Saravanan, S. (2025, April). Enhancing Student Learning with a Customizable Virtual Assistant. In *2025 3rd International Conference on Advancements in Electrical, Electronics, Communication, Computing and Automation (ICAECA)* (pp. 1-7). IEEE.

Aslam, M. (2024). AI and cybersecurity: An ever-evolving landscape. *International Journal of Advanced Engineering Technologies and Innovations*, *1*(1), 52–71.

Asrifan, A., Sadaruddin, S., Ashar, A., Nonci, J., Setiawan, T., & Erniati, E. (2025). Redefining Learning Pathways: The Impact of AI-Enhanced Micro-Credentials on Education Efficiency. In *Integrating Micro-Credentials With AI in Open Education* (pp. 281-312). IGI Global Scientific Publishing.

Athavale, V. A., Selvakumar, P., Poorani, S., Anand, T., & Rathore, D. S. (2025). Designing chatbots for educational leadership. *Chatbots in Educational Leadership and Management*, 181-204.

Ayeni, O. O., Al Hamad, N. M., Chisom, O. N., Osawaru, B., & Adewusi, O. E. (2024). AI in education: A review of personalized learning and educational technology. *GSC Advanced Research and Reviews*, *18*(2), 261–271. DOI: 10.30574/gscarr.2024.18.2.0062

Badmus, O., Rajput, S., Arogundade, J. B., & Williams, M. H. (2024). AI-driven business analytics and decision making. *World Journal of Advanced Research and Reviews*, *24*(1), 616–633. DOI: 10.30574/wjarr.2024.24.1.3093

Bagai, R., & Mane, V. (2024). Designing an AI-powered mentorship platform for professional development: opportunities and challenges. *arXiv preprint arXiv:2407.20233*.

Barczak, A. L., Mathrani, A., Han, B., & Reyes, N. H. (2023). Automated assessment system for programming courses: A case study for teaching data structures and algorithms. *Educational Technology Research and Development*, *71*(6), 2365–2388. DOI: 10.1007/s11423-023-10277-2

Bardia, A., & Agrawal, A. (2025). MindCraft: Revolutionizing Education through AI-Powered Personalized Learning and Mentorship for Rural India. *arXiv preprint arXiv:2502.05826*.

Basha, Mrs. N. R. Dr. H. S. A., & Thoti, K. K. (. (2024). AI-powered Recruitment and Employee Selection: Evaluating Bias and Fairness in Hiring Practices. [EEL]. *European Economic Letters*, *14*(1), 827. DOI: 10.52783/eel.v14i1.1107

Basri, W. S. (2024). Effectiveness of AI-powered Tutoring Systems in Enhancing Learning Outcomes. *Eurasian Journal of Educational Research (EJER)*, (110).

Batool, A., Zowghi, D., & Bano, M. (2025). AI governance: A systematic literature review. *AI and Ethics*, *5*(3), 3265–3279. Advance online publication. DOI: 10.1007/s43681-024-00653-w

Battilana, J., & Casciaro, T. (2012). Change agents, networks, and institutions: A contingency theory of organizational change. *Academy of Management Journal*, *55*(2), 381–398. DOI: 10.5465/amj.2009.0891

Bayly-Castaneda, K., Ramirez-Montoya, M. S., & Morita-Alexander, A. (2024, August). Crafting personalized learning paths with AI for lifelong learning: A systematic literature review. [). Frontiers Media SA.]. *Frontiers in Education*, *9*, 1424386. DOI: 10.3389/feduc.2024.1424386

Belcadhi, L. C. (2016). Personalized feedback for self assessment in lifelong learning environments based on semantic web. *Computers in Human Behavior*, *55*, 562–570. DOI: 10.1016/j.chb.2015.07.042

Benn, S., Edwards, M., & Williams, T. (2014). *Organizational change for corporate sustainability*. Routledge. DOI: 10.4324/9781315819181

Bharathiraja, S., Rajesh Kanna, B., Geetha, S., & Anusooya, G. (2023). Unmasking the digital deception-a comprehensive survey on image forgery and detection techniques. *The Australian Journal of Forensic Sciences*, •••, 1–49.

Bhuyan, S. S., Sateesh, V., Mukul, N., Galvankar, A., Mahmood, A., Nauman, M., Rai, A., Bordoloi, K., Basu, U., & Samuel, J. (2025). Generative Artificial Intelligence Use in Healthcare: Opportunities for Clinical Excellence and Administrative Efficiency. *Journal of Medical Systems*, *49*(1), 10. Advance online publication. DOI: 10.1007/s10916-024-02136-1 PMID: 39820845

Bian, Y., & Xie, X. (2021). Generative chemistry: drug discovery with deep learning generative models [Review of Generative chemistry: drug discovery with deep learning generative models]. Journal of Molecular Modeling, 27(3). Springer Science+Business Media. https://doi.org/DOI: 10.1007/s00894-021-04674-8

Blackmore, J. (2013). A feminist critical perspective on educational leadership. *International Journal of Leadership in Education*, *16*(2), 139–154. DOI: 10.1080/13603124.2012.754057

Bleher, H., & Braun, M. (2023). Reflections on Putting AI Ethics into Practice: How Three AI Ethics Approaches Conceptualize Theory and Practice. *Science and Engineering Ethics*, *29*(3), 21. Advance online publication. DOI: 10.1007/s11948-023-00443-3 PMID: 37237246

Bolick, A. D., & da Silva, R. L. (2023). Exploring Artificial Intelligence Tools and Their Potential Impact to Instructional Design Workflows and Organizational Systems. *TechTrends*, *68*(1), 91–100. DOI: 10.1007/s11528-023-00894-2

Bolukbasi, T., Chang, K. W., Zou, J. Y., Saligrama, V., & Kalai, A. T. (2016). Man is to computer programmer as woman is to homemaker? Debiasing word embeddings. *Advances in Neural Information Processing Systems*, *29*, 4349–4357.

Booyse, D., & Scheepers, C. B. (2023). Barriers to adopting automated organisational decision-making through the use of artificial intelligence. *Management Research Review*, *47*(1), 64–85. DOI: 10.1108/MRR-09-2021-0701

Borenstein, J., & Howard, A. (2020). Emerging challenges in AI and the need for AI ethics education. *AI and Ethics*, *1*(1), 61–65. DOI: 10.1007/s43681-020-00002-7 PMID: 38624388

Borstad, A. L., Appling, S. A., Kloos, A. D., Spangler, L., & Marc, D. T. (2023). Beyond Borders, Beneath Words: Using Natural Language Processing to Map Student Reflections on International Service Learning to Physical Therapy Values. *Journal, Physical Therapy Education*, •••, 10–1097. PMID: 40008869

Brennan, A., & Canny, A. (2023). Problematising Irish student-teachers'(dis) engagement with sociology of education in initial teacher education programmes. *Teaching and Teacher Education*, *130*, 104173. DOI: 10.1016/j.tate.2023.104173

Brown, A., & Garcia, M. (2023). Socio-cultural bias in AI: Implications for equitable learning analytics. *Journal of Educational Technology Equity*, *5*(1), 45–62.

Buckingham Shum, S., Lim, L. A., Boud, D., Bearman, M., & Dawson, P. (2023). A comparative analysis of the skilled use of automated feedback tools through the lens of teacher feedback literacy. *International Journal of Educational Technology in Higher Education*, *20*(1), 40. DOI: 10.1186/s41239-023-00410-9

Buolamwini, J., & Gebru, T. (2018). Gender shades: Intersectional accuracy disparities in commercial gender classification. *Proceedings of the 1st Conference on Fairness, Accountability and Transparency*, 77–91. https://proceedings.mlr.press/v81/buolamwini18a.html

Burstein, J., Shore, J., Sabatini, J., Moulder, B., Lentini, J., Biggers, K., & Holtzman, S. (2014). From teacher professional development to the classroom: How NLP technology can enhance teachers' linguistic awareness to support curriculum development for English language learners. *Journal of Educational Computing Research*, *51*(1), 119–144. DOI: 10.2190/EC.51.1.f

Campbell, J., & Koffi, B. A. (2024). The Role of AI-powered financial analytics in shaping economic policy: A new era for risk management and national growth in the United States. *World Journal of Advanced Research and Reviews*, *23*(3), 2816–2825. DOI: 10.30574/wjarr.2024.23.3.2963

Casad, B. J., Franks, J. E., Garasky, C. E., Kittleman, M. M., Roesler, A. C., Hall, D. Y., & Petzel, Z. W. (2021). Gender inequality in academia: Problems and solutions for women faculty in STEM. *Journal of Neuroscience Research*, *99*(1), 13–23. DOI: 10.1002/jnr.24631 PMID: 33103281

Castañeda, R., Mercadé, L., Gómez, V. J., Mengual, T., Díaz-Fernández, F. J., Lozano, M. S., ... & de Zárate, D. O. (2024). Empowering Education 4.0: Impact of Using ChatGPT as a Virtual Mentor on K-12 Students Learning Science.

Chaka, C. (2023). Fourth industrial revolution—a review of applications, prospects, and challenges for artificial intelligence, robotics and blockchain in higher education. *Research and Practice in Technology Enhanced Learning, 18*, 002-002.

Chakraborty, S., Misra, B., & Dey, N. (2024). *AI-Empowered Knowledge Management in Education*. Springer. DOI: 10.1007/978-981-97-2574-8

Charles, T., Zoelfakar, S., & Sebastian, S. (2025). Micro-Credentials in Vocational and Professional Training. In *Integrating Micro-Credentials With AI in Open Education* (pp. 217–250). IGI Global Scientific Publishing.

CHAURASIA. (2024). *S., SENGAR, A. S., TOMAR, A., & SINGH, R.* Aupdeshik–AI Powered Learning Platform.

Chen, B., Wu, Z., & Zhao, R. (2023). From fiction to fact: The growing role of generative AI in business and finance. *Journal of Chinese Economic and Business Studies*, *21*(4), 471–496. DOI: 10.1080/14765284.2023.2245279

Cheng, K., & Wu, H. (2024, April 18). Policy framework for the utilization of generative AI. In Critical Care (Vol. 28, Issue 1). BioMed Central. https://doi.org/ DOI: 10.1186/s13054-024-04917-z

Chen, X., Xie, H., Zou, D., & Hwang, G.-J. (2020). Application and theory gaps during the rise of Artificial Intelligence in Education. *Computers and Education: Artificial Intelligence*, *1*, 100002. DOI: 10.1016/j.caeai.2020.100002

Chen, Y., Yu, B., & Yu, Y. (2021). Analysing preservice teachers' reflection journals using text-mining techniques. *International Journal of Innovation in Education*, *7*(2), 122–143. DOI: 10.1504/IJIIE.2021.118046

Chetwynd, E. (2024). Ethical Use of Artificial Intelligence for Scientific Writing: Current Trends. *Journal of Human Lactation*, *40*(2), 211–215. DOI: 10.1177/08903344241235160 PMID: 38482810

Chine, D. R., Chhabra, P., Adeniran, A., Kopko, J., Tipper, C., Gupta, S., & Koedinger, K. R. (2022, June). Scenario-based training and on-the-job support for equitable mentoring. In *The Learning Ideas Conference* (pp. 581-592). Cham: Springer International Publishing.

Choi, Y. H., Liu, P., Shang, Z., Wang, H., Wang, Z., Zhang, L., Zhou, J., & Zou, Q. (2020). Using deep learning to solve computer security challenges: A survey. *Cybersecurity*, *3*(1), 1–32. DOI: 10.1186/s42400-020-00055-5

Chong, C., Sheikh, U. U., Samah, N. A., & Sha'ameri, A. Z. (2020, July). Analysis on reflective writing using natural language processing and sentiment analysis. [). IOP Publishing.]. *IOP Conference Series. Materials Science and Engineering*, *884*(1), 012069. DOI: 10.1088/1757-899X/884/1/012069

Choudhary, P., Sharma, K., Sharma, K., Borasi, M., Bhargava, P., Ali, I., & Rehman, K. (2024). Enhancing Mentorship through Technology: A Comprehensive Review of Current Practices and Future Directions. *Available at SSRN* 5070036.

D'Souza, R., Mathew, M., Mishra, V., & Surapaneni, K. M. (2024). Twelve tips for addressing ethical concerns in the implementation of artificial intelligence in medical education. *Medical Education Online*, *29*(1), 2330250. Advance online publication. DOI: 10.1080/10872981.2024.2330250 PMID: 38566608

Dai, C. P., Ke, F., Pan, Y., Moon, J., & Liu, Z. (2024). Effects of artificial intelligence-powered virtual agents on learning outcomes in computer-based simulations: A meta-analysis. *Educational Psychology Review*, *36*(1), 31. DOI: 10.1007/s10648-024-09855-4

Darvishi, A., Khosravi, H., Abdi, S., Sadiq, S., & Gašević, D. (2022, June). Incorporating training, self-monitoring and AI-assistance to improve peer feedback quality. In *Proceedings of the ninth ACM conference on learning@ scale* (pp. 35-47). DOI: 10.1145/3491140.3528265

Das, R. (2024). *Generative AI: Phishing And Cybersecurity Metrics*. CRC Press. DOI: 10.1201/9781003503781

Davar, N. F., Dewan, M. A. A., & Zhang, X. (2025). AI chatbots in education: Challenges and opportunities. *Information (Basel)*, *16*(3), 235. DOI: 10.3390/info16030235

David, N. (2024). AI-powered virtual assistant solution for supporting international students.

David, B., Chalon, R., & Zhang, X. (2022, September). Virtual assistants (chatbots) as help to teachers in collaborative learning environment. In *International Conference on Interactive Collaborative Learning* (pp. 135-146). Cham: Springer International Publishing.

de Marcellis-Warin, N., Marty, F., Thelisson, E., & Warin, T. (2022). Artificial intelligence and consumer manipulations: From consumer's counter algorithms to firm's self-regulation tools. *AI and Ethics*, *2*(2), 259–268. DOI: 10.1007/s43681-022-00149-5

Demir, B., & Özdemir, D. (2025). AI voice journaling for future language teachers: A path to well-being through reflective practices. *British Educational Research Journal*, berj.4174. DOI: 10.1002/berj.4174

Devi, M. N., & Subbulakshmi, B. (2025). Mentoring Chatbot. *Adopting Artificial Intelligence Tools in Higher Education: Teaching and Learning*, 187.

Dhananjaya, G. M., Goudar, R. H., Kulkarni, A., Rathod, V. N., & Hukkeri, G. S. (2024). A digital recommendation system for personalized learning to enhance online education: A review. *IEEE Access : Practical Innovations, Open Solutions*.

Dhayanidhi, G. (2022). Research on IoT threats & implementation of AI/ML to address emerging cybersecurity issues in IoT with cloud computing.

Díaz, M. M. M. B., Lim, J. R., Navia, I. C., & Elzey, K. (2022). A world of transformation: Moving from degrees to skills-based alternative credentials.

Díaz-Rodríguez, N., Ser, J. D., Coeckelbergh, M., de Prado, M. L., Herrera-Viedma, E., & Herrera, F. (2023). Connecting the dots in trustworthy Artificial Intelligence: From AI principles, ethics, and key requirements to responsible AI systems and regulation. *Information Fusion*, *99*, 101896. DOI: 10.1016/j.inffus.2023.101896

Dietvorst, B. J., Simmons, J. P., & Massey, C. (2015). Algorithm aversion: People erroneously avoid algorithms after seeing them err. *Journal of Experimental Psychology. General*, *144*(1), 114–126. DOI: 10.1037/xge0000033 PMID: 25401381

Dignum, V. (2022). Responsible Artificial Intelligence: Recommendations and Lessons Learned. In Social and cultural studies of robots and AI (p. 195). Springer International Publishing. https://doi.org/DOI: 10.1007/978-3-031-08215-3_9

Dimitriadou, E., & Lanitis, A. (2025). Evaluating the impact of an automated body language assessment system. *Education and Information Technologies*, *30*(3), 3509–3539. DOI: 10.1007/s10639-024-12931-5

Durak, G., & Cankaya, S. (Eds.). (2024). *Integrating Micro-credentials with AI in Open Education*. IGI Global. DOI: 10.4018/979-8-3693-5488-9

Elbadawi, M., Li, H., Basit, A. W., & Gaisford, S. (2024). The role of artificial intelligence in generating original scientific research. *International Journal of Pharmaceutics*, *652*, 123741. DOI: 10.1016/j.ijpharm.2023.123741 PMID: 38181989

Elkhodr, M., Wangsa, K., Gide, E., & Karim, S. (2024). A Systematic Review and Multifaceted Analysis of the Integration of Artificial Intelligence and Blockchain: Shaping the Future of Australian Higher Education. *Future Internet*, *16*(10), 378. DOI: 10.3390/fi16100378

Erdélyi, O. J., & Goldsmith, J. (2022). Regulating artificial intelligence: Proposal for a global solution. *Government Information Quarterly*, *39*(4), 101748. DOI: 10.1016/j.giq.2022.101748

Evenddy, S. S. (2024). Investigating AI's Automated Feedback in English Language Learning. *Foreign Language Instruction Probe*, *3*(1), 76–87. DOI: 10.54213/flip.v3i1.401

Fan, X., Luo, W., Menekse, M., Litman, D., & Wang, J. (2017, March). Scaling reflection prompts in large classrooms via mobile interfaces and natural language processing. In *Proceedings of the 22nd international conference on intelligent user interfaces* (pp. 363-374). DOI: 10.1145/3025171.3025204

Fayyaz, Y., Almehmadi, A., & El-Khatib, K. (2024). A hybrid artificial intelligence framework for enhancing digital forensic investigations of infotainment systems. *Forensic Science International Digital Investigation*, *49*, 301751. DOI: 10.1016/j.fsidi.2024.301751

Fernoagă, V., Stelea, G. A., Gavrilă, C., & Sandu, F. (2018). Intelligent Education Assistant Powered by Chatbots. *eLearning & Software for Education, 2*.

Fu, M., Pasuksmit, J., & Tantithamthavorn, C. (2024). AI for DevSecOps: A Landscape and Future Opportunities. *arXiv preprint arXiv:2404.04839.*

Fyfe, P. (2022). How to cheat on your final paper: Assigning AI for student writing. *AI & Society*, *38*(4), 1395–1405. DOI: 10.1007/s00146-022-01397-z

Gamieldien, Y., McCord, R., & Katz, A. (2023). Utilizing natural language processing to examine self-reflections in self-regulated learning. *Available at SSRN* 4487795. DOI: 10.2139/ssrn.4487795

Ganguly, A., Johri, A., Ali, A., & McDonald, N. (2025). Generative artificial intelligence for academic research: Evidence from guidance issued for researchers by higher education institutions in the United States. *AI and Ethics*, *5*(4), 3917–3933. Advance online publication. DOI: 10.1007/s43681-025-00688-7

Gholami, S., & Omar, M. (2023). Does Synthetic Data Make Large Language Models More Efficient? *arXiv preprint arXiv:2310.07830.*

Gholami, S., & Omar, M. (2024). Can a student large language model perform as well as its teacher? In *Innovations, Securities, and Case Studies Across Healthcare, Business, and Technology* (pp. 122-139). IGI Global. DOI: 10.4018/979-8-3693-1906-2.ch007

Golda, A., Mekonen, K., Pandey, A., Singh, A., Hassija, V., Chamola, V., & Sikdar, B. (2024). Privacy and Security Concerns in Generative AI: A Comprehensive Survey. *IEEE Access : Practical Innovations, Open Solutions*, *12*, 48126–48144. DOI: 10.1109/ACCESS.2024.3381611

Grab, M. O. (2025). Teaching for Equity: An Exploration of AI's Role in Culturally Responsive Teaching in Higher Education Settings. *Innovative Higher Education*, •••, 1–22. DOI: 10.1007/s10755-025-09801-4

Guan, C., Mou, J., & Jiang, Z. (2020). Artificial intelligence innovation in education: A twenty-year data-driven historical analysis. *International Journal of Innovation Studies*, *4*(4), 134–147. DOI: 10.1016/j.ijis.2020.09.001

Gubareva, R., & Lopes, R. P. (2020). Virtual Assistants for Learning: A Systematic Literature Review. *CSEDU*, (1), 97–103. DOI: 10.5220/0009417600970103

Gupta, A. S., Shreneter, K. P., & Sehgal, S. (2024, March). Visual Veracity: Advancing AI-Generated Image Detection with Convolutional Neural Networks. In *2024 11th International Conference on Reliability, Infocom Technologies and Optimization (Trends and Future Directions)(ICRITO)* (pp. 1-6). IEEE.

Gurgu, E., Bucea-Manea- oni , R., Avram, L. G., & Simion, V. (2020). Applicability of the ethics management tools in Romanian academia. *Independent Journal of Management & Production*, *11*(7), 2709–2732. DOI: 10.14807/ijmp.v11i7.1205

Hadid, A., Chakraborty, T., & Busby, D. (2024). When geoscience meets generative AI and large language models: Foundations, trends, and future challenges. *Expert Systems: International Journal of Knowledge Engineering and Neural Networks*, *41*(10), e13654. Advance online publication. DOI: 10.1111/exsy.13654

Hain, R. (2020). Principles and ethics in medicine. *Medicine (Abingdon)*, *48*(10), 631–633. DOI: 10.1016/j.mpmed.2020.07.009

Halmo, H. (2025). *Human-Centered, Tech-Enabled: Scaling Academic Advising in Higher Education Through Predictive Analytics and Organizational Change an Innovation Study* (Doctoral dissertation, New York University).

Hamza, Y. A., & Omar, M. D. (2013). Cloud computing security: Abuse and nefarious use of cloud computing. *International Journal of Computer Engineering Research*, *3*(6), 22–27.

Harahap, H., & Hamid, A. (2020). Analysis of The Importance of Omnibus Law "Cipta Karya" in Indonesia. [IJSRM]. *International Journal of Scientific Research and Management*, *8*(8), 236–250. DOI: 10.18535/ijsrm/v8i08.lla01

Hari, D., Zemljak, D., Kerneža, M., Kurbus, N., Krabonja, M. V., & Flogie, A. (2025). CONVERSATIONAL ASSISTANTS IN EDUCATION: ADVANTAGES, CHALLENGES, AND OPPORTUNITIES FOR THE FUTURE. *INTED2025 Proceedings*, 6675-6683.

Hashmi, M. F., Ashish, B. K. K., Keskar, A. G., Bokde, N. D., & Geem, Z. W. (2020). FashionFit: Analysis of Mapping 3D Pose and Neural Body Fit for Custom Virtual Try-On. *IEEE Access : Practical Innovations, Open Solutions*, *8*, 91603–91615. DOI: 10.1109/ACCESS.2020.2993574

Heidari, A., Jafari Navimipour, N., Dag, H., & Unal, M. (2024). Deepfake detection using deep learning methods: A systematic and comprehensive review. *Wiley Interdisciplinary Reviews. Data Mining and Knowledge Discovery*, *14*(2), e1520. DOI: 10.1002/widm.1520

Herington, J., Connelly, K., & Illes, J. (2023). Ethical Imperatives for Working With Diverse Populations in Digital Research. *Journal of Medical Internet Research*, *25*, e47884. Advance online publication. DOI: 10.2196/47884 PMID: 37721792

Hermann, E., & Hermann, G. (2021). Artificial intelligence in research and development for sustainability: The centrality of explicability and research data management. *AI and Ethics*, *2*(1), 29–33. DOI: 10.1007/s43681-021-00114-8

Hewage, C. T., Khattak, S. K., Ahmad, A., Mallikarachchi, T., Ukwandu, E., & Bentotahewa, V. (2022). Multimedia privacy and security landscape in the wake of ai/ml. *Social Media Analytics, Strategies and Governance*, 203-228.

Hirschberg, J., & Manning, C. D. (2015). Advances in natural language processing. *Science, 349*(6245), 261–266. DOI: 10.1126/science.aaa8685 PMID: 26185244

Holmes, W., Bialik, M., & Fadel, C. (2019). *Artificial Intelligence in education: Promises and implications for teaching and learning*. Center for Curriculum Redesign.

Hooda, M., Rana, C., Dahiya, O., Rizwan, A., & Hossain, M. S. (2022). Artificial intelligence for assessment and feedback to enhance student success in higher education. *Mathematical Problems in Engineering, 2022*(1), 5215722. DOI: 10.1155/2022/5215722

Hosseini, M., Rasmussen, L. M., & Resnik, D. B. (2023). Using AI to write scholarly publications. *Accountability in Research, 31*(7), 715–723. DOI: 10.1080/08989621.2023.2168535 PMID: 36697395

Hosseini, M., Resnik, D. B., & Holmes, K. (2023). The ethics of disclosing the use of artificial intelligence tools in writing scholarly manuscripts. *Research Ethics, 19*(4), 449–465. DOI: 10.1177/17470161231180449 PMID: 39749232

Howell, P. B., Cook, C. M., Miller, N. C., Thompson, N. L., Faulkner, S. A., & Rintamaa, M. F. (2018). The complexities of middle level teacher credentialing: Status report and future directions. *RMLE Online: Research in Middle Level Education, 41*(4), 1–12. DOI: 10.1080/19404476.2018.1456840

Hsia, L. H., Hwang, G. J., Lin, Y. N., & Hwang, J. P. (2025). Artificial intelligence-supported physical education during the pandemic: A physical skill auto-assessment and feedback approach based on a reflection-promoting mechanism. *Educational Technology Research and Development*, •••, 1–22. DOI: 10.1007/s11423-025-10452-7

Hu, C., Li, F., Wang, S., Gao, Z., Pan, S., & Qing, M. (2025). The role of artificial intelligence in enhancing personalized learning pathways and clinical training in dental education. *Cogent Education, 12*(1), 2490425. DOI: 10.1080/2331186X.2025.2490425

Huff, A. J., Burrell, D. N., Nobles, C., Richardson, K., Wright, J. B., Burton, S. L., Jones, A. J., Springs, D., Omar, M., & Brown-Jackson, K. L. (2023). Management Practices for Mitigating Cybersecurity Threats to Biotechnology Companies, Laboratories, and Healthcare Research Organizations. In *Applied Research Approaches to Technology, Healthcare, and Business* (pp. 1-12). IGI Global.

Hutson, J. (2024). Rethinking Plagiarism in the Era of Generative AI. *Journal of International Communication*, *4*(1). Advance online publication. DOI: 10.54963/jic.v4i1.220

Ionescu, S.-A., & Dıaconı a, V. (2023). Transforming Financial Decision-Making: The Interplay of AI, Cloud Computing and Advanced Data Management Technologies. *International Journal of Computers, Communications & Control*, *18*(6). Advance online publication. DOI: 10.15837/ijccc.2023.6.5735

Ironsi, C. S., & Ironsi, S. S. (2025). Efficacy of micro-credential learning environments for developing students' 21st century skills: Toward achieving sustainable development goals. *International Journal of Educational Management*. Advance online publication. DOI: 10.1108/IJEM-07-2024-0379

Islam, A., Ali, R., Singh, G., Islam, B., Islam, A., & Hossain, S. (2024, May). An Evaluation of AI-Enhanced Collaborative Learning Platforms. In *2024 International Conference on Communication, Computer Sciences and Engineering (IC3SE)* (pp. 207-211). IEEE. DOI: 10.1109/IC3SE62002.2024.10593320

Islam, M. A., & Rihan, N. M. (2024). AI and Blockchain as sustainable teaching and learning tools to cope with the 4IR. In *Blockchain and AI* (pp. 123–153). CRC Press. DOI: 10.1201/9781003162018-4

Jackson, I., Ivanov, D., Dolgui, A., & Namdar, J. (2024). Generative artificial intelligence in supply chain and operations management: A capability-based framework for analysis and implementation. *International Journal of Production Research*, *62*(17), 6120–6145. DOI: 10.1080/00207543.2024.2309309

Jacques, P. H., Moss, H. K., & Garger, J. (2024). A synthesis of AI in higher education: Shaping the future. *Journal of Behavioral and Applied Management*, *24*(2), 103–111. DOI: 10.21818/001c.122146

Jafari, D., & Yazdi, Z. S. (2024). Transforming Education with AI: The Development of a Personalized Learning Algorithm for Individual Learning Styles. *Journal of Algorithms and Computation*, *56*(2), 135–150.

Jalilov, O., Zawidzki, J., & Bez, M. (2024). TOWARDS SCALABLE MENTORING: EXPLORING INTERACTIONS IN HYBRID AI SYSTEMS. In *ICERI2024 Proceedings* (pp. 9678-9686). IATED.

Jdidou, Y., & Aammou, S. (2024). TRANSFORMING EDUCATION WITH AI: THE ROLE OF RECOMMENDATION SYSTEMS IN PERSONALIZED LEARNING. In *EDULEARN24 Proceedings* (pp. 7662-7669). IATED.

Jin, Z., Goyal, S. B., & Rajawat, A. S. (2024). The informational role of artificial intelligence in higher education in the New era. *Procedia Computer Science*, *235*, 1008–1023. DOI: 10.1016/j.procs.2024.04.096

Jirgensons, M., & Kapenieks, J. (2018). Blockchain and the future of digital learning credential assessment and management. *Journal of teacher education for sustainability, 20*(1), 145-156.

Johnson, M., Kumar, S., & Patel, R. (2021). Enhancing teaching decisions with AI: A study of data-driven interventions in middle school classrooms. *Journal of Educational Computing Research*, *59*(4), 747–768.

Jones, R., Omar, M., Mohammed, D., Nobles, C., & Dawson, M. (2023). Harnessing the Speed and Accuracy of Machine Learning to Advance Cybersecurity. In *2023 Congress in Computer Science, Computer Engineering, & Applied Computing (CSCE)* (pp. 418-421). IEEE. DOI: 10.1109/CSCE60160.2023.00074

Jones, R., & Omar, M. (2024). Revolutionizing Cybersecurity: The GPT-2 Enhanced Attack Detection and Defense (GEADD) Method for Zero-Day Threats. *International Journal of Informatics* [INJIISCOM]. *Information System and Computer Engineering*, *5*(2), 178–191.

Kabashkin, I., Mišņevs, B., & Zervina, O. (2024, September). AI-Driven and Ontology-Based Framework for Personalized Learning Pathways in Education. In *International Conference on Reliability and Statistics in Transportation and Communication* (pp. 494-506). Cham: Springer Nature Switzerland.

Kadri, S., Dorri, N., Osaiweran, M., Garyali, P., & Petkovic, M. (2024). *Scientific Peer Review in an Era of Artificial Intelligence*., DOI: 10.1007/978-981-97-4060-4_23

Kajiwara, Y., & Kawabata, K. (2024). AI literacy for ethical use of chatbot: Will students accept AI ethics? *Computers and Education Artificial Intelligence*, *6*, 100251. DOI: 10.1016/j.caeai.2024.100251

Kalashnikova, L. V., Lobanova, A. S., Hrabovets, I. V., Chernous, L. S., Chorna, V. A., & Davydenko, Y. O. (2025, March). Modern information and communication technologies in professional training of sociology students: Evolving needs and significance in the digital age. In *CTE Workshop Proceedings* (Vol. 12, pp. 381-398). DOI: 10.55056/cte.922

Kane, D. A. (2016). The role of chatbots in teaching and learning. *E-learning and the academic library: Essays on innovative initiatives, 131*, 131-147.

Kazim, E., & Koshiyama, A. (2021). A high-level overview of AI ethics [Review of A high-level overview of AI ethics]. Patterns, 2(9), 100314. Elsevier BV. https://doi.org/DOI: 10.1016/j.patter.2021.100314

Kenshinbay, T., Ghorbandordinejad, F., Bolatova, A., & Kiyassova, K. (2025). Enhancing Language Teacher Reflection through Narrative Techniques: Character Development and Critical Incident Analysis: Language Teacher Reflection through Narrative Techniques. *Bulletin of Language and Literature Studies*, *2*(1). Advance online publication. DOI: 10.59652/blls.v2i1.482

Kerimbayev, N., Adamova, K., Jotsov, V., Shadiev, R., Umirzakova, Z., & Nurymova, A. (2024, August). Organization of Feedback in the Intelligent Learning Systems. In *2024 IEEE 12th International Conference on Intelligent Systems (IS)* (pp. 1-7). IEEE. DOI: 10.1109/IS61756.2024.10705178

Khaleel, Y. L., Habeeb, M. A., Albahri, A. S., Al-Quraishi, T., Albahri, O. S., & Alamoodi, A. H. (2024). Network and cybersecurity applications of defense in adversarial attacks: A state-of-the-art using machine learning and deep learning methods. *Journal of Intelligent Systems*, *33*(1), 20240153. DOI: 10.1515/jisys-2024-0153

Khamis, R. (2024). AI-Powered Learning Experience Platforms: Investigating Personalized Learning in the Workplace.

Khan, Z. R. (2024). Ethics of Artificial Intelligence in Academia. In *Springer international handbooks of education* (p. 1551). Springer Nature., DOI: 10.1007/978-3-031-54144-5_188

Khasawneh, D. M. A. S. K. (2024). Improving the learning of language proficiency at tertiary education level through AI-driven assessment models and automated feedback systems. *Migration Letters : An International Journal of Migration Studies*, *21*(2), 712–726.

Khimi, W., Albarqi, K., Saif, K., & Elhag, S. A Systematic Review on Deep Fake Image Generation, Detection Techniques, Ethical Implications, and Overcoming Challenges.

Khormali, A. (2022). Advanced Deep Learning Methodologies for Deepfake Detection.

Khosrowi, D., Finn, F., & Clark, E. (2024). Engaging the many-hands problem of generative-AI outputs: A framework for attributing credit. *AI and Ethics*. Advance online publication. DOI: 10.1007/s43681-024-00440-7

Klingbeil, A., Grützner, C., & Schreck, P. (2024). Trust and reliance on AI — An experimental study on the extent and costs of overreliance on AI. *Computers in Human Behavior*, *160*, 108352. DOI: 10.1016/j.chb.2024.108352

Kohli, R., Pizarro, M., Garcia, L. G., Kelly, L., Espinoza, M., & Cordova, J. (2021). Critical professional development and the racial justice leadership possibilities of teachers of colour in K-12 schools. *Professional Development in Education*, *47*(1), 89–101. DOI: 10.1080/19415257.2020.1814387

Koshiyama, A., Kazim, E., Treleaven, P., Rai, P., Szpruch, Ł., Pavey, G., Ahamat, G., Leutner, F., Goebel, R., Knight, A. W., Adams, J., Hitrova, C., Barnett, J., Nachev, P., Barber, D., Chamorro-Premuzic, T., Klemmer, K., Gregorovic, M., Khan, S., & Chatterjee, S. (2024). Towards algorithm auditing: Managing legal, ethical and technological risks of AI, ML and associated algorithms. *Royal Society Open Science*, *11*(5), 230859. Advance online publication. DOI: 10.1098/rsos.230859 PMID: 39076787

Kovari, A. (2025). A systematic review of AI-powered collaborative learning in higher education: Trends and outcomes from the last decade. *Social Sciences & Humanities Open*, *11*, 101335. DOI: 10.1016/j.ssaho.2025.101335

Krajcer, Z. (2022). Artificial intelligence for education, proctoring, and credentialing in cardiovascular medicine. *Texas Heart Institute Journal*, *49*(2), e217572. DOI: 10.14503/THIJ-21-7572 PMID: 35481865

Kulugh, V. E., Aondover, K. P., & Faki, A. S. (2025). Artificial Intelligence-Powered Personalised Career Guidance System. *Dutse Journal of Pure and Applied Sciences*, *11*(1c), 92–104.

Kumar, C. R. (2025). AI-Powered Recruitment: Transforming Talent Acquisition in the Digital Age. *Journal of Informatics Education and Research*, *5*(1). Advance online publication. DOI: 10.52783/jier.v5i1.2166

Kumar, S., Kameswari, Y. L., Moram, V., & Pasha, M. (2025). Adaptive Learning in Modern Education Systems Leveraged by AI and Blockchain. In *Blockchain and AI in Shaping the Modern Education System* (pp. 44–71). CRC Press. DOI: 10.1201/9781003502739-3

Kyrylenko, Y. (2024). Chatbots and virtual assistants vs. human agents in IT customer support.

Lan, Y. (2024). Through tensions to identity-based motivations: Exploring teacher professional identity in Artificial Intelligence-enhanced teacher training. *Teaching and Teacher Education*, *151*, 104736. DOI: 10.1016/j.tate.2024.104736

Lasker, A. (2024). Exploring Ethical Considerations In Generative AI. *International Journal of Advanced Research*, *12*(4), 531–535. DOI: 10.21474/IJAR01/18578

Lee, J., & Park, Y. (2022). Teacher-AI collaboration in personalized learning environments: A multi-case study. *Computers & Education*, *182*, 104465. DOI: 10.1016/j.compedu.2022.104465

Lee, S., Chen, Y., & Alvarez, M. (2022). Linguistic equity in automated essay scoring: Challenges and innovations. *Computers & Education*, *187*, 104608. DOI: 10.1016/j.compedu.2022.104608

Lepri, B., Oliver, N., & Pentland, A. (2021). Ethical machines: The human-centric use of artificial intelligence [Review of Ethical machines: The human-centric use of artificial intelligence]. iScience, 24(3), 102249. Cell Press. https://doi.org/DOI: 10.1016/j.isci.2021.102249

Li, L., & Kim, M. (2024). It is like a friend to me: Critical usage of automated feedback systems by self-regulating English learners in higher education. *Australasian Journal of Educational Technology*, *40*(1), 1–18. DOI: 10.14742/ajet.8821

Li, P., & Ding, Z. (2025). Application of deep learning-based personalized learning path prediction and resource recommendation for inheriting scientist spirit in graduate education. *Computer Science and Information Systems*, (00), 43–43. DOI: 10.2298/CSIS241125043L

Liu, C. C., Hwang, G. J., Yu, P., Tu, Y. F., & Wang, Y. (2025). Effects of an automated corrective feedback-based peer assessment approach on students' learning achievement, motivation, and self-regulated learning conceptions in foreign language pronunciation. *Educational Technology Research and Development*, •••, 1–22. DOI: 10.1007/s11423-025-10484-z

Liu, S. (2025). Navigating Equality in Schools: The Sociological Impact of Leadership on Student Success. *Education and Urban Society*, *57*(3), 245–298. DOI: 10.1177/00131245241304404

Llorca, D. F., Charisi, V., Hamon, R., Sánchez, I., & Gómez, E. (2023). Liability Regimes in the Age of AI: A Use-Case Driven Analysis of the Burden of Proof. *Journal of Artificial Intelligence Research*, *76*, 613–644. DOI: 10.1613/jair.1.14565

Loganathan, M. E., Agalya, S. Y., Hariharan, K., & Bharathi, A. K. (2025). AI-Powered Alumni Portal: Connect, Learn, Thrive. *International Research Journal on Advanced Science Hub*, *7*(01), 1–9. DOI: 10.47392/IRJASH.2025.001

Luckin, R., Holmes, W., Griffiths, M., & Forcier, L. B. (2016). *Intelligence unleashed: An argument for AI in education*. Pearson Education. https://www.pearson.com/content/dam/one-dot-com/one-dot-com/global/Files/about-pearson/innovation/open-ideas/Intelligence-Unleashed-Publication.pdf

Lyu, S. (2024). *DeepFake the menace: mitigating the negative impacts of AI-generated content. Organizational Cybersecurity Journal: Practice*. Process and People.

Mac Fadden, I., García-Alonso, E. M., & López Meneses, E. (2024). Science Mapping of AI as an Educational Tool Exploring Digital Inequalities: A Sociological Perspective. *Multimodal Technologies and Interaction*, *8*(12), 106. DOI: 10.3390/mti8120106

Magooda, A., Litman, D., Ashraf, A., & Menekse, M. (2022, July). Improving the quality of students' written reflections using natural language processing: Model design and classroom evaluation. In *International Conference on Artificial Intelligence in Education* (pp. 519-525). Cham: Springer International Publishing. DOI: 10.1007/978-3-031-11644-5_43

Maheshwari, R. U., & Paulchamy, B. (2024). Securing online integrity: A hybrid approach to deepfake detection and removal using Explainable AI and Adversarial Robustness Training. *Automatika (Zagreb)*, *65*(4), 1517–1532. DOI: 10.1080/00051144.2024.2400640

Majeed, A., & Hwang, S. O. (2023). When AI meets information privacy: The adversarial role of AI in data sharing scenario. *IEEE Access : Practical Innovations, Open Solutions*, *11*, 76177–76195. DOI: 10.1109/ACCESS.2023.3297646

Marchisio, M., Barana, A., Fioravera, M., Rabellino, S., & Conte, A. (2018, July). A model of formative automatic assessment and interactive feedback for STEM. In *2018 ieee 42nd annual computer software and applications conference (compsac)* (Vol. 1, pp. 1016-1025). IEEE. DOI: 10.1109/COMPSAC.2018.00178

Martinez-Romo, J., Araujo, L., Plaza, L., & López-Ostenero, F. (2025, April). Generative AI for Education: A Retrieval-Augmented System for Effective Feedback in Self-Assessment. In *2025 IEEE Global Engineering Education Conference (EDUCON)* (pp. 1-9). IEEE. DOI: 10.1109/EDUCON62633.2025.11016446

Mavuso, N. C., Jere, N., & vanGreunen, D. (2023). A Customized Artificial Intelligence Based Career Choice Recommender System for a Rural University.

Ma, Y., Wang, L., Zhang, J., Liu, F., & Jiang, Q. (2023). A personalized learning path recommendation method incorporating multi-algorithm. *Applied Sciences (Basel, Switzerland)*, *13*(10), 5946. DOI: 10.3390/app13105946

Mbah, G. O.Geraldine O Mbah. (2024). Data privacy in the era of AI: Navigating regulatory landscapes for global businesses. *International Journal of Science and Research Archive*, *13*(2), 2040–2058. DOI: 10.30574/ijsra.2024.13.2.2396

Mehrabi, N., Morstatter, F., Saxena, N., Lerman, K., & Galstyan, A. (2021). A survey on bias and fairness in machine learning. *ACM Computing Surveys*, *54*(6), 1–35. DOI: 10.1145/3457607

Mekni, M. (2021). An artificial intelligence based virtual assistant using conversational agents. *Journal of Software Engineering and Applications*, *14*(9), 455–473. DOI: 10.4236/jsea.2021.149027

Mckni, M., Baani, Z., & Sulieman, D. (2020, January). A smart virtual assistant for students. In *Proceedings of the 3rd international conference on applications of intelligent systems* (pp. 1-6).

Mendoza, S., Sánchez-Adame, L. M., Urquiza-Yllescas, J. F., González-Beltrán, B. A., & Decouchant, D. (2022). A model to develop chatbots for assisting the teaching and learning process. *Sensors (Basel)*, *22*(15), 5532. DOI: 10.3390/s22155532 PMID: 35898035

Menekse, M., Putra, A. S., Kim, J., Butt, A. A., McDaniel, M. A., Davidesco, I., Cadieux, M., Kim, J., & Litman, D. (2025). Enhancing student reflections with natural language processing based scaffolding: A quasi-experimental study in a large lecture course. *Computers and Education: Artificial Intelligence*, *8*, 100397. DOI: 10.1016/j.caeai.2025.100397

Messina, C. M., Jones, C. E., & Poe, M. (2023). Prompting reflection: Using corpus linguistic methods in the local assessment of reflective writing. *Written Communication*, *40*(2), 620–650. DOI: 10.1177/07410883221149425

Mientus, L., Wulff, P., Nowak, A., & Borowski, A. (2023). Fast-and-frugal means to assess reflection-related reasoning processes in teacher training—Development and evaluation of a scalable machine learning-based metric. *Zeitschrift für Erziehungswissenschaft*, *26*(3), 677–702. DOI: 10.1007/s11618-023-01166-8

Miernicki, M., & Ng, I. (2020). Artificial intelligence and moral rights. *AI & Society*, *36*(1), 319–329. DOI: 10.1007/s00146-020-01027-6

Miller, T. (2019). Explanation in artificial intelligence: Insights from the social sciences. *Artificial Intelligence*, *267*, 1–38. DOI: 10.1016/j.artint.2018.07.007

Mishra, P., Oster, N., & Henriksen, D. (2024). Generative AI, teacher knowledge and educational research: Bridging short-and long-term perspectives. *TechTrends*, *68*(2), 205–210. DOI: 10.1007/s11528-024-00938-1

Mitchell, M., Wu, S., Zaldivar, A., Barnes, P., Vasserman, L., Hutchinson, B., & Gebru, T. (2020). Model cards for model reporting. *Proceedings of the Conference on Fairness, Accountability, and Transparency*, 220–229. https://doi.org/DOI: 10.1145/3287560.3287596

Mohammadkarimi, E. (2023). Teachers' reflections on academic dishonesty in EFL students' writings in the era of artificial intelligence. *Journal of Applied Learning and Teaching*, *6*(2), 105–113.

Mohammed, D., Omar, M., & Nguyen, V. (2018). Wireless sensor network security: Approaches to detecting and avoiding wormhole attacks. *Journal of Research in Business. Economics and Management*, *10*(2), 1860–1864.

Mökander, J. (2023). Auditing of AI: Legal, Ethical and Technical Approaches. *Digital Society : Ethics, Socio-Legal and Governance of Digital Technology*, *2*(3), 49. Advance online publication. DOI: 10.1007/s44206-023-00074-y

Monahan, R., MacCormac, A., & Minogue, J. (2024, July). Fostering Epistemic Agency: Strategies for Mitigating Implicit Bias in AI-Enhanced Education. In *Ed-Media+ Innovate Learning* (pp. 1011-1025). Association for the Advancement of Computing in Education (AACE).

Moradi-Kelayeh, N. (2025). *From Chalkboard to Chatbots: The Integration of Artificial Influence on Pedagogical Practices* (Master's thesis, Harvard University).

Morozevich, E. S., Korotkikh, V. S., & Kuznetsova, Y. A. (2022). The development of a model for a personalized learning path using machine learning methods. *Бизнес-информатика*, *16*(2, 2 (eng)), 21–35. DOI: 10.17323/2587-814X.2022.2.21.35

Mounkoro, I., Uberas, A. D., Cadelina, F. A., Saleem, M. U., Maryam, S., Almagharbeh, W. T., ... & Hidayatallah, Z. (2024). Integrating AI in Classroom Management: Improving Educational Efficiency and Teacher Workflows.

Moustafa, N., Koroniotis, N., Keshk, M., Zomaya, A. Y., & Tari, Z. (2023). Explainable intrusion detection for cyber defences in the internet of things: Opportunities and solutions. *IEEE Communications Surveys and Tutorials*, *25*(3), 1775–1807. DOI: 10.1109/COMST.2023.3280465

Mulyana, E., & Hakimi, R. (2018, July). Bringing automation to the classroom: A chatOps-based approach. In *2018 4th International Conference on Wireless and Telematics (ICWT)* (pp. 1-6). IEEE. DOI: 10.1109/ICWT.2018.8527810

Murikah, W., Nthenge, J. K., & Musyoka, F. M. (2024). Bias and ethics of AI systems applied in auditing - A systematic review [Review of Bias and ethics of AI systems applied in auditing - A systematic review]. Scientific African, 25. Elsevier BV. https://doi.org/DOI: 10.1016/j.sciaf.2024.e02281

Murtiningsih, S., & Sujito, A. (2024). Reimagining the future of education: Inclusive pedagogies, critical intergenerational justice, and technological disruption. *Policy Futures in Education*, •••, 14782103251341406.

Museus, S. D., & Jayakumar, U. M. (2012). Creating campus cultures. *Routledge, 10*, 9780203832417.

Nehyba, J., & Štefánik, M. (2023). Applications of deep language models for reflective writings. *Education and Information Technologies*, *28*(3), 2961–2999. DOI: 10.1007/s10639-022-11254-7

Ng, E. M. (2016). Fostering pre-service teachers' self-regulated learning through self-and peer assessment of wiki projects. *Computers & Education*, *98*, 180–191. DOI: 10.1016/j.compedu.2016.03.015

Nguyen, V. (2025). The Use of Generative AI Tools in Higher Education: Ethical and Pedagogical Principles. *Journal of Academic Ethics*. Advance online publication. DOI: 10.1007/s10805-025-09607-1

Nguyen, V., Mohammed, D., Omar, M., & Banisakher, M. (2018). The Effects of the FCC Net Neutrality Repeal on Security and Privacy. [IJHIoT]. *International Journal of Hyperconnectivity and the Internet of Things*, *2*(2), 21–29. DOI: 10.4018/IJHIoT.2018070102

Nieminen, J. H., Asikainen, H., & Rämö, J. (2021). Promoting deep approach to learning and self-efficacy by changing the purpose of self-assessment: A comparison of summative and formative models. *Studies in Higher Education*, *46*(7), 1296–1311. DOI: 10.1080/03075079.2019.1688282

Norori, N., Hu, Q., Aellen, F. M., Faraci, F. D., & Tzovara, A. (2021). Addressing bias in big data and AI for health care: A call for open science [Review of Addressing bias in big data and AI for health care: A call for open science]. Patterns, 2(10), 100347. Elsevier BV. https://doi.org/DOI: 10.1016/j.patter.2021.100347

Nunes, A., Cordeiro, C., Limpo, T., & Castro, S. L. (2022). Effectiveness of automated writing evaluation systems in school settings: A systematic review of studies from 2000 to 2020. *Journal of Computer Assisted Learning*, *38*(2), 599–620. DOI: 10.1111/jcal.12635

O'Toole, K., & Horvát, E.-Á. (2024). Extending human creativity with AI. *Journal of Creativity*, *34*(2), 100080. DOI: 10.1016/j.yjoc.2024.100080

Oakley Browne, T., Abedin, M., & Chowdhury, M. J. M. (2024). A systematic review on research utilising artificial intelligence for open source intelligence (OSINT) applications.

Oduro, S., Moss, E., & Metcalf, J. (2022). Obligations to assess: Recent trends in AI accountability regulations [Review of Obligations to assess: Recent trends in AI accountability regulations]. Patterns, 3(11), 100608. Elsevier BV. https://doi.org/ DOI: 10.1016/j.patter.2022.100608

Olex, A. L., Garber, A. M., Santen, S. A., Blondino, C., Goldberg, S., & DiazGranados, D. (2025). Utilizing natural language processing to analyze student narrative reflections for medical curriculum improvement. *Medical Teacher*, *47*(6), 970–975. DOI: 10.1080/0142159X.2024.2390034 PMID: 39161978

Omar, M. (2021). New insights into database security: An effective and integrated approach for applying access control mechanisms and cryptographic concepts in Microsoft Access environments.

Omar, M. (2022). *Machine Learning for Cybersecurity: Innovative Deep Learning Solutions*. Springer Brief. https://link.springer.com/book/978303115

Omar, M. (2024). From Attack to Defense: Strengthening DNN Text Classification Against Adversarial Examples. In *Innovations, Securities, and Case Studies Across Healthcare, Business, and Technology* (pp. 174-195). IGI Global.

Omar, M. (2024). Revolutionizing Malware Detection: A Paradigm Shift Through Optimized Convolutional Neural Networks. In *Innovations, Securities, and Case Studies Across Healthcare, Business, and Technology* (pp. 196-220). IGI Global. DOI: 10.4018/979-8-3693-1906-2.ch011

Omar, M., Zangana, H. M., Al-Karaki, J. N., & Mohammed, D. (2024). Harnessing LLMs for IoT malware detection: A comparative analysis of BERT and GPT-2. In *2024 8th International Symposium on Multidisciplinary Studies and Innovative Technologies (ISMSIT)* (pp. 1-6). Ankara, Turkiye. https://doi.org/DOI: 10.1109/ISMSIT63511.2024.10757249

Omar, M., & Zangana, H. (Eds.). (2025). *Digital Forensics in the Age of AI*. IGI Global., DOI: 10.4018/979-8-3373-0857-9

Omar, M., & Zangana, H. M. (Eds.). (2024). *Redefining Security With Cyber AI*. IGI Global., DOI: 10.4018/979-8-3693-6517-5

Omar, M., & Zangana, H. M. (Eds.). (2025). *Application of Large Language Models (LLMs) for Software Vulnerability Detection*. IGI Global., DOI: 10.4018/979-8-3693-9311-6

Omar, M., Zangana, H. M., & Mohammed, D. (Eds.). (2025). *Integrating Artificial Intelligence in Cybersecurity and Forensic Practices*. IGI Global., DOI: 10.4018/979-8-3373-0588-2

Öncü, S. E., & Süral, İ. (2024). Leveraging AI for Enhanced Support: Satisfaction Levels of Users Utilizing Virtual Assistant in Open Education. *Asian Journal of Distance Education*, *19*(1).

Padua, D. (2025). Artificial intelligence and quality education: The need for digital culture in teaching. *Journal of Educational* [ECPS Journal]. *Cultural and Psychological Studies*, (30), 181–193.

Palmer, I., Dunford, R., & Buchanan, D. (2016). *EBOOK: Managing Organizational Change: A Multiple Perspectives Approach (ISE)*. McGraw Hill.

Pando Cerra, P., Fernández Álvarez, H., Busto Parra, B., & Castaño Busón, S. (2023). Boosting computer-aided design pedagogy using interactive self-assessment graphical tools. *Computer Applications in Engineering Education*, *31*(1), 26–46. DOI: 10.1002/cae.22569

Patil, S. (2025). AI-driven personalized learning paths in MOOCS: Optimizing engagement and outcomes in digital education. In *Digital Transformation and Sustainability of Business* (pp. 387–395). CRC Press. DOI: 10.1201/9781003606185-90

Pavlik, J. V. (2023). Collaborating With ChatGPT: Considering the Implications of Generative Artificial Intelligence for Journalism and Media Education. *Journalism & Mass Communication Educator*, *78*(1), 84–93. DOI: 10.1177/10776958221149577

Pedro, F., Subosa, M., Rivas, A., & Valverde, P. (2019). Artificial intelligence in education: Challenges and opportunities for sustainable development.

Peer Mohamed, M. S. (2024). *Exploring ethical dimensions of AI-enhanced language education: A literature perspective*. Technology in Language Teaching & Learning.

Pereira, R., Reis, A., Barroso, J., Sousa, J., & Pinto, T. (2022, August). Virtual assistants applications in education. In *International conference on technology and innovation in learning, teaching and education* (pp. 468-480). Cham: Springer Nature Switzerland.

Perrotta, C., Selwyn, N., & Cramman, H. (2021). AI and the teaching profession: Navigating the disruption. *Teaching in Higher Education*, *26*(7–8), 1045–1059. DOI: 10.1080/13562517.2021.1928063

Picht, P. G., & Thouvenin, F. (2023). AI and IP: Theory to Policy and Back Again – Policy and Research Recommendations at the Intersection of Artificial Intelligence and Intellectual Property. *IIC; International Review of Industrial Property and Copyright Law*, *54*(6), 916–940. DOI: 10.1007/s40319-023-01344-5

Polydoros, G. V. (2025). Harnessing AI and Digital Tools for Micro-Credentialing in Mathematics Education: Enhancing Learning Outcomes for Students With Learning Difficulties. In *Integrating Micro-Credentials With AI in Open Education* (pp. 195-216). IGI Global Scientific Publishing.

Quan, T., Bracho, C. A., Wilkerson, M., & Clark, M. (2019). Empowerment and transformation: Integrating teacher identity, activism, and criticality across three teacher education programs. *Review of Education, Pedagogy & Cultural Studies*, *41*(4-5), 218–251. DOI: 10.1080/10714413.2019.1684162

Rachmad, Y. E. (2025). *The Future of Gen Z Careers: Competence and Certification Replacing Degrees*. United Nations Development Programme.

Rachmad, Y. E. (2025). *The New Era of HR Management: Prioritizing Competence Over Degrees*. United Nations Development Programme.

Radanliev, P. (2025). AI Ethics: Integrating Transparency, Fairness, and Privacy in AI Development. *Applied Artificial Intelligence*, *39*(1), 2463722. Advance online publication. DOI: 10.1080/08839514.2025.2463722

Rafi, M. U. (2025). Fundamentals of AI Learning Curriculum: Preventing Job Losses in the Era of Automation. *Available at SSRN* 5277211. DOI: 10.2139/ssrn.5277211

Raga, R. (2016). Reflections on the awareness and progress of natural language processing (nlp) research in the philippines. *Philippine Computing Journal*, *11*(1), 1–9.

Rajesh, R. (2024). *ARTIFICIAL INTELLIGENCE: BEYOND IDENTITIES. Routledge Handbook of Gender*. Culture, and Development in India.

Ramírez-Montoya, M. S., Quintero Gámez, L., Sanabria-Z, J., & Portuguez-Castro, M. (2024). Exploring complex thinking in latin American universities: Comparative analysis between programs and alternative credentials. *Journal of Latinos and Education*, *23*(5), 1744–1765. DOI: 10.1080/15348431.2024.2329671

Rane, N. (2023). Chatbot-enhanced teaching and learning: Implementation strategies, challenges, and the role of ChatGPT in education. *Challenges, and the Role of ChatGPT in Education (July 21, 2023).*

Rane, N., Choudhary, S., & Rane, J. (2024). Machine Learning and Deep Learning: a Comprehensive Review on Methods, Techniques, Applications, Challenges, and Future Directions. *Techniques, Applications, Challenges, and Future Directions (May 31, 2024).*

Rawas, S. (2024). AI: The future of humanity. *Discover Artificial Intelligence*, *4*(1), 25. Advance online publication. DOI: 10.1007/s44163-024-00118-3

Ray, V. (2019). A theory of racialized organizations. *American Sociological Review*, *84*(1), 26–53. DOI: 10.1177/0003122418822335

Reddy, N. S., Chaitanya, N. P., Varshitha, P. S., Varma, R. C., Reddy, P. K., & Dandu, J. (2024, August). Intelligent Chatbot For Educational Institutions. In *2024 7th International Conference on Circuit Power and Computing Technologies (ICCPCT)* (Vol. 1, pp. 1337-1343). IEEE. DOI: 10.1109/ICCPCT61902.2024.10673214

Reyes, R., Garza, D., Garrido, L., Cueva, V., & Ramírez Uresti, J. (2020). *Virtual assistants in education: model, implementation, and results. Novus2020.* Available at ResearchGate.

Rhode, J., Richter, S., & Miller, T. (2017). Designing personalized online teaching professional development through self-assessment. *TechTrends*, *61*(5), 444–451. DOI: 10.1007/s11528-017-0211-3

Rohatgi, S., Abinash, B., Joshi, S., Sushant, S., & Kumar, S. (2023). Introduction to Artificial Intelligence and Cybersecurity for Industry. In *Artificial Intelligence and Cyber Security in Industry 4.0* (pp. 1–22). Springer Nature Singapore. DOI: 10.1007/978-981-99-2115-7_1

Roshanaei, M., Khan, M. R., & Sylvester, N. N. (2024). Navigating AI Cybersecurity: Evolving Landscape and Challenges. *Journal of Intelligent Learning Systems and Applications*, *16*(3), 155–174. DOI: 10.4236/jilsa.2024.163010

Rossi, A., & Lenzini, G. (2020). Transparency by design in data-informed research: A collection of information design patterns. *Computer Law & Security Review*, *37*, 105402. DOI: 10.1016/j.clsr.2020.105402

Sahoo, D. K., Le, T. M., Kumar, A., & Chandel, A. (2025). AI-Powered Talent Development: Nurturing Skills and Leadership in Entrepreneurial Teams. In *Improving Entrepreneurial Processes Through Advanced AI* (pp. 241-266). IGI Global.

Salem, M., & Shaalan, K. (2023, December). ChatGPT: Advancing Education with Virtual Assistants. In *International Conference on Business Intelligence and Information Technology* (pp. 283-293). Singapore: Springer Nature Singapore.

Sá, M. J., & Serpa, S. (2020). The COVID-19 pandemic as an opportunity to foster the sustainable development of teaching in higher education. *Sustainability (Basel)*, *12*(20), 8525. DOI: 10.3390/su12208525

Sayyafzadeh, S. (2024). *Thumbnail Image Forensic Acquisition and Analysis in the Age of Artificial Intelligence* (Master's thesis, Florida Agricultural and Mechanical University).

Seifert, T., & Feliks, O. (2019). Online self-assessment and peer-assessment as a tool to enhance student-teachers' assessment skills. *Assessment & Evaluation in Higher Education*, *44*(2), 169–185. DOI: 10.1080/02602938.2018.1487023

Sengar, S. S., Hasan, A. B., Kumar, S., & Carroll, F. (2024). Generative artificial intelligence: a systematic review and applications [Review of Generative artificial intelligence: a systematic review and applications]. Multimedia Tools and Applications. Springer Science+Business Media. https://doi.org/DOI: 10.1007/s11042-024-20016-1

Shani, A. B., Noumair, D. A., Zandee, D. P., & Coghlan, D. (Eds.). (2025). *Research in organizational change and development*. Emerald Publishing Limited. DOI: 10.1108/S0897-3016202531

Shanmughan, P., & Joseph, J. S, B. N., SM, A., CS, A., & Jose, J. (2024, November). The AI revolution in micro-credentialing: personalized learning paths. In *Frontiers in Education* (Vol. 9, p. 1445654). Frontiers Media SA.

Shardlow, M., Sellar, S., & Rousell, D. (2022). Collaborative augmentation and simplification of text (CoAST): Pedagogical applications of natural language processing in digital learning environments. *Learning Environments Research*, *25*(2), 399–421. DOI: 10.1007/s10984-021-09368-9

Shivshankar, S., & Acharya, N. (2025). AI in assessment and feedback. In *Next-generation AI methodologies in education* (pp. 119–146). IGI Global Scientific Publishing.

Siham, E. K. (2024). Tech-Enhanced Ties: AI's Role in Cross-Cultural Peer Education. *PROCEEDINGS BOOK*, 671.

Silver, J. K., Dodurgali, M. R., & Gavini, N. (2024). Artificial intelligence in medical education and mentoring in rehabilitation medicine. *American Journal of Physical Medicine & Rehabilitation, 103*(11), 10–1097. DOI: 10.1097/PHM.0000000000002604 PMID: 39016292

Sindiramutty, S. R., Prabagaran, K. R. V., Akbar, R., Hussain, M., & Malik, N. A. (2025). Overview of Generative AI Techniques for Cybersecurity. *Reshaping CyberSecurity With Generative AI Techniques*, 1-52.

Singh, H. (2023). The New Era in Education: Web 3.0. *TAM METİN BİLDİRİ KİTABI*, 78.

Singh, V., & Ram, S. (2024). Impact of artificial intelligence on teacher education. *Shodh Sari-An International Multidisciplinary Journal, 3*(01), 243–266. DOI: 10.59231/SARI7669

Singla, J. (2024). Safeguarding the Future: Advancements in Cybersecurity. *Utilizing Generative AI for Cyber Defense Strategies*, 421.

Smith, L., Tan, E., & Morris, J. (2021). Teacher trust in AI: A mixed-method study on interpretability and control. *Educational Technology Research and Development, 69*(3), 1391–1413.

Steinert, Y. (2025). Faculty development: core concepts and principles. *Faculty development in the health professions: A focus on research and practice*, 3-28.

Steyvers, M., & Kumar, A. (2023). Three Challenges for AI-Assisted Decision-Making. *Perspectives on Psychological Science, 19*(5), 722–734. DOI: 10.1177/17456916231181102 PMID: 37439761

Stouten, J., Rousseau, D. M., & De Cremer, D. (2018). Successful organizational change: Integrating the management practice and scholarly literatures. *The Academy of Management Annals, 12*(2), 752–788. DOI: 10.5465/annals.2016.0095

Sullivan, A. L., Artiles, A. J., & Hernandez-Saca, D. I. (2015). Addressing special education inequity through systemic change: Contributions of ecologically based organizational consultation. *Journal of Educational & Psychological Consultation, 25*(2-3), 129–147. DOI: 10.1080/10474412.2014.929969

Sumon, R. I., Uddin, S. M. I., Akter, S., Mozumder, M. A. I., Khan, M. O., & Kim, H. C. (2024). Natural language processing influence on digital socialization and linguistic interactions in the integration of the metaverse in regular social life. *Electronics (Basel), 13*(7), 1331. DOI: 10.3390/electronics13071331

SWARGIARY. K. (2025). *Educational Sociology: Theory, Practice, and Contemporary Challenges*. ERA, US.

Takale, D. G., Mahalle, P. N., & Sule, B. (2024). Cyber Security Challenges in Generative AI Technology. *Journal of Network Security Computer Networks*, *10*(1), 28–34.

Tan, M. J. T., & Maravilla, N. M. A. T. (2024). Shaping integrity: Why generative artificial intelligence does not have to undermine education. *Frontiers in Artificial Intelligence*, *7*, 1471224. Advance online publication. DOI: 10.3389/frai.2024.1471224 PMID: 39512399

Tapalova, O., & Zhiyenbayeva, N. (2022). Artificial intelligence in education: AIEd for personalised learning pathways. *Electronic Journal of e-Learning*, *20*(5), 639–653. DOI: 10.34190/ejel.20.5.2597

Tariq, M. U. (2025). Empowering Learning Through Networked and Connected Education: Case Studies in Digital Engagement. In *Cases on Enhancing P-16 Student Engagement With Digital Technologies* (pp. 169-198). IGI Global Scientific Publishing.

Tatineni, S. (2020). Recommendation Systems for Personalized Learning: A Data-Driven Approach in Education. [JCET]. *Journal of Computer Engineering and Technology*, *4*(2).

Thong, C. L., Atallah, Z., Islam, S., Lim, W., & Cherukuri, A. K. (2025). AI-powered Tools for Doctoral Supervision in Higher Education: A Systematic Review. *Journal of Information & Knowledge Management*, 2530001.

Trajkovski, G., & Hayes, H. (2025). The Future of AI in Educational Assessment. In *AI-Assisted Assessment in Education: Transforming Assessment and Measuring Learning* (pp. 347–380). Springer Nature Switzerland. DOI: 10.1007/978-3-031-88252-4_9

Tran, P. D. T., Vu, K. B., Doan, M. N., Dang, Q. T., Dang, Q. V., & Ho, T. T. (2024). Personalized learning paths recommendation system with collaborative filtering and content-based approaches. *Science & Technology Development Journal: Economics-Law & Management*, *8*(2), 5243–5253.

Tun, Z. Y. (2024). Empowering human health with wearables: exploring the feasibility and efficacy of AI-powered health mentoring systems.

Tuomi, I., Cachia, R., & Villar-Onrubia, D. (2023). *On the futures of technology in education: Emerging trends and policy implications*. Publications Office of the European Union.

Tyagi, A. K., & Addula, S. R. (2024). Artificial Intelligence for Malware Analysis: A Systematic Study. *Artificial Intelligence-Enabled Digital Twin for Smart Manufacturing*, 359-390.

Uddin, A. S. M. A. (2023). The Era of AI: Upholding Ethical Leadership. *Open Journal of Leadership*, *12*(4), 400–417. DOI: 10.4236/ojl.2023.124019

Uddin, M. Z., Jamal, M. Z. U., Umair, M., Khader, M., & Kumar, M. U. (2024). AI-Powered financial modeling and valuation analysis: Unleashing data-driven insights. *International Journal of Multidisciplinary Research and Growth Evaluation*, *5*(2), 626–629. DOI: 10.54660/.IJMRGE.2024.5.2.626-629

van Woudenberg, R., Ranalli, C., & Bracker, D. (2024). Authorship and ChatGPT: A Conservative View. *Philosophy & Technology*, *37*(1), 34. Advance online publication. DOI: 10.1007/s13347-024-00715-1 PMID: 38419827

VanLehn, K. (2006). The behavior of tutoring systems. *International Journal of Artificial Intelligence in Education*, *16*(3), 227–265.

Vargas, N. C. (2024). Exploiting the margin: How capitalism fuels AI at the expense of minoritized groups. *AI and Ethics*. Advance online publication. DOI: 10.1007/s43681-024-00502-w

Vygotsky, L. S. (1978). *Mind in society: The development of higher psychological processes*. Harvard University Press.

Wagner, G., Lukyanenko, R., & Paré, G. (2021). Artificial intelligence and the conduct of literature reviews. *Journal of Information Technology*, *37*(2), 209–226. DOI: 10.1177/02683962211048201

Wang, R., Wei, S., Ohland, M. W., & Ferguson, D. M. (2019). Natural language processing system for self-reflection and peer-evaluation. In *the Fourth North American International Conference on Industrial Engineering and Operations Management* (pp. 23-25).

Wang, T., Zhou, N., & Chen, Z. (2025). CyberMentor: AI Powered Learning Tool Platform to Address Diverse Student Needs in Cybersecurity Education. *arXiv preprint arXiv:2501.09709*.

Wang, Q., & Xu, Z. (2022). Human-centered AI in education: Enhancing teacher agency in data-driven classrooms. *Computers & Education*, *183*, 104516. DOI: 10.1016/j.compedu.2022.104516

Wang, T., Bruckman, A. S., & Yang, D. (2025). The Practice of Online Peer Counseling and the Potential for AI-Powered Support Tools. *Proceedings of the ACM on Human-Computer Interaction*, *9*(2), 1–33. DOI: 10.1145/3711089

Watiktinnakorn, C., Seesai, J., & Kerdvibulvech, C. (2023). Blurring the lines: How AI is redefining artistic ownership and copyright. *Discover Artificial Intelligence*, *3*(1), 37. Advance online publication. DOI: 10.1007/s44163-023-00088-y

Weiner, S., Lake, R., & Rosner, J. (2024). *AI Is Evolving, but Teacher Prep Is Lagging: A First Look at Teacher Preparation Program Responses to AI*. Center on Reinventing Public Education.

Wen, Z., & Tong, D. (2023). Analysis of the Legal Subject Status of Artificial Intelligence. *Beijing Law Review*, *14*(1), 74–86. DOI: 10.4236/blr.2023.141004

Williams, P. (2019). Does competency-based education with blockchain signal a new mission for universities? *Journal of Higher Education Policy and Management*, *41*(1), 104–117. DOI: 10.1080/1360080X.2018.1520491

Wong, W. K. O. (2024). The sudden disruptive rise of generative artificial intelligence? An evaluation of their impact on higher education and the global workplace. *Journal of Open Innovation*, *10*(2), 100278. DOI: 10.1016/j.joitmc.2024.100278

Wright, J., Dawson, M. E.Jr, & Omar, M. (2012). Cyber security and mobile threats: The need for antivirus applications for smartphones. *Journal of Information Systems Technology and Planning*, *5*(14), 40–60.

Wulff, P., Buschhüter, D., Westphal, A., Nowak, A., Becker, L., Robalino, H., Stede, M., & Borowski, A. (2021). Computer-based classification of preservice physics teachers' written reflections. *Journal of Science Education and Technology*, *30*(1), 1–15. DOI: 10.1007/s10956-020-09865-1

Wulff, P., Mientus, L., Nowak, A., & Borowski, A. (2023). Utilizing a pretrained language model (BERT) to classify preservice physics teachers' written reflections. *International Journal of Artificial Intelligence in Education*, *33*(3), 439–466. DOI: 10.1007/s40593-022-00290-6

Wulff, P., Westphal, A., Mientus, L., Nowak, A., & Borowski, A. (2023, January). Enhancing writing analytics in science education research with machine learning and natural language processing—Formative assessment of science and non-science preservice teachers' written reflections. [). Frontiers Media SA.]. *Frontiers in Education*, *7*, 1061461. DOI: 10.3389/feduc.2022.1061461

Xue, B., Green, R., & Zhang, M. (2023). Artificial Intelligence in New Zealand: applications and innovation. In Journal of the Royal Society of New Zealand (Vol. 53, Issue 1, p. 1). Taylor & Francis. https://doi.org/DOI: 10.1080/03036758.2023.2170165

Xu, H., & Shuttleworth, K. M. J. (2023). Medical artificial intelligence and the black box problem: A view based on the ethical principle of "do no harm.". *Intelligent Medicine*, *4*(1), 52–57. DOI: 10.1016/j.imed.2023.08.001

Yang, Y., Zhang, Y., Sun, D., He, W., & Wei, Y. (2025). Navigating the landscape of AI literacy education: Insights from a decade of research (2014–2024). *Humanities & Social Sciences Communications*, *12*(1), 374. Advance online publication. DOI: 10.1057/s41599-025-04583-8

Yekollu, R. K., Bhimraj Ghuge, T., Sunil Biradar, S., Haldikar, S. V., & Farook Mohideen Abdul Kader, O. (2024, February). AI-driven personalized learning paths: Enhancing education through adaptive systems. In *International Conference on Smart data intelligence* (pp. 507-517). Singapore: Springer Nature Singapore. DOI: 10.1007/978-981-97-3191-6_38

Ye, X., Yan, Y., Li, J., & Jiang, B. (2024). Privacy and personal data risk governance for generative artificial intelligence: A Chinese perspective. *Telecommunications Policy*, *102851*(10), 102851. Advance online publication. DOI: 10.1016/j.telpol.2024.102851

Zangana, H. M. (2015). A New Skin Color Based Face Detection Algorithm by Combining Three Color Model Algorithms. *IOSR J. Comput. Eng, 17*, 06-125.

Zangana, H. M. (2017). A new algorithm for shape detection. *IOSR Journal of Computer Engineering (IOSR-JCE), 19*(3), 71-76.

Zangana, H. M. (2018). Developing Data Warehouse for Student Information System (IIUM as a Case Study). *International Organization of Scientific Research, 20*(1), 09-14.

Zangana, H. M. (2018). Implementing a System for Recognizing Optical Characters.

Zangana, H. M. (2019). Issues of Data Management in the Library: A Case Study.

Zangana, H. M. (2019). ITD Data Quality Maturity (A Case Study). *International Journal Of Engineering And Computer Science, 8*(10).

Zangana, H. M. (2022). Improving The Web Services for Remittance Company: Express Remit as a Case Study. *Academic Journal of Nawroz University (AJNU), 11*(3).

Zangana, H. M. (2024). Exploring Blockchain-Based Timestamping Tools: A Comprehensive Review. *Redefining Security With Cyber AI*, 92-110.

Zangana, H. M. (2024). Exploring the Landscape of Website Vulnerability Scanners: A Comprehensive Review and Comparative Analysis. *Redefining Security With Cyber AI*, 111-129.

Zangana, H. M., & Mustafa, F. M. (2025). Wavelet-Autoencoder Hybrid Model for Enhanced Image Denoising in Medical Imaging. In M. Aamir, U. Bhatti, Z. Rahman, J. Bhutto, & W. Abro (Eds.), *Deep Learning in Medical Signal and Image Processing* (pp. 487-508). IGI Global Scientific Publishing. https://doi.org/DOI: 10.4018/979-8-3693-9816-6.ch019

Zangana, H. M., Mustafa, F. M., Mohammed, A. K., & Omar, M. (2025). The Role of Change Control Boards in Ensuring Cybersecurity Compliance for IT Infrastructure. *JITCE (Journal of Information Technology and Computer Engineering), 9*(1). Retrieved from https://jitce.fti.unand.ac.id/index.php/JITCE/article/view/303

Zangana, H. M., Omar, M., Al-Karaki, J. N., & Mohammed, D. (2024). Comprehensive Review and Analysis of Network Firewall Rule Analyzers: Enhancing Security Posture and Efficiency. *Redefining Security With Cyber AI*, 15-36.

Zangana, H. M. (2017). Library Data Quality Maturity (IIUM as a Case Study). *IOSR Journal of Computer Engineering*, *19*(March), 29. DOI: 10.9790/0661-1902033844

Zangana, H. M. (2017). Watermarking System Using LSB. *IOSR Journal of Computer Engineering*, *19*(3), 75–79. DOI: 10.9790/0661-1903027579

Zangana, H. M. (2018). Design an information management system for a pharmacy. *International Journal of Advanced Research in Computer and Communication Engineering*, *7*(10), 52–55. DOI: 10.17148/IJARCCE.2018.71012

Zangana, H. M. (2020). Mobile Device Integration in IIUM Service. *International Journal (Toronto, Ont.)*, *8*(5).

Zangana, H. M. (2021). The Global Finical Crisis from an Islamic Point Of View. *Qubahan Academic Journal*, *1*(2), 55–59. DOI: 10.48161/qaj.v1n2a39

Zangana, H. M. (2022). Creating a Community-Based Disaster Management System. *Academic Journal of Nawroz University*, *11*(4), 234–244. DOI: 10.25007/ajnu.v11n4a1485

Zangana, H. M. (2022). Implementing New Interactive Video Learning System for IIUM. *Academic Journal of Nawroz University*, *11*(2), 23–29. DOI: 10.25007/ajnu.v11n2a1281

Zangana, H. M. (2025). Design and Implementation of a Novel Parallel Algorithm for Efficient Image Compression in High-Performance Computing. *EAI Endorsed Transactions on AI and Robotics, 4*. Advance online publication. DOI: 10.4108/airo.7832

Zangana, H. M., & Abdulazeez, A. M. (2023). Developed Clustering Algorithms for Engineering Applications: A Review. *International Journal of Informatics* [IN-JIISCOM]. *Information System and Computer Engineering*, *4*(2), 147–169.

Zangana, H. M., & Al-Shaikhli, I. F. (2013). A new algorithm for human face detection using skin color tone. *IOSR Journal of Computer Engineering*, *11*(6), 31–38. DOI: 10.9790/0661-1163138

Zangana, H. M., Bazeed, S. M. S., Ali, N. Y., & Abdullah, D. T. (2024). Navigating Project Change: A Comprehensive Review of Change Management Strategies and Practices. *Indonesian Journal of Education and Social Sciences*, *3*(2), 166–179. DOI: 10.56916/ijess.v3i2.735

Zangana, H. M., Mohammed, A. K., Sallow, A. B., & Sallow, Z. B. (2024). Cybernetic Deception: Unraveling the Layers of Email Phishing Threats. [INJURATECH]. *International Journal of Research and Applied Technology*, *4*(1), 35–47.

Zangana, H. M., Mohammed, H. S., & Husain, M. M. (2025). Addressing insider threats: The human factor in cybersecurity for financial institutions. *Journal of Innovation Information Technology and Application*, *7*(1), 88–96. DOI: 10.35970/jinita.v7i1.2686

Zangana, H. M., Mohammed, H. S., & Husain, M. M.Hewa Majeed ZanganaHarman Salih MohammedMamo Muhamad Husain. (2025). Banking Cybersecurity: Safeguarding Financial Information in the Digital Era. *Journal of Computers and Digital Business*, *4*(2), 56–63. DOI: 10.56427/jcbd.v4i2.751

Zangana, H. M., & Mustafa, F. M. (2024). From Classical to Deep Learning: A Systematic Review of Image Denoising Techniques. *Jurnal Ilmiah Computer Science*, *3*(1), 50–65. DOI: 10.58602/jics.v3i1.36

Zangana, H. M., & Mustafa, F. M. (2024). Hybrid Image Denoising Using Wavelet Transform and Deep Learning. *EAI Endorsed Transactions on AI and Robotics*, *3*. Advance online publication. DOI: 10.4108/airo.7486

Zangana, H. M., & Mustafa, F. M. (2024). Review of Hybrid Denoising Approaches in Face Recognition: Bridging Wavelet Transform and Deep Learning. *The Indonesian Journal of Computer Science*, *13*(4). Advance online publication. DOI: 10.33022/ijcs.v13i4.4209

Zangana, H. M., & Mustafa, F. M. (2024). Surveying the Landscape: A Comprehensive Review of Object Detection Algorithms and Advancements. *Jurnal Ilmiah Computer Science*, *3*(1), 1–15. DOI: 10.58602/jics.v3i1.29

Zangana, H. M., & Mustafa, F. M. (2025). A Novel Hybrid Wavelet-GAN Image Denoising System. In Bhatti, U., Aamir, M., Gulzar, Y., & Ullah Bazai, S. (Eds.), *Modern Intelligent Techniques for Image Processing* (pp. 409–424). IGI Global Scientific Publishing., DOI: 10.4018/979-8-3693-9045-0.ch017

Zangana, H. M., Mustafa, F. M., & Omar, M. (2024). A Hybrid Approach for Robust Object Detection: Integrating Template Matching and Faster R-CNN. *EAI Endorsed Transactions on AI and Robotics*, *3*. Advance online publication. DOI: 10.4108/airo.6858

Zangana, H. M., & Omar, M. (2020). Threats, Attacks, and Mitigations of Smartphone Security. *Academic Journal of Nawroz University*, *9*(4), 324–332. DOI: 10.25007/ajnu.v9n4a989

Zangana, H. M., & Omar, M. (2025). The Role of Leadership in Advancing Inclusive Health Technologies. In Burrell, D., & Nguyen, C. (Eds.), *New Horizons in Leadership: Inclusive Explorations in Health, Technology, and Education* (pp. 203–220). IGI Global Scientific Publishing., DOI: 10.4018/979-8-3693-6437-6.ch009

Zangana, H. M., Sallow, Z. B., & Omar, M. (2025). The Human Factor in Cybersecurity: Addressing the Risks of Insider Threats. *Jurnal Ilmiah Computer Science*, *3*(2), 76–85. DOI: 10.58602/jics.v3i2.37

Zangana, H., Al-Karaki, J., & Omar, M. (Eds.). (2025). *Navigating Law and Policy in STM Enterprises: Ethical Governance, Regulation, and Innovation Strategy*. IGI Global., DOI: 10.4018/979-8-3373-4862-9

Zangana, H., Al-Karaki, J., & Omar, M. (Eds.). (2025). *Revolutionizing Cybersecurity With Deep Learning and Large Language Models*. IGI Global., DOI: 10.4018/979-8-3373-3296-3

Zangana, H., Firas, M. M., & Omar, M. (2025). A Novel Hybrid Algorithm for Effective Image Restoration. *Vokasi Unesa Bulletin of Engineering. Technology and Applied Science*, *2*(2), 76–89. DOI: 10.26740/vubeta.v2i2.38118

Zangana, H., & Omar, M. (Eds.). (2025). *Ensuring Secure and Ethical STM Research in the AI Era*. IGI Global., DOI: 10.4018/979-8-3373-4252-8

Zangana, H., & Omar, M. (Eds.). (2025). *Leveraging Large Language Models for Quantum-Aware Cybersecurity*. IGI Global., DOI: 10.4018/979-8-3373-1102-9

Zawacki-Richter, O., Marín, V. I., Bond, M., & Gouverneur, F. (2019). Systematic review of research on artificial intelligence applications in higher education – Where are the educators? *International Journal of Educational Technology in Higher Education, 16*(1), 39. DOI: 10.1186/s41239-019-0171-0

Žerovnik, A. (2024). Technology-Enhanced Feedback System Usability in the Context of Self-Regulation Promotion. *Education Sciences, 14*(9), 948. DOI: 10.3390/educsci14090948

Zhao, C., Du, H., Niyato, D., Kang, J., Xiong, Z., Kim, D. I., & Letaief, K. B. (2024). Generative AI for secure physical layer communications: A survey. *IEEE Transactions on Cognitive Communications and Networking*.

Zhao, D. (2025). The impact of AI-enhanced natural language processing tools on writing proficiency: An analysis of language precision, content summarization, and creative writing facilitation. *Education and Information Technologies, 30*(6), 8055–8086. DOI: 10.1007/s10639-024-13145-5

Zhou, K. R., & Gattinger, G. (2024). The Evolving Regulatory Paradigm of AI in MedTech: A Review of Perspectives and Where We Are Today [Review of The Evolving Regulatory Paradigm of AI in MedTech: A Review of Perspectives and Where We Are Today]. Therapeutic Innovation & Regulatory Science, 58(3), 456. Springer Science+Business Media. https://doi.org/DOI: 10.1007/s43441-024-00628-3

Zreik, M. (2024). Harnessing AI for entrepreneurial idea generation: Navigating the new frontier. In *Generating Entrepreneurial Ideas With AI* (pp. 1–18). IGI Global Scientific Publishing. DOI: 10.4018/979-8-3693-3498-0.ch001

# About the Contributors

**Hewa Majeed Zangana** is an Assistant Professor at Duhok Polytechnic University (DPU), Iraq, and a current PhD candidate in Information Technology Management (ITM) at the same institution. He has held numerous academic and administrative positions, including Assistant Professor at Ararat Private Technical Institute, Lecturer at DPU's Amedi Technical Institute and Nawroz University, and Acting Dean of the College of Computer and IT at Nawroz University. His administrative roles have included Director of the Curriculum Division at the Presidency of DPU, Manager of the Information Unit at DPU's Research Center, and Head of the Computer Science Department at Nawroz University. Dr. Zangana's research interests include network systems, information security, mobile and data communication, and intelligent systems. He has authored numerous articles in peer-reviewed journals, including Inform: Jurnal Ilmiah Bidang Teknologi Informasi dan Komunikasi, Indonesian Journal of Education and Social Science, TIJAB, INJIISCOM, IEEE, and AJNU. In addition to his journal contributions, he has published more than five academic books with IGI Global, several of which are indexed in Scopus and Web of Science (Clarivate). Beyond publishing, Dr. Zangana actively contributes to the academic community through editorial service. He serves as a reviewer for the Qubahan Academic Journal and the Scientific Journals of Nawroz University. He is also a member of several academic and scientific committees, including the Scientific Curriculum Development Committee, the Student Follow-up Program Committee, and the Committee for Drafting the Rules of Procedure for Consultative Offices.

***

**Luay Albtosh** is a dedicated and accomplished professional currently pursuing a Ph.D. in Cyber Leadership. With a robust academic background and over a decade of industry experience, Luay Albtosh has established a strong foothold in the field of computer science. Luay Albtosh holds a master's degree in computer science, which laid the groundwork for a career marked by continuous learning and impactful contributions to the field. Throughout the years, Luay Albtosh has developed a profound expertise in various aspects of computer science, including cybersecurity, software development, and IT project management. In addition to academic achievements, Luay Albtosh has consistently demonstrated a commitment to excellence in professional endeavors. With more than 10 years of hands-on experience, Luay Albtosh has successfully led numerous projects, drove innovation and ensuring the seamless integration of technology solutions. This extensive experience has provided Luay Albtosh with a deep understanding of both the technical and strategic facets of the industry.

**Faradila Hasan** is an academician and Islamic law practitioner who was born in Manado on June 16, 1992. She currently serves as the Head of the Journal House at LP2M IAIN Manado and Chairperson of the Regional Board of Relawan Jurnal Indonesia (Indonesian Journal Volunteers) North Sulawesi, while actively working as a lecturer at the Muhammadiyah Islamic Institute of Kotabobagu. With over 8 years of experience in scholarly publication, Faradila has managed various high-reputation journals including Scopus-indexed journals, and has published dozens of scholarly articles in the fields of Islamic family law, Islamic economics, and gender studies. As a young figure actively involved in the development of scholarly publications in Indonesia, Faradila is also engaged in various community organizations such as the Indonesian Council of Ulama North Sulawesi, Fatayat Nahdlatul Ulama, and serves as the founder and chairperson of the Antmind Youth Empower Foundation. Her contributions to the academic world extend beyond research and publication to include serving as a resource person, moderator, and facilitator in various scholarly activities and academic writing training programs throughout Indonesia.

**Firas Mahmood Mustafa** holds a Ph.D. in Computer Engineering from Mosul University, Iraq. His academic journey began with a B.Sc. in Electrical Engineering (Electronics and Communication), graduating in the top quarter of his class. He earned an M.Sc. in Computer Engineering from Mosul University in 2000. Mustafa joined the Computer Science Department at AlHadba University in 2003 and completed his Ph.D. in 2007. From 2013 to 2017, he was with DPU University, and from 2017 to 2020, he chaired the CCE Department at Nawroz University. An active participant in Erasmus+ and IREX programs, he now teaches at DPU University, shaping future computer engineering professionals.

**Muhammad Nur**, beginning with a Bachelor's degree in the Department of Comparative Schools of Thought and Law at the Faculty of Sharia, IAIN Syarif

Hidayatullah Jakarta (1993–1997), his higher education path started. He then sought a Master's degree in Islamic Law/Sharia at the Postgraduate Program of IAIN Alauddin Makassar (1999–2001), and then finished his Doctoral Program (Ph.D.) in Islamic Law/Sharia at UIN Alauddin Makassar in 2013.

**Rismawati** is a distinguished academic and consultant with a robust focus on sustainability reporting. She currently holds the position of lecturer and Head of the Quality Assurance Institute at Universitas Muhammadiyah Palopo, where she has been pivotal in ensuring the quality of university processes and outputs since February 2020. Additionally, she serves as an Assurer for Sustainability Reporting at the National Center for Sustainability Reporting in Jakarta, specializing in the evaluation of sustainability reports for mining companies across Indonesia. Her academic qualifications are extensive, comprising a Bachelor's degree in Economics and Accounting, a Master's degree in Accounting Science, and a Doctorate in Accounting from Universitas Brawijaya, Malang. Rismawati is also a certified specialist in sustainability reporting, risk management, and tax planning, holding several prestigious certifications including Certified Sustainability Reporting Specialist (CSRS), Certified Risk Management Practitioner (CRMP), Certified Management Accountant (CMA) and Certified Enterprise Risk Analysis (CERA). In her professional capacity, she has provided consultancy services in financial management and tax compliance for companies such as PT. Reski Barito Timur and PT. Helay Raya. Furthermore, she has authored multiple publications on Social Accounting, Sustainability Accounting, Management Accounting and CSR, contributing significantly to the academic community. Her interests in reading, writing, and travel reflect her commitment to lifelong learning and professional growth in her field.

**Shubhanshi** is an academic and educator with a strong background in education and zoology. She completed her Ph.D. in Education from SHUATS, Prayagraj, with a focus on the relationship between mental health, job satisfaction, and the sense of responsibility of teachers. She has authored several book chapters on topics such as bio-energy, cyber-security, and the paradigm shift in Indian education due to information technology. Dr. Shubhanshi has also published numerous research papers in national and international journals, presented in national seminars, and received the Global Greens Paryavaran Sanrakshan Navodit Ratn Samman National Award in 2024. Her experience includes teaching and contributions to national workshops.

**Anny Widiasmara**, is a book writer who has a strong background as an accounting lecturer and researcher in the fields of financial accounting, behavioral accounting, and internal control. My dedication to the academic world is reflected in my comprehensive educational journey, including a Bachelor of Economics and Accounting, a Master of Accounting, and a Doctorate in Accounting that I obtained from Brawijaya University, Malang. In addition to my career in education, I am also actively developing professional competencies through various prestigious certifications. I hold a Certified Sustainability Reporting Specialist (CSRS) certification which shows my commitment to sustainability issues, as well as a Certified Tax Technician (CTT) competency in taxation which complements my understanding of financial aspects, taxation and business holistically. My in-depth teaching and research experience has inspired me to share knowledge and insights through writing. The books I produce are the embodiment of a strong theoretical understanding and practical application in the field, with the hope of making a significant contribution to the development of accounting science and business practices in Indonesia.

# Index

## A

## B



## C



## D



## E

# L



# M



# N



# P



# R



# S

# T



# V



# W

www.ingramcontent.com/pod-product-compliance
Ingram Content Group UK Ltd.
Pitfield, Milton Keynes, MK11 3LW, UK
UKHW050844101026
15624UKWH00018B/500

9 798337 359519